THE MUSICAL WORLD OF
FRANCES JAMES AND MURRAY ADASKIN

GORDANA LAZAREVICH

*To darling Erika + dear
Burton with love*

The Musical World of
Frances James and
Murray Adaskin

Murray Adaskin

Gordana Lazarevich

Frances Adaskin

UNIVERSITY OF TORONTO PRESS
Toronto Buffalo London

© University of Toronto Press 1988
Toronto Buffalo London
Printed in Canada

ISBN 0-8020-5738-1

Printed on acid-free paper

Canadian Cataloguing in Publication Data

Lazarevich, Gordana
The musical world of Frances James and Murray Adaskin

Bibliography: p.
Includes index.
ISBN 0-8020-5738-1

1. James, Frances – Biography. 2. Adaskin, Murray,
1906–   – Biography. 3. Women singers – Canada –
Biography. 4. Composers – Canada – Biography.
5. Music teachers – Saskatchewan – Biography.
I. Title.

ML385.L39 1988   780'.92'2   c87-095198-x

To Murray and Fran, in gratitude for entrusting me with
the story of their lives

Contents

PREFACE vii
ACKNOWLEDGMENTS ix
ABBREVIATIONS 2

1
The early years: Up to 1930 3

2
Two burgeoning careers in the decade of the great Depression 34

3
The Canadian performer in the 1940s 73

4
The making of a Canadian composer in the 1940s 134

5
A Prairie renaissance of the arts: 1952–1973 172

6
The compositions of the Saskatoon period 216

7
Two lives in busy retirement: Victoria, BC 243

APPENDICES
A. Musical examples 261
B. Catalogue of compositions by Murray Adaskin 283
C. First or early performances given by
Frances James of works by Canadian composers 295
D. Content of air-check discs recorded by Frances James for the CBC 297

NOTES 303
BIBLIOGRAPHY 313
INDEX 317

Preface

This story of two careers in music evolves against a backdrop of national and international events. The Adaskins were a product of their times but they were also leaders in their times. One cannot, therefore, give an account of their careers without reference to the social, political, and cultural circumstances that affected them. Although the book is not intended as a definitive cultural history of twentieth-century Canada, aspects of Canadian culture unfold with the biographical accounts.

In the first half of the twentieth century Frances James was this country's leading soprano, who based her career almost exclusively on Canadian soil. Through her activities a picture emerges of many of the institutions and individuals responsible for the promotion of musical culture in Canada from the 1920s through to the 1950s. Her lengthy association as concert artist with the Canadian Pacific Railway Company reveals an important and interesting episode in the history of pre–World War Two Canadian culture, when a business institution functioned as a major sponsor of music and art.

Starting with the CPR broadcasts from Banff in the 1920s and 1930s, through the early national broadcasts of the Canadian Radio Broadcasting Commission and, subsequently, the Canadian Broadcasting Corporation, the development of the singer's career reflects the development of radio broadcasting in this country. During the post-war reconstruction era Frances James's singing career and Murray Adaskin's early activities as composer unfolded within the context of a society in which the artists' fight for a Canadian cultural identity and for government recognition and funding eventually led to a major cultural breakthrough: the establishment of the Canada Council.

A study of the Adaskins' careers during the 1940s, therefore, unveils a cultural portrait of a nation. They witnessed and were the beneficiaries of the enlightened policies of the CBC toward Canadian music, and during Geoffrey

Waddington's and Terence Gibbs's association with the CBC Frances was a pioneer in introducing contemporary music to radio audiences. She was one of the earliest singers to tour Canadian communities from coast to coast, while engaging in an active concert career in Toronto, Montreal, and Ottawa. The breadth of repertoire acquired over the three decades of her concert performances would challenge most of today's singers.

As one of the founders of the Canadian League of Composers and an early member of the Canada Council, Murray too was involved with this country's emerging cultural institutions. During his two decades as professor of music at the University of Saskatchewan his creative approach to administration and teaching brought an unprecedented flourishing of musical activities to the small town in the midst of the vast Prairies. As a result of his indefatigable work on behalf of the Canadian composer, Saskatoon became a centre for contemporary musical performances in the Prairies and the West.

Not all the events in the narrative, however, relate to the broader social and political context. Chapter 2, for example, emphasizes the atmosphere of splendour the CPR created at the Banff Springs Hotel in the midst of the growing Depression that was affecting the rest of the country. The chapter describes social life in Banff in the 1930s, an artificial oasis in the Rocky Mountains to which socialites could escape from the pressures of the intensifying world problems.

Where possible, each chapter in the book covers one decade of the Adaskins' careers. Chapter 5 articulates the stylistic characteristics of Murray's music and the relationship between the composition and the environment that motivated its creation. A detailed technical analysis is, therefore, supplanted by a more general overview of the works, in an effort to present a picture of the composer's manifold activities. The richness of each facet of Murray Adaskin's creative personality is better conveyed in a humanistic than an analytical context.

Chapter 7, which relates the ongoing story of the Adaskins' retirement in Victoria, is chronologically too close to be evaluated within a historical perspective. The narrative really ends with Murray's retirement from the University of Saskatchewan, with chapter 7 functioning as an epilogue.

In presenting the musical achievements of Frances James and Murray Adaskin, and their impact on generations of music students and musicians across this country, the book re-creates their musical world. Above all, I hope it conveys the courage and vision of these remarkable musical pioneers.

Acknowledgments

The research for this project was conducted through interviews with Frances James, Murray Adaskin, some of their students, colleagues, and Saskatoon friends, and through the study of the Adaskin archives in both Victoria and the National Library in Ottawa. A large portion of the information was also obtained from the Archives of the Canadian Rockies in Banff, the Archives and Music Division of the National Library of Canada, the CPR Corporate Archives in Montreal, the CBC Archives in Toronto, and the archives of the University of Saskatchewan.

The author wishes to acknowledge the generous assistance of the following institutions or individuals: the Saskatoon Friends of Frances James and Murray Adaskin; Mrs Johanna Mitchell, Saskatoon; the President's Committee on Faculty Research and Travel from the University of Victoria; the Ontario Arts Council; the Social Sciences and Humanities Research Council. The following individuals provided information and friendly co-operation: Dr Helmut Kallmann, chief of the Music Division of the National Library of Canada and his staff: Dr Stephen Willis, Maria Calderisi-Bryce, and Don Uhryniw; Jon White, Ted Hart, and Don Bourdon of the Archives of the Canadian Rockies; Nicholas Morant of Banff; Omer Lavallée and David Jones of the CPR Corporate Archives; Gail Donald, Barbara Clarke, and Linda Litwack of the CBC Program Archives; Keith MacMillan, who gave me access to the files of his father, Sir Ernest MacMillan; John Gibbon, Tom Taylor, Paul Pedersen, Bruce Mather, John Weinzweig; Eli and Chrisse Bornstein, Ruth and Dr Louis Horlick, Margaret and the late Fred MacDermid, Blair and Mary Nelson, Bubs Coleman, Dr J.W.T. Spinks, Dr Lawrence House, all of Saskatoon; Trudy Carlyle; Margaret Abbott, Rod Sharman, Mark Ellestad, Dr Dale MacIntosh, all of Victoria. I am grateful to Dr Bryan N.S. Gooch of the English Department, University of Victoria, for his helpful comments as reader of the manuscript.

Special thanks are extended to Patricia Debly and Claire Friesen, graduate student assistants who provided typing services, Dr Glen Carruthers, Carol Bruner, and Dr Janet Bavelas, and Alex Black of the Department of Psychology, University of Victoria, for their co-operation and generous help with computer services, and Rosemary Mountain for copying the musical examples. I am grateful to P.K. Page for permission to quote excerpts from *The Travelling Musicians*, and to the following, who have given permission to quote from unpublished material: Udo Kasemets, George Zukerman, CBC Public Relations (Head Office), Keith MacMillan, Naomi Adaskin, and Community Concerts Inc, New York.

This book has been published with the help of a grant from the Canadian Federation for the Humanities, using funds provided by the Social Sciences and Humanities Research Council of Canada.

PICTURE CREDITS

John Murray Gibbon: Whyte Museum of the Canadian Rockies, Banff, Alberta; Frances James in the 1930s: I. Abresch; Banff Springs Hotel Trio: Nicholas Morant; Murray Adaskin with portrait by Paraskeva Clark: Gordon R. Sisson; portraits of Frances James and Murray Adaskin: Myfanwy Pavelich; Murray Adaskin in Saskatoon home: Marcel Ray

John Murray Gibbon

Staged publicity photo of the Trail Riders of the Canadian Rockies: Frances James, singing, with (counter-clockwise) Murray Adaskin, violin; Louis Crerar, harmonium; and John Adaskin, cello

Frances James at Lake Louise as Mary Queen of Scots, 1928

The Toronto Symphony Orchestra with Luigi von Kunits conducting in Simpson's Arcadian Court, late 1920s. Murray Adaskin is on the outside of the third desk of violins.

Frances James in the 1930s

The Adaskin family about 1940: (top row, left to right) Harry, Gordon, Frances Marr; (bottom row) Frances James, Murray, Naomi, Tamar, and John

Frances James and Louis Crerar in concert in Mount Stephen Hall, Banff Springs Hotel

The Banff Springs Hotel Trio, about 1935: (left to right) Murray Adaskin, Louis Crerar, Cornelius Ysselstyn

Samuel Hersenhoren, 1936   Roland Hayes, 1945

(Left to right) Charles Jones, Madeleine Milhaud, Darius Milhaud, and the Adaskins at Santa Barbara, California, 1950

Murray Adaskin standing in front of his portrait by Paraskeva Clark

CBC producer Ernest Morgan (left) and conductor Ettore Mazzoleni discussing Frances James's role in *Deirdre of the Sorrows*, 1946

Portraits of Frances James and (opposite) Murray Adaskin by Myfanwy Pavelich

Murray Adaskin in his Saskatoon home, 1950s

Murray Adaskin, 1986

THE MUSICAL WORLD OF FRANCES JAMES
AND MURRAY ADASKIN

Abbreviations

BBC	British Broadcasting Corporation
CAPAC	Composers, Authors, and Publishers Association of Canada
CBC	Canadian Broadcasting Corporation
CMA	Canadian Music Associates
CNR	Canadian National Railway
CPR	Canadian Pacific Railway
CRBC	Canadian Radio Broadcasting Commission
GE	General Electric
NFB	National Film Board
RCAF	Royal Canadian Air Force
TSO	Toronto Symphony Orchestra
UBC	University of British Columbia
UNESCO	United Nations Educational, Scientific, and Cultural Organization
YMCA	Young Men's Christian Association
YMHA	Young Men's Hebrew Association

1

The early years:
Up to 1930

Born in Saint John, New Brunswick, 3 February 1903, Mary Frances James represents a rare phenomenon within the social fabric of this country: a true Canadian both by birth and by geographic location of her lifelong activities, she is a fifth-generation United Empire Loyalist and a descendant of Anne Faucght, the first baby girl to be born after the landing of the Loyalists in Saint John. Faucght eventually married Robert James, an immigrant of Welsh descent.

Frances James's professional activities were to span the country from east to west in a true embodiment of the motto 'a mari usque ad mare,' providing a unique example of an artist in the first half of this century who chose to make her career in Canada to the extent where, in her own words, she could wear a 'made in Canada' label. Frances was the youngest of a family of four children that included two other girls and a boy. Following the birth of the third child by ten years, she considers herself 'an afterthought.' The oldest, Bess Louise James, was at first a publicity agent in the press department of the Canadian Pacific Railway (CPR) in Montreal and later in San Francisco and Chicago. A brother was second in line, followed by a second sister, Ruth, who became a nurse at the Royal Victoria Hospital in Montreal.

The four children were brought up in a strictly religious atmosphere. Frederick W. James, head of the household and an employee of the CPR Steamship Company, was a Methodist, his wife a Presbyterian. Church music played a major role in the children's education. Frances's brother and sisters sang in church choirs, firmly implanting the oratorio tradition in the young girl's musical consciousness. Her brother, in particular, had a beautiful voice but was reluctant to develop it on a professional level. Among Frances's earliest memories are those of singing along with her family; she remembers that the

Hallelujah chorus from the *Messiah* had an especially strong impact on her even at an age so young that, at best, she could pronounce only 'for the Lord God omnipotix rained.'

During Frances's childhood the James family changed location twice: a move to Halifax in 1903 was followed seven years later by a move to Montreal. It was in Montreal – where she spent the next sixteen years of her life – that Frances began her schooling and received most of her formal education. The family first lived on Esplanade Avenue, which extended from Pine to Mount Royal avenues, in an area of Mount Royal at the top of Fletcher's Field, at that time extensive parkland. Bleury Street divided the city into French- and English-speaking neighbourhoods. West of Bleury Street, where the James family lived, the residents were almost entirely English-speaking. Frances remembers the aristocratic elegance of Outremont, to the north of Mount Royal, where French was the dominant language, and the equally elegant Westmount, at that time inhabited almost entirely by the English-speaking. Much to her regret Frances was not exposed to the French language during those formative years.

As a teenager Frances attended the girls' high school on University Street, which not only had separate entrances for boys and girls, but offered segregated education. By then the James family had moved to a new residence in East Montreal by the St Lawrence River and near the Dominion Amusement Park; every day Frances had to travel an hour on the streetcar from her home to the school.

Frances's earliest music lessons were given by Duncan MacKenzie, a Scottish music master at the girls' high school, who recognized her talent. He advised her parents that she could start formal voice lessons at the McGill Conservatorium once she reached the age of sixteen; the female voice starts to mature only at that age and is not ready for technical work earlier. Frances's musical training at the Conservatorium began in 1919 and continued over the next five years. Her high school education, however, had to be interrupted at the age of seventeen when she developed a heart condition, and was never completed.

The McGill Conservatorium, which fostered an active concert life, was established in 1904 and was affiliated with McGill University. It provided the young singer with training in voice and theory within a rich musical atmosphere that contributed to her education. Three teachers at the Conservatorium exerted a profound influence on the development of the young artist: Clara Lichtenstein, Alfred E. Whitehead, and Walter Clapperton.

Clara Lichtenstein (1860–1946), who is purported to have taken lessons from Franz Liszt, came to Montreal in 1899 from Edinburgh at the invitation of Lord Strathcona, to take charge of the music department of the Royal Victoria College for girls, precursor of the Conservatorium.[1] Once the Conservatorium was established she was appointed vice-director of the institution, teaching piano, voice, and music history until 1929. It was through her that Frances, who had up to that time been exposed almost exclusively to English oratorio and church music, was first introduced to the German *lied* repertoire.

Alfred Whitehead (1887–1974), organist of Christ Church Cathedral in Montreal, taught organ, composition, and music theory at McGill University and the Conservatorium. Until 1942 he also conducted the city's well-known Cathedral Singers. As a composer, Whitehead always felt that he suffered from being in the shadow of Healey Willan, a near contemporary working in the same field.[2] Through him Frances obtained her knowledge of theory, and their professional relationship lasted throughout the 1930s, when she sang as soloist with the Cathedral Singers in the Brahms *Requiem* at Christ Church Cathedral (February 1937) and in *Messiah* at Notre-Dame Church (December 1937).[3]

At the Conservatorium Frances obtained a good basic technique that allowed her voice to grow naturally. Because of this superb training she never found it necessary throughout the course of her career to change her technique, but simply to build on it. She excelled at her studies, winning two Peterson scholarships, the highest awards granted by the music faculty of McGill, and was a frequent performer in Conservatorium concerts given in the city's Royal Victoria Hall. In these early appearances she sang *Scena for Soprano, Baritone, and Orchestra* by Dr D.H.C. Perrins, dean of the Faculty of Music, and, with the conservatory orchestra, such operatic scenes as *Ah Perfido* from Beethoven's *Fidelio* and arias from Gounod's *Faust*. Other concerts included songs by English composers, especially Peter Warlock, Cyril Scott, and Roger Quilter.

Frances's voice teacher at the Conservatorium was Walter Clapperton, organist at St James's Methodist Church, which had a seating capacity of more than 1,500. It was Clapperton who introduced her to the English song repertoire and broadened her oratorio and church music repertoire. He engaged her for her first professional job, at age seventeen, as soloist at St James's. When Clapperton resigned from his post after a dispute with the minister, accepting a position as organist in a fashionable church on Sherbrooke Street West, Frances continued her job as St James's. She finally resigned in 1926 because of friction with Clapperton's successor as organist and because the board members would not allow her two months off for a summer job at Lake Louise.

In 1925 Frances made the acquaintance of John Murray Gibbon, the general publicity manager for the Canadian Pacific Railway Company, who offered her a summer job at Banff and Lake Louise as a tourist information clerk and singer in the company hotels in those two resorts. A year later he engaged her as a performing artist in the Château Frontenac, the CPR hotel in Quebec City. The summers of 1925 and 1926, therefore, were spent in Banff, while the winters were spent in Montreal, with trips to Quebec.

In her first two summers in the West Frances presented concerts in Calgary (1925) and Winnipeg (1926), under the auspices of the CPR. A review in the *Winnipeg Tribune* in 1926 refers to her 'delightfully fresh and beautiful soprano of great power and range.'[4]

Her winter concerts at CPR's Château Frontenac took place in the Salon Verchères each Sunday night and twice during the week at tea-time. A review in Quebec's *Chronicle Telegraph* of a concert sung under the baton of Nico Poppeldorff in 1926 paints the following picture of her performance:

Folk songs do not make the program of a vocalist any simpler. The spirit with which they must be presented is unique. Words and music are different from all other branches of song and they must be rendered with [a] feeling of inherent natural love of music ... Miss James ... showed deep feeling and thorough comprehension of her programme, never once permitting her technical qualifications to obliterate or diminish her understanding of true folk songs. Three items were given by the artist. They were 'Gaillon la Gai le Rosier', 'A la Claire Fontaine' and 'Marianne S'en Va-t-au Moulin' ... Miss James rendered these items with ease and perfection.[5]

Frances's engagements in Banff and Lake Louise marked the end of her studies at McGill and precipitated the severing of her ties with Montreal. They marked, also, the beginning of a long association with the CPR, which, under John Murray Gibbon, became a major sponsor of culture in pre-war Canada. She spent the next five years building a career in the West, singing under the auspices of the CPR in Banff, Victoria, and Vancouver; she returned to Montreal in subsequent decades only as guest artist.

THE CALL OF THE WEST

It was a long way from the cultural verve of Montreal to Banff, a small frontier town nestled at the foot of the Rocky Mountains in the wilderness of the country's barely settled West. The contrast between the life-style of rugged individuals who explored the wilderness as mountaineers, outfitters, and guides, or of those who tamed the country's vast expanses by homesteading in the prairies, and the life-style of the city-dwellers in the East was as dramatic as the contrasts in the face of the country itself. It took a national railway to conquer the seemingly endless distances and to link the disparate geographic elements and the cities, towns, and countryside of Canada.

The railway that pushed into the West, where isolated centres of human endeavour alternated with vast, as yet unsettled spaces, was in need of travellers whose patronage would pay its expenses. A concerted campaign to attract tourists was seen as essential to the survival of the railway. One of the early directors of the Canadian Pacific Railway Company, Thomas J. Shaughnessy, established the CPR office of public relations. The subsequent publicity campaign, launched from the company's offices in England, Scotland, various European centres, and such U.S. cities as San Francisco, New York, and Chicago, focused on the natural beauty of the West, the breathtaking scenery of the Rocky Mountains, and their potential for such activities as mountain climbing, horseback riding, fishing, and hunting. Through the Canadian Pacific Press Bureau, George Ham, the first manager of public relations, supervised the designing of maps, folders, and pamphlets for distribution across the world in order to attract tourists. At the time of Frances James's first associations with Banff, the mountain wilderness of Banff National Park still claimed unexplored valleys and mountain peaks not yet climbed, whose romantic mysteries lured adventurers and world travellers.

The transcontinental trains that transported the tourists into Canada's 'wild West' offered a life of comfort and luxury to those who chose to travel first class. The parlour cars were furnished with richly embroidered upholstery, rugs, inlaid mahogany panelling, and brass lamps. The sleeping cars were roomy and luxurious. In the dining cars the ornate seats were decorated in leather, and the tables, covered with white linen topped with silverware, were attended by uniformed waiters who served food prepared by CPR chefs according to rigorous company standards.

In order to accommodate the tourists on their long transcontinental journey, a network of CP hotels sprang up in the major Canadian cities with special emphasis on the mountain hotels, which reflected an old-world elegance contrasting with the new-world ruggedness of their natural surroundings. According to a recent historian of the West, E.J. Hart, such tourist havens as the Royal Alexandra Hotel in Winnipeg or the Banff Springs Hotel in Banff 'helped to fill a cultural vacuum in a country as new as Canada, especially in the West, and gave the guests the opportunity to dress up in an aura of splendour and elegance.'[6]

The hotels, in fact, became tourist attractions in their own right – self-contained resorts offering active cultural fare. The Queen of the West was the Banff Springs Hotel. Originally designed by Bruce Price of Vancouver and completed in 1888, it emulated the luxury of the châteaux in the French Loire Valley, and became the most fashionable holiday resort area in Canada, ranking with other famous international resorts. Located in the midst of some of the most beautiful scenery in the world, the hotel combined the facilities of a

European spa with amenities of unsurpassed elegance, providing an array of outdoor activities ranging from short hikes to rugged mountain climbing or fishing. In time a summer music program was developed, offering to the guests a quality of music-making unmatched even in concert halls across Canada. Between 1925 and 1941 the CPR employed Frances James as the leading recitalist at the Banff Springs Hotel. The clientele included the international cultural elite, connoisseurs, and supporters of music who expected the quality of the hotel's musical fare to match the elegance of its surroundings.

The ingenious plan of sponsoring concerts as part of the CPR publicity campaign to attract tourists to the West was developed by John Murray Gibbon (1875–1952), a man who left an indelible imprint on Canadian culture. Born in Ceylon, Gibbon attended Oxford University, specializing in the relationship between poetry and music. In the summers he studied Sanskrit and Greek archaeology at the University of Göttingen, acquiring there his knowledge of German literature (particularly the poetry of Heine and Goethe), culture, and folk-songs.[7] These interests, combined with his love of painting and travel and his extensive linguistic abilities, contributed to the success of his creative endeavours in Canada.

Gibbon's earliest visit to Canada's West in 1907 was an experience that affected him profoundly for the remainder of his life. Upon his return to Canada two years later, he made his first trail ride on horseback in the Rockies with Tom Wilson, the first white man to see Lake Louise, Emerald Lake, and Yoho Valley, as his guide.

At first Gibbon served the CPR as publicity agent in London. In 1913 Sir Thomas Shaughnessy offered him the position of general publicity manager for the company at the Montreal headquarters. It was in Montreal, a decade later, that his path crossed that of young Frances James, whose sister Bess worked as a publicity agent in the company's press department. In addition to engaging the singer for the Banff and Lake Louise hotels, Gibbon utilized her talents in the Rocky Mountain powwows, musical events that occurred as the culmination of the wilderness hikes of the Trail Riders of the Canadian Rockies. The Trail Riders were an idea for the promotion of the CPR and its hotels, originating with the Scot. While snowed in with a group of outfitters, guides, and fishermen at Wolverine Plateau near Tumbling Glacier one summer day in 1923, Gibbon came up with the idea of creating an Order of Trail Riders of the Canadian Rockies, in which buttons would be awarded to riders covering distances of 500, 1,000, and 2,500 miles. These awards were to foster the riders' pride in their participation, encouraging them to return the following year.[8] Quite apart from its commercial aims, the purpose of the order was to maintain and improve old trails and construct new ones as an encouragement to horseback travel in the

Canadian Rockies. The organizers shared a love of the outdoors, a wish to conserve the park's flora and fauna, and an interest in fostering Indian customs and traditions.

One of the early trail rides under the auspices of this new organization occurred in August 1925 with J. Murray Gibbon as secretary; H.B. Clough, of the Rand McNally map company of Chicago acting as vice-president; and Charles D. Walcott, secretary of the Smithsonian Institution of Washington, acting as president. One hundred riders joined them on this occasion, carrying their own sleeping-bags for placement at night in tepees erected by the Kootenay and Stoney Indians who accompanied the riders in their full regalia. Harold Eustace Key, conductor of the Mendelssohn Choir of Montreal and director of music for the CP hotels, and Frances James accompanied the riders, furnishing music at the powwows. The original ride in Yoho National Park was three days long, from the Johnson Canyon, over the Wolverine Plateau, past Mount Goodsir and Lake McArthur to Lake O'Hara and the Wapta bungalow camp. This camp served as the location for the powwow, which was followed by a dance on the veranda, with a jazz orchestra bused in from Banff for the occasion. An Indian war-dance staged by chiefs from Stoney Indian and Kootenay tribes preceded the general dance.[9]

In his autobiography, Gibbon recounts how during the first trail ride of the group the Stoney Indians from Morley made and decorated the tepees required for their camping trips, which included a large circular tent called Sundance Lodge, suitable for powwows, particularly in inclement weather. During the first powwow at Yoho Gibbon invited Frances James, soloist at the Banff Springs Hotel, to sing to the accompaniment of the YMCA piano at Field, which was carted over the road to the campsite. The singsong held at the powwow was so success-ful that Gibbon designated it an annual feature. Harold Eustace Key, who knew where to obtain a portable harmonium such as is used by the Salvation Army, was the song-leader over a number of years.[10]

Frances recalls this occasion with some humour. Upon her arrival from Montreal at Field, BC, near the Emerald Lake Chalet, she had to complete the rest of the trip on horseback. With the help of a guide, she clambered onto the back of a horse for the first time in her life to cross an eight-thousand-foot mountain pass in order to meet up with the Trail Riders' party: 'It was a rainy day when we climbed the mountain; I was sitting on the horse, hanging onto a Western saddle in pummel fashion, looking down and thinking that any moment the horse was going to slip off the side of the mountain and I was going to go with the horse. Had it not been for the assurances of the guide who told me that the horse was a very sure-footed animal, I don't think that I would have survived the trip.'

Such were the trials of a city artist, combining her artistry with John Murray Gibbon's promotional ideas for the CPR in the wilderness! In her two years of singing at the powwows, Frances James covered more than one thousand miles on horseback. Both she, and in later years Murray Adaskin, earned the Trail Riders' Badge.

The songs were sung around the camp-fire, and Frances James led the group in a singsong of popular contemporary tunes, such as 'Annie Rooney,' 'Carry Me Back to Old Virginny,' and 'Sweet Adeline.' In his autobiography Gibbon recounts that the singsongs around the camp-fire began not later than 8:00 p.m., ending at ten when hot chocolate was served from pails by the guides. He even compiled a *Songbook of the Trail Riders of the Canadian Rockies*, which became the official song-book, in use for years after his death. He wrote a number of parody texts to familiar tunes to suit the locale. For example, the tune to 'O Sole Mio' acquired a new text about Lake O'Hara; similarly, 'The Bells of St Mary's' became 'The Trails of the Rockies.'

The powwows illustrate an initial stage – and a somewhat unorthodox mode – of Gibbon's unique style of operating: that of combining the business aspects of a major Canadian corporation, the CPR, with Canadian artistic endeavours. In the years that followed he was to apply this principle on a broader scale, designing major cross-Canada cultural events in the service of the CPR.

THE CPR: A CULTURAL INSTITUTION IN CANADA
BETWEEN THE TWO WORLD WARS

It took an outsider, a visitor to Canada from Scotland, to realize that the country possessed immense cultural resources that she was failing to exploit or encourage. John Murray Gibbon discovered that the rich traditional and folk arts of French Canada, if better-known to English-speaking Canadians, could contribute to the mutual understanding of the English and the French. He further realized that folk music had the power – as did few other human endeavours – to unify a country. By creating a means of displaying various folk arts, Gibbon planned to paint a great national canvas of a country unified through its diversities. His passion for music and art, his command of languages, and his flair for creative writing were to serve as tools for promoting this country's culture. Thus, in a unique manner, Gibbon was able to combine his knowledge of poetry, the classics, and the humanities, his love of Canada, and his position as publicity agent for the CPR.

The concept of the CPR folk art and music festivals evolved out of Gibbon's mandate to publicize the new wing of the Château Frotenac after the destruction of one portion of the hotel by fire. The press from New York, Boston, Philadelphia, Chicago, Toronto, and Montreal were to be invited and provided with suitable entertainment: dinner, and music representative of Quebec folk traditions. Charles Marchand, the noted French-Canadian folk-singer, was invited to perform on this occasion. Marchand, who felt that the journalists would disdain folk-songs, would only consent to sing if the audience could understand the text. Gibbon thus proceeded to translate a group of songs into English to the total satisfaction of Marchand.[11] Encouraged by his initial success, Gibbon decided to translate into English the thirty most popular songs in Marchand's repertoire in order to foster an understanding for French songs in Ontario. Published in 1927 by J.M. Dent and Sons as *Canadian Folk Songs Old and New*, they were arranged and harmonized by Oscar O'Brien and Geoffrey O'Hara.

When asked by the general manager of the CPR hotels in the early spring of 1927 to devise some form of publicity to attract tourists to the Château Frontenac, Gibbon suggested a four-day folk festival involving singers, fiddlers, and dancers, to be combined with an exhibition of Quebec handicrafts by spinners and weavers shown in the process of producing their wares. Charles Marchand, who by 1927 had formed the vocal quartet The Bytown Troubadours, was asked to participate.[12] Gibbon also enlisted the assistance of the famous folklorist Marius Barbeau. Barbeau, at that time associated with the Department of Anthropology at the National Museum in Ottawa, was in charge of six thousand recordings of folk-songs collected from the St Lawrence Valley area. Specializing in studies of French-Canadian and Indian folklore, Barbeau was a highly respected anthropologist and ethnologist who had personally recorded and transcribed numerous folk-songs on his field trips.

At Barbeau's suggestion that the festival should span national boundaries, some of the most prominent Toronto musicians were invited to join such well-known French-Canadian singers as Alfred Laliberté, Achille Fortier, and Victor Brault. The Toronto contingent included Sir Ernest MacMillan and Healey Willan, baritone J. Campbell McInnes, and the Hart House String Quartet.

Gibbon had the full support and the financial backing of the CPR administration – its president, Sir Edward W. Beatty, in particular – to employ whatever means necessary to promote the tourist trade. By thus drawing upon his vast pool of knowledge and using his fertile imagination, this visionary was able to combine commercial means and cultural ends, becoming the motivating force behind a general Canadian cultural awakening.

Such, then, was the genesis of a series of sixteen music and folk art festivals given across Canada over a span of five years, the largest celebrations of

Canadian culture before the centennial celebration of 1967. They provided a remarkable display of folk art, music in particular, unique in the cultural history of this country. Each of the festivals, three to five days in duration, was held at one of the famous CPR hotels: Château Frontenac, Quebec; Royal York Hotel, Toronto; Royal Alexandra Hotel, Winnipeg; Hotel Saskatchewan, Regina; Hotel Palliser, Calgary; Banff Springs Hotel, Banff; Hotel Vancouver, Vancouver; and Empress Hotel, Victoria.[13]

Each festival was held at a time of year appropriate to the city where it took place and to the general theme of the event. December presented the occasion for the two Victoria Old English Yuletide festivals in 1928 and 1929. Mid-January of 1929 and 1930 witnessed the Sea Music Festivals in Vancouver and Victoria, respectively. The third week in March of 1928 and 1930 saw the great West Canadian Folk-song, Folk-dance, and Handicraft Festivals in Regina and Calgary respectively. The third week in May of 1927, 1928, and 1930 ushered in the Canadian Folk-song and Handicraft Festival in Quebec, while the Winnipeg festival took place in June 1928. The Winnipeg New Canadian Folk Song and Handicraft Festival featured songs and crafts of peoples from central Europe. The five consecutive Banff Highland Gatherings, Scottish music festivals, occurred at the end of August annually from 1927 through 1931. In Toronto, in mid-November of 1929, the English Music Festival was held on the occasion of the inauguration of the newest CPR hotel, the Royal York.

Each region's festival had a distinct flavour of its own and was an elaborate production combining vocal and instrumental performances, folk-dances, sports competitions (as in Banff's Highland Gathering), and folk arts. Pageantry was an important ingredient in all of these. In the Quebec festivals, for example, weavers were brought in from isolated rural areas to demonstrate differing traditional methods of weaving such articles as rugs, bedspreads, and a typically Canadian sash, a garment dating back to the time of the voyageurs.[14] This activity occurred within rooms exhibiting paintings and other art objects on loan from the National Gallery in Ottawa or from private sources. The works of art were always in some way connected with the theme of the festivals. Even two cooks from Ile d'Orléans were brought in to prepare special traditional dishes at the hotel. The Quebec festival included paintings illustrating folk life and scenery of French Canada by such well-known artists as Clarence A. Gagnon, Arthur Lismer, A.Y. Jackson, and Cornelius Krieghoff. The festival events filled each day to the fullest, with non-musical events fitted around the daily matinée performance and formal evening recital. The events usually culminated in a ball involving all of the guests and relating in some way to the theme of the festival.

The program of each festival was meticulously planned by Gibbon to convey an overall idea of the interdisciplinary nature of the specific cultural event. His intention was to present as complete a picture as possible of a province's living folk tradition and its historical roots. To this purpose three different types of publicity material were prepared by the CPR music department: brochures up to thirty pages in length, program books detailing events for each day of the festival, and individual programs with full printed text. In the case of the Quebec festival, a translation into English was provided for every song performed. The brochures described the cultural events highlighted at the festival, giving their historical background and listing the performers with short biographies on each. These elaborate brochures, designed by Charles W. Simpson, included photographs of artists and performing groups and even reproduced sketches or paintings by famous artists. Some of the photos serve today as a unique source of documentation on Canadian artists from that period. The inclusion of the full text of songs represented Gibbon's philosophy that each be made as accessible to and understandable by the listener as possible.

While serving as entertainment for the tourists, the festivals had at the same time distinctly educational purposes: to acquaint Canadians with their own culture, transplanted from other sources to their homeland, and to display this culture to non-Canadian visitors. Each brochure included historical essays written by Murray Gibbon. The Victoria Old English Yuletide festival, for example, explained the medieval ceremonies of the burning of the Yule-log and the bringing in of the boar's head. The performance in Banff of the ballad opera *The Jolly Beggars*, based on melodies by the eighteenth-century Scottish poet Robert Burns, prompted Gibbon to discuss Burns's education and interest in music, quoting from the poet's letters to explain how he combined his tunes with his poetry.

Gibbon's historical essays in the festival brochures displayed his remarkable knowledge both of music from the past and of the activities of his musicologist and ethnomusicologist colleagues, who were researching and transcribing this music from old notation into that of the twentieth century. A case in point was his revival of the thirteenth-century *pastourelle* (pastoral play), *Le Jeu de Robin et Marion* by the trouvère Adam de la Halle, making this Canadian production the second performance of the work since the Middle Ages. In *Tribute to a Nation-Builder*, Gibbon states his reasons for arranging for the performance of this work. Remembering Charles Marchand's warning that folk music cannot be revived on a national scale because it is considered mere 'habitant stuff' or 'peasant music,' he decided to show that the tradition of some folk-songs dates back to the aristocratic troubadours and trouvères of the Middle Ages. For the performance of the medieval *pastourelle* he engaged the co-operation of Professor Jean Beck of the University of Pennsylvania and Wilfrid Pelletier, conductor of the Metropolitan Opera, who undertook to get the opera company to stage the production in Quebec.

Folk-songs, the musical substance of every festival, were presented in many different guises: unaccompanied, or accompanied only with a lute or some other string instrument; in arrangements for instrumental or vocal quartets; or as bases for newly composed choral compositions, orchestral suites, and ballad operas. A typical program from the Quebec music festival combined groups singing madrigals of the French Renaissance with soloists such as J. Campbell McInnes accompanied at the piano by Sir Ernest MacMillan, or Jeanne Dusseau, giving her famous rendition of *Ma Fille Veux-Tu un Bouquet?* from a collection of folk-songs edited by Marius Barbeau. Even the Hart House String Quartet played repertoire based on folk-songs, composed by Leo Smith, Ernest MacMillan, and Oscar O'Brien.

Milton Blackstone, violist in the Hart House String Quartet, suggested during the Quebec festival of 1927 that the CPR sponsor a competition and offer a prize for orchestral and vocal compositions based on French-Canadian folk music. At Gibbon's recommendation, the president of the CPR, Sir Edward W. Beatty, donated three thousand dollars for this purpose. An international jury was formed, consisting of such well-known personalities as Sir Hugh Allen of the Royal College of Music in London, Pierre Vidal of the Paris Conservatoire, Eric de la Marter of the Chicago Civic Symphony Orchestra, and Achille Fortier, the Montreal teacher and composer. Two of the winning compositions, Claude Champagne's *Suite Canadienne* and Ernest MacMillan's *Six Bergerettes du Bas Canada*, were *premièred* at the Quebec festival the following year.[15] The Beatty prize, therefore, represented one of the earliest formal commissions of Canadian compositions and reinforced the CPR's position as promoter of Canadian music.

The period of the CPR festivals can also be viewed as a significant movement towards the promotion of Canadian performing talent. One of John Murray Gibbon's many skills was that of impresario. He not only engaged the major performers of the folk and classical repertoire across Canada, but also had a keen sense for discovering such new talents as Frances James. Under his direction, the CPR became the employer of a veritable army of Canadian musical artists. Frances James, who emerged to dominate the vocal scene of the time, knew and interacted with all of them.

James's career was then in its early stages and was entirely sponsored by John Murray Gibbon and the CPR. Not only did she take part in all the festivals in Banff, Victoria, and Vancouver, but also she was employed as the official concert singer at the Banff Springs Hotel. She and John Deacon, also an artist at the hotel, performed alternately two weeks at the Château Lake Louise and two weeks at the Banff Springs Hotel. This marked the beginning of her acquisition of what developed into a remarkably broad repertoire. Each evening's concert required a different program, and duplication of the Lake Louise and Banff repertoire had to be avoided, because many of the guests visited both hotels.

The 1928–30 seasons were particularly busy for James: the period of June through September 1928 was spent at Banff; at Christmas she took part in the CPR festival in Victoria and two weeks later in the Vancouver festival of 1929; a tour across Canada followed as part of the Six Concerts of British and Canadian Music, which ended in Victoria with a solo concert in November and another in December. She participated in the 1929 Victoria Yuletide Festival, and several weeks later in the Sea Music Festival and the summer season in Banff.

The Banff Highland Gatherings differed considerably in content and theme from any of the other festivals. They celebrated the Scots' heritage and included music by various highland regiments in Canada. Highland dancing and bagpipe competitions prominently displayed the rich costumes of the various clans. Athletic games – such as tossing the caber or putting the shot – were annual events. In the evenings, concerts of Scottish music recalled the minstrelsy of the old Scottish courts and glorified the memory of the revered poet Robert Burns. These concerts included songs in Gaelic, to show that the language still lived in many parts of Canada and to display the beauty of the melodies of these old Celtic songs from the Highlands and the Hebrides.

Occasionally Gibbon sponsored internationally known figures at Banff; as in 1929 he brought from Scotland the famous baritone Robert Burnett, prize bag-pipers, and sisters Marjory Kennedy-Fraser and Margaret Kennedy. Marjory Kennedy-Fraser was a Scottish composer, singer, and specialist in songs of the Hebrides, while Margaret Kennedy was a singer and pianist.

Other Banff festival events included Sunday open-air church services at the Sun Dance Canyon, conducted by the colorful novelist Ralph Connor, also known as the Reverend Dr Charles W. Gordon. Reverend Gordon became famous for conducting the service while dressed in a kilt and standing on a platform in the middle of a water-hole at the Banff Golf Course, with his congregation lining the shore and sitting on the grassy hillocks nearby. His sermons are still remembered by people who attended them.

The musical highlights of the Banff festivals, however, were the ballad operas. Presented in lavish costumes and supported by small instrumental ensembles, these works were modelled on the eighteenth-century tradition of stage entertainments, consisting of spoken dialogue and musical numbers taken from the folk-song repertoire and harmonized by local musicians. Over the five years of these music festivals, the CPR commissioned a number of ballad operas, reviving this eighteenth-century tradition and creating a unique chapter in the history of the opera in Canada. Banff was the centre for performances of ballad operas based on topics from British history. *The Jolly Beggars* was presented there in 1928 and in 1930. Also performed in Banff in 1928 was *At the Court of James v*, on a text by John Murray Gibbon, in collaboration with R.S. Tait, Historiographer Royal of Scotland. *Prince Charlie and Flora*, written by Gibbon, with music arranged by Healey Willan and stage set designed by Charles W. Simpson, *premièred* in Banff in 1929 and was repeated there two years later. Willan's *The Ayreshire Ploughman*, based on traditional Scottish melodies, was written for the 1930 Banff festival, while 1931 saw the *première* of *Prince Charming*, with songs arranged by Sir Ernest MacMillan. Other ballad operas, such as *Bound for the Rio Grande*, based on English sea-shanties, were composed for the 1929 Vancouver festival and were repeated the same year in Toronto on the occasion of the opening of the Royal York Hotel.[16] Victoria presented three such operas: Willan's *The Chester Mysteries*, possibly based on his incidental music of 1919;[17] his *Indian Nativity Play*, with words by Captain Alexander Ramsay of Victoria; and Harold Eustace Key's *Christmas with Herrick*.

Some of the ballad operas featured only one soloist accompanied by a choral group, or used only male characters – as in Willan's *Order of Good Cheer*. Others, such as Victoria's *Indian Nativity Play*, served as means of combining music with pageantry. In many instances Gibbon provided the text, while the stage set was specially designed for each occasion by such CPR artists as Charles W. Simpson and by a now-famous member of the Canadian Group of Seven painters, Arthur Lismer. The musical directors were, in alternation, Harold Eustace Key and Alfred Heather, while the director of Scottish diction, where appropriate, was J. Campbell McInnes. The CPR-sponsored ballad operas, therefore, represented a true collaborative effort between contemporary Canadian painters, composers, authors, and musicians, all working under Gibbon's direction and supervision.

Frances James was the star performer in the Banff ballad operas. The 1928 program brochure cites her performances as the queen in *Mary Queen of Scots*. Her other operatic roles included one of the female vagrants in *The Jolly Beggars*, Agnes Fleming in *The Ayrshire Ploughman*, and Flora in *Prince Charlie and Flora*. *The Jolly Beggars* was a comedy using characters from the lowly walks of life: the poor, and such social outcasts as a maimed soldier, a fiddler, a tinker, the widow of a highland freebooter, a bard and ballad singer, the soldier's lass, and two female vagrants. *The Ayrshire Ploughman* was called 'a romantic ballad opera' and incorporated songs of Robert Burns. The part of Robert Burns was sung by J. Campbell McInnes, while other members of the cast included Frances James, Jean Haig, Beatrice Morson, Allan Wilson, Allan

Burt, Enid Gray, and Amy Fleming. *Prince Charlie and Flora* was originally written for six voices, plus an instrumental accompaniment of flute, violin, cello, and piano.[18] The seventeen songs, arrangements of traditional Scottish melodies, were sung and acted by Stanley Maxted, Catherine Wright, Finley Campbell, Herbert Hewetson, and Henry Button, in addition to Frances James. This opera seems to have been particularly successful.

Another ballad opera, Vaughan Williams's *Hugh the Drover*, had its Canadian *première* in Toronto in 1929 to mark the opening of the CPR's Royal York Hotel. It was produced by Alfred Heather in co-operation with the Toronto Conservatory of Music opera workshop, with Sir Ernest MacMillan as conductor and Arthur Lismer as designer of the stage sets. Hector Charlesworth, the Toronto critic for *Saturday Night*, judged this 'the most ambitious and the most brilliantly successful operatic production yet given under purely Canadian auspices.'[19]

Frances James, who by then had built up a reputation in Western Canada as a leading soprano, did not take part in this Toronto production because of her involvement with the Six Concerts of British and Canadian Music. Organized by the CPR during the 1929–30 season as an outgrowth of the music festivals, the concerts featured five groups of artists and the Hart House String Quartet. All had participated in the festivals and had attained great popularity. The Kennedy sisters, brought to Canada from the British Isles by Gibbon for the 1929 Banff festival, gave one of the concerts. Other artists included Stanley Maxted and Frances James, who shared a program, with Gwendolyn Williams, the official accompanist at the Banff Springs Hotel, at the piano; a violin-soprano-piano trio from Toronto – Florence Hood, Jean Rowe, and Winnifred MacMillan – John Goss, popular for his interpretation of ballads and sea-shanties; the Hart House String Quartet; and a father-and-son team, tenor and cellist Rodolphe and Lucien Plamondon.

The six groups of artists performed at CPR hotels in six Canadian cities: Toronto, Winnipeg, Regina, Calgary, Victoria, and Vancouver. While the official purpose of the concerts was to provide the hotel guests with music at times when the great festivals were not in operation, they also served a propagandistic and educational aim: to create an awareness of such British contemporary composers as Elgar, Stanford, Parry, Delius, Holst, Cyril Scott, Bax, and Dame Ethel Smyth. Gibbon, who was the organizer of these concerts, recognized that, although Canada was exposed to much good music through performances of New York and other non-Canadian artists, most of it was of European origin to the detriment of British music, which was suffering benign neglect. He thought that it was in the national interest for Canadians to have the opportunity to hear the music that was their legitimate heritage. Stanley

Maxted was engaged by Gibbon to sing the A.A. Milne children's songs, *When We Were Very Young*, set to music by Fraser Simson. Maxted had a special talent for dramatizing these songs in recital, and his presentation of them was very popular with audiences. Frances James's repertoire was more serious, including such songs from the classical repertoire as Mozart's *Exsultate, Jubilate*, the Bach-Gounod *Ave Maria*, a group of Russian art songs by Rachmaninoff and Gretchaninoff, and works by such modern English composers as Cyril Scott, Roger Quilter, and Michael Head. Music critic Dan A. Cameron of the *Regina Star* reviewed her 1929 Regina appearance: 'Miss James has a lovely voice, opulent in tone and intimately responsive to imaginative and dynamic suggestion. She has great natural charm, dramatic intensity, and a delicate musical sense, all of which make her a delightful singer.' These musical events were publicized by the CPR not just in the towns in which they occurred but also in newspapers all across Canada.

The list of singers and instrumentalists hired by John Murray Gibbon to perform in the CPR festivals and other CPR-sponsored cultural events reveals a cross-section of Canadian artists. The nature of their activities for the CPR affords an interesting glimpse into the nature of music-making in early twentieth-century Canada. It encapsulates the musical world surrounding the young Canadian soprano Frances James at the beginning of her career. Oscar O'Brien, Harold Eustace Key, Alfred Heather, Ernest MacMillan, the Hart House String Quartet, and Jeanne Dusseau were frequent participants in the festival programs.

Composer, pianist, folklorist, and arranger of hundreds of folk-songs, Oscar O'Brien (1842–1958) was particularly influential in the Quebec festivals. One of his songs on a poem by John Murray Gibbon, *Love Song from the Caravan*, dating from 1934, was later incorporated by Frances James into her radio series 'Heritage of Song,' thirteen radio concerts sponsored by the CPR.

Founder and director of the Mendelssohn Choir in Montreal, Harold Eustace Key (1881–?) was general musical director for the CPR hotels. Organist, choirmaster, singer, conductor, arranger, accompanist, and composer, he was involved with all of the music festivals. In Banff he conducted the ballad opera *The Jolly Beggars*, while in Victoria he arranged the music for *Christmas with Herrick*. As accompanist he performed with singers Cédia Brault in Quebec and Frances James in Victoria. At the Victoria Yuletide Festival of 1928, he sang the baritone part with the Victoria Festival Quartette, a group comprising Frances James, Josephine Wood, contralto, and Herbert Hewetson, tenor. Dressed in sumptuous Elizabethan costumes the quartet presented Christmas carols. One of Key's songs, *In Flanders Fields* (text by John McCrae), was also incorporated into Frances James's radio repertoire. Key's many arrangements include the first volume of Gibbon's *Northland Songs* (published by Gordon P. Thompson, 1936).

Another versatile musician in the employ of the CPR was voice teacher, tenor soloist, and opera producer Alfred Heather (1876–1932). He staged and produced two ballad operas in Banff, *Prince Charlie and Flora* in 1929 and *The Ayrshire Ploughman* in 1930, and directed the musical production of Vaughan Williams's *Hugh the Drover* in Toronto. Heather's vocal interests led to his frequent appearances at the festivals as tenor soloist, and to attempts to establish a permanent opera company. The vocal group that provided solos and choruses for the Banff ballad operas from 1929 to 1931 was called The Alfred Heather Light Opera Company.

Ernest MacMillan (1893–1973) was also a frequent participant. By 1926 he had succeeded A.S. Vogt as principal of the Toronto Conservatory of Music and a year later as dean of the Faculty of Music at the University of Toronto, and had already acquired a reputation for his annual performances of the *St Matthew Passion*, which became a Toronto tradition over a period of thirty years. In addition to his contribution as composer, he appeared at the 1927 Quebec festival as accompanist to J. Campbell McInnes in five folk-songs from collections by Marius Barbeau translated by Gibbon. The ballad opera *Prince Charming*, presented in Banff in 1931, was based on folk-songs arranged by MacMillan. His arrangements of Irish and French-Canadian songs of the sea were interpreted at the Vancouver Sea Music Festival by the noted soprano Jeanne Dusseau, to the accompaniment of the Hart House String Quartet.

The quartet performed at three of the festivals – Quebec in 1927, Vancouver and Toronto in 1929 – and was a featured group at the CPR-sponsored Six Concerts of British and Canadian Music, appearing in concerts across Canada. In addition to the quartet, another chamber group employed by the CPR during this period was the Banff Springs Hotel Quintette, formed under the auspices of the CPR to perform at the Banff festival of 1930. Three of its members were Adolph Koldofsky, first violin; Murray Adaskin, second violin; and Gwendolyn Williams, piano. While short-lived, the quintet served as the genesis, in 1932, of a piano trio consisting of Murray Adaskin, violin; Louis Crerar, piano; and John Adaskin, cello. Later known as the Toronto Trio, the group owed its existence and its employment over a period of twenty years to the CPR.

By enlisting the efforts of Canada's leading musicians, the CPR functioned as this country's first cultural organization. In addition to the already-mentioned artists, the cultural portrait of music in the late 1920s depicts a rich panoply of singers for the most part forgotten today. They were among the most eminent Canadian singers of the times, whose names must be mentioned in order to create a musical context for the early career of Frances James. These included baritones J. Campbell McInnes (1873–1945), John Goss (1894–1953), George Lambert (1900–71), and Ernest Morgan; tenors Stanley Maxted, John Deacon, Herbert Hewetson, and Rodolphe Plamondon (1876–1940), and bass Ulysse Paquin (1885–1972); sopranos Jean Haig, Enid Gray, Amy Fleming, Frances James, and Jeanne Dusseau (1893–); mezzo-soprano Cédia Brault; and contraltos Catherine Wright, Ruth Matheson, and Josephine Wood. They all performed in the CPR-sponsored music events of the late 1920s, and many became associated in the next decade with radio broadcasting.

Scottish-born J. Campbell McInnes had sung principal roles at major English music festivals prior to emigrating to Canada in 1919. He was also soloist with such leading North American orchestras as those in Philadelphia, Chicago, and Cleveland. He became director of diction for the American Opera Company and also taught diction in Toronto, developing a Canada-wide reputation as a specialist in that field. Between 1923 and 1938 he was known for his famous interpretation of the role of Christus in the *St Matthew Passion*, which he sang under Sir Ernest MacMillan's baton for fifteen seasons. McInnes was considered one of Canada's leading oratorio singers. By the time Gibbon solicited his services for the CPR festivals his reputation was already well established.

Before his involvement with the CPR McInnes had initiated in 1922 the popular Sunday Evening Concerts at Hart House in Toronto. They featured the Sunday Evening Songsters, a college-sponsored choir conducted by him, who presented ethnic folk-songs. He often led singsongs and antiphonal singing at Hart House, establishing himself as a powerful influence in the life of that institution and in the education of the young men who attended it.[20] McInnes participated in the CPR music festivals as director of a group of madrigal singers (Quebec 1927), as orchestrator of the ballad opera *The Jolly Beggars* (Banff 1928), as soloist in songs by Robert Burns (Banff 1931), and as male lead in *The Jolly Beggars* and *The Ayrshire Ploughman* (Banff 1930). At the Toronto festival he gave lectures on music. He also figured prominently as a radio artist throughout the 1930s in the early days of broadcasting. His legacy was succinctly summarized by Ralph Vaughan Williams, whose *Sea Symphony* (1910) and *Five Mystical Songs* (1911) were *premièred* by the singer: 'a lovely baritone voice, a fine sense of words and, above all, the power which few singers possess to make a time live.'[21]

Also active at the Banff festivals were George Lambert, Ernest Morgan, and Stanley Maxted. Lambert, who spent most of his career as a teacher at the Toronto Conservatory of Music, and who sang the role of Christus in Sir Ernest MacMillan's annual presentations of the *St Matthew Passion* from McInnes's retirement in 1938 until 1945, had just returned from his studies in Italy when he was engaged by Gibbon for the 1931 Banff festival. There he performed in the ensemble directed by Alfred Heather known as the Musical Crusaders. The nine-member vocal group, which included Frances James, sang choruses at evening concerts and provided soloists for the ballad operas. Frances James, who remembers Lambert as a very good singer and excellent musician, recalls his concern during his Banff stay as to whether he should follow a concert or a teaching career. After 1931 he chose to settle in Toronto and became one of Canada's foremost voice teachers and coaches.

Ernest Morgan's rich voice and dramatic interpretations of Canadian folk-songs had already made him a favourite with Canadian audiences by the time he sang in the 1928 ballad opera *The Jolly Beggars* in Banff. Born in Cardiff, Morgan came to Canada as a boy and incorporated a number of special interests into his career: he was a music and drama critic for the *Globe and Mail*, organist-choirmaster, actor, producer, and radio executive. He joined the CBC in 1933, initiating a broadcasting career that included a position as senior program director and music producer in Vancouver (1940–4) as well as supervisor of international exchange programs for the CBC in Toronto.[22]

Stanley Maxted began his singing career in England as a boy soprano. Until the First World War, when he joined the Canadian artillery, he lived in Toronto, and after the war he continued his voice studies in Toronto and Pittsburgh. Before his appearances at the Banff festivals he had already made his reputation in Montreal as an oratorio singer with a brilliant pure tenor voice. He participated in the Banff Highland Gathering and Scottish Music Festival of 1929, where he sang in Healey Willan's ballad opera *Prince Charlie and Flora*.

Maxted was Frances James's vocal partner in the six CPR-sponsored cross-country concerts of British and Canadian music. His vocal career was at its peak throughout the 1930s when he became one of the leading male radio artists. With Frances James he participated in a series of weekly programs called the 'General Electric Vagabonds,' combining light, popular music with folk-songs. He was also one of four singers engaged by Hector Charlesworth, director of the Canadian Radio Broadcasting Commission (1933–6), to sing professionally for the network. His career as radio artist in the 1930s was closely linked with that of Frances James. In 1937 Maxted left Canada to join the BBC as a war correspondent, and throughout the war years covered stories from Aberdeen to Zanzibar and also in the Pacific. He built up a reputation as an announcer of 'cool, slow-spoken reports from dangerous places,' and eventually settled as a broadcaster in England.[23]

John Deacon and Herbert Hewetson were also associated with the CPR's Banff music festivals and were members of the Alfred Heather Light Opera Company. Originally from Belleville, Deacon was heir to the well-known Deacon Shirt Company. The Banff operatic engagement followed his New York voice studies with Edward Johnson. His potential for a successful career at the Metropolitan Opera was never fulfilled because of his responsibilities to his father's business and his eventual directorship of the company.

At the time of her involvement with the CPR festivals, soprano Jeanne Dusseau had already acquired an international reputation and was at the height of her concert career. Ruth Thom (her original name) came to Toronto from Scotland as a child. By 1921 she was singing with the Chicago Lyric Opera, where she created the role of Ninetta in the world *première* of Prokofiev's *Love for Three Oranges*. Subsequently, she performed with symphony orchestras in Toronto, New York, Boston, and Cincinnati and toured Western Canada in Canadian folk-song concerts sponsored by the Association of Canadian Clubs.[24] In her guest appearances at the CPR festivals between 1927 and 1931 she performed renditions of numerous folk-songs, then achieved success with the Sadler's Wells Opera in London. As a brilliant Canadian concert artist she was much in demand in the Quebec festivals, four of the Banff festivals, and those in Vancouver and Toronto. After her retirement as a performer in 1942, Dusseau taught in New York and Washington.[25]

Jean Haig, Enid Gray, Amy Fleming, Catherine Wright, Ruth Matheson, and Josephine Wood were all singers with the Alfred Heather Light Opera Company in Banff and in Victoria, engaged by the CPR for the duration of the concert season. Jean Haig's career was well established by the time Frances James arrived on the Toronto scene in the early 1930s, and, like Frances James and Stanley Maxted, she became one of the artists figuring in the early history of radio broadcasting in Canada. She was employed by Hector Charlesworth for the Canadian Radio Broadcasting Commission, becoming a member of one of the commission's standing vocal quartets, which included Billie Bell, a contralto specializing in jazz singing, Stanley Maxted, and Wishart Campbell, baritone. On another occasion, with Frances James and Billie Bell, Haig formed a radio trio called the Triolets, singing arrangements of light- and folk-music by Percy Faith. Jean Haig was one of the official singers for all of the CPR musical and broadcasting activities in Toronto and Banff.

The CPR music festivals held between 1927 and 1931 assumed a dominant position in early-twentieth-century musical life in Canada. Products of a union between Canadian art and one of the largest Canadian pre-war business corporations, their benefit to Canadian culture by far exceeded the original intentions of the organizers and participants.

Above all, the CPR festivals presented a context through which the young soprano, Frances James, attained prominence, establishing herself in a career that was to be inextricably bound with the development of radio broadcasting and the Canadian concert scene until the 1950s.

MURRAY ADASKIN

Murray Adaskin was born on 28 March 1906 in the heart of Toronto's colourful Jewish district, where horse-drawn carts clattered noisily through the narrow streets and bustling shoppers picked over the fruit and vegetables sold in sidewalk stands. His father, Samuel Adaskin, was a Russian wood-turner and carver, a craftsman and artist of great skill and scruple, engaged in his own woodworking business in Riga (now part of Latvia), when he found it necessary to leave the country because of the persecution of the Jews by the Russians. He emigrated to Canada in 1903, leaving behind his wife and two young sons – Leslie and Harry – until he could save enough money to pay for their transoceanic trip. Nine months after his arrival in Canada, Samuel Adaskin and his family were united on the soil of their adopted country. Penniless, they settled in a rented house at Foster Place, a short street south of Dundas, off Elizabeth Street. A feather bed and a silvered samovar, transported from their native land, were their only material possessions.

Two childhood impressions left a strong imprint on Murray: the large electric power station that dominated their street, and the house in which he lived – a shack with a garden in the small backyard that also contained the outhouse. Having to visit the outhouse during the blustering Toronto winters was a challenging experience for the family. In their early days in Canada, the residence represented sheer heaven to the elder Adaskins. Not having been schooled in the English language in Russia, they found Toronto's Jewish district a haven where they could communicate with their neighbours in Yiddish or Russian.

Murray's brother John was born two years after him. A fifth child, Gordon, was born considerably later as a product of Samuel Adaskin's second marriage, which followed his wife's death in 1927. The family changed residence on a number of occasions, moving from Foster Place to a house on Ontario Street south of Carlton and one block west of Parliament Street, then to Claremont Street in the Italian district, where, through his playmates, Murray picked up swear-words in yet another language.

Samuel Adaskin had been brought up in a closely knit family with a strictly religious background. Thus, shortly after their arrival in Canada, the elder Adaskins started sponsoring the emigration of their family members to Canada; their parents, brothers, sisters, nephews, and nieces immigrated one by one, always finding a shelter with Murray's parents until they could learn the language and find a job. The Adaskin house – even the little shack at Foster Place – was always full of relatives, who shared with Murray's parents the modest meals and facilities. These humble people served as a model for

Murray's own generosity evident in later years towards his students, friends, and colleagues.

The Adaskin children's education in the Hebrew language and traditions was at first fostered by Murray's mother, who would seat them around the kitchen table and have them read from their Talmud in Hebrew while she moved around the kitchen. Although Murray at that time could not understand a word of what he read, his mother, who had memorized the entire Talmud, would correct him, satisfied that he had a reading knowledge of the language. Murray's early education was continued by his paternal grandfather, whom he remembers as a very wise but fanatically religious man.

The Jews in Russia at the time Murray's grandparents lived there frequently had no access to schools other than the *chadder*, the religious schools where they learned to memorize the Talmud in Hebrew. In the process they became very learned in the philosophy of the Hebrew religion. Calligraphy was an important part of this education, and Murray's later fascination with the beauty and intricacies of longhand writing stems from the calligraphic art of both his grandfather and his mother. His grandfather was a serious, scholarly man, a devout Orthodox, who would frequently be called upon by small congregations to be their cantor. On those occasions all four boys were recruited to sing in the choir. One of the tunes they sang in the synagogue was later incorporated into a fanfare composed by Murray on the occasion of the opening of the Saskatchewan Centre of the Arts in Regina in 1970.

Despite the family's relative poverty, the children's musical education was a priority. Both parents loved music. Samuel Adaskin delighted in chamber music, and Murray's mother sang Russian and Hebrew folk-songs as she worked around the house, as well as all the tunes that she heard her children practising. The parents wanted their sons to have the musical education they themselves had lacked. At first a violin was purchased, and later a piano. Three of the boys – Harry, John, and Murray – made a career in music and have left a strong imprint on Canadian musical culture. Leslie, who did not pursue an artistic career, spent twenty years as a salesman in the United States. Gordon, whose birth coincided with the year of Frances and Murray's wedding, distinguished himself as a painter. A professor in the school of architecture at the University of Manitoba, he is frequently called upon to instruct at the Banff School of Fine Arts.

As a cellist and trumpet player, John was the most versatile of the musical brothers. Murray remembers John's extraordinary musicianship: 'When he played a melodic line, it would melt your heart. From the first note he was in another world. At that time we children did not have the ability to reproduce that quality of sound.' Early in his musical career John was an orchestral musician, frequently playing in radio shows and in groups directed by Murray. In the late 1920s Murray conducted an orchestra for a small theatre company. John was a cellist in this orchestra and occasionally provided trumpet solos. He was cellist in Murray's trio when it was first formed in Banff in 1932.

John's talents were not just musical but also mechanical. At age seven he taught himself how to drive a Model-T Ford, and about the same time he built one of the first peanut-tube crystal radio sets in Toronto. The set could receive only nocturnal transmissions from Schenectady, NY, one of the first sending stations in America. Listening to this radio was a big family event; all gathered around, eagerly awaiting the broadcasts, which could be heard only with earphones. Murray remembers his brother's bedroom, out of bounds to everyone because of the abundance of wires required for the crystal set. Touching the wrong wire would give one a hefty shock in addition to upsetting John's special wiring system.

Later, during the early days of broadcasting in the National Carbon Company Studios in the 1930s, John's technical bent was made use of. The engineer would rely on the conductor, Geoffrey Waddington, to advise him about the instrumental balance during the broadcast. In these early days of music broadcasting the position of music producer had not yet been created, and the conductor was not able to judge the technical aspects of the balance of sound. John, because of his combined mechanical and musical abilities, was asked by Waddington to leave the cello section, sit beside the engineer in the recording booth, and advise the conductor as to which instrumental groups or solos should be brought out more. Eventually John became one of the top music producers in Canada.

Harry, as the oldest child, was first to embark upon musical studies. He started private violin lessons at age seven, and five years later studied with Bertha Adamson at the Toronto Conservatory of Music. A scholarship from the conservatory lightened the family's financial burden; despite the parents' support of their children's musical activities, finding the money was never easy. Harry continued his music instruction with Luigi von Kunits at the Canadian Academy of Music, and between 1919 and 1922 held the position of second violin in the Academy String Quartet. A few years later he became a member of the Hart House String Quartet, an association that lasted until 1938.

The Hart House String Quartet, consisting of Geza de Kresz (first violin), Harry Adaskin (second violin), Milton Blackstone (viola), Boris Hambourg (cello), was officially formed in 1925 under the patronage of Vincent Massey, thus becoming the first fully subsidized string quartet in Canada. The Massey Foundation guaranteed salaries and benefits, in return for which the members were to be full-time performers with the group.[26] Massey's one demand was that they never refuse a Canadian engagement in a small town that could not pay their fee; they played across Canada on numerous cross-country tours. For many years Hart House was their official headquarters, the Hart House Theatre in particular, where they gave series of six to eight annual concerts. In the 1930s these concerts came to be recognized as one of the focal points of Toronto's musical life and were always well attended. The quartet travelled frequently on extended tours through the United States and Europe, supported by a lucrative stipend from the Massey Foundation even through the years of the Depression.

The Adaskin parents were always very proud of their children's musical accomplishments, and Murray still remembers his father sitting in the front row of the Hart House Theatre listening as if in a sublime state to the late Beethoven quartets performed by the Hart House String Quartet. These compositions, written by a deaf, tormented genius, are not easy to understand, but they were Samuel Adaskin's favourite musical fare.

Murray was very close to his brothers, with whom he shared an innate sense of humour and a love of childish pranks. As fans of Charlie Chaplin movies, they never missed a show, often emerging from the theatre screaming with laughter. The Chaplinesque qualities – the sense of fun, and the total delight in life – remain part of Murray's personality up to the present day.

Harry was Murray's first violin teacher. When, after only eight years of public school, Murray wanted to discontinue his formal schooling in order to pursue full-time violin studies, his father, overjoyed that yet a second son wanted to follow the career of a violinist, gave him his full approval. Murray's formal education ended, therefore, in 1921 when he was fifteen. His true education, however, continued throughout the rest of his life. Riding to work on streetcars, at times for more than an hour each way, Murray purposely read books beyond his understanding, decoding them with the aid of a pocket dictionary that was his constant companion. Some words needed to be looked up many times before their meaning was clearly understood and they became incorporated into his vocabulary. This absorption in his reading material caused him sometimes to ride past his stop, so that a walk of several blocks to the theatre in which he was playing that day would almost make him late for the engagement.

Soon after he left school, Murray's career as a violinist began. Providing background music for silent movies was one of his earliest sources of income. Until 1931, when the talkies first appeared in Toronto theatres, silent movies from Hollywood dominated the entertainment market. The movie-houses employed anywhere from one keyboard player to a whole group of orchestral musicians with a conductor, providing a major source of income for a considerable number of Toronto artists. The job was highly paid, relative to other jobs at the time; a musician could earn between forty and sixty dollars per week. At first Murray played with a pianist in the pit of a small theatre in Mimico on the outskirts of Toronto, later at the centrally located Uptown Theatre in an orchestra with a conductor. Some of the larger Toronto movie-houses employing conductors at that time were the Uptown, the Regent, the Tivoli, and the Princess theatres.

The conductor's role required considerable skill in that the music had to be timed with split-second precision. Distributed with the film was a thick volume, a compendium of musical effects. The conductor looked at the music in advance, choosing selected measures appropriate to the action of the movie. He had a cue sheet with which he watched the film, co-ordinating the orchestra with the moving picture. The musicians, too, read from the compendium.

Buddy Collins, in particular, was a skilled conductor whose sense of timing was remarkable. Murray recalls a whole week when the orchestra Collins conducted had to be co-ordinated with a player piano spotlighted on the stage, playing Gershwin's *Rhapsody in Blue*. The co-ordination was difficult enough to achieve when the piano and orchestra played in alternation, but the real test for Collins, as conductor, occurred in sections when both played simultaneously.

During one particularly difficult year when, as a result of their mother's illness, all the Adaskin children were relied upon to contribute additional funds to the family budget, Murray spent twelve consecutive months playing two engagements a day and a regular Monday morning rehearsal. For a while Murray also played in the Georgian Room at Eaton's department store where, as leader of a small ensemble, he was required to conduct while playing his violin. He was the *stehgeiger*, the leader who gave cues with his fiddle. The dozen musicians in the orchestra provided music on the balcony of the Georgian Room during lunchtime, on a daily basis.

The theatre musicians, who were in daily contact with one another, formed a tightly knit circle in which pranks often alleviated the mechanical aspects of music making. On one occasion when Murray was conducting his own orchestra for a stock company theatre, he perpetrated a joke on his brother John, cellist with the orchestra, who occasionally played solo trumpet passages. Just before such a solo, Murray placed a nail in the mouthpiece of the instrument. As usual, he was conducting with his face to the audience and surrounded by his orchestra, because he was also first violinist. Turning to John and trying to keep a serious face, he gave him his entrance cue with the bow. The nail had clogged the hole in the trumpet causing John's eyes to pop as he blew into the silent instrument. The orchestra, of course, collapsed with laughter, much to the anger and frustration of the soloist, who proceeded calmly to extract the offending object by turning the trumpet upside down.

Similarly, on another occasion with the stock company theatre, the orchestra was called upon to provide music for a Persian garden scene. The music chosen was Albert Ketèlbey's *In a Persian Market*, 'the most rotten, cheapest piece we ever played.' Violinist Samuel Hersenhoren, who was not a member of that particular orchestra but was a close friend of Murray and the musicians, often sat in the pit to see the show. One day, he stumbled upon a water whistle lying on a table in the property room, right under the stage, near the stage door. It was the type of whistle that was capable of reproducing a number of bird sounds. In the midst of Ketèlbey's music the members of the orchestra were surprised to hear bird sounds. Looking around, they saw Hersenhoren poking his head in the pit blowing away on the whistle. Again the orchestra laughed hysterically under the manager's threatening glances.

Next to silent movies, live theatre was the most popular entertainment with Toronto audiences. Here, too, music played an important role, but was primarily performed at intermissions, between the acts of a play. From 1927 to 1930 Murray conducted his own orchestra at the Empire Theatre, preparing the music for the intermission, always trying to match the mood at the end of the act and to anticipate that at the opening of the next. Frequently he even wrote his own music, his first attempts at composing. On one occasion when a Chinese scene in a play required accompanying music, Murray copied a tune by ear from the first Chinese record that ever came to Canada. He then proceeded to play it on the violin and to orchestrate it for his group. His practical experience from these early days when his ear was his only guide laid a foundation for his later formal composition studies.

The Empire Theatre, located on Temperance Street, was a lovely old structure styled after the English theatres, with one balcony and a seating capacity of about one thousand. The theatre was always well attended, providing enough business for nightly performances and two weekly matinées. A new play was presented each week. The company performed comedies, serious plays, and Christmas pantomimes. Most of the leading actors were New Yorkers hired by the theatre manager, who also chose the ballet groups and the occasional dancing chorus line. Enjoying fame at the time were actresses Deirdre Doyle and Edith Tagliaferro, both of whom were regular members of the Empire Theatre Company. The players in the six-man orchestra included violinist Louis Sherman, who acted as Murray's sidekick, a pianist, a string bassist, a cellist, and a clarinettist. John Adaskin was the regular cellist, and Percy Faith, the arranger of the orchestra's music, occasionally substituted for Leo Barkin, the regular keyboard player. Murray worked at the Empire Theatre for four seasons.

During the nine years that followed his withdrawal from his public school studies, Murray continued his violin lessons with his brother Harry, while simultaneously working for a living. Because of the great demand for live music in Toronto, the local musicians had a ready market for their talents in movie-houses, tea-rooms, restaurants, theatres, and hotels. Every theatre and movie-house had an orchestra, providing the musicians with full-time employment and generous incomes. Many of them also played in the Toronto Symphony Orchestra, or the New Symphony Orchestra as it was known between 1923 and 1927.

From 1906 to 1918 Toronto had supported a symphony under the direction of Frank Welsman, with the players drawn primarily from the faculty and students of the Toronto Conservatory of Music. The concert-master of the symphony was Bertha Adamson, the leading Toronto violin teacher at the time.[27] In 1922 the orchestra was reactivated under the baton of Luigi von Kunits (1870–1931). Born in Vienna, von Kunits was schooled in the Sevčik, Bruckner, and Hanslick traditions, which he transmitted to his Canadian students. Upon his arrival in Toronto in 1912 he had established himself as violin teacher at the Canadian Academy of Music and as founder of the Academy String Quartet, with Harry Adaskin as second violin. The ensemble tackled such difficult and ambitious works as the late Beethoven string quartets and Schoenberg's first quartet, presenting the latter in its Canadian *première*.

Despite the problems facing the new orchestra in the 1920s morale was high among the players, who felt the necessity for a city the size of Toronto to have its own orchestra and who took its formation into their hands as a co-operative effort. Von Kunits led the New Symphony Orchestra (renamed the Toronto Symphony Orchestra during his directorship) until his sudden death in 1931, when he was succeeded by Sir Ernest MacMillan. Throughout the nine years of von Kunits's leadership concerts were given only in the late afternoon – from 5:15 to 6:15 p.m. – largely because of the musicians' commitments to theatre and silent movie performances. These 'Twilight Concerts,' as they came to be known, made it possible for audiences to attend in the period after the workday ended and before the evening meal, while enabling the musicians to pursue their major source of income in the evening.

In this period the symphony was not financially self-supporting. Audiences in Massey Hall were rather small, and as attendance varied from one concert to the next, salaries were meagre. Ticket sales provided the only revenue, which was then divided among the players. The fee, which also included payment for rehearsals, fluctuated between five and ten dollars per concert.

The early years witnessed some famous performances: in 1927 Madame Schumann-Heink sang her farewell recital to a full house, while in the following year Horowitz made his Canadian debut. Pianist Josef Hofmann played in the

Canadian *première* of a Prokofiev concerto, and the orchestra tackled Sibelius's first symphony.

Murray Adaskin's association with the orchestra started in 1922, while he was still a teenager. Harry, considered as head of the family, purchased his brother's first long trousers, as well as his first formal dinner jacket. Murray's memories of his earliest engagement with the symphony begin with the brothers' excursion to a store on Yonge Street to get fitted for the dinner jacket. While 1923–4 was Harry's only season with the orchestra, Murray continued until 1936. John played in the cello section intermittently between 1926 and 1938.

Several excellent string players populated the Toronto musical scene in the 1920s, many of whom continued their activities in that city throughout the subsequent decades. These included Adolph Koldofsky, Maurice Solway, Harold Sumberg, and Samuel Hersenhoren. Most were at the beginning of their careers, struggling to make a living while searching for an opportunity to further their string studies. Many were not yet professionally trained, taking whatever instruction they could obtain at the major musical institutions in Toronto. The most famous teachers were in cosmopolitan centres in Europe, and the dream of every young violinist was to study there with one of the world-renowned personalities. Money was a major obstacle for many of the aspiring young musicians, since at that time there were no government sources of funds and no sponsorship of artists. Some had to depend on parental support combined with the income earned free-lancing in Toronto. The Belgian violinist Eugène Ysaÿe was considered the most eminent teacher, and studying with him was many a young person's ideal. A number of Murray's colleagues spent time in Brussels with Ysaÿe, notably Adolph Koldofsky and Maurice Solway. Harold Sumberg studied for five years with Willy Hess at the Berlin Hochschule für Musik before joining the Toronto Symphony in 1927 and the staff at the Toronto Conservatory of Music.

Another member of the string section of the TSO dating from the 1920s was Geoffrey Waddington, who later became conductor of the CBC Symphony Orchestra and director of several music programs for the CBC. He arrived in Toronto from Lethbridge in 1921 to study at the Toronto Conservatory of Music, establishing himself as a violinist before embarking upon a conducting career. Murray recollects a concert given by Waddington at the conservatory: 'When Geoffrey was a senior student he played one piece that knocked every fiddler back on his heels. It was "La Capricieuse" by Elgar, a marvellous piece that demands the most perfect staccato bowing that one could produce. One must have a staccato just like angel's wings, a feature that all of us, fiddlers, were struggling to obtain. The Elgar is a very accessible, enchanting piece, a great showpiece that Heifetz used to play to perfection. Geoffrey played it in an unforgettable fashion.'

Some of Murray's other colleagues in the twenties included violinist Isadore Dubinsky, who played with the TSO for more than fifty years, violist Milton Blackstone, and cellist Cornelius Ysselstyn, native of The Hague, who made his career in Toronto in the decades that followed as a radio and chamber music artist. He became the regular cellist in Murray's Toronto Trio, appearing at the Banff Springs Hotel in the summers and Toronto's Royal York Hotel in the winters.

A colourful and much liked figure from this period was Salzburg-born Louis Waizman (1863–1951), who was in his sixties when Murray first made his acquaintance. Well trained in harmony and theory, Waizman studied composition at the Mozarteum where Richard Strauss was a class-mate. Upon his arrival in Toronto in 1903 he worked as a trombonist and a theatre musician, playing viola, cello, and piano.[28] He played viola in the New Symphony Orchestra, and taught theory and composition to some of the violinists in the orchestra. He was already advanced in age when he accepted the position of copyist and staff arranger for the CBC in the late 1930s.

The impression one receives of musical life in Toronto in the 1920s is of a community bustling with talented young string players, all very busy earning a living while studying on the side. In those pre-radio days, there was ample opportunity for live music to be heard. Working together on a daily basis engendered among the musicians a spirit of camaraderie and of the competitiveness necessary for constructive collaboration.

Toronto in the early 1920s supported three major schools of music: the Hambourg Conservatory, the Canadian Academy of Music, and the Toronto Conservatory of Music (later the Royal Conservatory of Music). Up to 1951 the Hambourg Conservatory, with branches throughout the city, was the major rival of the Toronto Conservatory of Music. For forty years it was operated by members of the talented Hambourg family, which included cellist Boris, violinist Jan, and pianist Mark. The institution fostered a cosmopolitan atmosphere through its large faculty, many of whom were imported from Europe. Such artists and writers as Arthur Lismer and E.J. Pratt frequently dropped by to discuss art and literature.[29] It even provided living quarters for some of its teaching staff. One of the European artists brought to Toronto by the Hambourg Conservatory was a colourful violinist of Polish origin by the name of Henri Czaplinski. Up to the time of Czaplinski's arrival, Luigi von Kunits, affiliated with the Canadian Academy of Music, was considered the principal violin teacher in Toronto, whose instruction was sought after by the brightest students. After Czaplinski joined the Hambourg faculty, the most talented students gathered around the newcomer, leaving von Kunits disgruntled. Unfortunately, although Czaplinski was an excellent fiddler, he soon developed a reputation of having dubious ethical standards. After some unscrupulous financial dealings he disappeared from Toronto without a trace. The Canadian Academy, which had a shorter existence than the Hambourg Conservatory, was absorbed in 1924 by the Toronto Conservatory of Music. Its directorate included Frank Welsman and Albert Ham, who also taught at the Toronto Conservatory. After the amalgamation of the two institutions, the Toronto Conservatory of Music became the largest school of music in the province.

While Murray Adaskin watched many of his colleagues leave for violin studies abroad, his financial situation and that of his family made it impossible for him to contemplate a similar move. Nevertheless, by the summer of 1929 enough money had been saved up to enable him to spend nine weeks in Europe, his first venture abroad. His initial intention to study with the famed Ysaÿe was foiled when he discovered upon his arrival in Europe that the great violinist was in a hospital in Lyons; he had developed gangrene and eventually had to have his leg amputated. In his absence, Ysaÿe's son, Gabriel, also a violinist, offered to teach Murray, an offer the young Canadian refused because of Gabriel's predilection for alcohol.

Murray's companion in Europe was Philip Clark, a Canadian working on preparatory papers for his accounting examinations at McGill University. Clark, who eventually became controller of revenue for the province of Ontario, loved music and the theatre and had been a frequent visitor at Murray's stock company theatre productions. He was somewhat older than Murray, and according to Murray 'probably a little more level-headed, keeping an eye on me and feeling a sense of responsibility for me. You should have seen some of those papers he had to write! While I was practising, Philip would be in another room doing his papers; it was a wonderful arrangement.' Clark did not return from Europe empty-handed. In Paris he met an artist by the name of Paraskeva, born and educated in Leningrad, and working in an art-glass store in the French capital. Two years later they were married in London and moved to Toronto. Paraskeva Clark became one of Canada's leading painters in the 1930s and 1940s, establishing a lifelong friendship with Frances James and Murray Adaskin in the years to come.

After the unsuccessful Brussels visit, Murray and Philip travelled to Paris, where the young violinist entrusted his musical studies to Marcel Chailley, father of one of the famous musicologists of our times, Jacques Chailley. Acutely aware of the tight budget that dictated the length of his European stay, Murray threw himself into his studies with vigour. His practice began at six o'clock in the morning and lasted all day as he prepared the repertoire given to him by his teacher. This period of study in Europe was one of the turning-points in his musical career. Eventually his money ran out and the companions had to return to Canada.

In the spring of 1929, shortly before the European trip, while Murray was directing his orchestra at the Empire Theatre in Toronto a traveller from Montreal came backstage, introducing himself as head of music for the CPR hotels. Murray, who knew nothing about the CPR or its hotels, granted the stranger his request to sit in the pit and listen to the group play. The stranger was Harold Eustace Key. The following day over lunch he invited Murray to be official violinist for the musical events at the Banff Springs Hotel. Upon hearing about the young musician's European plans, Key postponed the date of Murray's Banff engagement by one year, advising him not to miss the opportunity for summer study in Europe as another chance for such a trip might not present itself. And indeed, such an opportunity did not come again.

Fate has a way, however, of manipulating human lives. In this case, fate took the form of Harold Eustace Key's invitation to Murray to join the pool of artists already employed by the CPR.

In the summer of 1930 the Toronto violinist had his first glimpse of the magnificent Rocky Mountains, as he, his friend Adolph Koldofsky, and Koldofsky's future bride, Gwen, formed part of the Banff Springs Hotel Quintet, which gave concerts and accompanied the Alfred Heather Light Opera Company productions. In the same summer Murray had his first glimpse of the leading concert artist at the Banff Springs Hotel – the lyric soprano Frances James.

I heard Fran sing, and was just mesmerized by it. This was something in my life that I had not much experience in. Fran would have a half-hour recital after the quintet finished playing. I would stay in Mount Stephen Hall and sit in a corner. I didn't know Fran then, but I would listen to her, and I can remember her singing Debussy's 'Romance.' My brother John used to play a transcription of it for cello, and I so loved that piece, that when I heard Fran sing it, I could not believe my ears. It was so enchanting. Fran turned out those things in a marvellous way, singing every night in front of an audience. This is how we eventually got to know each other, and we fell in love. By the end of the summer we knew that we were going to be married eventually.

Both Frances and Murray spent the following winter in Toronto, where Frances's mother came from Montreal to share the apartment with her. It did not take long for Murray's prophecy to be fulfilled. In Banff on 16 July 1931, in the presence of Harold Eustace Key, Frances James and Murray Adaskin were united in a marriage that was to last them a lifetime.

2

Two burgeoning careers in
the decade of the great Depression

The first decade of Frances and Murray's married life coincided with a deepening economic depression in Canada. While the prairie farmers' crops were failing and unemployment began to plague the population, Banff, the remote western community in the Rockies, at first seemed unaffected by the ominous developments in the rest of Canada. The glitter and magnificence at the Banff Springs Hotel in the 1930s provided a spectacular contrast to the famine in the prairies, and the atmosphere created by the Canadian Pacific Railway Company for its hotel guests symbolized a cultural oasis in the Rockies. The company employed a veritable army of artists for the edification and entertainment of its clientele. Musicians, painters, and photographers mingled with the employees of the hotel in a strictly observed hierarchy. Throughout the 1930s Frances James and Murray Adaskin were leading artists at the Banff Springs Hotel, where they performed during the summer seasons until the hotel's closing in 1941.

Originally built in 1888, the Banff Springs Hotel is located at the outskirts of the town at the foot of Sulphur Mountain. It commands a spectactular view of the valley and its surrounding mountains: Rundle, Cascade, Tunnel, and Norquay. Through the years turrets and wings were added, and modifications to the general structure occurred right up to 1928. The hotel was a giant, continually changing shape in order to make better use of its promontory and to provide more accommodation for tourists. In 1922, for example, approximately 52,000 visitors had occupied rooms at the hotel during its June-September season.[1] It became a totally self-contained castle with little connection to the town. Most townspeople never ventured inside the premises.

The Banff Springs Hotel promoted a glittering life of luxury and elegance.

Because of its international clientele, its aura of cosmopolitanism was unmatched in Canada. Politicians and Holywood stars mingled with wealthy socialites from South Africa, The Hague, Paris, Austria, England, Japan, Borneo, Hong Kong, and the United States. The luxurious suites were at times occupied by such royalty as the king of Siam, the prince of Wales, and the duke of Kent. The prince of Wales (later King Edward VIII), who had also purchased a ranch south of Calgary, was a particularly frequent visitor at the hotel. The Banff Highland Gatherings occurred under his sponsorship.

Some of the American guests vacationed in the area for as long as a month, spending two weeks at the Banff Springs Hotel and two at the Château Lake Louise. The tourists, who for the most part were supporters of culture on their home ground, had sophisticated musical taste. Many were the musical elite from New York and Boston. Murray Adaskin remembers one wealthy patron of the Boston Symphony Orchestra who insisted on having a say in the choice of repertoire his trio was to perform; Beethoven's *Archduke Trio* was her favourite, and she wanted to hear it often.

Hollywood stars staying at the hotel during the 1930s included Jack Benny and Benny Goodman. Goodman caused considerable excitement when he landed in Banff in his private plane. He and his mother occupied a large suite at the hotel, where Murray recalls listening in fascination to the story of how Goodman, Szigetti, and Bartók rehearsed Bartók's *Contrasts for Violin, Piano, and Clarinet* for the *première* recording of the composition.

The interior elegance of the hotel appealed to the taste of its guests. There were generous applications of native pine and fir. The main lobby was an octagonal rotunda, lined with balconies that overlooked it.[2] Oriental rugs, period furniture, and original paintings filled the reading and smoking rooms, various other parlours and reception rooms, and the three most famous halls: the Alhambra Dining-Room, the Riverview Lounge, and Mount Stephen Hall. The dining-room projected a Spanish flavour, which was enhanced by white Moroccan filigree doors. In the Riverview Lounge, publicized in CPR brochures as one of the hotel's attractions, eight large arched windows afforded magnificent views over the river valley and the surrounding mountains. The sunken floors of Mount Stephen Hall were of polished terazzo. The great carved oak beams and stained glass windows made the hall an imposing setting for concerts. A long ramp from an upper balcony led to the dining-room entrance.

Evening attire was mandatory in the Alhambra Dining-Room. Only the select among the hotel's staff members were allowed to eat with the guests. These included the chief steward, chief accountant, housekeeper, manager, manager's secretary (who reigned over the office and the crew), and social hostess. Few of the artists were allowed to eat in the dining-room. Nick Morant, as the official CPR photographer, and Frances James, as the leading concert artist, were among the exceptions. Morant's wife and business partner, the Adaskin trio, and the other hotel musicians ate in the staff room. Because the staff numbered in the hundreds, the hotel imposed a strict caste system. Most of the serving staff at that time were college students. The bellboys constituted an elite of prospective doctors and lawyers. In the words of Nick Morant, they had to be treated with respect because one never knew when, in the future, one would need their professional services.

Among the artists, Frances James was the star. She presented formal concerts every evening at nine, singing solos as well as performing in ensemble pieces with other musicians. Murray and his trio played in Mount Stephen Hall in the late afternoons before dinner. On the musicians' Thursday nights off the concerts were replaced by lectures on various aspects of the surrounding wilderness by naturalist Dan McCowan. Later, Nick Morant lectured at the hotel for about ten years.

The Banff Springs Trio, later known as the Toronto Trio, was formed in 1932, with Murray Adaskin as violinist and leader, Louis Crerar as pianist, and John Adaskin as the trio's first cellist. Philip Spivak replaced John Adaskin and was himself replaced a few years later by Cornelius Ysselstyn, who remained with the trio for most of its existence. Two other cellists – Joyce Onovski and Marcel Ray – were on occasion alternate players with the trio in Toronto. The *Canadian Review of Music and Art* praised the trio as 'one of the foremost ensemble groups in Canada.'[3] Up to 1941 the group performed at the Banff Springs Hotel in the summer, and from 1938 to 1952 it performed at Toronto's Royal York Hotel in the winter. The trio also gave numerous concerts across Canada. Louis Crerar (d 1981) was considered not only a brilliant soloist but also one of the best ensemble pianists and accompanists in the country.[4]

Hotel guests at Banff were entertained in weekly dances by a dance band led by Horace Lapp (1905–86), a pianist who from 1924 to 1935 also composed and conducted his own music for stage shows in Toronto as member of Jack Arthur's various theatre orchestras. He later led a dance band at Toronto's Royal York Hotel.

The location of the artists' quarters in the Banff Springs Hotel denoted the degree of prestige they earned. Murray Adaskin and Nick Morant lived in adjoining rooms at the top of the tower in the south wing, considered the most elegant of artists' quarters. The musicians created a jovial and convivial atmosphere, with the artists frequently playing practical jokes on one another. Nick Morant remembers an occasion when he decided to test Murray's patience because the violinist had demanded quiet while practising in his room. Morant used a broom to make sweeping noises outside of the artist's door, occasionally banging into the door. The noise would stop when Murray interrupted his practising in order to listen and identify the external sounds. No sooner would he continue work when the noise resumed. After this happened several times, the furious violinist threw open the door, only to find the culprit grinning from ear to ear.

Guests at the hotel enjoyed a wide variety of activities. In addition to the musical performances, the ballroom dancing, and the naturalist's talks, they could visit the nearby hot springs, go sightseeing on one of the Brewster cars or buses, or play tennis or golf. Entertainment was even provided at the golf course, where, at the large water-hole in the middle of the course, the Reverend Charles Gordon delivered the occasional Sunday sermon and Frances James presented outdoor songs. There is a recording of her singing and whistling a cowboy tune to the accompaniment of an accordion, while sitting on a raft in the water-hole.

For the more rugged individuals the hotel offered sports farther afield. Big-game hunting in areas outside of the park, trail riding, and mountain climbing lured the more adventurous men and women. Available to guide the guests through their wilderness experiences and provide for their safety were the mountain people who lived in Banff, many of whom were employees of the CPR. The guides and outfitters in the 1920s and 1930s included among their ranks the Brewster family, Bill Potts, Walter Nixon, and Soapy Smith. Even Swiss guides were imported by the CPR. It was the preceding generation, however, who had created legends by discovering the lakes and mountain passes that bear their names today, and who paved the way for the tourist hikes and wilderness enjoyment. Most of those old-timers were still living in Banff and its environs during the 1920s and 1930s, contributing to the unique character the town had assumed by that time. Tom Wilson, James Brewster, Bill Peyto, James Simpson, and Mary Schaeffer were some of the explorers who discovered scenery that had previously been seen only by native Indians.

A second group of mountain people were the artists and painters who captured the beauty of the Rockies on canvas. The most notable Banff artists were Peter and Catharine Whyte. Peter (1905–66) was a native of Banff, who worked for the Brewster Transport company before embarking on his studies at the School of the Museum of Fine Arts in Boston. Catharine Robb Whyte (1906–79) was born in Massachusetts to a wealthy family who moved in the same social circles as the Rockefellers. She and Peter met while studying at the same Boston school and made Banff their lifelong residence. They loved the Rockies and demonstrated this affection through their drawings and paintings of the scenery. Peter also excelled in his portraits of local Indians, by whom he was held in great esteem.

Both Whytes used to sketch in the mountains with J.E.H. MacDonald, the founder of the Canadian Group of Seven painters, at that time also head of the Ontario College of Art. Although the Whytes were not officially in the employ of the CPR, John Murray Gibbon purchased a number of their paintings for the company. Their friends included such CPR artists as German-born Carl Rungius, living in Long Island, NY, whose specialties included painting sheep, goats, and rams in high passes; Walter Phillips, one of Canada's great water-colourists and wood-block print-makers; and official CPR photographers Nick and Willie Morant.

Nick Morant, who joined the CPR in 1929 and was the company's special photographer for forty years, possessed great versatility. He worked for *Saturday Night* magazine, for the *Winnipeg Free Press,* and even wrote stories about Mediterranean cruises to accompany his publicity photographs. The subjects of his publicity pictures include interiors of rail cars to show their elegance, alpine scenery in Banff and Yoho parks to publicize the natural beauties, and people, particularly celebrities, for the social pages. During the Second World War he took photos of war plants and was later among the first to record on film the United Nations meeting in San Francisco.

The paintings of the CPR artists and the photos of the company photographers played a large role in the publicity material the corporation assembled for brochures, pamphlets, and calendars. Nick Morant, who in 1986 still resided in Banff with his wife, Willie, is an articulate raconteur, with mischievous blue eyes and lively facial expressions, who vividly recalls the colourful days of Banff in the 1930s.

Another group of summer residents in Banff were the international journalists employed by the CPR to create publicity for the company's hotel and trains by describing events that occurred at the Banff Springs Hotel during each season. Paul Standard of New York, who became a lifelong friend of the Adaskins, was correspondent for the *New York Times* and the *Herald Tribune,* frequently reviewing musical events, including the concerts of Frances James. Following his employment with the CPR he established himself in New York as a successful calligrapher.

Murray and Frances were especially fond of Catharine and Peter Whyte. They admired their paintings and valued their friendship, which endured from the Adaskins' first wedding anniversary spent in the company of the Whytes, to the end of Peter's and Catharine's lives. Murray dedicated his *Serenade Concertante* (1954) to the Whytes, and the composition was played at Catharine's funeral because she loved it so much. Catharine and Frances carried on a lifelong correspondence.

These rugged individualists, artists, and journalists created the remarkable community that was Banff in the 1930s, an unusual gathering of personalities whose lives were dedicated to the mountains. Two societies, in effect, coexisted in the small town in the Rockies: the transient self-contained community of wealth and elegance centred in the Banff Springs Hotel, and the permanent community of mountain people living in the town of Banff and its vicinity.

Frances James and Murray Adaskin spanned both worlds. They befriended the hotel guests, socialized with the hotel musicians, and cemented lifelong relations with some of the Banff townspeople. Murray, in particular, knew how to talk to people from all walks of life. He was accepted by the cowboys and trail hands who were part of the world outside the hotel as much as by the hotel elite. Such, then, was life in Banff at the time that Frances James and Murray Adaskin decided to get married; it was a unique artistic and cultural community that, for the most part, owed its living to the CPR.

The Adaskins remember their wedding date with fondness and some hilarity. The occasion was kept secret from all but a few select friends. Louis Crerar was delegated to prepare the refreshments, while John Murray Gibbon and Harold Eustace Key and his wife came to the church to assist at the private wedding. A United church was chosen for the occasion. It was a Thursday, Frances's day off from singing. The wedding ceremony had to take place in the evening, however, following Murray's dinner session with the trio. Unfortunately, his musical engagement caused him to be fifteen minutes late for the wedding. Once the ceremony proceeded, convincing the bride that the groom was serious about his intentions, they both realized that Murray, because of his Jewish background, had never attended a Christian wedding ceremony and was quite ignorant of the procedures. At the suspenseful moment when the minister posed the question 'Do you take this woman to be your wedded wife?' there was a long silence, which to the bride seemed like an eternity. Finally Murray stuttered: 'Yes, thank you very much.' The bride went into hysterics of laughter much to the dismay of the groom and the best man, Harold Eustace Key, who, out of embarrassment, looked as if they were attending a funeral.

After the ceremony the small wedding party headed back to the hotel, where the regular evening activities were in progress. All the musicians, including the members of the Alfred Heather Light Opera Company, were invited to the party at which the marriage was announced by Gibbon, who offered a toast to the bride. This development, which came as a total surprise, so delighted the musicians that John Deacon in his excitement dashed out of the room straight to Horace Lapp, who was conducting his dance band. The leader stopped the music and announced the news to all the guests of the Banff Springs Hotel. The locale resounded with merriment and general jubilation. The hotel management gave the wedding party the luxurious Italian suite, which had two bedrooms, one sitting-room, and three bathrooms, and the wedding celebrations continued for three days.

Throughout the 1930s Frances James acquired a repertoire of great dimension and scope. Each night during her Banff seasons she presented five art songs in her recital in addition to those sung on request – a total of almost fifty compositions a week. During an average season she performed approximately seventy-five recitals. The Banff experience, therefore, served as a learning process, as she studied and accumulated new repertoire. She performed songs from several different categories: German *lieder*, songs from the French school, Russian and British art songs, as well as folk-songs. Frequently she combined forces with the Banff Springs Trio.

Murray often gave solo violin recitals, presenting such selections as Fritz Kreisler's compositions, Tartini's G-minor violin sonata, and violin transcriptions of compositions written for other instruments – Chopin *Nocturnes*, for example. One of Murray's early compositions was the violin obbligato line to the Bach-Gounod *Ave Maria*, sung by Frances. Many of these concerts were also broadcast by the CP radio station in Banff.

The quality of music making at Banff is best captured through the following contemporary press review:

Four young Toronto artists Sunday night pooled their distinguished talents in a memorable concert ... Relying entirely on the accepted classics, the Banff Springs Trio[,] ... assisted by the fresh-voiced soprano Miss Frances James, performed the music of one Russian and seven German composers, and the large audience, responded warmly ... The trio played Mendelssohn's Andante Espressivo in C-minor, three of Brahms' Hungarian dances, and Tschaikovsky's Capriccio Italien, their tone always sensitively balanced and their understanding of the music clear and spontaneous. In projecting it, they gave their audience much of the joy thay had in playing it.

Their capable rendition of Tschaikovsky's orchestral piece reduced to the humbler medium of three instruments deserves special praise. It was a daring thing to do and came off excellently by reason of close team work.

Miss James ... sings easily and has an uncanny control of pianissimo, so that often her tones are hushed to something just this side of silence. Her English group consisted of Handel's 'Wher'er You Walk', and Bach's 'Will Thou to Me Thy Heart Give', reportedly his only song set to an avowed love lyric. But as usual he invests this music with unearthly gentleness and compassion to which Miss James gave a tender, melting expression. She then sang in German Schubert's 'Gretchen am Spinnrade,' Richard Strauss' 'Breit über Meine Haupt Dein Schwarzes Haar' ... her German diction clear throughout. She rose to real heights in the Schubert song, revealing admirably the girl's growing despair and desolation ... The entire group was recalled many times by the audience ... Miss James' talents are a source of continuing recognition.[5]

This informative and elegantly written review was penned by Paul Standard, serving as an eloquent example of the type of prose he produced for Canadian newspapers as well as for the *New York Times*. It was written in his capacity as newspaperman for the CPR, and released in a number of Canadian papers such as the *Calgary Daily Herald, Vancouver Province,* and *Montreal Star.*

Murray Adaskin's exuberance and love of life were reflected in the initiation of humorous concerts at Banff, such as the performance of the *Toy Symphony,* described in this press review:

Haydn's Toy Symphony was performed for the first time in the Canadian Rockies in Mount Stephen Hall at the Banff Springs Hotel on Sunday evening. Eleven musicians participated, the Banff Springs Trio being assisted by five members of the hotel's dance orchestra, and three from among the hotel's musical guests.

In addition to the trio ... there were parts for cuckoo, toy drum, toy trumpet, second violin, double bass, nightingale, quail and rattle. The performance went beautifully from start to finish for all of its less than ten minutes.

The final movement, twice repeated in the original theme, ended in 'runaway' tempo, and brought down the house, which was packed to the doors.[6]

On 26 May 1939 King George VI and Queen Elizabeth arrived in Banff in the company of Prime Minister William Lyon Mackenzie King and a large entourage for a four-day vacation in the Banff–Lake Louise area. They were touring Canada and were on their way to the west coast. Although the visit occurred before the official June opening of the Banff Springs Hotel, the building was fully staffed, and John Murray Gibbon had invited from Toronto Murray Adaskin's trio, with Frances Adaskin and the tenor Joseph Victor Laderoute.

The Adaskins still vividly remember their concert for the royal visitors. That night Mackenzie King entertained the enormous press corps that followed the royal visit in a dining-room on the other side of the building. Royalty dined in a private room, which opened onto a veranda overlooking Mount Stephen Hall where the concert was being held. The queen emerged to sit on the veranda, serene in her beautiful pastel-coloured chiffon gown, with the trio performing directly underneath her. The king, who was in a very relaxed mood that night, sat in the back of the hall, mimicking the motions of the players in the trio and enjoying himself to the fullest. The concert pleased Her Majesty so much that, when the artists reached the end of their program, she sent an aide to ask them to continue.

After the concert the press corps joined the royal couple, and the king was particularly amused by the jokes of a journalist from Moose Jaw. Both the jokes and the name of the Saskatchewan town sent the king into paroxysms of laughter. Later that evening the royal couple made an appearance in the hall where Horace Lapp was conducting the dance band.

The whole royal visit took place in a delightful aura of informality. Apart from their entertainment in the hotel the guests received guided tours of the area by Jim Brewster, president of Brewster Transport. King George, fascinated by their guide's accounts of his hunting successes and of the stuffed animal heads he claimed to have in his home as trophies, expressed the wish to see them. Brewster brought the royal couple to his home, to the total mortification of his wife, who was preparing lunch for the farm-hands when she looked out the window to see the king and queen approaching the humble abode. This incident became one of Banff's colourful legends.

The glitter and bustle of life at the hotel diminished as the Depression deepened, and during the war years, starting with 1941, the hotel shut down. The emotional effects of the war even penetrated the granite barriers of the Rockies; Frances James gave a recital at Emerald Lake Chalet at Field, BC, in aid of the Queen's Canadian Fund for Air Raid Victims.[7]

The closing of the hotel's doors symbolized the end of an era in Canadian cultural history as well as the end of an epoch in the Adaskins' own musical lives. By that time Frances James had been in the employment of the CPR for sixteen years, while Murray Adaskin had worked for the company and its Banff hotel for twelve years. The consistently high quality of their summer concerts at Banff enriched the lives of hundreds of thousands of vacationers and many others in the area who heard the regular CP broadcasts from the hotel. Reciprocally, the Banff concerts served the Adaskins as an opportunity to study new repertoire, a process of self-education that resulted in their continual personal growth as musicians. Their association with the CPR and John Murray Gibbon did not end with the closing of the hotel, but continued into the 1940s through a number of radio programs broadcast by Frances James over the CBC network.

The Adaskins' successful engagements at the Banff Springs Hotel throughout the 1930s, however, constitute only one part of their activities throughout that decade. Before proceeding with a discussion of how they spent the war years, one must first take a look at their musical activities in Toronto in the thirties.

THE TORONTO MUSICAL SCENE

During the 1930s the career of Frances James mushroomed into a network of multifaceted activities. While the summers were committed to concerts in Western Canada under the auspices of the CP hotels, the winters were filled with major solo recitals in Toronto, numerous coast-to-coast tours sponsored by women's musical clubs and Canadian concert association series, performances of oratorios and other large vocal pieces with Toronto, Montreal, and Ottawa choral groups, and frequent appearances on local and national radio broadcasts.

The Toronto recitals took place in the city's major halls: the Art Gallery, the Great Hall of Hart House, and the Eaton Auditorium. Occasionally other artists participated in the program; concerts at the Art Gallery, for example, were shared with Murray Adaskin playing violin, or, on a later occasion, with Boris Hambourg, cello, and Frances Marr, piano. One type of concert given at the Art Gallery was an evening of French song, incorporating works from the thirteenth to the seventeenth century in arrangements by MacMillan, Ravel, and Warlock. Such an event would also include French-Canadian folk-songs and art songs by Debussy, Duparc, and Fauré.[8]

In 1937 Frances James, assisted by a string quartet, performed a concert at Eaton Auditorium dedicated entirely to the music of one composer – the Canadian-born Charles Jones. Not only did this type of homogeneous program represent an innovation in Toronto, but also, to base an entire concert on the music of a contemporary Canadian composer was an outright act of bravery for that epoch in the history of music in Canada. Augustus Bridle's review in the *Toronto Star* depicts the event in colourful strokes of the pen, documenting the content and the significance of the concert to the city's contemporary musical scene:

Seven Toronto musicians gave Charles Jones of New York, formerly violin student in Toronto, once of Orillia, his debut as a composer ... This youth of Welsh parentage has for years been among the younger moderns of New York. His debut programme was all as new to Toronto as Stravinsky's 'Firebird' and 'Petrushka' were ten years ago; as modern as Bax, Bartok or Schoenberg are now; a string quartet, a viola Capriccio and five songs – all at the end of a week that began with Stravinsky; ... a day ahead of Enesco's debut here from Paris – also as violinist composer. And only two months ago we had the American premiere of Gielgud's 'Hamlet,' the first Canadian performance of Walton's sensational symphony, shortly before that the world premiere of Willan's Symphony No. 1 and two weeks ago the first showing anywhere of Shirley Temple in a Shanghai picture.

This Canadian try-out of Charlie Jones was the first of its kind here in at least ten years, and of its kind the most significant. Not many Canadians have written string quartets; in Toronto only MacMillan, Leo Smith, Healey Willan, and Von Kunits. This one of Charles Jones was played as an opener by Harold Sumberg, Tom Brennand, Hyman Goodman, Marcus Adeney. It also ended the programme, opinion being that the audience would be surer of what it was all about after the second time.[9]

Charles Jones later settled in New York as a teacher of composition at the

Juilliard School of Music. The Adaskins' lifelong friendship with him was reinforced throughout the late 1940s when Murray took composition lessons with him and with Darius Milhaud at the Music Academy of the West in Santa Barbara, and in Aspen.

Another ensemble concert at Eaton Auditorium in the 1930s featured Frances James with accompanist Gwendolyn Williams Koldofsky and violinist Adolph Koldofsky. Critic Hector Charlesworth was in the audience:

The Women's Musical Club of Toronto, in addition to introducing noted foreign musicians, devotes one afternoon every season to a programme by Canadian artists ...

Miss James is known through radio to Canadian listeners, but this medium does not permit her to reveal the charm of her personality, and platform style, nor the finesse of her interpretative gifts. Her voice is soft and sweet and beautifully modulated, and she especially impressed critical listeners by her renderings of Schubert and Brahms. Evidently she had worked on each number until she was able to convey its precise atmosphere. Especially fine was her rendering of Schubert's 'The Young Nun,' leading to an exquisite and dignified climax, and she was captivating in such tender and gracious lyrics as 'The Trout' and Brahms' 'The Maiden Speaks.'[10]

Other Toronto recitals were given by the singer at the Heliconian Club, where in 1941 she performed the Canadian *première* of Hindemith's song-cycle, *Das Marienleben* (first version), with Arnold Walter at the piano. Her début in Hart House took place in the institution's Great Hall in 1935. A stone building of Gothic style within the complex of the University of Toronto, Hart House was a bastion for male students whose facilities fostered cultural discussions, guest lectures, concerts, and debates. In addition, it contained all the facilities for activities outside a student's curriculum: squash courts, barber-shops, private dining-rooms, swimming-pool, rifle range, three common rooms, billiard-room, two gymnasiums, quarters for wrestling and fencing, chapel, library, and music-room with a large collection of records. A five-hundred-seat theatre and a concert hall were open to the general public.

Hart House offered numerous cultural events to its members as well as to the public. The Group of Seven painters exhibited many of their works on its walls with the express purpose of helping students develop a taste for contemporary Canadian art. Lismer, Varley, Jackson, and Harris frequented the sketch rooms, providing criticism and lectures, and occasionally teaching art classes. Today the institution is a repository of an important collection of Canadian paintings purchased from those artists.

The Sunday-evening Hart House concerts attained great popularity among Toronto audiences. J. Campbell McInnes initiated the concerts in 1922, and the momentum created at that time carried through the next decades as well. Performances by the Hart House String Quartet and Healey Willan's Tudor Singers became annual events. Many of the leading Toronto musicians were featured in these concerts: Leo Smith, Luigi von Kunits, the piano duo of Reginald Godden and Scott Malcolm, and Sir Ernest MacMillan.

Frances James's recital in Hart House, therefore, signified for the artist a major professional event. Murray recalls his impressions of that event:

I can still remember Fran having been ill with nerves that day, and I thought, 'my God, is this the life we are going to have? Do I have to live through this with every concert?' I almost died I was so worried about her. I accompanied her to the theatre. She was beautifully dressed, and Fran had a way about her – she did not walk out on stage, she glided onto the stage. I have never seen anyone else do that before. She had a wonderful way of doing it with a beautiful expression, full of smiles. It was unconscious; I don't think that she was aware of it. I looked at her and I thought 'is that my wife that has just been dying of stage fright?' She opened her mouth, and with that first note I knew that she was over it. There were to be no more nerves.

Well, that was Fran, and I was soon to learn that when we went through those pre-performance jitters, I had no reason to worry about anything.

Some six years earlier Murray had made his violin début at Hart House in a program of Bach, Handel, and Brahms. Later, in the mid-1930s, the Toronto Trio also made its official début there. It happened that the day after the performance the newspapers carried a story of three men who had robbed a bank. The headline was Toronto Trio Jailed for Robbery. Sir Ernest MacMillan, who was always quick to recognize a humorous situation, sent Murray a clipping of the headline with the inscription: 'tut, tut, and after such a successful debut!'

Frances James alternated her Toronto engagements with a series of annual cross-country tours. During the 1935–6 season, seventeen recitals were given in Ontario towns alone, augmented by performances in Saint John and Vancouver. Held under the auspices of the Canadian Concert Association Series, the Ontario concerts took the artist on a tour of Niagara Falls, Galt, Belleville, Welland, Owen Sound, Sarnia, Chatham, Thunder Bay, Fort William, and other places. A number of recitals were also given under the auspices of women's musical clubs. Usually run by talented women with an intense interest in fostering and supporting music in their communities, this Canadian-wide network of clubs sponsored domestic and international artists. Throughout the 1930s and 1940s they ranked among the most active sponsors of solo and small ensemble vocal and instrumental recitals across Canada, fulfilling a particularly important function in introducing artists to the smaller and more isolated Canadian communities. At times these concerts assumed the character of social events, with local newspapers reporting who among the community's elite graced the event with their presence. The artist and her accompanist were frequently guests of the club's president at whose home they also received accommodation. The same person would host the social event following the concert, introducing the artists to the local luminaries.

Not all these concerts were held in the evening: for example, those sponsored by the Montreal Ladies Morning Musical Club were held at the Ritz-Carlton Hotel at 11:00 a.m. Some, such as the Vancouver Women's Musical Club, presented mid-afternoon recitals, starting at 3:30 in the Oak Room of the Hotel Vancouver. A January 1937 newspaper article refers to Frances James's Vancouver recital as the 317th such concert held by the club, suggesting an active organization with a long musical tradition.

These musical groups functioned as sponsors in an epoch of Canadian musical life where professional management agencies for Canadian artists were still scarce. Occasionally, a company town would sponsor a concert series for the edification and entertainment of the staff. In March 1936, for example, Frances James and the Toronto Trio were guests at such a series at Copper Cliff, near Sudbury, Ontario.

Through John Murray Gibbon, the Canadian Pacific Railway continued to sponsor cultural events as promotional features, although the frequency of those activities had declined considerably from that in the previous decade. A Montreal concert for members of the Royal Empire Society in 1936 featured the singer in a 'Travelogue of Canada,' devised by Gibbon. According to the *Montreal Gazette*,

[the audience was] conducted across Canada from the Atlantic to the Pacific ... in a unique musical travelogue called 'Canada in Song and Picture.' The event took place at the dinner concert of the society at the Windsor Hotel.

Mr. Gibbon constructed his travelogue in a novel manner. Claiming that Canada possessed few songs internationally known, he selected a number of melodies from the most catholic sources and set to them texts of his own composition, poems which took as their subject the various places touched upon during the imaginative journey.

These were sung by Frances James ... while a camera projected upon a screen reproductions in color of pictures of the different locations, painted by Canadian artists, and selected mostly from the National Gallery of Ottawa ...

With Mr. Gibbon as guide, the audience proceeded from the Atlantic coast represented on the screen by pictures of G. Horne Russell, R.F. Gagen and William Brymner, and by the lyric 'On the Cool Atlantic Shore' which Mr. Gibbon set to the tune of a sea shanty.[11]

Throughout the 1930s, therefore, Frances James's activities as concert artist were many and varied. Her career, which in the previous decade had been formulated entirely under the auspices of the CPR, had now assumed new direction. Building upon her already well-established reputation as concert singer in the western part of Canada, she was establishing a reputation in Toronto and other parts of the country as a leading Canadian soprano. Her concerts displayed a remarkable breadth and variety of repertoire, which, in addition to folk-songs, usually included a group of German, French, and English art songs. Among the German composers, Schubert (*An die Musik, Gretchen am Spinnrade*, and *Die Forelle*) and Brahms (*Das Mädchen Spricht* and *Botschaft*) were her favourites. Songs by Debussy, Duparc, and Milhaud (*Fumée* and *Fête de Montmartre*) already pointed toward her predilection for twentieth-century repertoire; English songs ranged from Handel's arias (*Art Thou Troubled?* from his opera *Rodelinda*), to Quilter, Bax, and Delius. Folk-songs usually included arrangements by Willan and MacMillan: for example, selections from *Northland Songs* by John Murray Gibbon and Sir Ernest MacMillan. Her innovative and path-breaking programming led to a growing emphasis on the performance of Canadian composers' works, as exemplified in the Charles Jones recital. One of her favourite concert encores was *The Shepherd* by Murray Adaskin.

Frances's primary accompanist in this period was Gwendolyn Williams Koldofsky. Born in Bowmanville, Ontario, in 1906, Gwendolyn Koldofsky was one of Canada's top pianists and accompanists from the time of her return from her studies in England in 1926 until 1945, when she accepted a post at the University of Southern California to head the Faculty of Accompanying, where she was still teaching in 1987. Originally accompanist for Jeanne Dusseau, she toured Canada and the United States with the singer until her professional engagement by John Murray Gibbon as a CPR artist. Many reviews praised her skills as pianist and her remarkable musicianship. She was one of the official accompanists at Banff throughout the 1930s, and in the winters she played numerous concerts in Toronto and its environs for Frances James.

During the 1930s Toronto was one of the largest centres of cultural energy in Canada. To a visitor from outside of Canada such as British musicologist Rosemary Hughes, who spent the academic year 1934–5 in Toronto, the intensity and quality of musical life in the city were impressive. Her description of the musical events re-creates the atmosphere and colour of the times of which Frances James and Murray Adaskin were a product. In the *Toronto Conservatory Review* of August 1935, she enumerates the music activities she observed during her stay, which included performances by local soloists and large ensembles, and concerts by visiting dignitaries. She describes the Promenade Concerts in Varsity Arena, conducted by Reginald Stewart and attended at times by as many as seven thousand people. She also mentions Reginald Stewart's Bach Society performance of the *St John Passion,* an annual event in the thirties, with J. Campbell McInnes as Christus and Hubert Eisdell as Narrator. She praises as outstanding the same two male singers in the eleventh annual presentation of the *St Matthew Passion,* conducted by Sir Ernest MacMillan in Convocation Hall. She was also impressed by the singers of the Mendelssohn Choir under the baton of H.A. Fricker: 'at first I found the dignified and traditional atmosphere of the choir and the wonderful standard of the individual members rather overawing ... charging in to practice in flapping gowns and wrestling with the *Missa Solemnis* under the shadow of the brontosaurus skeletons in the University Museum.'

In Eaton Auditorium she heard the Tudor Singers under the directorship of Healey Willan, the group's founder and conductor, while at Massey Hall she enjoyed the winter symphony concerts at which both the serious and humorous elements reigned. She recalls a particularly amusing interpretation by Sir Ernest MacMillan of a polka. The symphony programs included Sibelius, Dvorak, Walton, and Wagner (with Lotte Lehmann singing the *Liebestod*), and one concert was devoted entirely to British music by Elgar, Delius, and Holst. The Detroit Symphony Orchestra visited that year, as did Myra Hess. Local artists heard were the Hart House Quartet, Geza and Norah de Kresz, and Emmy Heim. All of these activities gracing Toronto stages during one musical season prompted the British observer to praise the richness and vitality of the city's musical life, the wealth of fine local musicans, and the enthusiasm of the listeners.

Choral music, in particular, had assumed an important position on Toronto's musical scene. The *St Matthew Passion,* conducted by Sir Ernest MacMillan, was among the most important annual musical events in Toronto. Reginald Stewart's performances with the Bach choir of the *St John Passion* and Dr Herbert Fricker's renditions with the Mendelssohn Choir of such major choral masterpieces as Bach's *B Minor Mass* and Beethoven's *Missa Solemnis* also dominated the musical events. To have three conductors of the stature of Fricker, MacMillan, and Stewart in one city during the same decade was remarkable, resulting in considerable rivalry between MacMillan and Stewart, and leading to factionalism among Toronto audiences, followers of one or the other of the two conductors. The Promenade Symphony concerts, founded by Adolph Koldofsky, developed from 1934 onward under the baton of Reginald Stewart as a summer counterpart to the Toronto Symphony concerts, whose regular conductor was Sir Ernest MacMillan. They continued under Stewart's leadership until his resignation in 1941.[12]

In 1934 Frances James made her earliest appearance with Reginald Stewart's

Bach Society. She performed the Bach cantatas (including *Sleepers Awake*) in Timothy Eaton Memorial Church and sang in the *St John Passion*, which she did intermittently throughout the decade.[13] On each occasion the roles of Christus and narrator were interpreted by J. Campbell McInnes and Hubert Eisdell respectively. Murray Adaskin recalls McInnes's performance of Christus: 'If you had ever heard that, you would never be satisfied with any other interpretation. I have never heard another one that quite reached the emotional heights of his gorgeous singing.' The eminent Toronto critic Hector Charlesworth records the 1937 performance of this work in his usual informative mode:

The simplest of the four versions, the 'St. John Passion,' is the most pathetic, and it would be but gilding refined gold to dwell on the loveliness of Bach's musical treatment of the incidents ... Noblest of all are the polyphonic chorus which opens the work and the glorious chorale which concludes it. Though comprising but eighty, the Bach Choir is very fine in vocal quality, and its volume of tone is surprisingly impressive. There was, moreover, an intense quality and mastery of detail in Mr. Stewart's direction, which at all times evoked vitality and brillance in expression.

As in previous presentations of the Bach 'Passion' the dominating figure was J. Campbell McInnes ... the grandeur and nobility of his declamatory style was never more apparent ... A very difficult task fell on the able tenor Hubert Eisdell who, as the Evangelist, had to sing hundreds of lines of the narrative ... his enunciation was always clear and incisive ... Very high praise must be accorded the singing of arias by Eileen Law, alto and Frances James, soprano. Both possess beautiful voices and sang with exalted expression befitting the text.[14]

The more popular *St Matthew Passion* was conducted annually by Sir Ernest MacMillan for thirty consecutive years (1923–53). It was the first major work in which Murray Adaskin played as an orchestral violinist, an engagement that he repeated fifteen times between 1923 and 1938. Murray was initially hired as musician for the *St Matthew Passion* on the recommendation of J. Campbell McInnes. He recalls the first performance held in Timothy Eaton Memorial Church on St Clair Avenue:

I always sat with Adolph Koldofsky – I guess it was because we sat together in the symphony too – and Adolph flipped a page back that happened to be loose. It went floating into the audience, right into the front while we continued playing. Everyone was terribly serious, and Adolph and I had to keep a straight face which for me was almost impossible. Someone very thoughtfully just stood up and handed it to us, and we put it back on the stand under MacMillan's stern gaze. His performances were always done very solemnly, with no applause until the end. They were always lovely performances with excellent singers.

Although in the decade that followed, Sir Ernest MacMillan used Frances James as a regular soloist in *Messiah*, in the 1930s he had not yet discovered her talents as an oratorio singer despite her already acquired national reputation as a soloist in choral works. One of her earliest professional engagements with MacMillan occurred in the historic first complete Toronto performance of act 3 of Wagner's *Die Walküre*. As an admirer of the German composer's music, MacMillan welcomed the opportunity to introduce Toronto audiences to Wagner's musical style. The critic Augustus Bridle, who was in the audience, describes this rather unusual addition to the regular TSO concert season, revealing, in the process, another aspect of musical performance practice of the pre-war era:

The last forty minutes of the symphony programme last night sent everybody home excited. 'Wagner!' they gasped. 'After all, he has the greatest finales!'

This one was Act III of 'The Valkyrie,' never before done as a concert here; not in 32 years as opera – since Savage brought a Wagner cycle here in English, a feat which would wreck any impresario now. Behind a black-draped bar on the top rail-bird promenade at backstage stood the seven Valkyria with scores on the ledge, each Valkyr with a small megaphone, which, in magnified ensembles, when they all sang, looked like bottles of Shepherds' horns ... In front of the orchestra were Brunnhilde (Jeanne Hesson), brilliant in many impassioned and argumentative solos; Sieglinde (Frances James), splendidly lyric and frenetic, and Wotan, who as sung by Norman Cordon from Chicago was a majestic vocal performance. [15]

It was in 1939, at the instigation of Emmy Heim, the voice teacher at the conservatory with whom the artist was taking coaching lessons and who was a close friend of MacMillan, that the conductor gave Frances an aria to sing in the *St Matthew Passion*: 'It was the last soprano solo in the massive work – which is two-and-a-half hours long – and it was one of the most difficult songs ("For Love Would My Saviour Die"). It suited me beautifully because it was very lyrical and required a pianissimo sound in the high range, but I had to wait for two-and-a-half hours to sing it. It was a terrible strain.'

Frances James was a soloist in a number of other large-scale choral works, for instance, Bach's *B Minor Mass*, Handel's *Messiah*, and the Brahms *Requiem* conducted by Dr Alfred Whitehead in Montreal; and Beethoven's *Missa Solemnis* with Dr Herbert Fricker in Toronto. The Montreal appearances occurred in 1937 and 1938 with Whitehead's Cathedral Singers, a popular

Montreal group. Frances recalls the cavernous bowels of Christ Church Cathedral in Montreal: 'The choir sang up in the gods; there were five thousand souls sitting and I was standing up there by a brass rail. It was dizzying to look that mile away to all those people, as we were up in the heavens, right with the angels; we could not have gotten any closer to the top. I hung on to the book with one hand and the brass rail with the other.'

An event about which Frances reminisces with fondness was the occasion in January 1936 when she received a phone call from Herbert Fricker, with whom she had previously had no contact. The conductor asked her whether she could sing a high B-flat. After Frances, who was in a state of amazement at the way the entire conversation was proceeding, answered positively, he asked her to come to Metropolitan United Church at ten o'clock the next morning. 'I appeared at this enormous church in Toronto, and he actually hit a B-flat on the organ and asked me to sing it. I did not have a chance to warm up, but it turned out to be another instance where I sang the pitch more accurately and clearly than ever before in my life. It is at this point that he asked me to do the *Missa Solemnis*.' Fricker, like MacMillan, used his favourite singers in performances of these major choral works. In the *Missa Solemnis*, however, because of a series of B-flats in sections of the soprano solo, Fricker's favourite soloist declined to perform such a taxing line; as a result he contacted Frances James, who had made a reputation as a soprano with a remarkably flexible high range.

While the 1930s witnessed a burgeoning of musical activities, the greatest impetus to the diffusion of her reputation on a national scale derived from her involvement with radio broadcasting.

THE INFANCY OF RADIO BROADCASTING

Both Frances James and Murray Adaskin shared in the evolution of radio broadcasting; Frances started in 1930 with the CPR's first broadcasts from Banff, while Murray began somewhat earlier with the CN transmissions of the Toronto Symphony Orchestra programs. A major portion of Frances's career developed through her performances as radio artist. To a great extent, therefore, the development of her career parellels the evolution of broadcasting in this country. Murray's appearances on radio originated from his activities as violinist with the Toronto Trio and as member of various radio orchestras. In later years, his compositions received numerous radio performances.

The twenties can be viewed as the experimental phase in the field of communication, years when radio was still a novelty, reaching primarily into the large eastern centres to the exclusion of portions of the West and the less populated areas. Few frequencies were exclusively Canadian, and most of those suffered interference from the powerful American and Mexican stations.[16] Canadians in the early twenties listened for the most part to American programs. The popular KDKA from Pittsburgh, PA, was a favourite in eastern Canada. One of the earliest broadcasting licences in Canada was issued to a Montreal station later called CFCF. As the decade progressed, however, dozens of broadcasting stations appeared across the country, and by 1928 Canada could account for more than sixty such licensed units.[17]

The Canadian National Railway Company (CNR) was a major force in radio programming during the 1920s. Realizing the necessity for travellers on transcontinental trains to have contact with the outside world, the company equipped parlour cars on the moving trains with radio receiving sets manned by uniformed operators. The first newscast was transmitted to a moving train on 9 October 1923.[18] The CNR, therefore, marked the beginning of network broadcasting in Canada and remained the major network until the formation of the Canadian Radio Broadcasting Commission (CRBC) as a working organization on 1 April 1933. By that time, the CNR had acquired and operated stations in Moncton, Ottawa, and Vancouver, and had leased twelve private stations across the country from Halifax to Red Deer. In 1924 it opened studios at the King Edward Hotel in Toronto, and a year later the Hart House String Quartet gave its inaugural concert, initiating a series of broadcasts over CNR stations. Three years later the group made a cross-country tour under CNR auspices, broadcasting Beethoven quartets in memory of the centenary of the composer's death.

The broadcasts combined music with school programs, news, plays, and reviews of world affairs. The first operetta broadcasts, such as Gilbert and Sullivan's *The Mikado* (1925) and *The Gondoliers* (1926), were transmitted from Montreal, where Walter Clapperton was active as conductor of the McGill Operatic and Choral Society.[19] A major CNR-sponsored event was the 'All-Canada Symphony Hour,' a series of twenty-five broadcasts by the Toronto Symphony, conducted over the national network in the 1929–30 season by Luigi von Kunits. Canadian and internationally known soloists were featured in these Sunday afternoon transmissions, which originated from Simpson's Arcadian Court in Toronto.

By 1931, the radio receiving set service on CNR trains had to be discontinued because of the effects of the increasing austerity of the Depression. As a result of the findings of the Aird Commission, which recommended the establishment of a nationally owned network, the CNR eventually ceased broadcasting and sold its three stations to CRBC.

While it did not own stations, the Canadian Pacific Railway Company in its turn sponsored and distributed programs. The first series of broadcasts sponsored by the CPR was in May 1930 over the Calgary station CFCN, featuring a cowboy band. Unlike its rival company's broadcasts, the CPR programs were primarily aimed at publicizing its facilities and attracting tourists. Most were designed by John Murray Gibbon as a continuation of his promotional ideas of the twenties. The thirteen-week 'Musical Crusaders,' initiated in October 1930 and broadcast from Toronto, was the first series of its kind sponsored by the CPR, and also marked the first time that a Canadian-sponsored program was beamed over a network of fourteen American stations.[20] Charles Jennings was the producer of the shows. The series was announced at the back of one of the CPR festival brochures as taking place on Sunday afternoons from 4:15 to 4:45:

[It] introduces a group of musicians who are making a cruise round the world on the 'Empress of Australia.' Written and planned by Stanley Maxted, well-known Canadian tenor, and produced by Alfred Heather, assisted by members of his Light Opera Company, including Stanley Maxted ... Harvey Donay ... Beatrice Morson, Jean Haig, Billie Bell and Mary Frances James, *Musical Crusaders* originates in the new studio of the Royal York Hotel, and is broadcast over coast-to-coast network in Canada and over the network stations in the Eastern and Middle-western States.

Two other series were created by the CPR at this time: 'Melody Mike's Music Shop' and 'Friday Evenings.' The former was a variety program with a large following, which introduced many Canadian singers to the public, while the 'Friday Evenings' series combined vocal or light symphony programs, conducted by Alfred Heather and Rex Battle, with Fred Culley's Royal York Dance Orchestra.

'Canadian Mosaic,' a series of thirteen programs produced in 1938, was the direct outcome of John Murray Gibbon's book by the same title, published in 1938 by McClelland and Stewart. In the book Gibbon traced the history of the ethnic groups populating Canada. In the radio series his goal was to highlight the contribution to Canadian life made by the various racial groups, again as a means of promoting the CPR. Each week was devoted to an excursion into a different country featuring folk-music of that region. Charles Jennings, who shortly afterward became vice-president of the CBC, was announcer for this program as well. The songs chosen for the series were based on the material Gibbon had collected for his folk-song festivals. Many of them were arranged by Sir Ernest MacMillan, and Frances James, accompanied by the Toronto Conservatory String Quartet, was a regular singer on the show.[21] It was broadcast through the CBC network from a studio at the top of the Royal York Hotel.

Commercial broadcasting was a popular phenomenon of the 1930s. Particularly successful were such shows as the 'Imperial Oil' program, orchestral concerts conducted by Reginald Stewart (1930); the 'General Electric Vagabonds' (1931); the 'Coca-Cola Hour'; and the 'Neilson Hour,' sponsored by the Neilson chocolate company. The 'General Electric Vagabonds' was a weekly show that mixed light popular music with folk-song arrangements and selections from the classical repertoire. Ernest Dainty was conductor of the thirty-three piece band, with Charles Jennings as announcer. Frances James, who at this stage in her career rarely refused an engagement, was a frequent singer with the program either as soloist or in duets with Stanley Maxted. Other guests soloists included the piano duo of Reginald Godden and Scott Malcolm, cellist Boris Hambourg, pianist Ernst Seitz, baritone Frank Oldfield, and a saxophone trio.

Augustus Bridle's review of one of the programs in the *Canadian G.E. Monogram* reflects the temper of the times:

Half the radio programs I hear bore me because the performers think all audiences live in Hicktown. A good share of the other half bore me because they are technically highbrow. The Canadian General Electric program last night, which was inaugurated over a trans-Canada chain of 20 stations − struck a rhythmic swing in the opening number of Ernest Dainty's Vagabond orchestra, that carried right through a definite agreeable colour scheme, as naturally continuous as the episodes in a good story. It was not a recital by so many artists, but a lively sequence of musical moments all in the same picture.[22]

The *Canadian G.E. Monogram* was nothing less than a propaganda sheet, publicity for the company and its programs in order to promote sales of its products. It also published listeners' comments engendered by the polls it conducted across Canada soliciting public opinion about the company's music programs. According to the *Monogram*, 80 per cent of the audience polled responded either positively or enthusiastically to the radio shows. This type of publicity campaign and the pride in its high-quality radio show reflected a concern on the part of the GE company typical of an era that is now long past. Like the CPR, the GE company also had a publicity department and an advertising manager.

Throughout the 1930s Geoffrey Waddington was distinguishing himself as a leading conductor for the majority of the mushrooming English radio programs. For this purpose he used a standard group of musicians who formed part of his radio orchestra and who constituted the main body of players in the prolific broadcasting shows. Murray Adaskin, a member of Waddington's orchestra, recalls that Waddington, originally director of music, was pushed into a position of planning concerts and broadcasts as well as conducting the orchestra. As he was not a trained conductor, the players, who were all of the same age group – young and therefore brash – would freely impart advice on how a specific composition should be performed. They were all sharing in the development, through experimental stages, of the new communications medium. Through his more than twenty years of experience with the CBC, Waddington became an excellent and much valued conductor.

Murray remembers with affection Waddington's remarkable modesty:

In those days, none of the people who were conducting were formally trained; that is, one did not go through the study of score analysis and score reading or of the mechanics of dealing with an orchestra of sixty tough musicians with strong personalities. The conductors simply had to learn all of that through experience. So when another conductor told Geoff that he could learn a score simply by reading it without necessarily having to play or hear it, he confided in me with enormous envy; it upset him because he felt he could not do it. And I said, 'Geoff, would you tell him for me that I have worked, I have done score reading, I have looked at countless scores and taken them apart like a butcher dissects an animal, and tell him for me that he's a big liar. It's only when he hears the work in performance that he really knows what is in the score.' Geoff needed that, but that was the kind of modesty that would lead a person to drink.

Geoff felt that his whole background was wrong, and later, when younger conductors would go and study abroad with such people as Monteux, for example, he felt even more insecure about his abilities. I had long conversations with Geoff on these things and I would point out to him that we became violinists in a very non-violin world. It was hard for us to go to New York or abroad to pursue our studies with a great teacher because we had no money. We really had to do it the hard way. Sure, it takes you longer; perhaps you have lost ten years of success and fulfilment, but what about the fun you have had trying to do it on your own!

I did a lot of that kind of talking with him because we became very good friends, and when he was in the depths of depression, that's when I was always called into the act. The important thing is that he had a vision and he worked very hard for it, and this was the CBC Symphony. He formed it with the idea that it would have its own resident orchestra, and it was a marvellous orchestra with the best players in Toronto, which at that time, one could easily say, had the best musicians in Canada. Then he decided that it would be the orchestra to play new Canadian works.

Although the musicians involved in radio shows in the early days of broadcasting developed a close rapport in which friendship and pranks were symbolic of a youthful *joie de vivre*, their work was taxing and placed high demands on them.

I remember the weekly broadcasts of the 'Coca-Cola Hour' and the 'Neilson Hour,' where you rehearsed all day in preparation for the show, with Percy Faith writing all the extra bits of music at the very last minute. In those days Geoff would say to Percy, 'Go out and do a break for the brass.' We would be playing some jazz tune, and he would just write out the parts on little strips of paper, then proceed to put it on the stands while the rehearsal was in progress. In the middle of a piece, during a thirty-second break in the strings, the brass or the saxophone would play the freshly composed segment without any interruption to the flow of the music. Such was the precision required in those rehearsal studios, and although things were wild, free, and easy, one worked under tension. But when you are young these experiences are challenging.

I remember the famous 'Coca-Cola Hour,' which employed singers. One tenor came to ask Geoff to transpose the piece down a third. Geoff would wink at us and say, 'Okay, fellows, down a major third,' and the wink meant for us to play it exactly the way it was written. The tenor would sing it, thank Geoff, and inform him that the orchestra did not need to do that transposition tonight for the broadcast. We all had to keep a straight face. Or we would have to transpose mainly because we had the music for some voice setting other than the range of the singer that showed up. These were all arrangements by Percy Faith, and we would have to transpose the piece down a fourth or minor third. That orchestra would do it without a single foul-up, they were so experienced. There is no way of acquiring that kind of experience today, but at that time it was just common practice. It happened in vaudeville shows, in theatre pits, and similar occasions.

All of these broadcasts described occurred, of course, in the days before the musicians' union was established. The musicians, asked to come to an early-morning rehearsal, at times would have to sit around until noon waiting for the parts to be copied out. There was also no set time for the rehearsal to end. The decade of the 1930s was the era of live-music broadcasting, when musicians could earn a living by performing full-time in radio shows. In those early days of experimentation in and development of the medium, radio proved the major source of income for Toronto musicians. The 'Neilson Hour' and the 'Coca-Cola Hour' were broadcast for years.

Another program with a long broadcast history was 'The Melodic Strings,' conducted for more than ten years by a flamboyant Cossack. Initiated in 1933, by the end of the decade the program marked its three-hundredth regular weekly concert. Crimean-born Alexander Chuhaldin (1892–1951), violinist, teacher, conductor, and composer, was concert-master of the Imperial Grand Opera in Moscow before emigrating to Canada in 1927. In Toronto he both taught at the Conservatory of Music and conducted his orchestra in a primarily classical repertoire. Murray Adaskin, who took violin lessons from him for a short time, became a regular member of Chuhaldin's broadcast orchestra. By

1939 the group had reached such a high level of proficiency that Benjamin Britten, impressed with its high standards, wrote *Young Apollo* for it, dedicating the work to Chuhaldin. The composition *premièred* in a 1939 broadcast, with the composer at the piano.

A momentous occasion in the history of broadcasting in Canada occurred in April 1933 with the inauguration of the Canadian Radio Broadcasting Commission. The commission played a key role in the development of a national perspective, and became an effective instrument in nation building. Headed by a three-man committee under the directorship of Hector Charlesworth – music critic and editor of *Saturday Night* – the CRBC represented the first publicly owned and controlled national radio system in Canada. Its mandate was to develop the national network by building new stations across Canada and taking over privately owned ones.

In the three-and-a-half years of its operation, the CRBC accomplished much. The quality and reception of broadcasts were improved, programs were beamed into previously isolated areas in Canada's interior, and ambitious programming was offered in both languages. Programming included symphony concerts, opera, chamber and choral music, drama, educational shows, recitals, bands, children's programs, organ music, special events, variety, comedy, novelty, news and weather, sports, and the Northern Messenger Service. The fact remained, however, that by 1936 the national network still reached less than half the population; further, while the CRBC transmitted regular broadcasts by the New York Philharmonic, the Toronto Symphony Orchestra was heard very seldom. [23]

On 2 November 1936 the Canadian Broadcasting Corporation (CBC) was established, replacing the CRBC and assuming the status of a public corporation with a nine-member board of governors. Leonard Brockington of Winnipeg was appointed chairman, with W.E. Gladstone Murray as general manager. Two musical advisers, Sir Ernest MacMillan and Wilfrid Pelletier, conductor of the Metropolitan Opera orchestra, were also appointed. Production was divided into five regions: the Maritimes, Quebec, Ontario, the Prairie Provinces, and British Columbia.

The establishment of the CBC sparked an explosion of musical broadcasting by Canadian talent, particularly from the two major cultural centres, Toronto and Montreal. Several musical directors were reaching prominence across the airwaves. One was Montreal's Jean-Marie Beaudet, who conducted major oratorios and orchestral series with the seventy-two musicians of the Montreal Symphony Orchestra. In 1938 Beaudet was appointed national music director of the Quebec and Montreal regions. He was a strong supporter and proponent of contemporary Canadian music, a predilection that became particularly prominent during the next decade. His programs were heard live simultaneously on both the English and French networks.

In Toronto Geoffrey Waddington's reputation as a major radio conductor continued to grow as his association with broadcasting intensified through the formative years of the CBC. Particularly known were his programs 'Echoes of the Masters' (1936) and the 'CBC Music Hour' (1938). The latter was a series of Sunday broadcasts of light symphonic repertoire, using a group of thirty-six musicians. His 'Strike up the Band' featured Frances James as soloist on several occasions.

A popular conductor of choral groups at this time was Alfred Whitehead. His broadcasts with the CBC Singers were heard on the CBC national network. Canadian chamber groups also transmitted their artistry on the air, among them the McGill Quartet, the Toronto Conservatory String Quartet, the Hart House String Quartet, the Hambourg Trio, and Murray Adaskin's Toronto Trio. Eighty-eight chamber music programs were broadcast in 1936 alone.[24] Other groups attaining prominence in the early days of the CBC were Chuhaldin's Melodic Strings, le Quatuor de Montréal, L'Ensemble Instrumental de Montréal, Concert Champêtre, the Tudor String Quartet from Winnipeg, the Calgary String Ensemble, and the Lunenburg Ladies' Trio, led by Marjory Payne, who attained prominence as conductor in Halifax.[25]

Commercial programs featuring variety shows continued to occupy considerable time on the air-waves. By 1939 these included the 'Chase and Sanborn' program with Nelson Eddy, the 'Carnation Contented Hour,' and the 'Jell-O' program with Jack Benny. Various other types of light music were popular radio fare at the end of the decade: Luigi Romanelli's orchestra transmitted dinner music from the King Edward Hotel, Horace Lapp conducted dance music at the Royal York, and the Toronto Trio played in weekly fifteen-minute luncheon music broadcasts, also from the Royal York Hotel.

By the end of 1938 the CBC network was broadcasting an average of 520 hours per week. The already active publicity department that promoted the activities of the corporation in newspapers and periodicals was reorganized into a press and information service. The CBC *Annual Report* of 1939 states that the mandate of the press office was to 'regionalize the various press releases – so that the information could be written specifically for the district concerned and in accordance with the style of publication for which it was intended.' Regional representatives were appointed in British Columbia and the Maritimes. The amount of space in the Canadian press devoted to the CBC and its activities increased.

The objective of bringing to Canadian audiences programs by the country's leading symphony orchestras and choral groups was aggressively pursued. On

30 December 1939, for example, the CBC transmitted *Messiah* performed by Fricker's Mendelssohn Choir and members of the Toronto Symphony, with Frances James as the soprano soloist. The summer concerts of the Promenade Philharmonic and the winter season of the TSO were also broadcast. Throughout 1939 concerts by the symphony orchestras of Toronto, Montreal, and Vancouver were broadcast. The producer for the TSO broadcasts was John Adaskin, whose skill at balancing the various instrumental sections resulted in radio sound of excellent quality, setting unusually high broadcasting standards for a period hampered by technical deficiencies.

Murray summarizes his brother's technique:

We did the first Toronto Symphony broadcast in Massey Hall, where he set up a system of microphones high in the hall but in strategic places that could pick up the orchestra sound in a most remarkable way. His pick-ups became very famous and his setting stayed on in the hall for years. He could get what they called a prescience to the sound that made you feel as if you were right there. The sound was alive, not in the least mechanical. He was able to recreate such a high fidelity because of his wonderful ear. This is how he became almost a confidant of Sir Ernest MacMillan, who relied on him on many occasions.

Sir Ernest MacMillan had taken over the directorship of the Toronto Symphony Orchestra in 1931 after the death of Luigi von Kunits.

A major turning-point in the orchestra's history occurred in 1933 when silent movies were replaced by 'talkies.' Almost overnight, the whole employment structure for musicians collapsed, when they were no longer bound to their evening movie engagement. The TSO capitalized on this new turn of events by turning from 'twilight' to evening concerts, which enabled it to offer longer programs and more ambitious repertoire. It demanded its members attend morning rehearsals on an almost daily basis for its bimonthly concerts, for a total salary of between fifteen and thirty dollars a month. With the additional revenue from radio performances, however, the musicians were able to make a living throughout the 1930s.

During his winters in Toronto, Murray Adaskin played frequently as a violinist in radio orchestras and as a member of the TSO. Other musicians associated with the TSO's concerts in the previous decade also continued their association with the organization. More joined in the 1930s to contribute to the pool of such well-known Toronto names as Hyman Goodman, Albert Pratz, Eugene Kash, Elie Spivak (concert-master 1931–48), Harold Sumberg, Samuel Hersenhoren, Maurice Solway, Isadore Dubinsky, Donald Heins (assistant conductor 1931–42), Marcus Adeney, Leo Smith (principal cello), and Philip

Spivak. Toronto could, therefore, boast having some of the best string players in Canada assembled within one community.

The symphony devised fund-raising campaigns in the form of Christmas Box Concerts, where the players donated their services for the pension fund of the Orchestra Association. These delightful occasions, blending slapstick action, humorous performances, and the singing of Christmas carols, provided annual merriment until 1957. Sir Ernest MacMillan's tremendous sense of humour at such concerts is still fondly remembered by many. These concerts provided an ideal outlet for the clowning acts of several members of the orchestra, whose pranks throughout the symphony season seemed inexhaustible.

During one memorable Christmas Box Concert in 1935, Murray Adaskin conducted the orchestra dressed up as Charlie Chaplin. His shenanigans were fuelled by the outbursts of laughter from the children in the audience who found his art of falling off the stage irresistible. Another humorous occasion involved John Adaskin, who, during a fund-raising campaign, provoked considerable hilarity by performing a tin-horn concerto based on four pitches, while disguised as a gangster.

Humour, however, could be quickly dissipated by clashes of personality. Murray remembers how, on the occasion of the first night of the Christmas Box concert, Leo Smith came backstage and threw his arms around the impersonator of Charlie Chaplin, saying: 'Dear boy, in spite of all your fooling, you make the orchestra sound better than Sir Ernest MacMillan.' The cellist just could not miss an opportunity to criticize the conductor, who by then had become his arch-enemy. Even though Leo Smith had been one of the main teachers in the conservatory of which MacMillan was the director, and the cellist played in the orchestra conducted by MacMillan, they had not spoken to each other for years. The reason? Leo Smith had built a lovely house in Rosedale; the adjoining property was purchased by the conductor, who in later years proceeded to build a house higher than his neighbour's. The fact that the taller house obstructed the sun from Smith's caused the cellist to harbour permanent bad feelings towards the conductor.[26]

Murray Adaskin's association with the Toronto Symphony ended in 1936, after thirteen seasons during which he had experienced and contributed to the organization's growth and development. One summer shortly after Murray suffered a serious bout with appendicitis in Banff, which he survived through luck rather than the skill of attendant doctors, he was unpleasantly surprised by a letter from Sir Ernest MacMillan. It was a request for Murray to abandon his third desk seat on the outside of the first violin section of the orchestra in order to afford some of the younger members the opportunity to rotate locations. Murray found MacMillan's request totally incongruous. At that time in his late twenties, he did not exactly consider himself an 'elder' member of anything; in addition, he had actually expected to be moved forward a stand. Despite the fact that his summer of illness had left him penniless and that the income from the symphony was essential, he decided to resign. This situation created upheaval in the orchestra, for the players looked upon their violinist colleague as an invaluable asset to the organization. The concert-master and at least a dozen players attempted to dissuade Murray from what they saw as a rash decision by offering him their seats. In protest at the conductor's request, however, Murray quit the orchestra, much to the consternation of Sir Ernest MacMillan, a course of events that nevertheless did not seem to affect their friendship in later years.

The Toronto violin players were a closely knit group. One of their much anticipated social events was the Adaskins' annual fiddlers' party. In 1945 when the Adaskins built their summer cottage at Canoe Lake, many were to congregate in the peaceful haven of this Algonquin Park hideaway.

Although professionally engaged, the Toronto fiddlers never missed an opportunity to take violin lessons with any internationally known figure who happened to visit the city. In the mid-1930s the violist William Primrose had distinguished himself through his recordings of the Paganini *Caprices*. Admiration for his artistry prompted Murray and five of his string-player friends – including Albert Pratz – to bring the great violist to Toronto to give six weeks of master classes. For Murray each day of the six weeks was packed with practice and lessons, a difficult feat for someone who also held a number of full-time jobs playing in local orchestras. The group often took turns having dinner with Primrose at their homes. Murray recalls the occasion of their last meal together. The string players were in the middle of dinner at a restaurant when a phone call came for the violist from New York. Arturo Toscanini, who in 1937 was in the process of forming the NBC orchestra, had just heard the recording of the Paganini *Caprices* and had decided instantly that Primrose was to be a member of his orchestra. The manager had first phoned England, which the violist had visited prior to his Toronto teaching engagement. He proceeded to phone Montreal and then the Toronto Conservatory of Music, where he obtained the telephone number of one of the string group; it was finally the wife of one of the fiddlers who gave the manager the restaurant's telephone number. That night Primrose took the train to New York, and the next day he auditioned for Toscanini. Such was the expediency and precision with which the Italian maestro expected matters to be resolved. Primrose shared the first viola stand in Toscanini's orchestra for the duration of the orchestra's existence.

Murray engaged in formal violin lessons on only one other occasion. Shortly before the Primrose episode, he had heard of the brilliant Canadian violinist Kathleen Parlow (1890–1963). Originally from Calgary, she was the first

English-speaking person to study with Leopold Auer in St Petersburg. Her European concert career followed. She had settled in New York by 1936, when Murray decided to spend three weeks studying with her.

I lived in the Ansonia Hotel on Broadway, around 70th Street, the only place where you could practise all day long. All I heard from my windows were trombone players and pianists, violinists and singers. The place was full of musicians and all the sounds intermingled simultaneously. The musicians who had actually lived there permanently also numbered among their ranks the retired members of the Flonzaley String Quartet.

I did nothing but practise my head off, and I had two meals a day because I could not afford to have three. Otherwise I could not have stayed in New York as long as I had planned.

Upon his return to Toronto, Murray recommended Kathleen Parlow to Sir Ernest MacMillan for the post of principal violin teacher at the conservatory, which had been empty for some time. He felt that since she was no longer touring the concert stages of the world, her position as teacher of violin in New York was not challenging or fulfilling enough for her, and, since she was a Canadian by birth, the logical step for her would be to return to Canada. MacMillan first brought her to the conservatory for some lecture recitals, at which he provided the piano accompaniment. At the last recital he made the announcement that he had appointed Kathleen Parlow as head of the violin department. She moved to Toronto in 1941, to be immediately swamped with such eager violin students as Harry and Murray Adaskin, Hyman Goodman, Eugene Kash, Samuel Hersenhoren, and many others.

It was in the summer of 1938 while playing his regular Banff engagement with the Toronto Trio that Murray was approached by a Mr Matthews, the head of the CPR hotels, with the offer of a permanent position for him and his trio as regular musicians at Toronto's Royal York Hotel. This was three years after Murray had resigned from the Toronto Symphony Orchestra and the timing for the impecunious musician could not have been better.

As part of his job, Murray made innumerable transcriptions. Matthews, who travelled frequently to all the CPR hotels across Canada, would offer Murray's repertoire to the musicians in those hotels as an example of the kind of programming they should be considering. As a result Murray received inquiries from all over the country and orders for copies of his transcriptions. He thus inadvertently became music director for the CPR hotels.

The position at the Royal York Hotel, which spanned fourteen years, turned out to be a most interesting and rewarding experience for the violinist and his trio. The group was required to play a total of three hours a day, one-and-a-half hours each at noon and at dinner. In the tower of the hotel was Murray's studio, which contained a piano; there he practised and wrote his transcriptions. Later, in the 1940s when he started composition lessons with John Weinzweig, the studio was an oasis that allowed him to concentrate on his work undisturbed.

The trio had decided to play anything that was at all performable, ranging from classical to popular, in order to satisfy the requests and tastes of the hotel's guests. In the course of time each member of the group had developed a facility for transcribing his own instrumental part. Murray explains: 'In between performances Louis Crerar would be doing some writing on a piece of manuscript paper; I would be standing at the piano, unobtrusively jotting down things for the cellist, for whom we would always write out his part. Within minutes we were able to supply any piece that anyone wanted.'

Because of their regular trans-Canada broadcasts, the trio was heard by many publishers, who would then send, unsolicited, volumes of popular song sheets. Similarly, the group was swamped by mail with requests for arrangements and subsequent transmissions of favourite musical numbers.

The enormous dining-room at the Royal York could accommodate a large number of people. It was considered the best eating place in Toronto despite the steep price of $2.50 per dinner. Many of the leading international artists giving recitals in Toronto would stay at the hotel and eat their meals there. Murray and his trio never knew when Rachmaninoff, Mischa Elman, or Sir Thomas Beecham would be among the diners enjoying the sweet sounds of his Stradivarius. Many of the luminaries indeed came up to the trio after their dinner, complimenting them on the high musical standard of their performance. Murray relates many anecdotes based on his experiences as musician at the Royal York Hotel. He recalls that the background noise of clattering dishes in the dining-room was always considerable, frequently augmented by powerful crashes, as an unlucky waiter dramatically smashed the entire contents of a tray as he slipped on the smooth floor.

In the closing months of the thirties came the transition from the Depression to the Second World War. While the economic effects of the former era left their scars on the hotel business in Canada, the physical and psychological effects of the war constituted a threat to the hotel's very existence. Murray remembers the day war was declared, when the manager called the entire staff, including the musicians, and with tears in his eyes, reflected upon the potentially drastic effect the cutbacks would have on business. Murray, however, thought that the opposite would occur, and predicted that businessmen would be travelling even more than before in an attempt to supply half the world with ammunition, uniforms, food, and clothing:

Within a month the hotel was so full that travellers were sleeping in the front lobbies on chesterfields, with officers and troops making the hotel their lay-over point. A wealthy lady came from Australia, took a suite of rooms at the Royal York, and was there during the whole period of the war, looking after the Australian air force boys. She entertained them and did everything in her power to help them out. Similarly, the Norwegian air force boys would at times take up half the dining room in celebration of certain war events.

We played their pieces for them, such as 'Waltzing Matilda' for the Australians, and special selections for the Norwegians. I got to know one of the Norwegian flyers, who later became an aide to the king of Norway, and we corresponded for a long time thereafter. The place was like a beehive and it remained that way for the duration of the war.

The Toronto Trio provided fleeting moments of pleasure, therefore, to many servicemen faced with an uncertain fate.

The late 1930s presented a difficult time for artists. Yet the period was a remarkable milestone in the history of Canadian cultural awakening. Spiritual enrichment through music served as an antidote to the bleakness of life. For Canadians isolated by the vast expanses of this country's geography, the development of radio broadcasting ushered in an era of nation building through communication across the air-waves. With the development of broadcasting came the dissemination of musical culture into the remote areas of this country. The growing Depression, therefore, did not seem to affect negatively the development of Canada's musical culture.

IN PRAISE OF CANADIAN PAINTING IN THE THIRTIES

Another group of artists also contributed to the richness of Toronto's cultural fabric in the pre-war years, for the 1930s witnessed a profusion of painters, many centred in Toronto, most of whom are now legendary names in the history of Canadian art.

The city's art circles and the painters who frequented them constituted an important part of the Adaskins' lives. There was a rich cultural interchange of ideas between the artistic and the musical community, and the Adaskins' love for Canadian art stems from this time of their frequent contacts with the artists. Every major concert was attended by a large number of visual artists and, reciprocally, every new exhibition or showing was welcomed with interest by the Adaskins and their musical friends. Each group was genuinely interested in the artistic and creative endeavours of the other. Painters Will Ogilvie (1901–), Bertram Brooker (1888–1955), Lawren Harris (1885–1970), A.Y. Jackson (1882–1974), Charles Comfort (1900–), Arthur Lismer (1885–1969), Paraskeva Clark (1898–1987), sculptors Florence Wyle (1881–1968), Frances Loring (1887–1968), Elizabeth Wyn Wood (1903–1966) and her husband, Emmanuel Hahn (1881–1957) – these are some of the artists who lived and worked in Toronto and struggled to make a living during the Depression years. All of them loved music, and some, like Charles Comfort, were accomplished musicians themselves. Early in the 1920s Comfort was faced with a crossroads in his career – a choice between the violin and the paintbrush. Although the latter prevailed, music always remained an essential part of his life.

Harris, Jackson, and Lismer were members of the Group of Seven, which had been formed in 1920 and whose influence was still strongly felt throughout the 1930s. According to art historian Charles Hill, 'the Toronto-based Group of Seven was the embodiment of the nationalist cause, and A.Y. Jackson remained its leading spokesman. He believed that an art determined by geography and created by artists "with their feet in the soil" would naturally be a true expression of Canada, and that the revitalization of Canadian art would come about through the continued exploration and interpretation of its landscape.'[27] Whenever A.Y. Jackson returned from a sketching excursion, the artists and a handful of musicians were invited to view his new works and sketches, an occasion always accompanied by a party. He travelled all over Canada, visiting places never before seen by the majority of the Toronto musicians, who would listen in fascination to his experiences. During his travels Jackson would sell his sketches, a practice that enabled him to collect enough money to finance the remainder of his trip.

Alfred Casson (1898–), a close friend and associate of Franklin Carmichael (1890–1945) who was introduced to the Group of Seven at the Arts and Letters Club shortly after the group's formation, was invited in 1926 to join their membership. Although he was the only one who did not share the group's particular interest in music, he and the Adaskins met frequently at dinner parties and receptions. In later years, when Frances and Murray had built their cottage at Canoe Lake in Algonquin Park, Casson captured in an oil painting the essence of their view of the lake, the islands, and the land in the vicinity. This painting was given by the artist to the Adaskins and now forms part of their collection.

Paraskeva Clark, who settled in Toronto in 1931, at first succumbed to the influence of the Group of Seven, until she asserted her own philosophy in sympathy with leftist causes. Educated in Russia after the revolution, she supported social struggle by the oppressed, and during the 1930s befriended Norman Bethune, involving herself in the raising of funds for the Loyalist cause in Spain and the revolution in China. Montreal-based Louis Muhlstock (1904–) identified with Paraskeva Clark, and his work frequently highlighted the unemployed and other underprivileged members of society. Both Muhlstock and Clark were politically active.

Paraskeva and Philip Clark were close and lifelong friends of the Adaskins, and in the early years following the musicians' marriage the two couples lived across the hall from each other in the same apartment building on Lonsdale Road. One of Paraskeva's paintings in the Adaskins' possession – a still life of flowers – dates from this period (1934), but two major portrayals of the artists, 'Portrait of Murray Adaskin' and 'Portrait of Frances James Adaskin' date from 1945 and 1952 respectively. She also made an oil sketch of Canoe Lake entitled 'Adaskin Summer Cottage.'

Louis Muhlstock, who worked for his family's fruit-importing firm in Montreal, lived under severe financial restrictions, at times substituting potato sacks for canvas, or wrapping paper for drawing paper because of his inability to purchase supplies.[28] Murray remembers trips to Montreal in later years when he would visit Muhlstock in his house, where the walls were absolutely covered with his paintings. The painter would quip sarcastically that he had the largest collection of Louis Muhlstocks in the world. A painting of a nude by the artist now graces the walls of the Adaskins' home.

On the occasion of their Toronto gatherings the city's creative artists exerted an influence on one another's art and philosophy. The painter Gordon Davies and his wife entertained a great deal, and artists and musicians mingled in the Davies's home, establishing a warm rapport. In 1936 Davies painted a portrait of Frances that figures prominently in the Adaskins' private collection as a reminder of the many happy and hilarious evenings spent in their home.

The sculptor Elizabeth Wyn Wood and her husband Emmanuel Hahn, who designed the canoe with two people on the 1935 silver dollar, were prominent members of the Toronto art community. Frances and Murray's friendship with the Hahns, which began in the 1930s, lasted until Wyn Wood's death. On a visit to the Hahns in the 1940s the Adaskins fell in love with a magnificent work, a large white plaster plaque mounted on a metal pipe frame showing an island in relief. It was stored against the wall in Wyn Wood's studio with a big blanket around it. When the artist told them she was tired of storing it, the Adaskins bought the striking creation for a minimal sum, and today consider it the most beautiful acquisition in their home. At one time the National Gallery was interested in obtaining it from the Adaskins, who after all these years still cannot bear to part with it.

The Winnipeg artist Lemoine FitzGerald (1890–1956), who was invited to join the Group of Seven in the early 1930s, was still an unknown painter when Frances sang in Winnipeg during one of her western tours. Through his daughter, the singer learned that the painter was shy to the point of being a recluse, and incapable of promoting his own art. Frances, who recognized the artist's great talent, offered to take some of his paintings with her to Toronto, to introduce his work to art circles there and to sell it to her friends. She returned to Toronto with a roll of his unframed paintings. After the Adaskins purchased the ones that particularly appealed to them, they phoned their friends, and sold all the paintings in one afternoon for about forty dollars apiece. FitzGerald accepted the cheque for the successful transactions with incredulity.

Because of their interaction with painters during the 1930s, the Adaskins acquired many of their works of art either as gifts from the artists themselves or as purchases to help the artists during difficult economic times. Visual artists were one of the creative groups in Canada who suffered extensively during the Depression. Because of a lack of support by a public who considered art as non-essential luxury items, some artists were literally starving. The budget of the National Gallery of Canada was drastically reduced, affecting further the purchase of Canadian paintings. Private patronage of art was a rarity in Canada at the time. Among the few collectors of art, two stand out: J.S. McLean, president of Canada Packers Ltd, and Vincent Massey. Before his departure from Canada to accept the post of high commissioner in Great Britain, Massey had acquired a large number of paintings that were to constitute his great Canadian collection. Already in the twenties he had purchased a collection of forty-five Tom Thomson oil sketches that had been on exhibition at the Arts and Letters Club. Even though at that time the sketches were selling for between twenty-five and forty dollars each, few of the illustrious members of the club found them worthy of purchase. Murray explains the situation as follows: 'This kind of drawing was so different from what the club members were used to. They were accustomed to any outdoor landscape painting that had a cow grazing in a peaceful English-type meadow, which is great in England, but is definitely not the way Canada looks. These men [the Group of Seven] had discovered a way of painting Canada as it really was, a rugged part of the world with its own great beauty.'

In addition to his Tom Thomson acquisition, Massey purchased in 1934 the entire collection of some 250 paintings by David Milne (1882–1953), an artist who was then totally unknown. In his memoirs, Massey reconstructs his initial acquaintance with Milne's paintings: 'Alice and I visited an art dealer's shop in Toronto to view a collection of pictures by various painters that were offered for sale. One of these pleasured us greatly. Its subject was simple enough: a bunch of white flowers – trilliums I think – placed in some sort of jug on a windowsill, overlooking the roofs of a small town – purple, green, the off-white of the trilliums, and throughout the canvas – it was an oil – masses of grey and even black strikingly and effectively employed.'[29]

To compensate Milne for the inordinately low purchase price they paid, the Masseys devised a way of further helping the artist, not only financially but also in the spreading of his reputation: they offered some of the canvases they had purchased to the gallery that had originally sold them to the Masseys, with the mandate that they be sold again and a proportion of the proceeds be placed in a David Milne fund. Vincent Massey thus established himself as the true patron of this artist.

Not all Canadian artists, however, were fortunate enough to have such a patron: a magnanimous gesture of this kind would have been a rarity in any country. In fact those artists who did hold jobs or received commissions during the Depression were exceptionally fortunate. Charles Comfort was one of the few. He received a number of private commissions to design large murals. The North American Life Building (1932), the Toronto Stock Exchange (1936), and the Captain George Vancouver mural at the Hotel Vancouver (1939) were of his provenance. During this time he also lectured in the history of art department at the University of Toronto.

Some artists, Arthur Lismer and A.J. Casson, for example, were employed in the commercial field. Lismer's activities with the CPR in the late twenties and early thirties have already been noted. Throughout most of the 1930s he was also supervisor of art education at the Toronto Art Gallery. Frances and Murray had contact with him on the many occasions when they gave concerts at the Art Gallery. Casson was art director with the distinguished Toronto firm Samson Matthews. The position he held for thirty-five years entailed art printing and the process of silk-screen design. During the war, as part of the war effort, A.Y. Jackson and Charles Matthews commissioned large silk-screen canvases to send to the Canadian forces camps overseas as reminders of their home country. The Canadian government and the National Gallery helped to support this project, as did such major Canadian corporations as Imperial Tobacco, Imperial Oil, and Neilson's.

Charles Matthews always went to the top artist when he had a job to be done, and his firm employed a number of Canadian artists before and during the war. This type of commercial work was at times the only source of revenue for Toronto painters. On one occasion Player's cigarettes, a client of Charles Matthews, needed a design for their package. It was Casson who designed the sea captain who graced those packages through subsequent decades.

An art collector who was of great assistance to Toronto artists during the Depression was Douglas Duncan (1902–1968), who operated the Picture Loan Society. The project was initiated in 1936 by a group of artists and their friends, with the purpose of promoting the works of the younger generation of Canadian artists. The gallery exhibited pictures and loaned them for a monthly rental fee of two dollars; they could be kept indefinitely. There was an option to buy, in which case the price of rental was subtracted from the purchase price. Duncan was a man of exquisite taste, who exerted tremendous influence on the art scene of the 1930s. Murray and Frances Adaskin frequented his house on numerous occasions, marvelling at his large collection of Milne's artworks, which he would display by leaning them against the wall. The Adaskins' purchase of Milne's water-colour 'Trillium and Columbine' (1937) dates from this period.

In 1935 in Victoria, Murray and Frances made the acquaintance of Emily Carr (1871–1945), who did not belong to the Toronto art community, although she visited the city in 1927, 1930, and 1933.[30] Frances had been a regular visitor to Victoria for almost a decade, but Murray had never been there when he suggested that they pay their respects to Carr before the start of their summer engagement in Banff. The Adaskins, who recognized her greatness, were saddened by the reputation she had acquired in her home town as a confused eccentric who was not in command of all her 'upstairs marbles.' Murray recounts their experience with the painter:

[The Victorians] knew her as the lady who bought a baby carriage, dressed her monkey in a girl's costume, and took the monkey shopping in the carriage. Well, since there was no such thing as a grocery cart, it made all the sense in the world for her to use a carriage for this purpose. In fact, the idea was innovative and ahead of her time.

She had many animals, including this monkey whose name was Woo. Since it was a female, she dressed it up in a little skirt and bonnet and was quite fussy about the animal's attire. Since monkeys are destructive little animals, full of curiosity – they'll climb into anything, pull apart anything they can – she had to take the animal shopping with her. To her Victoria neighbours at the time she was just a funny old lady, an old maid pushing a monkey in a baby carriage, a mode of behaviour that they found utterly shocking.

Our Victoria hosts decided to drive us up to Emily Carr's house and leave us there. They had no interest in coming in and meeting the lady. In front of the house, on her hands and knees on the lawn, was a person dressed as a charwoman, pulling out dandelion shoots. I went to her and inquired whether this was Emily Carr's residence. 'Yes, I'm Emily Carr,' she said to our considerable surprise. She had a band around her head, and a big apron that came right down to her feet, just like my grandmother who came from Russia used to wear.

So I told her who we were and that we were leaving in a few days, and that we simply wanted to pay our respects to her. Well, she could not have been more hospitable or charming, and when I told her that I was Harry Adaskin's brother, that opened a new world for me. We entered her big studio where the chairs were hanging from the ceiling on pulleys. She let a couple of them down, wiped off the dust with her apron, and then proceeded to make tea for us. We had a lovely chat, and she showed us many of her paintings. Fran and I learned an important lesson then, one of the great lessons of our lives: when an artist shows you his or her paintings it is perfectly all right to inquire about the price and consider purchasing some. We so respected her and were overawed by meeting a great artist that we could not get ourselves to deal with such mundane things as prices or purchase of her work. We could have walked out with arms loaded with these drawings, her wonderful charcoal drawings on brown paper that we later saw at an exhibition in Toronto.

We had a charming time with her. She told us of her camping trip that was to take place the day after next, and invited us to come out and visit her. She would send a student to conduct us to the location, an offer that we were quick to accept. She owned a wagon that resembled a gipsy caravan, and she would call a trucking firm that would hitch the caravan to the back of the truck and drive out to some place in the Metchosin area. It was an ideal location, in solitude up on a hill, on a beautiful bank. She would ask the trucking company to return for her in two weeks' time. She had all the food she needed and was surrounded by her animals – cat, dog, bird, and monkey. Her caravan contained a bed for each animal, but Woo was the one that was always in human company, dressed in her little skirt and hat.

We sat on the hillside overlooking the water, absolutely enchanted by the magic of the place. We just sat around and chatted endlessly, for it was so beautiful to hear her talk. She had her own way of using the English language. She had not begun her writings yet; that was to come later.

That was the last time I saw her. Fran visited Vancouver some years later when Emily Carr was in the hospital there and sent her flowers. We received a pencilled letter from her, one of the last that she ever wrote, a lovely, full page of writing. She had sent it to Lawren Harris, who was living in Vancouver at the time, with the request to pass it on to us as she did not know our address.

When her first book, *Klee Wyck*, was published, our friends in Victoria began to realize that this was a rather important woman, and they sent us a copy for Christmas. Well, after that, one book after another began to come out after she could no longer paint. These were mainly her diaries that she kept all her life. She had no one to talk to, so she talked to herself through these diaries. What a wonderful way of talking!

Emily Carr taught me one of my early lessons; when you are in a community where you know a great figure resides whom you admire, there is nothing wrong in going to the door and paying your respects. It is a compliment and the most beautiful praise that a human being can get. With Emily Carr, we were not invited, we did not call ahead of time – in fact she did not even own a telephone – so that actually going there was the only way to see her. It turned out to be the richest experience I can imagine. How many people alive today can say that they saw the painter in her caravan?

Murray and Frances's love of Canadian art is directly connected to their close association and contact with these major artists of the 1930s. Their interest in art collecting started at the time they were married. Their only criterion in acquiring an artwork was not its potential value as an investment but the attraction that the work held for them. They would buy a painting because they knew the artist. Occasionally they would realize that they had outgrown a certain artist's style; their perception of a painting would change just as one's perception of the surrounding world changes. To the Adaskins 'a work of art has to hover, to have an essence and a being. If a painting began to lose these qualities for us, it was time to remove it.'

The artists of the 1930s enriched the inner lives of the Adaskins to such an extent that art provided the same spiritual uplift as music. For more than fifty years art has provided the very essence of their existence. In 1975 Murray composed a homage to his friends from the Depression era in his work for strings and harpsichord entitled *In Praise of 'Canadian Painting in the Thirties.'* The work, consisting of three movements – 1 Paraskeva Clark (Lento e cantabile), 2 Louis Muhlstock (Adagio), 3 Charles Comfort (Allegretto-Tempo Giusto) – was inspired by a 1974 exhibition in Vancouver called 'Canadian Painting in the Thirties.' Under the auspices of the National Gallery of Canada and the guidance of Charles Hill, many paintings of the important artists of that decade were assembled to reflect this difficult, yet intensely creative period in Canadian cultural history.

For the Adaskins, walking into that Vancouver exhibit was an emotional experience akin to stepping back in time. Murray describes the effect the exhibit had:

When I walked in, the first paintings that greeted us were the works that we had seen a million times in their original studios. I would say that seventy per cent of the paintings – and that is a conservative guess – were works that I had known by artists who moved in the same artistic community with us.

It conjured up so many memories of the artists themselves and how we would meet them at parties; suddenly you would remember that you were at their homes... One of them lived in the north part of Toronto, which at that time was out in the country. There was a streetcar that went along Yonge Street to his place. His name was C.W. Jefferys, whose marvellous watercolours depicted scenes from early Canadian history, and I remember going out to visit him on a Sunday afternoon. A group of us went to see him, and we sat in his garden.

In a letter to Charles Comfort on the occasion of the *première* of his composition, Murray described what prompted him to write this new work:

The works by all three of you [displayed at the Vancouver exhibition] have given Fran and me almost a lifetime of joy and all three of you have been our personal friends. Somehow I wanted to add my voice to all those who have praised the exhibition in their own way. And while I must tell you that there was no intention on my part to try and make the music describe each of my friends – yet I know that my deep affection and admiration must, somehow, perhaps underneath the notes, say something of my personal feelings towards you in the only really affectionate and meaningful way I know. However, as always, we will have to let the listener interpret in his own way.

In contrast to Murray's warm memories of this bygone era, the seventy-seven-year-old Paraskeva Clark, one of the leading participants in the events of that era, reflected on it with irony. In a letter to Murray written on the occasion of the completion of his composition she states that she no longer paints. Her era is gone and only memories remain. She has been forgotten, she says, and although the exhibition of Canadian paintings of the thirties generated considerable publicity, the event has occurred too late in her life to excite her.[31]

Thus through an exhibition, the past intermingled with the present, affording the new generations a glimpse into a bygone era, while eliciting emotional responses in those who shaped the era.

3

The Canadian performer in the 1940s

We shall go on to the end, we shall fight in France, we shall fight on the seas and oceans, we shall fight with growing confidence and growing strength in the air, we shall defend our island, whatever the cost may be, we shall fight on the beaches, we shall fight on the landing grounds, we shall fight in the fields and in the streets, we shall fight in the hills; we shall never surrender.

This powerful and well-known message was delivered by Winston Churchill on 4 June 1940, a few weeks before the surrender of France and the beginning of England's ultimately successful resistance to German attempts to bomb it into submission during the Battle of Britain. Some nine months earlier, after Hitler's invasion of Poland in early September 1939, Britain had entered the war. Canada was not far behind in sending its troops overseas. Churchill's speech symbolized the general fervour with which the enemy's invasions were countered, a spirit that also prevailed in Canada as the whole country eagerly followed events on the European battle fronts.

Every day Canadians waited at their radio sets for the latest reports on the hostilities. Murray remembers Churchill's speech quoted above and those dramatic, tension-filled wartime days when Lowell Thomas, a popular radio announcer from the American network, read the 7:00 p.m. news. The Toronto Trio, whose engagements at the Royal York Hotel began at 7:30 p.m., would listen eagerly to the news each night while dressing in their concert attire. Murray shared his friends' concern at that terrible time, as well as their admiration for the great British leader, Winston Churchill. He still recalls when England, bereft of its French ally, fought on alone – to emerge victorious.

In addition to sending their troops overseas, Canadians responded to the events that shook the world by raising money in support of the war effort. The Victory Loan campaigns were massive fund-raising drives, featuring both nationally and internationally known stars from the concert and entertainment world, who donated their services to the cause. These mammoth variety shows broadcast nationwide by the CBC network were produced by John Adaskin, who was by then one of the major producers in Canada. The conductors of the CBS and NBC radio orchestras were brought in from the United States for the concerts in Massey Hall.

The country's mood inspiring these Victory Loan campaigns is exemplified in the following 1943 newspaper excerpt:

The driving spirit of Canada's Fourth Victory Loan Campaign, has been impressively captured in the words and music of 'Back the Attack,' a stirring and rhythmic dedication to the country's $1,100,000,000 drive, written by J. Murray Gibbon … and Murray Adaskin, Toronto composer and violinist.

Presented in catchy march tempo, the number is actually a Victory Loan peptalk set to verse and music, at the same time possessing all the qualities of a standard song hit. Title and words of the song, which represent the work of Mr. Gibbon, were inspired by the campaign's slogan 'Back the Attack,' the words appearing at intervals throughout the chorus …

The melody, composed by Mr. Adaskin, gives martial flavour to the song, which should go a long way towards promoting the sale of bonds through the medium of radio broadcasts and presentation by various bands and orchestras.

The song … [stresses] … the importance of Canadians putting their shoulder to the wheel and making the maximum sacrifice to assure the campaign's success. [1]

Artists continued to function as an important source of fund-raising and morale boosting throughout the war years. A series of art events – War Services Sunday – was sponsored throughout 1943–4 by the Montreal Art Association. One of the concerts constituting part of the series was given in the city's art gallery by Frances James, with Alexander Brott, violin, and Marie-Thérèse Paquin, piano. [2] Painters were fighting, metaphorically, with their brushes, lending their support for the war effort through their art. A 1943 editorial in the *Canadian Review of Music and Art* noted that thanks to the national efforts of A.Y. Jackson, some 7500 pictures, mainly reproductions of Canadian paintings, hung in mess halls, recreation rooms, and huts of Canadian military personnel on active service. Artists donated their work, which was then reproduced by such corporate sponsors as railways, tobacco firms, life insurance companies, as well as the National Gallery. The works of art functioned not only as a means of brightening the drab surroundings of the military barracks, but as a point of contact for the armed forces with Canadian culture. [3]

Another organization that played an essential role during the war years was the Canadian Broadcasting Corporation. Already in late August 1939, with increasing international tension and gathering momentum toward war, the CBC changed its program pattern practically overnight in order to meet public demands for extended news services and political commentaries. The national broadcasting network assumed a vital function in promoting communication between Canada's leaders and its listeners and in sustaining the country's morale through appropriately planned programs. A CBC overseas program unit was established immediately upon the outbreak of war, reporting on the activities of Canadian and Allied troops through the short-wave facilities of the BBC. Realizing the importance of its broadcasting service, the CBC even made security arrangements to protect its transmitter plants against sabotage.[4]

Many programs featuring both musical variety and classical music were specifically dedicated to the war effort; 'The Army Show,' 'The Navy Show,' 'Canadian Music in Wartime,' and radio dramas are examples of the available listening fare. 'The Army Show,' with announcer Allan McFee and conductor Geoffrey Waddington, started as a musical revue for the Canadian forces. Later the name was adopted by the entertainment units serving the army. The radio series, broadcast during 1942–3 and written for the most part by Johnny Wayne and Frank Schuster, mixed light music with comedy. 'The Navy Show' was directed by Nelson Lay from Ottawa. Like its counterpart, it also toured Canada entertaining the armed forces. The New Zealand operatic bass Oscar Natzke was one of the show's stars. This colourful personality was a musically unschooled blacksmith with a naturally resonant voice, who in 1935 was offered a scholarship to study in England with the famous Albert Garcia. After having crammed ten years' worth of study into five, Natzke began to tour England, North America, and Australia as a concert and radio recitalist.

He came to the United States at the beginning of the war to sing in Wagner's *Die Meistersinger* at the Metropolitan Opera. When the international situation caused the opera production to be cancelled Natzke found himself impecunious and stranded on the North American continent. He made his way to Canada, where he was immediately engaged by Sir Ernest MacMillan as Frances James's singing partner for a Handel oratorio radio series. Those still did not provide full-time employment; when Murray Adaskin recommended him to Nelson Lay for 'The Navy Show,' Natzke welcomed the opportunity eagerly. After the war he was a popular recitalist on CBC's 'Distinguished Artists' series, while permanently engaged in New York with the New York Civic Opera Company. He finally did get to sing in *Die Meistersinger* at the Metropolitan Opera, but, as fate would have it, his career ended as abruptly as it had started: he died of a heart attack on the stage of the Met while singing the role of Hans Sachs.

The period from 1940 to 1945 gave rise to a phenomenon unique to the war years: radio dramas based on topics relating to the British Commonwealth, aspects of Canadian history, and experiences of peoples of European origin who chose Canada as their adopted country. These programs were usually presented in series of six or thirteen broadcasts, unified by such titles as The British Empire (1942), New Homes for Old (1941), Brothers in Arms (1942), White Empire (1945), Comrades in Arms (1942–5), Our Canada (1942–3), to mention some of the most popular shows. The pioneering aspect of the dramas was the fact that the CBC was responsible for bringing together for the first time in Canada the poets, writers, and composers who created these works. The thirty-minute broadcasts were at times little more than overt propaganda for the good living conditions in this country, radiating an aura of optimism in the midst of war devastation on the international scene, and romanticizing the opportunities and freedom extended by Canada to all its people. Alistair Grosart was the script-writer for many of the dramas, Samuel Hersenhoren was the conductor, and John Weinzweig was the composer of much of the music.

Live music was an essential component in these programs. The CBC hired musicians to provide the opening and closing theme music, cues of several measures denoting a change of scene, and music at the end of a scene to indicate a transition from one portion of the story to another. John Weinzweig composed approximately one hundred musical scores for radio shows at the rate of one to three per week. The demand for fresh music was so high that he barely had time to finish one score before another had to be started. His most prolific output of radio scores occurred between 1941 and 1943, when he entered the service. His posting to the Rockcliffe Air Station just outside of Ottawa enabled him to continue his musical activities, which included teaching theory to the bandsmen of the RCAF Central Band. He even gave the occasional composition lesson to Harry Somers, who commuted from Toronto for that purpose.

Weinzweig considers his five-year period of writing music for radio dramas as experience of inestimable value in learning about instrumental timbre and orchestral scoring. The art-form afforded him the opportunity to combine his interest in ethnic music with his compositional process. He always kept a notebook on hand in which he copied folk-songs heard along the way, drawing upon these resources where appropriate to the topic of a specific radio show. In a dramatization of life in India, for example, as part of the series on the British Empire, Weinzweig incorporated some Indian ragas, possibly the first time such music was heard in a Canadian composition in this country.

A similar use of folk-music occurred in the drama on Russia in the 'New Homes for Old' series. The program dramatized the personal story of Captain Boris Orloff, who, caught in the upheaval of the Russian Revolution, decided to emigrate to Canada in search of freedom. By the time his story was dramatized,

Orloff had been a Canadian citizen for twenty-two years. Weinzweig's music for this drama included passages from the Russian anthem, the Communist 'Internationale,' and 'O Canada' to assist recall of or to enhance specific moments in the drama. Violinist Paul Scherman was the narrator, and Captain Boris Orloff spoke in person at the end of the program to verify the facts in the story.

Contrived as these programs may seem to us today, they nevertheless served as an expression of the times, fulfilling a need for national ego-boosting in a very difficult period of Canada's social and cultural history.

Another radio series popular during the war period was 'Our Canada,' produced in 1942, thirteen stories about what the Canadian people have done to make their country a nation and a democracy. The composer for the series, John Weinzweig; author Gerald Noxon; producer Mavor Moore; and narrator Lorne Greene have all since distinguished themselves in the artistic community. Weinzweig's music presented a series of kaleidoscopic pictures with such titles as 'The People,' 'The Land,' and 'Bonds of Steel,' some of which were incorporated a few months later into the radio broadcast 'Music for Radio,' a program made up of works written especially for the medium, saluting such composers as Weinzweig, Howard Cable, Barbara Pentland, and Godfrey Ridout. The conductor was Samuel Hersenhoren.[5]

The CBC's wartime drama broadcasts assumed another important function within Canada's cultural history: over a period of five years the medium served as a forum for the composition and performance of music by Canadian composers. Through its policy of support for Canadian talent, it provided a source of income for a generation of young composers, as well as valuable experience and an opportunity to have their music heard. John Weinzweig, in particular, excelled as a Canadian artist during the early forties, embarking on a career in which he distinguished himself as one of this country's foremost composers.

The twenty-five-piece orchestra that provided music for the wartime radio dramas contained many of the string players active on the Toronto scene throughout the previous decade, including Murray Adaskin, who played in most of the shows. It consisted of the best players in town and provided a standard of musical performance unusually high for the genre and for the period.[6]

The feelings of nationalism generated by the social climate of the war years were expressed in numerous other broadcasts of music by Canadians. A phenomenon unique to the times, these programs in a sense reflected the necessity for the country to take stock of its native talent. 'Canadian Snapshots,' inaugurated on 13 December 1939, was a series of fifty programs that combined news and scenes from all across Canada with music by fifty composers. Conducted by Samuel Hersenhoren, these concerts included music by Louis Applebaum, Francean Campbell, Ernest Dainty, John Murray Gibbon, Hector Gratton, Eldon Rathburn, Ernst Seitz, and thirteen-year-old Clermont Pépin. The series was the first attempt by the CBC to feature a panoply of Canadian composers over a protracted period of time. By 1941, the broadcasting corporation articulated its policy on Canadian music:

To the serious young composer of concert or symphonic music, an auditorium, audience and orchestra of proportions suitable to the adequate performance of his works are rarely available. In Canada, a determined effort is being made to remedy this state of affairs. The CBC has assumed as a duty the seeking out and encouraging of exceptional creative talent in the field of musical composition.

A symphony orchestra and top-ranking conductor have been selected and an audience of greater proportions than could be housed in any concert hall on the continent will be reached when *Tribute to Canadian Composers* is broadcast.

Samuel Hersenhoren is a prime mover in the systematic research, which has discovered outstanding ability among the younger composers of Canada: John Weinzweig, Godfrey Ridout ... Barbara Pentland, Walter McNutt.[7]

CBC support for Canadian music continued over the next four years. Healey Willan's radio opera *Transit through Fire* was the first large-scale work of its kind commissioned by the corporation. It received its radio *première* in 1942 with Frances James in the lead role. The music of Barbara Pentland, Arnold Walter, Robert Fleming, Frank D. Harris, and Graham George was also transmitted to Canadian audiences in a number of separate programs during the war years.[8] In August 1944 Jean-Marie Beaudet, supervisor of music for the CBC, inaugurated and directed the Canadian composer series, 'Music of the New World.' The eight programs were launched at the invitation of the NBC, as part of the Inter-American University of the Air summer series, and were broadcast over both the NBC and CBC networks. Of the fifteen works, ten were radio *premières*, including Alexander Brott's *War and Peace* and Maurice Blackburn's *Canadian First*. John Weinzweig was represented by his *Interlude in an Artist's Life*.[9]

An example of inspirational programs of special wartime significance was provided by the 'British Ballad Opera' series of 1942. Its purpose was to present Canadian listeners with the best specimens of English opera. The eight works chosen ranged over three centuries of British music to include Purcell's *Dido and Aeneas*, Handel's *Acis and Galatea*, Gay and Pepusch's *The Beggar's Opera*, Vaughan Williams's *Hugh the Drover*, Arthur Benjamin's *The Devil*

Take Her, Michael Balfe's *The Bohemian Girl*, Sir Edward German's *Merrie England*, and Rutland Boughton's *The Immortal Hour*. Internationally known singers and conductors were featured along with the best Canadian talent. Singers Rose Bampton, John Brownlee, and Raoul Jobin, imported from the Metropolitan Opera, combined forces with such Canadian stars as Oscar Natzke, Frances James, Jean Haig, Amy Fleming, and William Morton. The general direction was under the supervision of Jean-Marie Beaudet.

The opera series generated considerable interest in the media, as illustrated in the following extract from an article by Robertson Davies in *Saturday Night*:

The CBC has undertaken to produce a short opera in English each Sunday evening ... The organization deserves high praise for this enterprise, which should do much to lend distinction to the winter radio season.

The first performance was given last Sunday and the piece was Handel's *Acis and Galatea*. Some of the singing was admirable and some was not. Frances James, who sang Galatea, seemed to have more real understanding of the music than anyone else and sang it with accomplishment and considerable wit. The rest of the group did not appear to know that *Acis and Galatea* is meant to be amusing and they sang it with a high seriousness which was not suitable to it. Oscar Natzke, except for his failure in understanding, sang magnificently as Polyphemus; his voice is big, true, and sonorous, and he has made it wonderfully flexible. Eugene Goossens conducted and, like most conductors of radio performances, seemed painfully conscious of Time's winged chariot hurrying near ...

Upon the whole, however, the performance was deeply pleasing and we are grateful to the CBC for it and for the promise of ... treasures ... on approaching Sundays.[10]

In December 1941, producer John Adaskin commissioned Healey Willan and the author John Coulter to write a new one-hour radio opera. The work, intended to initiate a revival of Canadian opera, was to employ soloists, chorus, and a full symphony orchestra. It was to be performed at the end of the CBC season of British ballad operas. In his memoirs *In My Day*, Coulter explains that as a result of the bleak and pessimistic atmosphere of the war years, *Transit through Fire* was chosen as a contemporary topic reflecting the Depression. It was 'a libretto spikey with anger and aquiver with compassion.'[11]

Willan completed the opera in a fortnight and the artists set to work preparing it for its May radio *première*. Sir Ernest MacMillan conducted the TSO and the Mendelssohn Choir. Albert Whitehead was the coach of the chorus, while Frances James and Howard Scott sang the leading roles with other roles interpreted by William Morton and J. Campbell McInnes. The work was met with great acclaim. Letters from listeners poured in, and one critic even alluded to it as 'the first great Canadian masterpiece of the war.'[12]

The critic in the *Toronto Star* who reviewed the preview rehearsal also expressed himself in positive terms:

Coulter's theme is the futility of modern college education facing the frustration problems of modern life and finding a peaceful solution only in the life of the soldier in the world's greatest struggle for freedom. Willan tackled a difficult text written by an expert in dramatic scenario; but he also is a maestro in the art of making a drama-script jump into new vitality through music.

His score is a marvel of text illumination. People who know little about musical techniques are easily charmed in this unconventional opera with the beauty and strength of the music ...

Frances James, as Joan ... gave remarkable beauty of tone, and sympathetic utterance to musicalized words whose emotional power was obvious in the clearly spoken language. Her experience in broadcast singing made her work in this just about a perfect soprano interpretation – such crystalline purity of tone is seldom equalled in opera.[13]

The highly successful work was rebroadcast one year later with the same cast, under the baton of Ettore Mazzoleni, who was soon to become principal of Toronto's Royal Conservatory of Music. On the concert platform of Convocation Hall at the University of Toronto, Howard Scott sang the role of William in his air-force uniform. Coulter reports: 'It was the last time we were to see or hear him. Some months later, having gone up on his first training-flight in England, he was killed. Canada and the world had tragically lost what ... was to become one of the great voices.'[14]

Although a considerable portion of the CBC's music broadcast time was dedicated to topics directly or indirectly related to the war, the corporation endeavoured to present its listeners with a broad spectrum of other types of music programs, ranging from light to classical and folk-music repertoire. During this heyday of live music broadcasting, the level of Canadian content was exceptionally high. The majority of artists performing on CBC radio were Canadian, from the Toronto and Montreal areas in particular, although such international luminaries as Sir Thomas Beecham; Michel Piastro, concertmaster of the New York Philharmonic; Wanda Landowska; and occasional stars from the Metropolitan Opera also made radio broadcasts during their guest appearances in Toronto.

Works by Gilbert and Sullivan and other British light operas, conducted by Geoffrey Waddington and George Stewart, were perennial favourites. While the regular broadcasts of the Metropolitan Opera Company continued to be transmitted, little classical opera emanated from Canadian studios. With Jean-Marie Beaudet as supervisor of music for the CBC, Montreal seems to have been a very active musical centre, occasionally broadcasting French opera series with such artists as Cosima Malenfant, Lionel Daunais, and Jeanne Desjardins. The symphony orchestras of Toronto, Montreal, and Vancouver were frequently heard on radio, as were Les Concerts Symphoniques de Montréal (1941) and The Little Symphony of Montreal (1943), both conducted by Bernard Naylor. Such string orchestras as the New World Chamber Orchestra (twenty-one strings conducted by Samuel Hersenhoren) and groups conducted by Paul Scherman and Harold Sumberg seem to have found favour during this period.

The folk-music revival that had been gathering momentum during the 1920s and 1930s under the influence of John Murray Gibbon, had lost some of its intensity during the war years. Although folk-music series continued to be broadcast on the CBC, their spectrum had narrowed to focus on music from the British Isles or French Canada. Gibbon's presence was still felt on the cultural scene, and Frances James remained his favoured artist for the programs he instigated.

Gibbon's radio programs reflected his support of the war effort and his respect for the British soldier, language, and tradition. This was particularly evident in the thirteen-week CBC series 'Heritage of Song,' broadcast coast-to-coast over the national network in 1941. The programs were designed by Gibbon to show the indebtedness of British poetry to the music set to this poetry. The songs, chosen as much for the quality of their words as for that of the music, range from the Elizabethan period to the twentieth century. Although Gibbon wrote the script for the continuities of each program, he did not tamper with the original text or music, which included popular folk-songs, such as 'Greensleeves'; arrangements by British composers of traditional songs, such as Roger Quilter's 'I Sing of a Maiden'; and songs and ayres by such composers as John Dowland, Henry Purcell, and Henry Lawes. The songs were arranged by Bernard Naylor for vocal duet and piano, with soloists Frances James and William Morton and with Louis Crerar at the piano. The producer of this highly successful series was John Adaskin.

Organizing radio broadcasts of choral concerts also constituted part of Gibbon's activities of this period. 'New World Ballads' (23 February 1940), consisting of sixty ballads on Canadian themes, was broadcast from Montreal and Toronto, as was 'Songs of Liberty' (May 1941), employing a male chorus of eight voices, accompanied by two pianos. Designed by Gibbon and directed by Albert Whitehead, 'Songs of Liberty' illustrated what the United States had produced in musical praise of liberty. The musical arrangements were by Healey Willan and piano accompaniment by Reginald Godden.

The CBC program schedules from the war years serve as interesting documents not only of the types of musical fare broadcast at the time, but of the musical forces involved in the creation of those programs. While a whole panoply of Canadian talent is revealed in all fields of musical endeavour, several names stand in the forefront of musical activity: Samuel Hersenhoren, John Adaskin, John Weinzweig, Jean-Marie Beaudet, Sir Ernest MacMillan, and Frances James. Hersenhoren was a particularly innovative and productive musician of the time, the extent of whose efforts in promoting Canadian music has yet to be recognized. John Adaskin's activities as wartime CBC radio producer were remarkable not only for the quality of each production, but also for their sheer quantity.

The period in Canadian radio history from the advent of broadcasting through to the end of the war years gave rise to another phenomenon in Canadian cultural history: the radio artist. Frances James was among the singers whose reputations were made or enhanced in this period by singing in coast-to-coast radio programs. Throughout the war, William Morton was Frances James's most frequent vocal partner in folk-song and light music programs, in light opera productions, as well as in Healey Willan's *Transit through Fire*. Thus, a vocal partnership that began in the days of the CPR festivals continued over several decades.

Although it was the medium of radio broadcasting that fanned her already well-developed reputation as a Canadian soprano, Frances James differed from her contemporaries during the war years by appearing in only the most prestigious radio programs. When in 1943 Sir Ernest MacMillan initiated a series of broadcasts of Handel's oratorios, she was asked to sing the soprano lead in three of the six works. The event itself was important in Canadian broadcasting history, as masterpieces such as *Judas Maccabaeus, Semele, Joshua, Samson, Solomon,* and the pastoral opera *Acis and Galatea* were aired, some for the first time in Canada. Her performance of the soprano lead in *Transit through Fire* further associated Frances James with milestones in Canadian broadcasting history, as this work marked the first time that a Canadian opera was commissioned by the CBC.

The wartime period, therefore, represented a new phase in Frances James's career. While she still occasionally performed programs of folk-song arrangements, her broadcast repertoire centred on the art song, Canadian compositions, and choral and operatic roles. She had outgrown the type of programming that was still being prepared by John Murray Gibbon, and when asked by him in 1945 to participate in his newest project – a lecture-recital of Brahms and Schubert songs in which a newly written English text substituted for the original German – she refused.

Gibbon's greatest interest as poet was the writing of totally new verse to a pre-existing piece of music. At first, as in *Magic of Melody*, published by Dent in 1932, he took such instrumental compositions as Gluck's 'Dance of the Blessed Spirits' from the opera *Orfeo ed Euridice*, Chopin's *Etude in A-flat*, a Schubert *Moment Musical*, and Schumann's 'Träumerei' to use with his own poems, which demonstrated a unity of mood and intent with the original music. He played these pieces on a phonograph, projecting the poems onto a large screen and giving them a public reading simultaneously with the musical performance. This concept was carried a step further when he decided to replace the original lyrics of a German *lied* with new text in English entirely unconnected in meaning to the original.

During the war years Gibbon's liberties with song texts had acquired a new rationale: German words were becoming unpopular. He felt, however, that the best ten thousand melodies to which they were sung had to be kept alive. The only solution, it seemed to him, was to adapt them to English words. To this purpose he prepared the song collection, *Brahms and Schubert Songs Transplanted*, and presented them in a lecture under the title 'Killing the German Language.'[15] He further planned to introduce the collection as a CBC radio series, with Frances James as the lead singer. The soprano, to whom the whole concept of applying anti-German sentiments and political ideology to works of art was anti-intellectual and totally unpalatable, refused to participate. She could not subscribe to the absurd concept of 'killing the German language,' and her artistic scruples would not allow her to sing such arias as Papageno's 'Ein Vogelfänger bin ich ja' from Mozart's *The Magic Flute* to the text 'Old Ontario.' When Frances apprised Charles Jennings, who by this time was vice-president of the CBC, of the philosophy behind Gibbon's planned radio series, the series was cancelled. Gibbon was unforgiving. The twenty-year friendship between him and Frances James came to an abrupt end, but not before he felt assured that he had the last word on the subject. In one of his letters to Frances he states that German is bound to die as an international language and that it will in the future be used mainly by singers and by those who are born to speak it as a family language. In his opinion, German is not a singable language, and it abounds with 'horrible gutterals and sibilants.'[16]

In a later letter Gibbon reminded Frances that she had been singing 'transplanted German Songs' for some time, as for instance 'Down Vancouver Way' replacing 'Kennst du das Land,' 'By Indian Trail' replacing Schubert's 'Der Lindenbaum,' and 'Canoe Song' – an old German pilgrim song.

Then, four months later, on 13 April 1945, John Murray Gibbon dramatically made his final statement to Frances. In a terse note that included a newspaper clipping he wrote that a German *lied* appropriate to the enclosed clipping, sung in German, would be 'Du bist die Ruh' (You are the peace). The clipping was entitled 'Unearth Nazi Death Camps, 5,817,000 Prisoners Died.' Such was the reaction of an embittered old man, who at age seventy had lost the vision that had guided his phenomenal pioneering efforts in the awakening of folk cultures in Canada several decades earlier.

Gibbon retired from the CPR in 1945 after thirty-eight years of service to the company. A year later the Canadian Authors' Association and the Composers, Authors, and Publishers Association of Canada paid homage to him with a distinguished gathering of political leaders, musicians, authors, and artists. He was presented an award of one thousand dollars for his outstanding contribution to Canadian culture.

And indeed, Gibbon's contributions to pre–World War Two musical culture in this country were remarkable. During the war he attempted to aid the war effort in his own way. Frances James, too, owed the early stages of her career to Gibbon. By the 1940s, however, her career had assumed new direction as a reflection of the cultural needs of the times, which diverged from Gibbon's views.

THE MAKING OF A CANADIAN SINGER

In the 1940s Frances James attained the pinnacle of her artistic achievement. She cemented her reputation as this country's most distinguished soprano and conquered the concert and radio world in her numerous appearances at Canada's most significant and successful musical events. During the post-war reconstruction period she triumphed on radio, when the CBC sponsored such major programs as the 'Wednesday Night' and 'Distinguished Artists' series and the thirteen week 'Midweek Recital' series, which featured thirteen solo recitals by Frances James. When the CBC established its own opera company, presenting some of the most innovative programming in the history of Canadian radio broadcasting, Frances was engaged as the lead soprano in such operas as Britten's *Peter Grimes* and *Albert Herring* and Stravinsky's *The Rake's Progress*. Her reputation as radio artist of the 1930s, compounded by the increased momentum of her musical activities throughout the 1940s, made her name familiar to millions of listeners across Canada who relied upon the CBC as their major source of communication with the rest of the world. She was much in demand as concert artist with symphony orchestras and choral groups in Toronto, Montreal, and Ottawa, and her performances of *Messiah*, in particular, met with great critical acclaim. She became the leading exponent of Canadian vocal music, giving first performances of numerous songs written by contemporary composers.

The 1940s saw the emergence of a generation of Canadian composers who carved out new musical directions and who took an active part in the creation of cultural organizations that today play essential roles in Canadian music. The post-war period was indeed a pioneering era both for such composers as Harry Somers, John Weinzweig, Barbara Pentland, Jean Coulthard (Adams), Kelsey Jones, and Murray Adaskin, and for Frances James, the first singer to present this new repertoire to Canadian audiences in coast-to-coast concerts and radio broadcasts alike, and the first champion of Canadian vocal music.

Her vital interest in contemporary music was further reflected in her presentation of works by Paul Hindemith, Darius Milhaud, Benjamin Britten, Igor Stravinsky, and Aaron Copland; she frequently gave them their first Canadian performance. In short, she was the most enterprising Canadian vocalist of her time in the presentation of unfamiliar works. Her numerous cross-country tours, annual events until 1952, introduced her artistry to the interior of the country's provinces. No other Canadian singer of the period toured Canada to the extent that Frances James did throughout the forties.

The contemporary press depicted the artist as a tall and glamorous woman, exuding charm, dignity, and poise. Charm was the word that described her public persona in the majority of the newspaper reviews. She would walk out on stage and, directing her gaze toward one person in the audience – in that way establishing a spiritual bond with her audience – she would begin to sing. One reviewer even commented on the artist's 'delightful capacity for taking her listeners into her confidence, at once putting them at their ease.'[17]

Wearing clothes appropriate to a particular concert program was an essential ingredient of Frances's artistic personality. Regardless of her financial situation, her choice of wardrobe was always a priority: it was as important to look like an artist as it was to sound like one. Simplicity and elegance were her guiding principles in the selection of a gown for a recital; the dress, which was never to assume a focal point of its own, was to be in harmony with the occasion, enhancing the event. During radio broadcasts of opera Frances always wore hats appropriate to her roles, as aids to the creation of the moods she was attempting to project. She was well known for the hat made from yards of tulle representative of seaweed netting that she wore for her role in *Peter Grimes*, while on the occasion of the preview of the radio production of *Deirdre*, a social column in the *Toronto Star* commented: 'When Frances James sang parts of soon-to-be-heard Canadian opera *Deirdre of the Sorrows* at Mrs. Gordon A. Davis' home Saturday, most of her feminine listeners wondered where she had found the romantic hat. Was it a John Frederics? Or a Lily Daché? All you could see was a garland of 12 lush American Beauty roses, here and there the odd green leaf, with not a sight of the black mohair crown. It was all-Canadian, Miss

James said, the work of a Toronto milliner she's been going to for years.'[18] In fact, she was listed in the periodical *New Liberty* as one of the hundred best-dressed women in Canada.[19]

A compound image of Frances James's vocal artistry emerges from contemporary newspaper reviews across Canada: 'Her voice has lovely quality, flexibility, wide range of tone color and adequate volume. It is produced without apparent effort, and intonation is faultless. Her enunciation was a joy to all listeners and the envy of other singers in the audience, every word being crystal clear and undistorted. Miss James has brains as well as talent and technique, and can project moods and create atmosphere in telling fashion.'[20] Many of the reviewers refer to the richness of her voice, contrasted with a 'flute-like' quality in the upper tones. They admired her ability to sing softly in sustained passages: 'Miss James has amazing command of pure, toneful pianissimo of great carrying power and head tones like fairy bells, crystal clear in her top register. Even when voice and words become just a tiny echo of sound, there is no suggestion of whisper or indistinctness.'[21] Or, as another reviewer expressed it, 'Every time Miss Frances James does a programme she provides us with further evidence that she is one of the very best singers in Canada. Her voice is not remarkable in itself; it is her artistry, her command of the subtlety of nuances and phrasing, which raise her so far above the level of most of her contemporaries. Her recent "Wednesday Night" programme of Debussy confirmed the fact that she is one of the few English-speaking artists who can sing French – which is very different from merely singing in French.'[22]

Through her specific choice of programs Frances James exhibited a highly intelligent musical mind; her primary guide in the selection of her repertoire was the inherent musical value of each piece rather than the pressure of conforming to standard practice. Her entire career was an embodiment of the philosophy that personal growth means learning, and learning means personal growth.

She had no hesitation throughout her career to reach out to outstanding vocalists for advice and coaching. Her reputation as a distinguished concert artist did not deprive her of humility and willingness to take lessons from any person who could help to further her technique or her interpretation of a vocal composition. She discovered early that the technique obtained during her Montreal days with Walter Clapperton provided a solid foundation upon which to build. She did feel the need, however, for professional guidance and coaching in some of the larger pieces in her repertoire in order to improve and broaden the limits of her technical palette.

During the 1930s and 1940s, Frances approached a number of prominent singers when a specific problem with a composition that she was about to perform publicly needed working out. Because Toronto at that time lacked a permanent voice teacher of international reputation Frances had to request occasional coaching lessons from prominent singers who happened to visit the city and stay for any length of time. Jeanne Dusseau, Emmy Heim, Lisette Patterson, and Oscar Natzke were four of the more outstanding personalities who coached her.

Lisette Patterson, or Madame Pat, as she was affectionately known, was a polyglot language instructor who taught French at Upper Canada College. Originally from Alsace-Lorraine, she married a colonel in the Canadian army during the First World War, settling in Canada after its end. This cultured woman, who also taught Vincent Massey, coached the soprano in French and German song texts. Frances remembers Madame Pat 'as a very difficult taskmaster. I would come out of lessons in tears because, knowing that I had lived in Montreal, she felt that I had a French-Canadian accent. My accent was really not French-Canadian at all, because I had originally learned French with a Scottish high school teacher. When Madame Pat was at her most enthusiastic she would scream at me for not producing pure French sounds, and I soon got to understand that she was at her fiercest when I was closest to assimilating her point.'

Frances studied with Oscar Natzke during the war, when she needed coaching on *Messiah*. They were both engaged by the Ottawa Choral Society to perform in the oratorio, and the soprano took this opportunity to draw upon Natzke's experience and expertise:

I started with the old war-horse, 'Rejoice Greatly.' This guy was so rough that, suddenly, in the middle of the first long run he lit a match and put it in front of my face. He wanted to show me where I was losing breath, and as soon as the flame flickered it was a sign that I was losing my air. Then, another time, I went into his studio chewing gum. He ordered me in a rough tone of voice to take it out and demanded never to see me chewing gum again. I explained that in broadcasting that was the way I kept my throat moist, to which he responded that by chewing gum I was overextending the glands, which would result in having a dryer throat than ever. He was right: I never chewed gum again.

Two remarkable musical personalities profoundly affected Frances James's artistic career: the noted Viennese soprano Emmy Heim (1886–1954) and the black American tenor Roland Hayes (1888–1977). Quite by coincidence both of these artists shared spirituality of countenance, lovely quality of voice, and wisdom in their advice to those who sought counsel. Frances's relationship with these two people developed into warm and lifelong friendship, based on her respect for each as human being, artist, and pedagogue. Their artistic philosophy and overwhelming sense of humaneness served Frances as an unending source of inspiration.

Emmy Heim first came to Toronto in 1934 at the invitation of Sir Ernest MacMillan, who was a personal friend, directly from Vienna, where she had been an active participant in the cultural events preceding and during the period of the First World War. Vienna was the cradle of revolutionary musical developments when, under the leadership of Arnold Schoenberg and his colleagues, a new expressionist movement was instigated, which replaced the traditional tonal system by experimentation with atonal music. She was friends with Schoenberg and his student Alban Berg, as well as with the writers Rainer Maria Rilke and Hugo von Hoffmannsthal. Her concert career in Hungary, Czechoslovakia, and other European centres was disrupted by the events of the war but not before she developed a reputation as a specialist in classic and romantic German and Viennese song literature both of the past and of her Viennese contemporaries. Many of Schoenberg's songs, which she subsequently taught to her Canadian students, directly transmitted the composer's own interpretative ideas.

Heim's first sojourn in Canada was brief because of her husband's dissatisfaction with life in Canada. Although she returned to Toronto alone in 1938, she did not settle in the city permanently until 1947. She thrived on her association with her Canadian students. She felt that because they lacked a European cultural background, Canadian singers exuded a refreshing exuberance and enthusiasm toward their repertoire, quite in contrast to the snobbish sophistication of her European students, who showed signs of over-exposure to the songs. Frances was Madame Heim's first Canadian pupil. She learned from the Viennese artist a love and understanding of the German *lied* at an almost spiritual level. To Heim such composers and poets as Schubert and Goethe were not figures of the past but friends whose spiritual world had to be understood at the sensual level if one was to perform their songs with conviction. For this purpose it was imperative to train all the senses: the eyes had to learn to see the beauty of nature depicted in the music; the nose had to be able to smell the flowers and perfume described in the poem. She wanted her students to be aware of the interdependence of the senses and to link the senses to the melodies and harmonies of a song. To Emmy Heim understanding a song meant feeling the creative heat and excitement a composer felt when setting a poem to music. She expected the performers to feel the mystery of the language strongly enough to convey it to their audiences through the colour of their voices, for to Emmy every feeling could be expressed through song.

This remarkable artist had an insatiable thirst for life and an unquenchable passion for music.[23] Her main philosophy was to transmit to her pupils what she herself had been given and to teach her 'children' not how to sing, but how to 'dig for more wealth in their own souls.' Her purpose was to educate the human being in each of her pupils.

Right up to her death Emmy remained Frances's musical adviser, even during the last two years of her painful struggle with sickness, when, after the Adaskins' move from Toronto to Saskatoon in 1952, Heim moved into their house on Winchester Street. During her last moments the Viennese artist found comfort and solace in reading and teaching Schubert *lieder*. Through letters, which often became discourses on music, she advised Frances on aspects of Schubert's vocal repertoire. In a letter of 17 November 1952, Heim wrote: 'Darling, I am so proud of you and, of course, of myself too. Now you are starting to grow. And in the right way too. Without conceit, but with joy and confidence. Once you have discovered that you as a personality can give personal things (no imitations) you will find more and more wealth in your soul that you can give to others. And that is what we are here for.'

To understand Emmy Heim's teaching is to gain an insight into Frances James's artistry. The intangible qualities of humaneness and spirituality that the Canadian soprano transmitted in her repertoire to her audiences and later, during her teaching career, to her students and every other person who had the fortune to be within her artistic sphere, constitute part of Emmy Heim's legacy.

It is rare enough for a human being to be exposed to one such remarkable person as Emmy Heim during her lifetime. Frances, however, had the good fortune to encounter in Roland Hayes yet a second person with similar qualities. The son of Georgia slaves, Hayes attained a reputation as an outstanding singer on a national as well as international scale. He was the first black American singer to succeed in the world of Western concert music, and his pioneering efforts within a society prejudicial toward his colour paved the way for future generations of black American singers such as Marian Anderson and Dorothy Maynard. Hayes performed a wide-ranging repertoire that explored a variety of styles and historical epochs. To him, music of all ages constituted a living entity. This included *bergerettes* from the Middle Ages, *chansons* by Guillaume de Machaut, madrigals by Renaissance composers, and songs of Caccini and Caldara for the most part forgotten today by the concert singer. Each program also included a complement of Negro spirituals, some arranged by Hayes. Performed by him, these spirituals acquired a special meaning. The early music repertoire was rendered with a beauty of tone, simplicity, and sincerity rare for a period when singers tended to infuse any vocal piece written before 1800 with emotional over-indulgence. His voice would change colour to accommodate the style of each song, and his interpretation of the naturalistic Mussorgsky songs was as effective as that of the tender medieval *bergerettes*.

His phenomenal diction and fine artistry were still much in evidence in a recording made at a time when his voice had lost some of its flexibility.[24] He also had a beautiful falsetto.

Contemporary music beyond Debussy and Fauré did not constitute part of Hayes's repertoire. His special feeling for the songs by these two composers, however, was transmitted to Frances James in much the same way as was Heim's love for the German *lied*. Hayes, who had studied with Fauré, acquired an insight into the French composer's interpretation that he then transmitted to those aspiring artists who worked with him. And indeed, as a result of Hayes's influence, Frances's interpretation of songs from the French repertoire was widely acclaimed by Canadian audiences and was considered one of her specialties. Both Hayes and Heim shared a common artistic philosophy that music must be approached with sensitivity and lyricism, that a thorough understanding of the text was necessary to the successful characterization of the song, and that clear diction was an essential component of a performance.

Frances approached Roland Hayes in the summer of 1944 after reading MacKinley Helm's book *Angel Mo' and Her Son Roland Hayes*.[25] The humaneness of the book prompted her to write the singer about accepting her for coaching lessons. His response was indicative of the greatness of the person: 'Replying to your kind letter of July 30 ... I am not really in the teaching business but sometimes, when I have the time, I do help certain individual artists who are definitely beyond the need of voice placement and other preparatory study to interpretative singing ... There is just something in your letter that makes me feel that I should say "yes."'[26]

Frances went to Boston in September 1944 for two concentrated weeks of daily lessons with Hayes, a pattern that was repeated over the following three years. Hayes lived in Brookline, Massachusetts, and Frances's coaching took place in his large living-room, elegantly and richly furnished with art objects. He had a rare Dutch clavichord, a magnificent Spanish chest presented to him by the queen mother of Spain, and a museum collection of exotic African instruments, on most of which he could himself perform. The grand piano was located at the back of the drawing-room, on a platform approached by climbing three steps. Hayes would sit on the other side of the room, using very few words throughout the lesson while conveying messages with his hands. Frances remembers his mesmerizing personality and the unusual beauty of his hands. At the time of her studies with the great American tenor, she was preparing a program for a recital at the Gardiner Museum in Boston. It was her first major American concert and she felt that some vocal coaching for the occasion would prove profitable. The success of her Boston concert in 1944 prompted another engagement the following year.

Frances found Hayes a most flexible teacher with respect to programming, as exemplified in her performance of Hindemith's mammoth song cycle, *Das Marienleben*, based on the text of Rainer Maria Rilke. She had started working on the second (1946) version of Hindemith's music and one day brought it to her lesson. After she had sung no more than the first part of the first song, Hayes came running out of his chair at the back of the room, shouting 'Stop, stop, stop, it will ruin your voice!' She put the song cycle aside and they proceeded to work on other repertoire. It was not until one year later, when Hayes visited the Adaskin home on the occasion of his concert engagement in Toronto, that he asked Frances to sing *Das Marienleben*. After she recovered from her surprise and reminded him of the previous year's comments, he responded that he had since had an opportunity to change his mind about the composition. Even though he abhorred the idea of contemporary music in his own programs he was willing and able to learn the piece in order to assist Frances with it.

Hayes felt that singing contemporary music could ruin my voice. Quite to the contrary, not only did it not ruin my voice but it made my reputation in Canada as an interpreter of contemporary music – I loved it. I remember the first time I did 'Air de Lia' from Debussy's *L'Enfant Prodigue*, it had an interval of a tenth in it, a jump quite unheard of in this period. I just loved that interval; in fact I never stopped to consider its vocal difficulty. It was marked on paper, and I sang it. I don't think anything can ruin your voice if you have good control and you know what you are doing.

In a situation that paralleled her relationship with Emmy Heim, Frances James and Roland Hayes carried on an extensive correspondence, which demonstrated the American artist's sensitivity toward his environment in general and great affection toward the Adaskins in particular. Despite his own busy schedule Hayes always followed Frances's career with sincere interest, and through his letters – often written from hotel rooms on concert tour – rejoiced at her success: 'Please know, dear Frances, that I am ever and always deeply appreciative of the person as well as the splendid artist you represent so wonderfully';[27] or 'You are singing in Vancouver soon and as always you have my strong and unwavering belief in your art and ability to carry through with flying colors.'[28]

In their vocal coaching both Heim and Hayes emphasized interpretation over technique. When the time came for the lyric soprano to do some strictly technical work because of the nature of the operatic roles that she was preparing for the CBC, Hayes recommended that Frances take some coaching lessons with Maria Kurenko. Madame Kurenko was a Russian expatriate who emigrated to New York with her art dealer husband after the Russian Revolution. Before settling in New York she was a coloratura soprano of extensive European concert experience. She too sang unusual repertoire with much expression, combining vocal mastery of coloratura passages with musicianship and interpretative skill. Frances, who studied with her intermittently from 1947 to 1953, would go to New York for ten days at a time. She stayed at the Great Northern Hotel, owned by Jack Dempsey, where Kurenko had established permanent residence and where Frances also took her lessons. She would have two lessons a day, working on technique in the morning and repertoire in the afternoon.

The main purpose of Frances's coaching with Kurenko was to master the role of Ellen in Britten's *Peter Grimes* and Lady Billows in his *Albert Herring*. Both of these roles required more of a dramatic than a lyric sound, and it was through Frances's technical work with Madame Kurenko that her voice opened up and acquired dramatic overtones. Later, in preparing the role of Anne in Stravinsky's *The Rake's Progress*, Frances reverted, under Maria Kurenko's guidance, to a lighter and more coloratura voice for the eighteenth-century Mozartean sound required in this neoclassic opera.

Frances James's approach to learning a new piece was both intuitive and intellectual. Never satisfied with learning only the voice line of a composition, she felt that the only way to gain an understanding of the piece was to learn the entire work. In a *lied* this signified being intimately acquainted with the piano texture, colour, and harmonies – the flow and structure of the whole. In an operatic work it meant knowing the whole opera: all the arias and the orchestral parts, even if her role was restricted to only three arias. As a musician she demanded an understanding of a composition at all levels in order to be able to interpret her vocal part with conviction. She acquired her depth of musical perception primarily through frequent exposure to orchestral sounds at symphony concerts. She preferred orchestral and chamber music concerts to voice recitals because instrumental music heightened her awareness of the instrumental colours and capabilities. The smoothness and lyricism of tone reproduced by a violin served as an inspiration to her in her own spinning out of a long, sustained vocal line. In her lessons with Madame Kurenko, Frances remembers, the artist stressed the importance of the horizontal as well as the vertical sound, and that a successful performance entailed an understanding and combination of both of these dimensions.

Frances James's concert work throughout the 1940s falls into several different categories: performances as guest soloist with choral groups; major appearances with the Toronto Symphony Orchestra under the baton of Sir Ernest MacMillan; regular performances of *Messiah* in Toronto, Montreal, and Ottawa; solo recitals of the French, German, and contemporary art song literature; recitals of all-Canadian music; and *première* performances of contemporary non-Canadian music, especially of songs by Hindemith. Major radio broadcasts were included in these activities. While a majority of concerts took place within the Toronto-Montreal-Ottawa triangle, two to three months of each year were spent on cross-country tours. This was also the period of some major concert engagements in the United States.

The critic H.A. Aldrick of the *Winnipeg Free Press* offers a contemporary assessment of Frances's activities:

Within her own field she is superior to any other Canadian artist. Miss James in the realm of lieder and art-song, is not only without a Canadian-born equal, but takes a legitimate place among the best of contemporary recitalists in the same field regardless of country of their birth ... Only last week, again, radio listeners had another opportunity of noting how superb Miss James can be in music to some extent outside of her specialized sphere of art-song and lieder. The occasion was her taking the solo role in Finzi's *Dies Natalis*. How beautifully she caught the spirit of Traherne's poignant poetry, how magnificently she sang the composer's setting of it, how she achieved the effect of sustained intensity of expression throughout – such achievement was the mark of a truly admirable artist.

But it is as an exponent of the great songs of Schubert, Wolf, Debussy, Strauss and others, that Miss James is on the heights ... Whether it is Heine or Verlaine, for example, the verse itself is illuminated by a sense of linguistic nuance rarely encountered in singers using a language other than their own ... At its most eloquent, Miss James' achievement 'in toto' is accordingly always an enthralling and unforgettable experience to the sensitive listener ...

Another aspect of Miss James' art is her association with contemporary music, including that by both Canadian-born composers or those resident in the country ...

The various qualities enumerated above are sufficient in themselves to make her a most attractive singer. But her art has deeper shafts, the merging point of which is a spirituality so penetrating that one's entire being cannot be other than strangely stirred.[29]

The *Dies Natalis* mentioned by Aldrick was a cantata set to Jacobean poetry by the twentieth-century English composer Gerald Finzi, for soprano and string orchestra. The work received its Canadian *première* by Frances James and the Little Symphony of Montreal under the baton of Bernard Naylor, and it was performed twice in Montreal and once in Ottawa.[30]

Cambridge-born Bernard Naylor (1907–1986) came to Montreal in 1942 after a distinguished career in England as organist, lecturer in music, conductor, and composer. As founder and conductor of the Little Symphony, he performed music by Sibelius, Hindemith, Britten, and Finzi, who were at the time little known in Canada. Although his visits to Canada were interrupted by lengthy sojourns in England, he spent ten years in Winnipeg and after 1968 retired in Victoria. Naylor was one of Frances James's accompanists whose pianistic abilities were a source of high praise by the singer: 'There was something about his playing that drew out of you the very best that you could possibly do. He is a great musician and is a product of a wonderful training; but when he got to the piano or started to conduct, it brought out an ingredient in him that made one rise above the material.'

Throughout the 1940s Frances was frequently engaged by Sir Ernest MacMillan in a number of musical enterprises that ranged from singing with the Toronto Symphony Orchestra to representing Canada at a cultural exchange event in Washington in 1944. Sir Ernest was one of Canada's leading musical figures, a man whose enormous contribution to this country's musical culture has yet to be definitively described and evaluated. His countless activities touched every facet of Canadian musical life over a period of more than half a century. Conductor, composer, organist, pianist, administrator, educator, adjudicator, he affected the lives of practically every musician in Canada because his interest in his country's culture and his boundless energy led him into personal involvement with every aspect of Canadian culture.

Frances James developed a warm working relationship with Sir Ernest, a binding tie that lasted up to the conductor's death in 1973. The following excerpt from a letter written by Sir Ernest to Frances three years before his death expresses some of his feelings toward her: 'It was good to get your letter and to recall the many times we have made music together. You contributed so much to our musical life and there must be thousands whom you made happy by your fine singing. I remember amongst many other occasions how bravely you stepped in at the last minute for Lois Marshall to sing "Messiah" without rehearsal.'[31]

Throughout the 1940s Frances sang often in Massey Hall under Sir Ernest's baton in concerts that included the conductor's own *Ode to England* (1941), Vaughan Williams's *Benedicite* (1944), Bach's *St Matthew Passion* (1944),[32] Gabriel Pierné's *Children's Crusade* (1945), and Debussy's *Chansons de Bilitis* (1948). Of her numerous renditions of *Messiah* during those years, five were at Massey Hall with the TSO and Sir Ernest MacMillan.[33]

22 January 1941 marked a gala performance of MacMillan's cantata *Ode to England*, composed by him twenty-three years earlier while a prisoner of war at Ruhleben camp in Berlin. A choral and orchestral setting of Swinburne's ode of the same title, the manuscript was originally sent by MacMillan from his internment camp to Oxford University, which granted him a doctoral degree *in*

absentia. This doctoral thesis received its Toronto *première* in 1921 under H.A. Fricker's baton, with the Mendelssohn Choir and the Philadelphia orchestra. Frances James's performance of it twenty years later proved a momentous occasion for both historical and patriotic reasons: it was the first time that the work was conducted by the composer, and Swinburne's inspirational words in praise of England harmonized with the sentiments of the audience concerning the world crisis and the conflagration in Europe.

One engagement with the TSO and Sir Ernest MacMillan in particular stands out in Frances James's mind as the highlight of her performances with the orchestra: her guest appearance at its subscription series on 17 and 18 February 1948. That year she was on the roster of TSO guests, which included such luminaries as Victor Malcuzinski, Jan Peerce, Zara Nelsova, Isaac Stern, Dame Myra Hess, and Rudolf Serkin. For the occasion Yousuf Karsh took a photograph of her, which appeared on the cover of *Saturday Night*. Frances participated in two musical events that evening: the first performance in Toronto of Mahler's *Symphony No 4 in G Major* and in Debussy's *Chansons de Bilitis*, based on a text by Pierre Louÿs.

In addition to these major appearances with the TSO, Frances was asked to sing in annual Toronto performances of Handel's *Messiah*, which she also performed on many occasions with Ottawa's Choral Society and in Montreal under the direction of Alfred Whitehead. The 1942 Toronto performance of *Messiah* marked the first important appearance of the Mendelssohn Choir under its new conductor, Sir Ernest MacMillan. Since its formation in 1894, the choir had been led by only two conductors: its founder, Augustus Vogt, and Herbert Fricker. Dr Fricker's illness in the preceding years had affected the choir's growth potential so that by the time Sir Ernest took it over it numbered only eighty-four voices. The chorus was particularly weak in the tenor section, since many of the male singers had left to serve in the war. For this occasion the choir was augmented by members of Bloor Street, Deer Park, Timothy Eaton Memorial, and Sherbourne Street United Church choirs. During the wartime performances of *Messiah* in Toronto and Ottawa, Frances James, Eileen Law, William Morton, and Oscar Natzke constituted a favoured quartet of soloists, and Morton in particular was an active interpreter of the tenor role throughout the decade.

In a review for the *Toronto Star*, Augustus Bridle expressed admiration for Frances James's artistry during the 1942 performance: '[She] has never done lyric work here with such dramatic breadth of style, and few oratorio sopranos control high head-tones as she did in "Redeemer Liveth" and "Come Unto Him."'[34] The following year Hector Charlesworth judged the performance 'one of the finest presentations of Handel's *Messiah* heard in Toronto within the present century,' while Frances James 'rose to ethereal intonation at certain moments.'[35]

For the 1949 performance of the oratorio, Sir Ernest had engaged the rising young Canadian soprano Lois Marshall. By four o'clock of the second day of the performance it became obvious that because of a cold that incapacitated her, Marshall would not be able to sing that evening. Frances received a phone call from a rather desperate-sounding Sir Ernest, asking her to step in at the last moment. The soprano, who had just returned from a performance of *Messiah* in Ottawa, agreed to help out the conductor in this last-minute substitution: 'Even though *Messiah* is not anything that you just pick up off the piano and start singing, I agreed to do it. It was four o'clock in the afternoon, and the performance – which was to be broadcast from coast to coast, was at eight. I knew that I was the only person who could do it because I had performed it with him on four other occasions. I got myself ready, and did a warm-up. I am sure that the excitement took me on, for the simple reason that I don't think I had ever sung *Messiah* better.'

The years 1944 and 1945 constituted particularly busy concert seasons for the Canadian soprano. Her out-of-town tours included engagements in Trois-Rivières, Montreal, Edmonton, Boston, Detroit, Washington, as well as at the University of Western Ontario in London and Queen's University in Kingston.

The 1944 concerts in Washington, DC, were given under the auspices of the city's Chamber Music Guild as part of an exchange of Canadian and American musicians. The idea, originating with the founder of the guild and Sir Ernest MacMillan, was to promote cultural relations between the two neighbouring countries. The program was shared with violinist Michel Piastro, concert-master of the New York Philharmonic, and both artists were accompanied at the piano by Arpad Shandor, a well-known New York pianist and a one-time accompanist of Jascha Heifetz. Frances's choice of Debussy's *Ariettes Oubliées* for that occasion was met with acclaim.

Frances James's activities in the oratorio and classical art song repertoire were supplemented by performances of twentieth-century music. Her sincere interest in contemporary music led to her becoming one of its earliest champions in this country. Canadian composers were particularly close to her heart, and a liberal representation of Canadian songs constituted standard fare in her cross-country concerts and radio broadcasts. In the frequent press interviews preceding her concerts she would voice her opinions on the public's attitude toward contemporary compositions, establishing a reputation as a spokesman for this music. She was often quoted as saying that Canadian composers were being shouted off the stage, comparing the public's hostility toward the new music to that which the Group of Seven encountered some twenty-five years earlier. She always felt that it was the performer's duty to help the composer by presenting as much Canadian music as possible. She advised her audience not to judge a piece upon first hearing, but to form an opinion only after repeated hearings. Her repertoire included songs by more than twenty Canadian composers, some seventy-five songs in all, not counting her *premières* of Willan's two operas and MacMillan's *Ode to England*. (For a listing of these works, see appendix C.)

On tour she usually interspersed Canadian compositions with standard repertoire. Concerts given in Toronto at times focused on a retrospective look at one composer, such as the Toronto Art Gallery concert of 26 February 1941, devoted entirely to the music of Arnold Walter (with Harry Adaskin and Cornelius Ysselstyn as assisting artists). Other Toronto concerts presented at the Art Gallery or the conservatory would include music by two or three Canadian composers, such as the 18 November and 2 December 1944 performances of songs by Robert Fleming, Jean Coulthard, and Barbara Pentland.[36] Jean Coulthard's *Two Songs of the Haida Indians* (Queen Charlotte Islands, BC), sung by Frances James at the art gallery, were originally composed in 1942 to a text by Constance Skinner. The earliest of a number of Coulthard's songs performed by Frances, they are dedicated to her.

An innovative series that was to leave an imprint on Toronto's cultural life was the establishment in 1946 of the Forest Hill Community Centre Concert and Theatre Series. Featuring theatre, ballet, concert stars, string ensembles, and opera, the series was made possible through the voluntary efforts of a group of citizens from one of the more affluent Toronto areas, with Charles Jennings as honorary chairman and Herman Voaden as chairman. The policy of the series was to feature all-Canadian talent 'with an accent on youth,' and to commission Canadian works. The inaugural concert of 11 November 1946 *premièred* Harry Somers's *Three Songs*, based on Walt Whitman's *Leaves of Grass*, with the composer at the piano. The reviewer Rose MacDonald found it especially interesting: 'that Miss James sang – with great taste – a little song cycle by a young Toronto musician, Harry Somers, who was directly commissioned to do the cycle by the collaborators in the project ... This was a type of modern music with which Miss James is perfectly at home. The performance of the cycle was so successful that Miss James and Mr. Somers repeated it, which with music being newly heard, was an excellent idea.'[37]

An important Canadian *première* in the following year was John Weinzweig's *Of Time, Rain, and the World* at Wymilwood, as part of the Sunday evening concert series sponsored by the Victoria College Union. Earle Moss was the accompanist for this performance.

One of the most important events of the 1940s was the presentation at

Harbord Collegiate on 17 April 1947 of compositions by Murray Adaskin, Harry Somers, Barbara Pentland, and John Weinzweig. This path-breaking event in the history of Canadian music is discussed more fully in chapter 4.

Frances James's *premières* of Canadian vocal compositions were not solely restricted to her Toronto concerts. She frequently used her tours as occasions for first performances, as for example, the October 1947 guest appearance for the Ladies' Musical Club in Halifax. Included in the program were Coulthard's *Two Songs of the Haida Indians* and two of the newly composed songs from Bernard Naylor's *C. Day Lewis Suite*: 'Beauty's End Is in Sight' and 'Twenty Weeks Near Past,' with the composer at the piano. Similarly, during her eastern tour four years later she sang Kelsey Jones's song cycle *Euridice* ('Pastoral,' 'The Serpent at the Wedding,' and 'Euridice').

While Murray Adaskin's *The Shepherd*, composed for her and *premièred* in Banff in 1934, was one of her favourites, she was deprived of the pleasure of performing her husband's songs because his modesty about his abilities to set text to music prevented him from composing in this genre. Today Murray reflects on this situation: 'Two things stood out in my mind at that time, quite wrongly: one was that I did not feel that I had that instinctive feeling for language as some of the English and some contemporary American composers did; the second was that I always felt I was not quite ready to do justice to the kind of song that Fran sang. I now realize that it was a great mistake, just one of those things ... In my next life I'll make up for it.' His *Epitaph*, set to words by Guillaume Apollinaire and composed in 1948, did not receive its *première* until four years later, when Frances sang it for a recording made by the International Service of the CBC.

The cultural identity of a city may be defined as a sum total of its artistic activities during any one epoch in the city's history. Toronto's musical identity in the 1940s was carved by the endeavours of the people who adopted the city as a permanent residence. An attempt has been made in the preceding pages to depict the varying groups of musicians who created part of this cultural energy, and who, upon arriving in Toronto, directed the cultural experience acquired in their varying places of origin into the collective creation of a musical fabric unique to the city.

Arnold Walter (1902–73) was such a figure in the mosaic of Toronto's musical life. Composer, pianist, and musicologist, he was educated in Prague and Berlin. A citizen of the world – he had lived in Majorca and London – he chose to settle in Toronto in 1937 as music master at Upper Canada College. Some years later he assumed the directorship of the Faculty of Music at the University of Toronto. Frances made the acquaintance of Dr and Mrs Walter shortly after their arrival in the city, and through Dr Walter, who had a consuming interest in Paul Hindemith's music and ideas, she was introduced to Hindemith's song cycle, *Das Marienleben*. The large work, based on a series of lyrics by one of the greatest European poets of the century, Rainer Maria Rilke (1877–1926), is a set of mystical songs of great breadth and vision, completed in 1923. A second version was revised by the composer in 1948.

Frances studied the songs throughout the late 1930s, working with Dr and Mrs Walter on the music and the text. It was one of the first compositions she took to Emmy Heim upon the Viennese soprano's arrival in Toronto, and was the work that she began to sing for Roland Hayes some years later, when he interrupted her with the comment that it would ruin her voice. Hindemith's composition was assimilated into the soprano's already vast repertoire and became especially meaningful to her. She presented it in its first Canadian performance in 1943 at the Toronto Society for Contemporary Music, the first all-Hindemith program heard in the city, and the concert was repeated under the auspices of the same organization two years later. On that occasion Frances also gave the work its Canadian radio *première* by broadcasting it nationally over the CBC network. It is of interest to trace the reaction of the Toronto critics to this rather momentous event:

Meeting in the Heliconian Club, which was filled very nearly to capacity for the occasion, the Society for Contemporary Music listened to a programme of Hindemith's music, some of it extremely rare on this continent. Apogee of the programme was the Song Cycle for soprano and piano, The Life of the Virgin Mary, eight songs sung by Frances James with Dr. Arnold M. Walter playing the piano part.

So rare is this extraordinarily interesting and beautiful work that no copies thereof were available so that photostats had to be made from the copy in possession of the New York Public Library.

The Cycle is profoundly moving in its writing ... and to the artists who made its performance here possible there must be a deep sense of gratitude ... The work is very much a challenge to any two artists who might attempt it, and both Miss James and Dr. Walter gave distinguished interpretations.[38]

Even the somewhat conservative critic of the *Toronto Star*, Augustus Bridle, had praise for the song cycle, which he called 'the most radical' thing on the program: 'the singer made an elevated rhapsody of the work that would be hard to surpass in Europe.' Hector Charlesworth, critic for *Saturday Night*, surpassed his colleague's mellifluous praise: 'One ceased to think of modernism and of Hindemith's espousal of fads like atonality, in listening to his song cycle, *Life of the Virgin Mary* ... It is a sincere, beautiful work, marked by structural grandeur and exquisite detail ... [Dr. Walter] was a pillar of strength at the piano;

and Frances James, one of the finest of Canadian sopranos, showed rare artistic intuitions in her tender and expressive rendering of the sequence of poems.'[39]

The opportunity presented itself for Frances James to meet the composer during his visit to Toronto in 1946, when at the instigation of Arnold Walter, Hindemith was invited to hold a class and a lecture at the Toronto Conservatory of Music. After his lecture she sang the song cycle for him during a musicale at Harry Adaskin's house that featured Hindemith's music. Hindemith was impressed with her interpretation, and his praise so flustered the singer that when Dr Walter offered her a ride back to the conservatory with Hindemith she accepted it, completely forgetting her husband, who was in the room: 'When we got to College and University Avenue, I was let out of the car, and as I was on my way home I continued walking east on College. With my head still in the clouds, I barely noticed the car that pulled up to the curb, and a head that poked through the window saying, "Do you remember me? I'm your husband"!'

At the time Frances James met Paul Hindemith, the composer was in the final stages of his revision of the song cycle. The second version, completed in 1946 but not published until two years later, functioned as a summation of his compositional practices and of his quest for organic unity. In an essay, he expressed his preference for the second version, stating that the original form of the cycle lacked dramatic coherence and did not always treat the voice in the kindest fashion. Later in 1946, when the composer invited Frances to Yale – his home after leaving Nazi Germany – for a preview of his new version of the song cycle, she did not delay in taking him up on the offer. She spent an entire day working with him on his music, and following afternoon tea and schnapps they went to his studio, where with the composer at the piano Frances sang songs from the French and German repertoire: 'I could not believe it, that such a famous person would pick me out – me, a complete Canadian product that he discovered in Toronto. This contact opened up a new field and made my career something more distinguished than it could ever have been had I not met him. This opened the door for all the other contemporary things I did in Toronto, and led to my being looked upon as an expert in contemporary music.'

Three years after her Yale visit Frances received a letter from Gertrude Hindemith, inquiring whether she had been working on or performing Hindemith's second version of *Das Marienleben*. The New York soprano Jennie Tourel had generated considerable interest in the new version through her 1949 *première* of it in Town Hall in spring 1949, after which Hindemith was swamped with inquiries as to whom else he could recommend for future performances of the song cycle.

One of these inquiries was from Victor Zuckerkandl, a Viennese intellectual who taught classes in poetry and music at St John's College in Annapolis,

Maryland. The institution, known as 'the college of the hundred books,' had a strong classical orientation and demanded a knowledge of the one hundred most important literary works. Zuckerkandl, who had taught Rilke's poems to his students, now wanted to add the musical perspective to the students' knowledge of the poetry.

Through Hindemith, then, the contact between Frances James and Victor Zuckerkandl was established. After a short period of correspondence they discovered that they shared a common friend in Emmy Heim, with whom Zuckerkandl had studied in Vienna. That discovery, plus the fact that Frances had been recommended to him personally by Hindemith, prompted him to invite her to Annapolis in 1951 to perform the song cycle. The college had a series of Friday night lectures where distinguished persons from different disciplines addressed the students. The guest preceding Frances's visit was Eleanor Roosevelt.

Frances had been officially engaged to perform the second version of the song cycle at the Friday evening concert. However, because of the tremendous interest shown by the students during their discussions of the work, the next day she performed the first version of *Das Marienleben* as well – a major feat during the space of one weekend!

Zuckerkandl's high esteem for Frances James resulted in an invitation for a return visit to Annapolis the following year, where she gave a concert devoted entirely to songs by Hugo Wolf, with Zuckerkandl at the piano.

In the summer of 1949, two years before her first Annapolis performance, Frances had joined Murray in Santa Barbara, where he was studying with Darius Milhaud at the Music Academy of the West. Sometime during the summer she had an opportunity to perform publicly the new version of Hindemith's *Das Marienleben*. The well-known American violinist Roman Totenberg heard it and liked it very much. The following winter, while Frances was visiting New York, Totenberg casually invited her to sing portions of the work for some of his friends at his home. At the end of the musicale, Frances was approached by a representative of Lyrichord Records with an offer to make a recording of the definitive version of Hindemith's *Das Marienleben*. He was Peter H. Fritsch, owner of a small recording company and a man of vision, courage, and enterprise.

Frances James's recording of Hindemith's work, made without pause or retakes, was released in 1951 to generally excellent press reviews. Jerome Bohm of the *New York Herald Tribune* liked the soprano's clear and intelligently voiced performance, although Hindemith's composition itself did not overly move him.[40] The most informative review, excerpted below, was afforded by Milton Wilson in the *Canadian Forum*:

The release by Lyrichord of two LP records of Hindemith's song cycle *Das Marienleben*, sung by Canadian soprano Frances James accompanied by George Brough, should be an important musical event not only for Canadians but for everyone who possesses a gramophone and wishes to hear a great contemporary work in a powerful performance ... This story of the life of the Virgin Mary, from before birth to after death, has a dramatic structure more closely patterned than most operas and is, indeed, a sort of chamber opera for single voice and piano. There is little repetition of material from song to song, but the effect of continuity and development, of controlled rise and fall, is brilliantly maintained ...

Hindemith's song cycle makes exacting demands on a singer: stamina, control, an unswerving sense of pitch, and the sort of musical intelligence that appears not only in intonation and phrasing but in the accommodation of the part to the whole. Frances James successfully meets these demands and clearly establishes her position as a leading interpreter of contemporary vocal music. George Brough has a great deal to do on the piano, including the long and powerful introduction to No. 9 and the grief-stricken epilogue to No. 10. He provides the clear texture and firm phrasing which the work requires. The very effective translation on the jacket is by Lister Sinclair. As for the recording itself, the surfaces have shortcomings, but the voice and piano are well balanced, and the sound has just enough echo to fit the quality of the work without being distracting.[41]

In releasing a record of modern music unfamiliar to audiences at the time, Fritsch exhibited unusual courage and high ideals. Unfortunately, placing musical integrity above the realities of the contemporary market led eventually to a financial loss for the company, which found itself in the same danger of bankruptcy that other similar private enterprises faced. The recording business in the early 1950s was not financially lucrative, and the situation was compounded by the competition exerted by larger companies espousing such modern technology as stereophonic sound.

Fritsch exhibited a warm, sincere personal interest in the career of Frances James. He was a pioneer who recognized the musical value of the modern repertoire propounded by the Canadian singer. While realizing that the song cycles by Milhaud, Hindemith, and Britten sung by Frances James did not have much commercial value as far as record sales were concerned, in his belief that these masterpieces must be heard Fritsch worked out a scheme for producing a set of records featuring Frances James and involving Geoffrey Waddington as conductor of orchestral works. His brave plans were defeated by the exorbitant production expenses and by the audiences' lack of interest in contemporary works.[42]

Paul Hindemith always remained deeply appreciative of Frances James for her pioneering efforts in introducing his music in Canada and performing it in the United States. Through the Hindemith-Zuckerkandl connection Frances James had reached out beyond the borders of her native country to display her artistry on the international scene. A number of factors – none of which pertained to the quality of her artistic expression – presented obstacles to the development of an international career. The main difficulty was to attempt an international concert career without the promotional skills of a major business manager. Coupled with it was the narrow-minded attitude of a conservative audience toward contemporary works. In addition, an interpreter of the art song repertoire did not hold as much glamour for audiences as did an opera singer. Without proper financial backing a Canadian artist in the late 1940s encountered severe restrictions in the development of an international career. It was through the CBC that Frances James encountered the medium fully receptive to her superbly artistic interpretations of the modern repertoire.

NEW DIRECTIONS IN CANADIAN MUSIC BROADCASTING

During the years immediately succeeding the war Canada embarked upon the task of rebuilding its economic resources and of nation-building in general. The Canadian Broadcasting Corporation reflected this trend in national growth and expansion by building additional transmitters across the country, and by introducing the first French and English FM outlets. Program development became a priority, and it is in this area that some of the most innovative and imaginative musical programs in the history of the CBC were created. One of the major new cultural events was the introduction of the 'CBC Wednesday Night' series, presented weekly from 7:30 to 11:00 p.m. and based on a concept unique to the North American continent. While the content changed each week, these live broadcasts incorporated half an hour of music, followed by a spoken play one to two hours in duration, a fifteen-minute news broadcast including reports from various parts of Canada, the United States, and England, and a final half-hour of music. Documentaries, discussions, lectures, and full-length CBC-produced operas were some of the components.

In addition to featuring internationally known performers, the series, initiated in December 1947, presented to its audiences the best in Canadian artistry.[43] Discussions of domestic issues alternated with those of international importance. Plays by Canadian playwrights were interspersed with world masterpieces; on this series during one season, for example, were such classics as Henrik Ibsen's *Hedda Gabler* and *Ghosts*, Shakespeare's *Hamlet*, T.S. Eliot's *Murder in the Cathedral* (adapted for radio by Lister Sinclair), with Steven Leacock's comedies, or Eric Nicol's satire of the holiday season, *Two Weeks at*

Wit's End. Andrew Allan was producer for many of the radio dramas, while author Lister Sinclair rose to prominence during this period, writing his own plays or adapting others for radio. Special monthly programs featured music by Canadian composers, in observance of a CBC policy 'to give encouragement to composers of promise, as well as recognition to those whose work, often recognized in other countries, was not well-enough known in Canada.'[44]

The 'CBC Wednesday Night' programs were entirely non-commercial, designed to be stimulating and substantive, and to present works that were seldom heard. Davidson Dunton, chairman of the CBC board of governors, issued a statement in Ottawa on 21 November 1947 that 'the CBC has the responsibility of endeavouring to meet varied tastes among Canadian listeners ... It believes ... that there are a considerable number of listeners who would welcome a whole evening on one network of a more advanced and challenging type of broadcasting. And it believes that it is to the general advantage of the broadcasting and listening public to endeavour in this way to show wider possibilities of radio as a force in the cultural life of Canada.' Although, by the CBC's own admission, the content and length of the weekly programs were demanding of the attention of the listener, the corporation experienced a growth in listening audience over the years. The varied fare of these programs seems to have attracted a large field of listeners from the United States and across Canada, a remarkable testament to the function of first-class broadcasting within a society that, in the late 1940s, was not yet dulled by the invasion of the television phenomenon. The quality of the production and the excellence of both music and non-music programs made the series outstanding. Its experimental nature and the flexibility and imaginativeness of its producers contributed to the widening scope of the programs.

Throughout the 1940s and into the following decade, the CBC functioned as a major patron of Canadian culture. Live classical music was an essential component of its broadcasts. By 1948 approximately one-half of the total annual music broadcast time (about twelve hundred hours) was devoted to classical music.[45] Canadian musicians and composers were being encouraged through both the International Service and the domestic service of the CBC. New programs were introduced with the express purpose of discovering and fostering young Canadian talent. Such talent-finding series as 'Opportunity Knocks,' 'Singing Stars of Tomorrow,' and later 'The Trans-Canada Talent Festival,' where young musicians through auditions competed for a number of prizes, served as an aid in building the careers of many of this country's top musicians.[46] Winning compositions sponsored by the Composers, Authors and Publishers Association of Canada (CAPAC) were also broadcast by the CBC. As a result of enlightened policies and the sincere concern of a few key figures such as conductor Geoffrey Waddington; program director of the Trans-Canada network Harry J. Boyle; directors John Adaskin, Ernest Bushnell, and Charles Jennings; producer Terence Gibbs; conductor, producer, and musical supervisor Jean-Marie Beaudet; and later, producers Tom Taylor and John Peter Lee Roberts, the CBC became a major source of commissions of Canadian compositions.

Even music appreciation for children was introduced in the late 1940s. On Saturdays two such programs were broadcast over the CBC Trans-Canada network (Vancouver and Toronto), incorporating stories of operas, ballets, lives of composers, and descriptions of orchestral instruments. Pre-school children learned simple songs and rhythmic concepts through 'Kindergarten of the Air.' Radio broadcasting in the post-war era had indeed assumed a new status within Canadian society as a culture-building medium. At the instigation of producer Terence Gibbs the first all-Canadian radio opera company was established (CBC Opera Company), and the phenomenon of radio opera (that is, opera composed and produced specifically for radio performances) was launched.

The late forties and early fifties constituted a period of bold experimentation in the field of music broadcasting, in which a few producers with imagination and enthusiasm introduced many events that are, in retrospect, of considerable historical importance. In addition to commissioning the first full-length Canadian opera, *Deirdre of the Sorrows*, with music by Healey Willan and text by John Coulter, the CBC aired Canadian and North American *premières* of operas by Benjamin Britten (*Peter Grimes, Albert Herring, Let's Make an Opera*), Arthur Benjamin (*A Tale of Two Cities*), Luigi Dallapiccola (*The Prisoner*), and Igor Stravinsky (*The Rake's Progress*). It broadcast Canadian and North American *premières* of songs by such major contemporary composers as Paul Hindemith, Darius Milhaud, Benjamin Britten, Arnold Schoenberg, and Aaron Copland.

One Canadian singer played a key role in this rich and fertile period of innovative post-war radio broadcasting by the CBC: Frances James was Canada's leading soprano in most of these historic performances. Her career was thus inextricably bound with the new directions assumed by the CBC in a symbiotic relationship in which the broadcasting company's new directions were, to a certain extent, shaped by the singer's interest in contemporary repertoire.

One of the path-breaking series was entitled 'Midweek Recital,' twenty Wednesday-evening art song recitals broadcast over the Dominion network, sung exclusively by Frances James, accompanied by Louis Crerar. The series, introduced on 20 March 1946 and produced by Norbert Bauman, was the first of its kind to be offered in Canada. Its novelty lay in the fact that the broadcasts featured only one artist and that these half-hour recitals focused on *lieder* and contemporary art song repertoire. The repertoire, at times devoted to the songs of one composer, was entirely designed by the artist. These unusual, intellectual, and highly specialized programs represented a bold idea in radio broadcasting at a time when variety constituted popular fare with the listeners. Among the 150 art songs presented on this series, Frances James included the *Nine English Songs* of Paul Hindemith, composed in 1942. This CBC performance constituted their Canadian *première* and contributed to the artist's reputation as an expert in contemporary music on the Canadian scene.

In the same year Frances James participated in another momentous event in the history of music in Canada by singing the lead role in *Deirdre of the Sorrows*. Of immense proportions, lasting three and one-half hours, this work received its world *première* on 20 April 1946, after months of rehearsals and years of preparation. The occasion was studded with precedent-setting events: it was the first full-length opera to be written and produced in Canada; its use of the English language made it much more coherent to its Canadian audiences than the foreign-language operas broadcast regularly from the Metropolitan Opera in New York; its use of an all-Canadian cast was of major significance, proving to the listeners that Canada had top-ranking singers capable of carrying out such an undertaking, which ranked as one of the most ambitious in the history of Canadian broadcasting; and it was one of the most costly productions to date. The critic Thomas Archer considered the performance technically far superior to any heard from the Metropolitan in recent years, and judged the quality of the production as setting new standards in operatic broadcasting.[47]

Coulter and Willan, whose previous one-hour radio opera *Transit through Fire* addressed a contemporary topic, decided upon a Celtic myth for their second collaborative work. The tragic story, set among ancient Druids, involves Deirdre, an Irish foundling, whose beauty attracts the rivals King Conochar and Prince Naisi, both of whom meet with disaster. On the occasion of its radio *première* the cast included Frances James (Deirdre), tenor William Morton (Naisi), baritone Lionel Daunais (Conochar), contralto Nellie Smith (Levercham), baritone George Lambert (Cathva), and bass Ernest Barry (the Bard). The production was assisted by members of the Toronto Conservatory of Music Opera School and was conducted by Ettore Mazzoleni, the principal of the school. Alfred Whitehead was chorus-master and Ernest Morgan the CBC producer in charge of opera.

A number of pre-production performances of portions of the opera were presented in Toronto with the double purpose of informing the audience and providing a practice run for the artists. On one occasion the libretto was recited on stage at the Arts and Letters Club by professional actors, with Frances James and George Lambert singing some of the arias involving Deirdre and Conochar.

At a reception at the home of Gordon and Doris Davis, Coulter, Willan, and Mazzoleni described their part in the production, followed by Frances's interpretation of Deirdre's 'Lament' from act 3.

This first major Canadian opera abounded in emotional intensity and Wagnerian overtones. Although previously Healey Willan had written ballad operas and incidental music for plays and the one-hour opera *Transit through Fire*, *Deirdre* signified the first full-length opera for the composer, who was noted for his lifetime of work in the field of church music. The new work as well as the skill of the performers met with critical acclaim:

Miss James had a specially formidable task set for her. The role of Deirdre hovers vocally somewhere between Elsa and Eva or Aida and Gilda. Like Violetta in *La Traviata* Deirdre must be both lyric and dramatic. She has to execute vocalises and she has to negotiate soaring lyrical phrases. She has to sing with Melisande restraint and she must be capable of incisive dramatic attacks. Miss James undertook the charge with splendid courage considering her vocal limitations, and there could be nothing but admiration for the way she brought it off as a whole. And, as is usual with her, conscientious and detailed study was evident in everything she did.

Mr. Morton had on the whole an easier assignment. The role of Naisi seemed to fall gratefully into his vocal range both technically and expressively. In all the enthusiastic throes of the fresh, pleasant young hero, Mr. Morton presented him with rightly intelligible diction. He did not let us forget how singable English can be when adequately treated.

But I would on the whole pass the honors to Lionel Daunais for his Conochar. It was singing of classical proportions in the sense that classical singing is like sculpture in sound. Mr. Daunais not only sang musically and poetically, but he rounded off Dr. Willan's phrases with distinguished elegance. He never forgot he was a singer first and a vocal actor second. He practised restraint as well as dramatic feeling. It was a rare case of striking a true balance between music and drama. Just why Mr. Daunais is not at the Metropolitan it is hard to understand. But it is for the good of Canada that he is not.

Finally it may be added that, in these days, when the standard of radio is not too high the CBC's venture with *Deirdre* is a singularly noble labour of love. The point is that, whatever the ultimate merits of *Deirdre* itself, the production has set a continental standard and set it both in the intrinsic undertaking and in the execution thereof. Here is one network in North America ready to assert at a considerable expense and effort that it is the duty of the most powerful means of modern mass communication to bring a measure of culture in a representative way to its listeners. Whether or not those listeners will take advantage of such generous offerings has nothing to do with the merits of the policy. So far as that goes other North American networks will undoubtedly take note of this great Canadian experiment and at least offer their admiration, aside from what they will learn from it.[48]

It had been Willan's and Coulter's fervent wish that *Deirdre* receive a staged performance. Coulter even went to Dublin in 1948 with the score and a recording of the CBC performance in hand, in the hope of procuring a staged production there. Despite the enormous interest in performing the opera at the forthcoming Dublin Festival of the Arts, the project did not materialize because of lack of funds. Dublin's invitation for Coulter, Willan, Mazzoleni, and the principal singers to take part in the overseas production could not be financed by Canada. A major cultural funding agency like the Canada Council had not come into existence, and the whole venture was doomed. Frances sang in the opera's second Canadian radio performance in 1951 with a partially changed cast and in a shortened musical and textual version. It was not until eighteen years after its radio *première* that *Deirdre* received its first staged presentation by members of the Toronto Conservatory Opera School.

One year after the radio production of *Deirdre*, the CBC launched its 'Distinguished Artists' series as part of the 'CBC Wednesday Night.' Between its inception in 1947 and 1953 Frances performed frequently on the 'Wednesday Night' series as a leading soprano in opera presentations, as soloist on the 'Distinguished Artists' series, and as guest in such music programs as 'The Layman's History of Music.' A considerable portion of her recordings dates from her performances on this CBC series (see appendix D).

The 'Distinguished Artists' series presented in concert domestic and foreign orchestras, as well as solo artists. Frances's appearances usually highlighted Canadian *premières* of works by contemporary composers. On 11 February 1948, for example, she sang the first radio performance of Bernard Naylor's suite for high voice and piano from the C. Day Lewis collection of poems entitled *From Feathers to Iron*. A year later she gave a *première* broadcast of John Weinzweig's three songs *Of Time and the World*, written for and dedicated to her by the composer. In 1953 she introduced the *Six Songs* by Chester Duncan, at that time professor of English at the University of Manitoba. Other Canadian *premières* of contemporary works included *Les Illuminations* by Benjamin Britten and *Rêves* by Darius Milhaud.[49] She was one of the first singers to perform Arnold Schoenberg's music in Canada. Three of his songs – 'Erhebung' (op 2 no 3), 'Aufgeregten' (op 3 no 2), and 'Traumleben' (op 6 no 1) were heard on the 'Distinguished Artists' series on 11 February 1948.

Frances's Canadian *première* of Darius Milhaud's *Rêves* (written in 1942) was the culmination of a number of her other concert performances of this work. She loved the songs, which she considered well suited to her lyric soprano voice. The poetry, indicated as being anonymous, was written by Milhaud's wife, Madeleine. Darius Milhaud (1892–1974), recognized after the death of Maurice Ravel as a leading French composer, had left his homeland during the war to accept a teaching post at Mills College in Oakland, California. By the time the Adaskins made his acquaintance, he was spending the summers teaching composition in the Music Academy of the West at Santa Barbara, alternating years at Mills College with the Conservatoire National in Paris where he was head of the composition department. (Both Harry Somers and, later, Bruce Mather studied with him there.)

After Frances's initial performances of *Rêves* in Santa Barbara, and her Canadian radio *première* of the songs, she broadcast them again in 1951. Milhaud, who had come to Toronto that year to conduct a concert of his own music for the 'CBC Wednesday Night' series, heard Frances's performance. At the moment when she successfully executed pianissimo notes high in her *tessitura*, Milhaud, who was sitting in the audience, made a gesture of sending her a kiss in the best French tradition. In order to show his appreciation for what he considered an exquisite performance, he inscribed the singer's score: 'to Frances James Adaskin, who sings these Dreams as in a lovely dream,' to which Madeleine Milhaud added, 'et moi aussi.'[50]

Frances's accompanists for a number of the 'Distinguished Artists' solo concerts included Earle Moss, Mario Bernardi,[51] and, later, Boyd McDonald. The orchestral concerts in which she participated as soloist – in programs ranging from all-Delius to Debussy's *La Demoiselle Elue* and Liszt's *Die Lorelei* to Gerald Finzi's *Dies Natalis* – were usually conducted by Geoffrey Waddington.

Britten's *Les Illuminations*, based on poems by Arthur Rimbaud, was performed at the instigation of producer Terence Gibbs. Shortly after his arrival in Toronto from England in 1948, upon hearing Frances's performance of Debussy's *Chansons de Bilitis* with the Toronto Symphony Orchestra, Gibbs phoned her with the request that she sing the Britten work. Frances, who knew and loved the work, had put it aside as unsuitable for her voice. She recalls the evening when Gibbs telephoned her:

I said, 'It's very kind of you to ask me, but I do not think that I could perform that work.' Gibbs responded, 'Yes, I think that it is for you. Please think it over, because we will not be able to do this work unless you are the one to sing it.' It just happened that Emmy Heim was having dinner with us that night and when I told Murray and Emmy about the phone call, they both responded instantly: 'You go right back and tell him that of course you will do it. We'll start rehearsing right after dinner.'

I am very glad I sang this composition. It was extremely difficult as Britten, like Wagner, does not spare the singer for a moment.

The performance of Britten's songs provided Frances with an opportunity to get acquainted with the composer's vocal style, and when Gibbs approached her a short time later with the offer of the role of Ellen in Britten's opera *Peter Grimes*, she was ready for the taxing role.

The Canadian *première* of *Peter Grimes* on 12 October 1949 was one of the more highly publicized events by the CBC. Originally composed for a *première* at the Sadlers Wells Opera House in 1945, *Peter Grimes* had received two broadcasts from the Metropolitan Opera prior to its CBC radio performance. It was generally felt that the Met broadcasts did not do the exciting and colourful work justice. Aware of the enormous musical demands placed by this opera on all participants, Gibbs was nevertheless confident that the Toronto production could easily rival the recent American performances.[52]

The libretto of *Peter Grimes* was written by Montague Slater, who derived the story from an early nineteenth-century poem by George Crabbe about life in a Suffolk fishing village. The drama about the weak person who finds himself at odds with society contained elements of savage realism, captured in the music in a most striking way. Hugh Thomson, critic for the *Toronto Star*, found the vocal and choral writing 'effectively dramatic, but Britten really excelled in his orchestration, which was picturesque in the extreme, especially in the many interludes which established changes of scene and mood.'[53]

In an effort to familiarize the listening audience with the contemporary work, the broadcast was preceded by a number of events relating to the opera: a dramatic presentation of the text was given on radio two weeks prior to the broadcast, and an orchestral program of sea music from the opera was aired one week before the *première*. The music for the dramatized version was arranged from Britten's opera by Louis Applebaum, with Geoffrey Waddington conducting the special score. Like the production of *Deirdre* several years earlier, *Peter Grimes* represented a sizeable investment on the part of the CBC, involving considerable risk at a time when listeners' tastes were still predominantly conservative. Such advance preparation paid off with the listening audience: the production received instant critical acclaim in newspapers across the country from music lovers, critics, and musicians alike. Radio listeners, who by the time of the broadcast had become well acquainted with the work, responded favourably even while the performance was in progress.[54] Because of its tremendous initial success, the entire opera was repeated live over the CBC a week later, and this second performance was also broadcast over station WNYC in New York City. This program received the Canadian Radio Award, the first award to be given for a musical production.

The reviewer in *Saturday Night* rated the singers:

... the most satisfying single performance was undoubtedly that of Frances James who sang the role of Ellen Orford with faultless technique and filled it with pathos and tenderness and pity. William Morton, in the title role, was only a little less impressive; a certain amount of initial straining was more than compensated for by his magnificent handling of the bitterly poignant final scene. Edmund Hockridge, as Captain Balstrode, illustrated – as he has done many times before – that he is a remarkably fine singer ... The chorus completely mastered a score of positively horrifying complexity, calculated to break the heart and shatter the nerves of the most hardened chorister.[55]

Benjamin Britten, who was on an ocean liner on his way to engagements in New York at the time, could not be present at the Canadian *première* of his opera. He did hear the recording, however, when he visited Toronto several weeks later for the performance of his *Saint Nicolas Cantata* with Peter Pears. His impressions of the Canadian production were strong enough to prompt him to record them in writing. He praised the singers' diction and character interpretation, and the efforts of producer Terence Gibbs. He referred to Frances James's intelligence and gift as a musician as well as her sympathetic interpretation of Ellen's character.[56]

The success of the Canadian production of *Peter Grimes* is all the more remarkable for a country that, by 1948, had not yet developed its own professional opera company. Most professional opera seen in Canada was imported from the United States. While performances of ballad operas and operettas abounded – as witnessed in Banff in the late 1920s or on radio throughout the 1930s and 1940s – and occasional staged operas were presented in Montreal, these were localized efforts. The Metropolitan Opera broadcasts, beamed into Canada from New York, constituted a primary source of continued contact with masterpieces of the operatic literature.

In recognition of this hiatus in the cultural life of this country, upon his arrival in Canada from Britain, the CBC producer Terence Gibbs became the driving force behind the creation of the CBC Opera Company. In the summer of 1948, Gibbs, who prior to his arrival in Toronto had supervised the recording of Gluck's *Orfeo ed Euridice* by the Glyndebourne Opera House, was assigned by the CBC to produce that opera for radio, using members of the Royal Conservatory of Music of Toronto. It did not take him long to realize that the high standard of Canadian singing in Gluck's opera warranted the creation of some permanent organization. Once created, such a radio opera company could use the 'CBC Wednesday Night' time slot as a vehicle for opera productions.[57]

The Royal Conservatory of Music in Toronto, which had acquired after the war a highly competent professional opera staff, had established an opera school for the training of singers. Ettore Mazzoleni was the principal of the conservatory, and Nicholas Goldschmidt was the opera school's first music director. The stage director was Herman Geiger-Torel, who brought to Toronto his considerable expertise as director of opera at Teatro Colón in Buenos Aires. Gibbs capitalized on this profusion of professional musical talent assembled in Toronto at the time of his arrival to create the CBC Opera Company, the first attempt to form a professional opera organization with Canadian talent. The board of directors, including Charles Jennings, then CBC's general supervisor of programs, Dr Arnold Walter, Harry Boyle, Geoffrey Waddington, Nicholas Goldschmidt, and Gibbs, functioned as the authority on musical content, scheduling of programs, and financial matters.

The genesis of the CBC Opera Company can thus be attributed to the energies and vision of the English producer and the willingness of the corporation's management to broadcast operas on the 'Wednesday Night' series. The first opera season (1948–9) witnessed the production of *Orfeo ed Euridice, La Bohème, La Traviata*, and *Don Giovanni*. The next season included five operas, the first of which – Benjamin Britten's *Peter Grimes* – represented a bold new departure from the established repertoire.

The CBC Opera Company continued its regular series until the end of the 1954–5 season. A repeat performance of *Deirdre* (1951), Canadian *premières* of Stravinsky's *The Rake's Progress* (1953) and Luigi Dallapiccola's *The Prisoner*, and the North American *première* of Arthur Benjamin's *A Tale of Two Cities* (1954) constituted some of the more unconventional broadcasting fare during this period. The cast of the 1951 performance of *Deirdre* differed from that of five years earlier. While Frances James and William Morton were, once more, the leading singers, the new names included Donald Brown, Glenn Gardiner, Bernard Johnson, Andrew MacMillan, and Trudy Carlyle.

The role of Levercham, Deirdre's nurse, marked Carlyle's debut with the CBC Opera Company. From 1950 to 1957 her career blossomed with amazing rapidity. During this brief and concentrated period she distinguished herself as a major singer of contemporary music in Toronto, an amazing feat for an artist whose career was cut short in 1957 by illness as suddenly as it was created.

After her discharge from the army in 1946, Calgary-born Trudy Carlyle had joined the Toronto Conservatory of Music Opera School. She was in her late twenties when she began regular voice lessons with Emmy Heim, and she was the first student accepted by Frances James. The guidance, artistry, and teaching philosophies of both these artists functioned as beacons during the mezzo-soprano's short career. Heim's legacy was an understanding of the spiritual aspect of music, while Frances James taught the importance of technique and discipline, a respect for the physical process of singing. Based on these two complementary philosophies and imbued with her own innate sense of musicianship, Carlyle developed a feeling for the long, sustained vocal line, and a beautiful warm and passionate voice resembling in quality that of Kathleen Ferrier.

Carlyle's position in the history of music in Canada resembles – within a telescoped time frame – that of her teacher and mentor, Frances James. After the Adaskins' departure from Toronto in 1952, it was Carlyle who became for a few years one of the major exponents of contemporary music in Toronto, interpreting a number of Canadian songs at concerts of the Canadian League of Composers. Mario Bernardi was Carlyle's most frequent accompanist, particularly in the numerous 'Distinguished Artists' concerts presented on 'CBC Wednesday Night.' The CBC recordings of these concerts reveal not only a varied repertoire of Mahler, Schumann, Berg, Webern, Schoenberg – particularly from the *Gurrelieder* – and the Emily Dickinson songs of Copland, but also a musical partnership of the highest calibre between the piano and the voice.

Stravinsky's *The Rake's Progress*, performed on 22 April 1953, marked the end of Frances James's appearances with the CBC Opera Company, because of two contributing factors: the Adaskins' move to Saskatoon, and the CBC's change in policy regarding opera broadcasts. In 1952 the Adaskins had moved from Toronto to Saskatoon, where Murray accepted the post of professor and head of the music department at the University of Saskatchewan. This move to the Prairies signified for Frances a physical removal from the centre of musical activities at a time in Canadian cultural history when Toronto and Montreal represented the cultural focal points of Canada, and when an artist had to reside in the 'East' in order to succeed in the musical world.

It was Terence Gibbs who once more approached Frances with the request to sing the lead in Stravinsky's opera. She accepted the engagement even though the consequences of her distance from Toronto had begun to manifest themselves. At first, Frances could not find a pianist skilled enough to help her in the preparation of her role. In addition, the requirement of a Mozartean sound in the three big soprano arias in this neoclassic opera presented the singer with a major challenge, after having developed a big dramatic sound over the previous several years in her preparation of the Britten songs and operas. Furthermore, the singer, accustomed to working on an opera with the entire cast over a protracted period of time and becoming intimately acquainted with the music, found this no longer possible. First, she went to New York for coaching lessons with Madame Kurenko in an effort to relearn the technique for the type of lyrical soprano needed in the Stravinsky work. Then, two weeks before the performance, she went to Toronto for rehearsals having to learn the entire opera in that short span of time. While the obstacles were not insurmountable, direct participation in the Toronto scene became increasingly more difficult with the passage of years. Terence Gibbs's position with the CBC changed, and by 1955 the regular CBC opera series had ended. Although opera performances on radio and television continued sporadically, 1955 marked the end of an exciting period in Canadian music broadcasting.

It took a man with the musical experience and sophistication of Terence Gibbs to recognize the needs of Canadian music radio programming. His energy and youthful exuberance, coupled with his vision of the cultural potential of broadcasting in post-war Canada, contributed some extremely innovative and unconventional air time. He produced more than forty radio opera broadcasts and was instrumental in the development of some of the CBC's major music series. Through his efforts this epoch in music broadcasting following the war years and immediately preceding the development of television marks a milestone in Canadian musical culture. The later development of television broadcasting affected adversely the quality of radio programs.

Almost twenty years later, shortly before his death in 1971, Terence Gibbs referred nostalgically to this period of Frances James's radio appearances and the performance of *Peter Grimes* as the happiest decade of his life. In a letter to the Adaskins, Gibbs comments on the televised performance of the opera from Aldeburgh, conducted by the composer himself: 'my only wish was that Fran had been there singing Ellen – a performance that has not been surpassed.'[58]

Terence Gibbs's and Geoffrey Waddington's legacy may be summarized in their advocacy of contemporary music, their belief in the Canadian composer in particular, and their instigation of major programs designed to feature Canadian artists as well as to discover new Canadian talent. Artists not only had the opportunity to be heard on the Trans-Canada network but they also regarded the CBC as a cultural institution enabling them to make a living in their own country.

THE PLIGHT OF THE CONCERT ARTIST

While the success of a musical career is based on a solid foundation of talent combined with favourable coincidences, the reality of the concert world demands dimensions beyond these two factors. Publicity is an essential ingredient in career building. The 'selling' of talent by professional concert managers or other individuals who, by virtue of their profession as radio producers or conductors, are in a position to lend the artist support and visibility leads to ultimate recognition of the artist by the general public.

Throughout her career, Frances James had the support of a number of personages who recognized her talents and were in a position to offer her performing opportunities. Just as John Murray Gibbon and the CPR played a major role in the early part of her career, the Canadian Broadcasting Corporation affected the direction of her mature career. A great portion of her time was devoted to radio performances, and to a certain extent she owes the success of her mature career to the CBC.

Despite the enlightened policies of the CBC toward its Canadian artists, however, the lot of a performer in this country, who during the post-war era attempted a concert career by touring Canada, was not an easy one. No resident Canadian artist of the period could make a living exclusively by giving concerts. A reverse process of career building seems to have existed: instead of the performer first establishing a reputation as concert artist, in Canada his or her reputation was established almost exclusively over the radio. In fact, without the radio, the artist would quite likely not have been heard at all.

Canadian audiences, particularly those in the smaller communities removed from the major eastern centres of cultural activity, seem to have nourished doubts about the ability of domestic musicians as well as about the quality of music written by domestic composers. They had not yet grasped the musical potential of home-grown talent. This attitude forced a number of Canadian performers to leave their country to establish a career in the United States and Europe, where society seems to have been somewhat more receptive to recognizing talent.

But what of Canadian artists who, like Frances James, stayed in Canada because of a belief in this country's cultural potential and a nationalistic desire to contribute to the Canadian musical scene? In order to promote themselves, Canadian artists needed to appear in major concert halls across the country, and they needed a management agency to assume responsibility for bookings, promotion, and financial arrangements. Such agencies acting on behalf of domestic artists were practically non-existent during the post-war period. For artists to conduct their own promotion and bookings across Canada was a time-consuming task, depleting the energy available for study and enhancement of their art. Rental of a major concert hall was financially impossible for most performers. The high cost of publicizing a concert presented an additional financial obstacle, coupled with the difficulty of filling a hall with an audience. Although professional managers existed in the major cities, they were mostly interested in booking performers of international reputation. Most of the concerts in smaller communities across the Dominion were sponsored by local organizations whose primary objective was to bring good live music to the townspeople where it would otherwise not have been heard because of the distance of the community from the mainstream of musical activity. These local service organizations usually used the proceeds to support a needy cause.

One of the most active service organizations was the already mentioned network of Women's Musical Clubs existing in cities across Canada. Associations of amateur musicians and music lovers in general, they represented some of the oldest musical organizations in Canada. One of their functions throughout the forties and fifties was to foster the appreciation of music within their communities by organizing professional concerts and by raising scholarship and bursary funds to help talented young local musicians headed toward a career in music. The associations also acted as sponsors to a variety of nationally and internationally known artists and musical groups.

The Women's Musical Club of Winnipeg, for example, is one of the four oldest in Canada. Frances James was their guest a number of times, and in 1950 she won accolades in both local newspapers. The program performed on that occasion and the enthusiastic audience response reflected in the review are indicative of an unusually high level of musical sophistication for a town supposedly isolated in the vastness of the Canadian Prairies. It is also a tribute to the local Women's Musical Club, which was, through its long-standing tradition of artistic sponsorship, to a certain extent responsible for the level of musical sophistication in Winnipeg. The soprano's program included a selection of songs by Hugo Wolf and Claude Debussy. Canadian works represented on the occasion were Bernard Naylor's 'Three Songs' from *King Solomon's Prayer* and two songs from Barbara Pentland's *Song Cycle*. The 'Embroidery Aria' from Britten's *Peter Grimes* and two of Hindemith's *Nine English Songs* were also performed.

The *Winnipeg Tribune* summarizes Frances's artistry:

The recital by Frances James, given before members of the Women's Musical Club Monday afternoon in the Concert Hall of the Auditorium was the epitome of song artistry.

A highly individual artist, with an apparently limitless repertoire, Miss James brings to her artistry the utmost of intelligence and imaginative conceptions. She is a singer whose equal in these respects one could not name among Canadian vocalists. Her singing brought back memories of the French-Canadian soprano, Eva Gauthier, who was also highly individual and original, and, like Miss James, a modernist at heart; also the French soprano, Madeleine Grey, whose singing of Debussy was a remarkable evocation of subtle inflections and poetic atmosphere.

Although the writer had heard Miss James in most of her CBC radio triumphs, including the Canadian premiere of Britten's opera, *Peter Grimes*, last October, he had never heard her in person until Monday. Her radiance of personality and womanly graciousness added to the spell cast by the beauty of her voice and artistry. Only once or twice in a decade or more does an artist of such calibre present a programme so striking in originality and one demanding the very highest resources of voice and temperament.

Miss James' consistently bright accuracy of intonation after her opening song was a steady delight, and so was the display of dynamic control which produces an impeccable pianissimo and a spine-chilling forte with equal certainty of aim. And the mental attitude which prompts her to design and model each item of her repertoire with skilled precision is naturally of invaluable service in the characterization of songs ...

It seemed to the writer that some of the highest among many peaks reached during the programme belonged to the opening Hugo Wolf songs. In these, and especially 'In dem Schatten meiner Locken' and 'Auf einer Wanderung,' Miss James seemed to realize with psychic insight the strange, indescribably beautiful imaginings of the composer. But it is part of her art that she finds and communicates the essential character of whatever music she touches. Mr. Naylor's accompaniments earned an equal share of acclaim for masterly interpretation and the spirit of tripping rhythm and gay romance of the 'Auf einer Wanderung' was happily emphasized.[59]

The Women's Musical Clubs were the most frequent source of sponsorship for Frances James's annual cross-country tours. These included the Ladies' Morning Musical Club in Montreal and the clubs in Vancouver, Regina, Calgary, Lethbridge, Toronto, Quebec, and Saint John. Other small community groups, such as the Imperial Order of the Daughters of the Empire and the Kinsmen's Club, also organized concerts to support and promote the arts locally. Frances was their guest in such communities as Edmonton, Port Arthur, Liverpool, and Annapolis Royal, Nova Scotia. The Victoria Musical Arts Society (successor to the Victoria Ladies' Musical Club), the Fort William Music and Arts Club, and the Edmonton Varsity Musical Club also hosted a number of the soprano's concerts.

Frances James's cross-country tours frequently included engagements at universities, sponsored by the local college student council. She performed at the University of Western Ontario, Queen's, Dalhousie, and the University of British Columbia. On the occasion of a February 1947 concert at UBC sponsored by the University Branch of the Canadian Legion, she found herself in the midst of a controversy involving the church and Sunday concerts in the city. A Vancouver organization – the Lord's Day Alliance – had succeeded in having a law passed forbidding Sunday concerts for which a fixed charge was to be made. The church's concern was that concerts, theatres, and other entertainments would interfere with the public's church-going activities. The Canadian Legion at the university, numbering about 2,500 veterans of the recent war, were oblivious of the existence of this law, and had organized a series of Sunday concerts featuring well-known Canadian artists, with the intent of raising funds in aid of needy members of their branch. The first concert was to feature Frances

James, and the tickets for this widely publicized event were almost sold out. Shortly before the day of the concert, representatives of the Lord's Day Alliance forced the leaders of the UBC Branch, Canadian Legion, to cancel the whole series. Because of the speed at which the events took place there was no opportunity to notify the soprano of the cancellation of her concert. She had already boarded the train to Vancouver. To her surprise, she was greeted upon her arrival in Vancouver station by a crowd of students and reporters asking her for her reaction to this incident. Frances, who knew nothing about it, was quick to adjust to the situation. One paper quoted her as saying: 'Did you expect me to be temperamental ... you may be sure I'll sing for you. I'll sing if I have to sing on the campus; there's lots of space and fresh air there.'[60] A new concert date was arranged, to the artist's considerable relief, because it afforded her additional rehearsal time with her accompanist, John Avison.

The touring concert artist frequently encountered a number of similar obstacles, which required considerable flexibility and adaptability to existing conditions on the part of the artist. Frances, who spent a month each spring touring the West and the equivalent length of time in the fall touring the East, depended on the train as her principal means of transportation. She had to contend with late arrivals resulting from occasional ten- to twelve-hour delays, as well as the vagaries of Canadian weather affecting well-ventilated trains in sub-zero temperatures and forcing her to sing at times in unheated halls. At one concert she sang while snuggled in the warmth of her fur stole.

The annual cross-country tours held little glamour. Often concerts were given every two to three days, each in a different community that could most conveniently be reached by train. No financial gain resulted from these tours; in fact, they often represented a considerable monetary loss to the singer, whose fee, averaging $150 per concert, had to cover her own and the accompanist's expenses as well as the accompanist's fee. Frances James, who always believed in the importance of good stage appearance, had the additional expense of purchasing appropriate concert gowns. Her annual cross-country tours would not have been feasible financially had it not been for Murray, who functioned as her sponsor by paying for each tour's deficits.

Other drawbacks occasionally encountered on these tours included the local organization's scheduling of her concert on the same night as another major event, such as a hockey game or a visiting popular entertainment show, so that she found herself competing with other events for an audience. During a tour through the Okanagan Valley, every concert she presented coincided with a hockey night.

Professional concert halls were rarely found in smaller Canadian communities during the post-war period. Many concerts, therefore, were presented in church halls and school auditoriums. Hotel ballrooms, university convocation halls or gymnasiums, Canadian Legion halls, and art galleries constituted the more luxurious concert accommodations. Understandably, the acoustical conditions in these were less than satisfactory, a point frequently raised by reviewers, who felt that the halls did not do justice to a singer of Frances James's calibre.

The mark of a great artist is the ability to adapt to local conditions and to make the best of a given situation. Frances James was determined to sing in the best way she could, in recognition of the local sponsors' efforts to organize her performances in their community. Adverse conditions did not seem to affect her. The audience was paying to hear her sing, and she felt a sense of responsibility toward them regardless of the performance conditions. Frequently before a concert she would be asked for an interview on the local radio station, or she would sing in a local radio broadcast. She always obliged out of a sense of civic duty.

While on most of her tours Frances gave solo recitals, during 1949 the Adaskins ventured into a joint cross-country recital tour. The following schedule summarizes the rigours of such a venture:

Jan 29 Marathon Paper Mills, Marathon, Ont
Feb 1   Third Avenue United Church, Saskatoon
Feb 3   Banff Junior Chamber of Commerce, Banff
Feb 7   Vancouver, a CBC broadcast
Feb 9   Women's Musical Club, Hotel Vancouver Ballroom
Feb 14 School auditorium, Shawnigan Lake School
Feb 16 Musical Arts Society, Empress Hotel, Crystal Ballroom, Victoria
Feb 21 Mount Royal Symphony Orchestra, Grand Theatre, Calgary
Feb 22 Edmonton

The Adaskins' fall tour to the east of Canada in the same year enlisted the services of the accompanist Earle Moss:

Oct 21 King's Hall School, Compton, Quebec
Oct 26 Ladies' Morning Musical Club, St Vincent's Auditorium, Saint John, NB
Oct 28 IODE, Vocational School Auditorium, Woodstock, NB
Oct 29 Netherwood School for Girls, Rothesay, NB
Oct 31 St Andrew's Music, Art and Drama Club, St Andrew's, NB
Nov 1   IODE, Annapolis Royal, NS
Nov 3   Zion Baptist Choir, Yarmouth, NS
Nov 4   IODE, Liverpool, NS
Nov 7   Council of Students, Dalhousie University, Halifax

In order to maintain high musical standards during a concert tour, Frances James chose her accompanists with great care. Over the course of her career she worked with several distinguished pianists. Her accompanists throughout the 1930s – Gwendolyn Williams and Louis Crerar – have already been mentioned. John Newmark, the German pianist, chamber musician, and accompanist, who arrived in Toronto during the war years, accompanied the artist on a cross-country tour in 1944. Frances, who was the first Canadian singer to employ Newmark as accompanist, recalls the pleasure of working with such an accomplished musician. Not yet employed full-time, Newmark would spend hours in the library copying out music for her, and the two of them would rehearse five hours at a stretch, indulging in the pleasure of making music and learning new repertoire.

For her Montreal concerts over a number of years, Frances's accompanist was the renowned French-Canadian pianist, coach, teacher, and translator Marie-Thérèse Paquin. Others included Bernard Naylor, the Vancouver-based conductor John Avison, Dorothy Swetnam (wife of the Calgary conductor Clayton Hare), and Mario Bernardi. Frances would join Dorothy Swetnam in Calgary for a recital there, which was followed by a tour through Okanagan Valley towns. In Toronto Frances gave concerts with Leo Barkin, George Brough, and Earle Moss at the piano.

Toronto-based George Brough was the Adaskins' accompanist on their 1949 Western tour, and it was Brough whom Frances called upon in an emergency to join her in New York for the recording of Hindemith's *Das Marienleben*. The person with whom she had worked on those songs all summer in Santa Barbara in preparation for the recording session proved so unreliable that ten days before the recording date in New York she found herself without an accompanist. George Brough, whose sight-reading facility contributed to his reputation as an expert accompanist, agreed to learn the taxing piano part of *Das Marienleben* in ten days. He is the pianist on the historic first recording of the Hindemith song cycle for Lyrichord records. Brough also accompanied Frances in Annapolis in 1951, when she sang Hindemith's song cycle for Zuckerkandl's class at the college.

With minimal or no financial reward, and with all the hardships inherent in cross-country tours, the question arises why an artist of the calibre of Frances James persisted with the annual visits to the Canadian interior. During the 1940s she had conquered the Canadian musical world; she had performed with major Canadian orchestras; she had sung in the most prestigious concert halls that the country had to offer; and she was a performer of stature on the CBC Dominion network. Yet she regularly toured coast-to-coast, dedicating almost two months of her busy concert schedule to travelling. Why did she not follow the example of a number of Canadian artists, and seek an international reputation by performing in Europe and the United States?

Both Roland Hayes and Madame Kurenko had urged Frances to present a New York début in Town Hall, but the expense involved in such an undertaking made the project unfeasible for the soprano. Launching a career in the United States was dependent on finding a good agent to promote the artist and to ensure that reviewers attended the début recital. Because she sang *lieder* almost exclusively, Frances's options were limited to the concert rather than the operatic stage, which narrowed down her potential audience. The other option open to a performer intent on an international concert career was to join the roster of artists managed by such a major international agency as Columbia Concerts Incorporated, with its headquarters in New York. This option did not hold much appeal for Frances, who, as a Canadian artist, felt an obligation to contribute to the cultural development of her country. Her cross-country tours constituted a labour of love, and her sense of nationalism guided her in her efforts to introduce good music – that of Canadian composers in particular – to communities in the interior whose opportunities of hearing live music were limited. She also believed in acting as a free agent and having her own managers book concerts rather than having to depend on placement by a management agency. Above all, she believed that the opportunity to develop a career in Canada must be given to every Canadian artist who chose to stay in this country.

Until the late 1940s Frances had not encountered any problems obtaining concert bookings in the interior. The Canada-wide radio broadcasts had made her name familiar to the directors of the service clubs who booked her engagements. Other Canadian artists, however, who wished to follow in her footsteps and who did not enjoy a similar reputation, met with increasing difficulty in booking concert tours. Two major management agencies were operating in the smaller Canadian communities, and while they were both instrumental in introducing live music into these towns, Canadian artists not hired by these agencies found themselves in competition with them. The Celebrity Concert Series operated out of Winnipeg, while the Community Concert Series, a division of Columbia Artists' Management, was an American organization, operating out of New York.

The concert series in Winnipeg was originally conceived by Fred M. Gee (1882–1947) who, over his thirty-six years as impresario, managed to create in the Manitoba capital one of the largest concert series on the North American continent, with an annual subscription as large as 3,500.[61] Gee's management tradition was continued after his death by his son, A.K. Gee, under the name of Celebrity Concerts Canada, Inc. The concerts broadened out into a network reaching into Ontario, Manitoba, Saskatchewan, and Alberta. Neither the Winnipeg-based Celebrity nor the New York-based Community Concert Series specialized in featuring Canadian performers. Pierrette Alarie and Leopold Simoneau were the few Canadians on the series.

While Celebrity Concerts booked engagements with service clubs that in turn sponsored the performer and contributed any revenue raised to domestic civic projects, the Community Concert Series operated in a different manner. Under its president, Ward French, the enterprise was the equivalent of a musical cartel, exerting control over the concert activities of a large number of professional musicians in the United States. The organization started to tap the Canadian market around 1930, applying business tactics and creating a cartel in Canada similar to that at home. The audiences in a small community would contribute annual dues of five dollars for a concert membership fee that entitled each member to attend all the concerts in the series. The membership campaigns were conducted over the span of one week, and only members were allowed to attend the concerts. No separate tickets were sold. The campaigns were run by volunteers from the community, usually capitalizing on women's volunteer efforts to sell memberships to friends and neighbours.

The amount of money raised in that fashion established the category and number of artists sent by the agency to the town; in other words, the town received a package of whatever type of artistic talent it could afford. The higher the sum, the greater the fame of the visiting artist. A local committee usually had a choice in the identity of the star performer, but because of the packaged format of the series it had little choice in the identity or quality of the other artists in the series. This was the decision of the New York concert agency, which often sent totally unknown performers whose fee was fixed at a lower rate than that of star performers. In Canada, the organization was most active in Ontario, Quebec, and the Maritimes.

Frances James, who was the only Canadian singer to have toured Canada from coast to coast annually for almost two decades, possessed intimate knowledge of the problems facing a Canadian performer who wished to make a living by giving concerts on home territory. Recognizing the restrictions that such an organization as the Community Concert Series placed on opportunities for Canadian artists who were not on the circuit of such a series, the soprano initiated a correspondence with Ward French. Her intention was to acquaint him with the plight of the Canadian performing artist.

The correspondence that evolved over the last nine months of 1948 documents an incident of considerable importance in Canadian cultural history. It reveals how one Canadian artist, singlehandedly challenged and opposed a representative of the most powerful management agency on this continent. The battle ultimately won by Frances James was fought on behalf of future generations of Canadian artists. Through perseverance, adherence to her principles and her full belief in the high quality of the Canadian artist, and through her ultimate submission of a brief on the matter to the Massey Commission, Frances James contributed toward breaking the powerful United States management monopoly. The correspondence between Frances James and Ward French deserves a place in the annals of Canadian music history. It must be remembered that the period of this exchange represents the height of the singer's career, when she was recognized as an artist of stature and as Canada's leading soprano.

April 6, 1948

Dear Mr French:

I have just completed a small tour in Western Canada and feel extremely alarmed that due to the number of concerts given by Community Concerts Incorporated I am finding it increasingly difficult to secure dates in my own country. I appeal to you to ask what can be done for resident Canadian artists who have not made their name in the United States.

I am a soprano of wide reputation and experience in concert, radio and as a soloist with orchestras in Canada. Some years ago it was my pleasure to meet you in your office in New York. You gave me advice then for introducing myself to the American scene, but for many reasons I have been unable to carry this out. I understand Community Concerts has now seventy cities in Canada organized for series of concerts. Would it not be possible for me to be heard in some of these without my first having to be established in the United States? I should be delighted to go to New York to audition for you. I would suggest you get in touch with Mr. Arpad Shandor who has played for me and could identify my work.

I would be glad to hear from you.

Yours sincerely,
Frances James

April 15, 1948

Dear Miss James:

I'm sorry you are alarmed over the growth of Community Concerts in Canada. This growth has been normal and natural. It's the result of previous years of pioneer work in helping cities establish their own Community Concert enterprise. I simply represent a clearing house and a service station for each city. The fact that you have not received recognition through Community Concerts in Canada is in no way unusual nor does it have anything to do with the American scene.

You have been in the musical world long enough, I think, to know that the musical world is an international one, and most of the important and major concert enterprises in every city clear their artists internationally through the five or six international music centers, such as London, Paris, Rome, New York and, at one time, Berlin. (Stockholm has become important in the last few years in that respect, too.) But it's simply a question of the clearing house at the crossroads. As an illustration, London, Ontario booked five attractions for next season last week and in checking through, I discovered that only one attraction is American born.

Should you come to New York one of these days, I would be very happy to see that you have a first-rate audition with Columbia Concerts. I say, first-rate, because I would be glad to have you skip over the regular audition committee so that a few of the important managers could hear you. I am very much interested in Canadian talent, more so than in American talent, because, musically, I am very close to Canada. However, Canadian talent has to compete in the international world, in order to get recognition which will book them on the important concert series in Canada. This is no different than it is in America. Young American artists have to do the same thing, and so do young French artists and young Italian artists. Mona Paulee, Jean Watson, Raoul Jobin, Pierrette Alarie and [Leopold] Simoneau, and many other young Canadian artists made the grade that way, and more will in the future. Perhaps among those will be you – who knows?

If you are coming to New York any time in the future, please let me know well in advance, and I will be glad to see that you get every possible consideration.

Cordially,
Ward French

May 24, 1948
Dear Mr. French:

Thank you for your letter of April 15th. I regret the delay in replying but I have been away. It is good of you to write so fully of my problem and I note that you are interested in Canadian talent. This I know for it was while Malcolm and Godden, pianists were on your lists that I visited you in New York, and I remember your high praise of them. We have many fine artists residing in Canada and they are finding it quite as difficult as I am getting concerts.

With reference to you 'representing a clearing house' by helping cities establish their own Community Concerts, do not say it is not unusual that I, a Canadian, have not received recognition or that this development has nothing to do with the American scene. You sell your artists, American, European and those Canadians who are residing in the United States and have made their names there, but a Canadian who remains in his own country may not perform here without first being recognized by your concert bureau. All of those thousands of dollars are going out of the country to your artists while I, a Canadian, cannot make a living by my singing alone because these towns you control cannot engage me without your approval. In talking to members of a Maritime Community Concert city they expressed concern that it is not possible to engage artists like myself in their series and asked me what could be done.

I quite realize that the musical world is an international one and know about the music centres, where artists may be appraised but why cannot we be judged by the musical centres in Canada, namely Montreal and Toronto and make this sufficient recommendation to perform in the smaller cities in our own country? Your suggestion that I sing for the important managers is a gracious one and I am quite ready to do that and appreciate your kind offer. Is their approval all that is necessary or, following an audition, if they feel I am capable, does that mean the usual New York recital and additional thousands of dollars for promotional work? This I cannot afford to do nor am I interested at this time, for the enormous number of debut recitals in New York today make it impossible for most artists. One has to be either a genius or a phenomenal ingenue and I am neither. I am well above the average recitalist and have had considerable success in that field. I feel I can compete in the international field but I cannot meet the financial requirements at this time ...

> With kind regards,
> Frances James

June 9, 1948

Dear Miss James:

Thank you for your nice letter. I wrote you fully because I am vitally interested in the subject matter of your discussion. I appreciate your struggle for a career, just like I appreciate the struggles of hundreds of other aspiring artists, and even though I have given a lifetime to the promotion of concerts, I know I have fallen far short of creating a situation which will make it possible for more than a small percentage of those who dearly want a career to satisfy their inner ambition. But among those who have profited from my efforts, you will find a generous percentage of Canadians. I have always been as interested in the Canadian artist as I have been in the American artist.

One vital, fundamental factor however, which is usually overlooked when it comes to criticizing Community Concerts is that the Community Concert plan was not devised as a means of making it possible for young artists to have careers. It does not belong to the artists. It does not belong to me. It belongs to the listeners. It was created for the listeners – the people who want to enjoy music. The benefit derived by the artist is incidental. The plan was not created for artists, any more than hospitals are built for doctors. Hospitals are built for patients, and a certain number of doctors naturally find careers because of this, but the young, struggling doctors who don't find careers, don't condemn hospitals. The truth of the matter is that the trouble with you and hundreds like yourself is that there aren't enough customers to consume the number of aspiring careers which are always present. That is the situation I have tried to remedy over the years, and have had some success in so doing, but I have fallen far short of any goal that would satisfy all the hundreds of young, aspiring artists who are looking for the reason why their careers haven't come through.

It is natural that those Canadians who attain success gravitate to New York. New York is one of the international musical crossroads of the world. A career cannot be made in just one country. ROSE BAMPTON, an American singer, is now on a long Mexican tour. She comes back the later part of this month and then leaves for South America, where she will be concertizing all summer. JEAN WATSON is a girl who was born and raised in Toronto, but, who, on her own initiative, solved the problem of getting started on her career, and is now managed by Columbia Artists Management, and who, through New York as the international music center, has been booked in Europe, as well as in America.

There is one point you make in your letter, which I would like to correct, and that is 'You sell your artists, American, European and those Canadians who are residing in the United States and have made their names there, but a Canadian who remains in his own country may not perform here without first being recognized by your concert bureau.' This is not true. I have tried time and time again to interest the committees of Canadian Community Concert Associations in local Canadian artists but have never been successful. They want Canadian artists, but they want those Canadian artists who have reached and made a success in the international field, not just the local field. This is true, not only of Canadian cities; it is true the world over. You also say, 'All of those thousands of dollars are going out of the country to your artists while I, a Canadian, cannot make a living by my singing alone because the towns you control cannot engage me without your approval.' This is also not true. Towns do not need my approval of an artist to engage him. It is written in their organization agreement that they can engage any artist they wish to engage. I simply act as a broker.

I may be criticized by some for having pioneered the organized audience plan in Canada, but I'm not criticized by the people who have benefited by it, such as the thousands of music lovers who have enjoyed the benefits of the organized audience plan. They are the people for whom I have worked and whom I have tried to serve. At least I should be given credit for the fact that I have given Canada a good idea, from which so many thousands of music lovers have profited in enjoyment and cultural advantages.

I do feel keenly the point you have made in your letter and, at least, I have felt that I wanted to exchange letters with you far enough to express some of the problems that exist on the other side of the fence, for whatever it may be worth. I wish you the very best of success and only wish I could find some way of helping that success along. If and when I could have that chance, it would be my pleasure.

August 3rd, 1948

Dear Mr. French:

I have been a long time replying to your letter of June 9th. I want to assure you that I will not prolong this correspondence. I very much appreciate your courtesy in explaining 'the other side of the fence' and while I am still not convinced, I will not weary you by continuing this debate.

I want to let you know that you have not been corresponding with a disappointed artist but that I am one of the more fortunate resident Canadians who have had fine engagements and given a lot of beautiful music from coast to coast in Canada. But I and my colleagues could handle more concerts if the American Concert Plan did not exclude us from their series in Canada. So many communities are unable to sponsor more than their subscription concerts. I do feel that it would be a smart idea for the Community plan to engage one Canadian artist in each community. For ten artists in 75 cities that would surely be a nice nucleus for a season's engagements.

My reason for writing you was not for myself alone. I feel very keenly the lot of a number of my colleagues and of the younger generation of artists to come but I realize that much has to be done in our own country to show the leading citizens who sponsor only outside artists that they have a few right at home who both need and deserve a hearing. Canada should encourage its own talent and give it confidence and the necessary courage to branch out to other shores, not as faltering would-be artists but artists ready to meet the rigours of that exciting music world. I do not blame your organization for starting and advancing this fine idea of bringing music to communities but I do blame our own people for wholeheartedly accepting while sacrificing their own musicians. We are learning though and can use the example the United States has given us. Her own young artists receive all their education in their own country and are launched there and make their names. I hope we will wake up soon and do the same before too many Jean Watsons leave us forever.

August 20, 1948

Dear Miss James:

Thank you for your very nice letter of August 3rd. You write very intelligently and I understand perfectly what you mean and I am sympathetic with it. The more young Canadian artists can be developed and given a chance in the music world, the happier I will be. I have certainly contributed as much as I can. I do think that Canada, in relation to her population, has contributed her share to the music world and will continue to do so, particularly when she has such a fine group coming up all the time. Perhaps some day when I am in Toronto you could have luncheon with me and we could have a visit. I think we could have a very interesting conversation.

I know just how the picture can look to all young Canadian artists, but I don't think I am as bad as some of them think I am. After all, I went into Canada with the Community Concert plan when there was just practically nothing in the Canadian cities as far as permanent and financially sound concert activities were concerned. I pioneered it for eighteen years and I feel very close to the Canadian musical life and have a host of bosom friends there. If it hasn't provided as many opportunities to artists as the Canadian artists feel it should, I can only say that this situation is not unique to Canada. There are hundreds of American artists who feel that way right here in the United States. I have given it a lot of thought and can only deduct that there are just too many young people aspiring for a career in ratio to the need for their services.

I spent a lifetime trying to correct that, but the more I expand the market, the more artists teachers have turned out, so I have sort of given up hope of ever rectifying it. Please don't be hard on your own people. The committees are the same in the United States, Mexico, and I guess the world over. When they get the budgets to engage artists, they want to pick the most outstanding for the money on hand and that overshadows their desire to use their Community Concerts for the purpose of furthering young careers. I do think the net results on the whole have been very satisfactory and worthwhile. There are many Canadian artists who are enjoying successful careers today who got their starts on Community Concerts.

If you are coming down to New York any time in the future, drop me a line and let me know. This is an invitation for a luncheon and we can talk over this problem. As I see it, you are a very intelligent gal and have given it a lot of thought and I have never been accused of being rigid.

October 5, 1948

Dear Mr. French:

... I accept with pleasure your kind invitation for luncheon either in Toronto or New York. I would prefer New York and can arrange to go early in November at your convenience. Should you also wish me to sing I would appreciate knowing in advance to arrange for an accompanist.

I was interested to hear from Mr Elie Spivak of his interiew with you. It was a pleasant coincidence that he too was taking his Canadian concert problems to you.

With kind thoughts,
Yours very sincerely,
Frances James

October 27, 1948

Dear Miss James:

...If you are coming to New York in November, I will be very glad to hear you and have other Columbia Managers present to hear you. I do not want to take the responsibility of encouraging you to make a special trip because that always sort of puts me on the spot. It will have to be your own gamble and not mine, but I will assure you that you will have the best kind of hearing possible; and furthermore, if you measure up from a competitive standpoint with the others in the field, regardless of nationality, I am sure you will have the best consideration. In other words, let me put it frankly. I cannot urge a Columbia Manager to take you under his management because you are a Canadian, but I will turn it around in the opposite direction. If you have what it takes to compete with others in the field, then your being a Canadian will be an advantage to you. Let's put it that way. At least, after our nice friendly correspondence, it will be a pleasure to meet you any time.

> Best personal regards,
> Cordially,
> Ward French

November 22, 1948

Dear Mr. French:

Thank you for your letter of October 27th.

Some unexpected broadcasting has made my departure to accept your very kind invitation to audition a little indefinite. I realize that you will soon be working on next season's lists and wonder how much longer I can delay auditioning and still be in time for consideration should your Columbia managers think my singing interesting to them?

I very much want to come and certainly will take full responsibility in making a special trip and will not put you on the spot – except perhaps in your kind invitation to luncheon! Seriously though, I am fully prepared to give you and your managers the opportunity of hearing me. If I hadn't had confidence that I could compete with those singers on your lists I would never have written you. I might refer you to a newspaper review I sent you on May 24th on just this subject by a competent critic in Calgary, Alberta. He felt I was much more qualified to give a fine recital than two well-known imported artists that season. There is a growing feeling in Canada of inferior singers giving inferior programs on concert series across the country.

I am enclosing a copy of a letter I received last week. In private life I am Mrs. Murray Adaskin and I wrote to an executive of the International Nickel Company to secure a date there when I am on tour in Western Canada in February. This is a Club which before the war had monthly concerts for their employees and where I gave at least three concerts. You can imagine my feelings to receive this [negative] reply, especially 'Should there be any change in our policy we will be glad to get in touch with you.'[62] This happens all the time, Mr. French, and is seriously limiting my opportunity to pursue my art. You really must help qualified resident Canadians.

> With kind thoughts,
> Yours very sincerely,
> Frances James

December 3, 1948

Dear Miss James:

Thank you for your nice letter.

I'm sorry you couldn't get down sooner to sing for the Columbia managers, if you were intending to take that gamble at all, because November would have been the better month as now that December is here, the list has been pretty well made up. However, that doesn't entirely preclude anything. It never does in this business.

We are starting our annual Community Concert Conference next Monday, the 6th, which will last until the 20th of December, and during those two weeks I will be practically out of circulation. I wish you could have at least gotten down this week before the conference would have started. My time will be all taken up with business sessions in the mornings, musicales in the afternoons and parties in the evenings, and this is as big a whirl as any human being can encompass in twenty-four hours of each day for two weeks and still keep his equilibrium. Therefore, the earliest we could make an appointment would be on the 21st and since that's pretty close to Christmas you probably won't want to come down to New York at that time of the year. I'll wait then until I hear further from you.

With kindest regards, I am
Cordially,
Ward French

December 6th, 1948

Dear Mr. French:

Thank you very much for your letter of December third.

You have my sympathy for the frightening orgy you must now endure during your annual Community Concert Conference. After such an ordeal I hate to tell you that December 21st would suit me well to come to New York as I am free of professional engagements during that week. I admire your courage and good sportsmanship to make the suggestion so soon following such an exhausting conference. I can arrange to be in New York from December 20th to the evening of December 23rd so if you will make an appointment for me and ask your secretary to advise me at the earliest convenience I would appreciate it. The matter of train and hotel reservations may be difficult at that time.

Will you also please advise how such an audition is arranged, the length of programme and any other details I might find useful?

Your Canadian singer, Jean Watson, gave a beautiful performance yesterday in the Mahler Symphony with the New York Philharmonic.

With kind thoughts and every good wish that you will keep a steady equilibrium until after December 21st.

Yours very sincerely,
Frances James

December 13, 1948

Dear Miss James:

I am setting up an audition for you for Tuesday, December 21st, at Steinway Hall at 3 o'clock. Hope this gives you enough time to make your train and hotel reservations.

I suggest that your prepare enough material to make about a half hour of singing. I suggest a couple of German lieder, a couple of French songs, two or three English songs, and an aria; and from these headings, would choose the things you feel most comfortable in singing ...

Cordially,
Ward French

Frances James's audition took place in Steinway Hall before an assembled group of managers in the employment of the concert agency. She chose as her accompanist Arpad Shandor, with whom she had worked for the Washington concert four years earlier and who enjoyed a reputation as one of the best accompanists in the United States. Her audition program included songs by Mozart, Schubert, and French and Canadian composers in a cross-section approximating her typical repertoire when on tour across Canada. Despite the management's request for her to sing an aria, she refused to do so on the grounds that her recital program never included operatic arias. To sing them outside of their operatic context with the orchestral part reduced to piano accompaniment was against her artistic scruples. After congratulating Frances on her performance and comparing her interpretation of *lieder* to that of Lotte Lehmann, they offered her a contract with the management agency of $450 per concert. That sum was to be broken down into two segments: the artist's fee and the cost of production. Her fee was to amount to $150, while the remaining $300 would be used for publicity and fee for the management agency. As a singer, she was responsible for paying her own accompanists. The disproportionate components of the fee, coupled with Ward French's demeanour toward her throughout the nine months of correspondence with him, incensed the soprano, who turned down the offer and returned to Canada.

From the tone of his letters and from the episode of the New York audition, Ward French may seem to have been a businessman whose concerns were not with the cultural welfare of small communities but rather with the profit-making aspect of his company. He was in the business of selling talent, and he seemed to capitalize upon the Canadian market, which was at that time wide open. He also recognized the revenue-making potential of community volunteers, whose unpaid labour to raise subscription money contributed income for the New York management agency. His patronizing tone toward Canada's leading singer showed an insensitivity toward Canadian artists in general and demonstrated a musical judgment of questionable value.

The Community Concert Series in general represented a u.s. monopoly over the Canadian concert scene through a network of smaller communities, tending to starve out Canadian talent by reducing the opportunity for a domestic artist not on the American management's circuit to perform on home ground. A domestic artist wishing to perform in concerts across Canada frequently encountered the response that the season in a particular town was completely booked by Community Concerts and that the concert budget was depleted.

The whole concept that concerts in smaller Canadian communities should be arranged by a New York agency was eventually refuted in the Canadian press. There was considerable outcry both in *Collier's* magazine and in the *Globe and Mail* over the right of a large management agency to hold a monopoly over the quality and quantity of community concerts in the United States and Canada.[63] It is equally astonishing, in retrospect, to realize that a small group of people, headed by Ward French, was largely responsible for shaping the musical tastes of such a large number of communities across this continent. The need for a Canadian artist to go to the expense of travelling to New York for an audition in order to be able to sing in Canadian towns also came into question. In 1949 this situation was remedied through the establishment of audition centres in Toronto and Montreal.

As a result of the controversy, Ward French published an 'Open Letter to Officers and Committee Members of Canadian Community Concert Associations,' in response to all the accusations. The document includes statements about the benefits of the Community Concert Series Associations to the public in the Canadian interior, the profusion of aspiring performers whose numbers exceed the needs of the audiences who subscribe to the concert series, and the fact that performers acquire greatness only upon attaining an international reputation. In an effort to demonstrate that there has been no discrimination against Canadian artists, French lists the names of those whose contributions to the international scene he found impressive: 'I feel a deep responsibility, not only to Canadian musical interests, but to my many personal friends in Canada. However, since Community Concerts has never been able to solve the problem in the United States of local artists, I don't see how it can ever solve the general chronic problem of local Canadian artists, which is the same.'

The document concludes with a recommendation: 'We want to be sure that some of Canada's exceptional talent does not escape our attention. Therefore, Columbia plans to set up annual auditions in Toronto and Montreal, and we plan to start these this coming September. Just *good* artists will not make the grade. Only where we discover exceptional qualifications for competition in a world market, will these artists be offered Columbia management, and then they will be offered to the international music audiences on a par with the best the world has to offer.'

All the points in Ward French's 'Open Letter' seem to be directly related to his correspondence with Frances James, right down to her challenge of the necessity for Canadian artists to travel to New York in order to audition for prospective concert tours in Canada. At the height of the controversy the controller of revenue of Ontario discovered that during all the years of Community Concerts Incorporated operations in Canada, no Canadian tax had been paid nor had the organization produced a scholarship for deserving young local talent. The money raised in Canadian communities went directly to New York. Concurrent with the revelation of this information, Frances James submitted a brief to the recently constituted Massey Commission on her experiences as a Canadian artist in the concert field. In 1950 a *New York Times* article carried the news that Ward French had been relieved of his duties. No public explanation for this act was given by the board of directors of Community Concerts Incorporated.

Because of the formation of the Royal Commission on National Development in the Arts, Letters and Sciences (Massey Commission) in 1949, Canada was sensitized to questions of cultural importance; the commission's function was to conduct an inquiry across the country into the state of the arts during this post-war period. The years leading up to the formation of the commission can be viewed as a period of struggle for a Canadian cultural identity. Seen within that context, Frances James's encounter with the American Community Concerts organization met with considerable interest and dismay in the artistic world. The singer's fight was on behalf of all Canadian artists and her experiences were of great interest to the members of the commission. She was asked to prepare a statement on the difficulties encountered by a Canadian musician in receiving adequate training in Canada, and on the problems facing the artist in retaining a Canadian identity once the training had been completed. She submitted her brief to the royal commission on 1 March 1950, and a considerable amount of her information was incorporated into the commission's report.

4

The making of a Canadian composer
in the 1940s

MURRAY ADASKIN'S YEARS OF APPRENTICESHIP

The 1940s marked the third decade of Murray Adaskin's professional activities as a violinist in chamber and orchestral music. The decade also signified a turning-point in his career, as the musician who had been gravitating toward writing all along decided to begin composition lessons in earnest. At the age of forty he made the bold move that was to change the course of his career.

By the time Murray started his composition lessons with John Weinzweig in 1946, he had behind him eleven seasons with the Toronto Symphony Orchestra, at least ten consecutive seasons of performing in *Messiah* under the baton of Sir Ernest MacMillan, and thirteen years of radio experience, along with fifteen annual performances of the *St Matthew Passion*. He was the leader of the nationally known chamber group, first called the Banff Springs Hotel Trio and then the Toronto Trio, which had given concerts not only in Banff and Toronto but also across Canada. His performance with radio orchestras for many commercial and non-commercial shows date from the infancy of broadcasting in Canada and associate him with the development of radio right up to the new programming developments of the CBC in the years after the war.

The chamber group was unique in Canada not only for its longevity – it existed for twenty-one years – but also for the quality of music it performed. It alternated summers in Banff (up to 1941) and winters in Toronto, with the Toronto activities becoming a year-round commitment between 1941 and 1952. The trio performed all the masterpieces of the classical repertoire for its instrumental combination, as well as many arrangements of pieces from the classical, folk-song, and light music repertoire. The trio also gave daily trans-Canada radio broadcasts, achieving a national reputation.

In addition to the group's regular activities at the Royal York Hotel, it also performed in the city's major halls, such as Hart House, the Art Gallery, and the Conservatory. Its touring schedule had to be geographically restricted to smaller Ontario towns such as Peterborough and Sudbury, because the regular engagement at the Royal York Hotel prevented the players' being absent for lengthy periods of time. During the Banff years, the trio frequently gave concerts across Canada in towns located along the westward route. On those occasions the group often combined forces with Frances James.

At times Murray also appeared as soloist apart from his trio, particularly in concerts with Frances, as in their 1949 cross-country tour. Murray, who always made a point of playing as many Canadian compositions as possible, featured his own violin sonata as well as Jean Coulthard's *Two Shakespeare Sonnets*, set to music for voice, violin, and piano and originally dedicated to the Adaskins. In later years he played the Weinzweig *Violin Sonata* many times.

Murray owned a Stradivarius, which he played with all the loving care such an instrument demands. He still remembers Kathleen Parlow's words that while a Guarneri can be played well immediately, it takes considerable time to learn how to play a Stradivarius. One must learn how to coax the beauty out of it. For his performances with the Toronto Trio Murray used his Stradivarius.

The story of the acquisition of the violin and the events that occurred subsequently constitute an interesting episode in a life whose direction was frequently shaped by destiny and coincidences. In 1938 Murray paid one of his occasional visits to New York, with the intent of selling his violin and purchasing a better one. On his visit to the Wurlitzer violin department he saw and played an exquisite Stradivarius. Although the beauty of the sound haunted him, he did not allow himself to get overly excited because the price tag of ten thousand dollars placed the violin completely beyond his range. During the same New York visit he was invited to the home of F.N., a rich American benefactor who had first met and befriended Murray while vacationing at the Banff Springs Hotel. Upon hearing about the instrument, his American friend insisted that the musician acquire the Stradivarius. Since Murray could not even consider such a price, the American purchased it as a gift to his Canadian friend and as a token of his esteem for the musician's artistry, which had afforded him many enjoyable moments in Banff. Murray's protests were to no avail. He not only found himself the possessor of an original Stradivarius but returned to Canada armed with a personal letter from the benefactor indicating Murray's legal ownership of the instrument.

Some years later, when Murray was living in Saskatoon, he heard of his American benefactor's death, which was precipitated by his unfortunate drinking habit. Since he had no immediate family, the man had bequeathed all of his estate to a friend. Shortly thereafter, Murray received a letter from the lawyer of F.N.'s friend, saying that in his will F.N. had also mentioned the Stradivarius. This instrument was therefore legally the friend's inheritance, stated the lawyer, and should be returned by Murray immediately. The violin was Murray's most prized possession, to which he had grown totally attached. Parting from it would have been not only painful, but unthinkable. Since the idea of embarking upon a lawsuit was inimical to the very essence of his philosophy, there was only one recourse. Murray sent F.N.'s letter explaining Murray's legal ownership of the Stradivarius to the lawyer, requesting that he destroy it, and offering to purchase the violin from the estate for whatever was the fair price at that time.

The lawyer, stunned by the facts and by Murray's honesty, agreed to sell him the violin at a very modest price. Despite its reasonableness, however, the price once again presented a financial obstacle to the musician, who had just embarked upon his new university career. For this transaction Murray solicited the help of a friend in Saskatoon, Fred Mendel, the owner of a major meat-packing plant, a great patron of the arts, and a remarkable human being. Mendel immediately procured a loan for the musician to cover the entire amount, restoring the Stradivarius to its rightful owner. As collateral for Mendel's generosity in acting as guarantor for the loan, Murray insisted that Mendel accept the oil painting of David Milne's *Trillium*, which constituted part of the musician's private collection. On one occasion, shortly after Murray had discharged about sixty per cent of the debt, Mendel invited the Adaskins to dinner and announced to the dumbfounded violinist his intention to pay off the outstanding balance personally. Moreover, he returned the Milne painting, stating that he would not even have accepted it originally as collateral had he not known that his assuming the painting was the only condition under which Murray would consider the loan.

This gesture typified Fred Mendel's kindness and humanity. In him Murray found a sincerity and generosity to be respected and loved. It is gratifying that a man of the highest moral standards, like Murray Adaskin, should have experienced human kindness in the midst of so much human greed. It is a case of poetic justice, therefore, that he, himself a generator of human kindness and source of inspiration to countless people, should have received such generosity. The Stradivarius remained in Murray's possession until his arrival in Victoria.

Throughout his three decades as a performing musician Murray's proclivity toward composing became increasingly evident. His early practical experiences as a conductor and later as a performer in radio shows where transpositions and musical arrangements were standard procedure taught him more about orchestration than he could have learned in any class-room. His work with the Toronto Trio demanded the creation of instant arrangements of classical and popular music to suit the combination of instruments. In his concerts with Frances James he frequently composed violin obbligato lines to accompany the voice. This practical experience resulted in a facility for writing for orchestral instruments and an outstanding sense of orchestral colour.

As early as 1934 Murray had composed a song for his wife on the occasion of their third wedding anniversary, basing it on Blake's poem, 'The Shepherd.' Some time later he wrote a piece for Alexander Chuhaldin's Melodic Strings. In celebration of the one-hundredth performance on the CBC by that group, Chuhaldin had the idea of dedicating an entire concert to compositions by the orchestral players. Murray's piece for string orchestra was subsequently performed by the group. .

His earliest attempts at formal composition lessons occurred toward the end of the 1930s, when he approached Leo Smith for instruction in harmony, theory, and counterpoint. Smith was one of the few teachers of harmony in Toronto at the time. Murray remembers him as a sweet, dreamy character, who was considered to be a good cellist although somewhat old-fashioned, and whose performances were liberally peppered with glissandi between all the positions.

I would come into the room to find him with his hands behind his back looking out the window of the Conservatory onto College Street. I was instructed to enter without knocking, and upon my having done that, he would just stand there in dead silence, without moving. I would sit down, begin perspiring, wondering what was going to happen next, and after what seemed like an eternity he would suddenly turn around and say, 'What is Oswald Roberts doing these days, dear boy?' Now, Oswald Roberts was a good cellist, who played in the symphony and radio orchestras around town. Only after having answered his question would we then get down to work.

The first thing that he hammered into me was to avoid consecutive fifths, fourths, and octaves, never even attempting to offer an explanation for this practice. Now at that time, I was playing purely intuitively. If anybody had asked me the difference between a major and a minor scale, I probably would not have been able to answer them. I knew, however, that Debussy's music enchanted me, and it was full of these forbidden intervals. Had Leo Smith only explained to me about the differing approaches to theory throughout the history of music it would have relieved me of my confusion.

Needless to say, Murray's lessons with Leo Smith were not of long duration. His next attempt at formal lessons occurred some time later with Sir Ernest MacMillan. The conductor, who was impressed with Murray's composition for Chuhaldin's string orchestra, offered him a scholarship to study with him. Finally, Murray thought, he would be able to find out how and why one deals with consecutive fifths and octaves!

The first question Sir Ernest asked me was whether I knew Bach's 'Air on the G String.' I had played it innumerable times, but when he requested that I write it out by memory I became so confused that it did not occur to me that the accompaniment was in octaves. I had never been asked to do that in my life. That was my first lesson.

In other lessons he would sit down at the piano and play entire excerpts from Wagner operas. It was nice to hear, but it did not bear much relationship to what I was after: it did not teach me anything. At subsequent lessons he would give me a bass line and ask me to fill the three voices above it.

After about ten lessons I quit. I was having trouble with my eyes, and straining was giving me terrible headaches.

Murray quit because he found that these lessons provided him with no more answers than the previous attempt, and he used the eye condition as a reinforcing factor. In 1946 he decided to have another attempt at composition lessons. Percy Faith, a colleague of Murray's, had recommended Louis Waizman. The day he was to have his first lesson with Waizman, Murray was persuaded over lunch with Reginald Godden to approach John Weinzweig. Godden, who had befriended Harry Somers, a student of Weinzweig, strongly recommended the composer. 'It was as if someone made a gong go off in my head,' says Murray. 'I went right to the telephone, cancelled my lesson with Waizman, phoned John Weinzweig, and asked him if he had room for one more student. He said "Yes," and that is how it all started. It was really Reg Godden who put me on the right track, in fact he put many people on the right track.'

John Weinzweig was one of the first Canadian composers to experiment with elements of serial technique. He was considered at that time to be the most avant-garde musician in Toronto, exploring new directions in composition in a city whose musical tastes were dominated by such traditionally oriented composers as Healey Willan. Weinzweig had developed the reputation of an outspoken proponent for Canadian music and as an outstanding teacher. Trained in Canada – Healey Willan, Leo Smith, and Sir Ernest MacMillan were his early teachers – he obtained his M MUS degree at the Eastman School of Music at twenty-five. When Murray began composition studies with him, the student was seven years older than his teacher.

During his lessons Murray always confronted Weinzweig with reams of material. In one year he covered harmony, theory, and counterpoint. Although Murray found the exercise of writing fugues somewhat less than scintillating, he proceeded to write several, for the practical reason that he wanted to learn how to develop musical material. From his studies of counterpoint the composer discovered how to deal with and develop four, five, and six voices.

Murray's studies with Weinzweig extended over a period of four years. They were enjoyable years and represented a crucial transition in his career from that of a performer to that of a composer. Even today Murray feels indebted to Weinzweig for his encouragement and support during this transitional period. Weinzweig was one of the few people who took the musician's efforts to compose seriously.

Murray's short hours at the Royal York Hotel allowed him to spend his afternoons working on composition assignments. On the top floor of the hotel, he had a studio with a rented upright piano, where he was able to work undisturbed. 'Fran always gave me my lunch in my briefcase. Everybody thought that I had music in it, but I really had my lunch with a thermos of tea in it. I would open up all the food and sit down at the piano doing my harmony exercises for John. First harmony and theory, then counterpoint, orchestration, and score reading. I did a lot of work, and started bringing him original compositions every afternoon.' Eventually the intensity of the composition studies placed a high demand on Murray's time during the weekends. He found a substitute to play for him at the hotel on the weekends in order to be able to compose.

Murray and Weinzweig, who enjoyed a close personal friendship at the time, watched with excitement every new composition that was produced and performed in Toronto. They shared their enthusiasm at witnessing new styles developing and musical directions expanding. Weinzweig's *Divertimento No 1* for flute had just been composed when Murray began his lessons with him. It became one of Murray's favourite works, one that he could sing from cover to cover.

Several compositions were written by Murray during his four-year period of studies with John Weinzweig: the *Sonata for Violin and Piano, premièred* by the composer at the Harbord Collegiate Concert on 17 April 1947, with Louis Crerar at the piano; the *Suite for Orchestra* in three movements, dedicated to Geoffrey Waddington and first broadcast under the conductor's baton by the CBC Symphony Orchestra on 22 June 1949; *Epitaph*, a song for soprano and piano to a text by Guillaume Apollinaire; and the *Suite for Strings*, dedicated to Weinzweig. *Epitaph*, composed in 1948 and dedicated to Frances James, was first performed by her on 13 June 1952, for the International Service of the CBC. Based on a text touching in its simplicity, it records the words engraved by the poet Apollinaire on the gravestone of Henri Rousseau (1844–1910), French painter and former Customs officer:

> Hear us, kindly Rousseau,
> We greet you.
> Delaunay, his wife, Monsieur Queval and I.

Let our baggage through the customs to the sky.
We bring you canvas, brush and paint of ours,
During eternal leisure, radiant
As you once drew my portrait, you still paint
The face of the stars.

The *Suite for Strings*, composed in 1949, received its first performance on the CBC Vancouver station, under the baton of Albert Steinberg. Murray's only piece in a twelve-tone idiom, this suite never quite satisfied him. He felt uncomfortable with that style of writing and considered it an idiom inimical to his musical impulses. When, some twenty years later, Boyd Neel expressed interest in performing the *Suite for Strings* with his chamber group at the Aldeburgh Festival in England, Murray did not wish to have it publicly performed.

In 1949, Charles Jones, whose friendship with the Adaskins had continued over the years despite his move to New York City, asked Murray whether he would be interested in a scholarship for summer study with Darius Milhaud at the Music Academy of the West in Santa Barbara. Jones, who was by then well established as a composition teacher in New York, was the French composer's teaching associate in the summers at Santa Barbara. In the early 1950s both Milhaud and Jones transferred their summer activities to the Aspen Summer Music School in Colorado, where the French composer's presence served as a stimulus to students from all over America.

Darius Milhaud was one of the few twentieth-century composers to explore a broad variety of forms and styles. Operas, ballets, incidental music, symphonies, concertos, choral works, chamber music, and songs were composed by him with seeming ease. Early in life he rebelled against German musical ideas, those of Wagner in particular, while the music of Debussy and Mussorgsky became his compositional guides. In the early twenties he was drawn into a group of composers, artists, and writers considered as the French avant-garde. The composers Georges Auric, Louis Durey, Francis Poulenc, Germaine Tailleferre, and the Swiss Arthur Honegger, who shared a concert program on one occasion, were dubbed *Les Six* by a critic, a name that seems to have clung to them despite the fact that their paths led them eventually in divergent directions. Erik Satie and Jean Cocteau were among Milhaud's early soul mates.

Milhaud came to Oakland, California, after the fall of France in 1940, and taught composition at Mills College. Although seven years later he resumed his teaching career in Paris, he continued his Mills College activities in alternate years until his retirement. Milhaud's interest in experimenting with new musical directions never diminished, and this enthusiasm was transmitted to his students.

Jones's suggestion that Murray study with Milhaud was prompted by Murray's completion of his *Suite for Orchestra*, which Jones felt should be sent to the French composer for his examination and appraisal. Simultaneously with this development, Weinzweig had received a letter from Aaron Copland, announcing his willingness to teach a Canadian student at the Tanglewood Summer School. Weinzweig had intended to recommend Murray Adaskin to Copland. Upon hearing about the Santa Barbara offer, however, he urged Murray to accept it without hesitation. Murray remembers those exciting years:

Harry Freedman and I were fellow students of John's. We used to often walk home after our composition lessons, and I found those walks very interesting because we would discuss the kind of music we were planning to write, how we were going to go about it, and who our favourite composers were.

I would have loved the experience of studying with Copland, since I am very fond of his personality and of his music. It just seems to go down with me in the most natural and wonderful way. Perhaps that is why I so enjoyed Ives when I first discovered him.

The summer of 1949, then, presented Murray with his first opportunity to study composition outside of Canada. He had respected Charles Jones's compositional artistry and was overwhelmed at the thought of studying with someone of Milhaud's stature. The school was about fourteen miles south of Santa Barbara, and the classes took place at Carpenteria in a building handsomely situated in the hills. Murray's class during that first nine-week course with Milhaud included among its eight members Josepha Heifetz, daughter of the violinist, and Burt Bacharach, who later distinguished himself in the field of popular music. Murray first glimpsed the great man when Milhaud, so large he seemed 'a mountain in repose,'[1] with jet-black hair and a serious facial expression, wheeled himself into the studio in his wheelchair. Milhaud was the victim of a walking disability. He seldom left his wheelchair, except to mount a podium to conduct his own works, a process painful to watch as the massive composer slid his way across the stage with the help of two canes.

Murray soon found out that the serious countenance was a mask that hid an impish and almost sardonic sense of humour, the same type of humour revealed in Milhaud's many compositions. The Canadian composer remembers the day a local photographer about to take a picture of Milhaud asked him to smile. 'Composers have nothing to smile about' was Milhaud's stern response, while simultaneously turning to his class and winking at them. On another occasion an elderly gentleman, one of the wealthy patrons of the school, handed a bouquet of flowers to the composer. After a friendly exchange of words, as the visitor turned his back, Milhaud, who was allergic to flowers, made a sour grimace. Just at that moment the man turned around, to find the most angelic expression on the composer's face. All of this occurred in front of the class, who tried with great difficulty to contain their laughter.

Murray remembers, too, the day an admirer handed Milhaud a photograph of the composer in order to obtain his autograph. Milhaud looked at the man, proceeded to take out his pen, and very calmly drew a cat moustache over his likeness. Then he signed his name and handed the photo back to the horrified man. 'I have no idea why Milhaud did this,' Murray says. 'He had a kind of a perverse sense of humour. This man was a stranger, and Milhaud did not know what to write for him. So he created something funny. He was always completely honest, a delightful character who hated any kind of sham.'

It did not take long for Murray Adaskin and Darius Milhaud to establish a special rapport, a bond that lasted until the French composer's death. During the first year of his studies at the Music Academy of the West Murray composed his *Canzona*, for violin and piano, to which he later added a second movement, calling the composition *Canzona and Rondo*. In Murray's own words:

In the *Canzona* we were aiming for the long line. I remember reading about it in one of Copland's books, where he stated that while writing a long line was the goal of every young composer, not everyone was capable of attaining that goal. It could be that because I was a violinist, I instinctively thought in terms of the long singing lines, which are manifested in the *Canzona*. About two-thirds of the way through the piece I came back to the opening theme but in a different key. I used this theme for a few bars, then I held one note while the piano underwent an interesting modulation resulting in a return to the original key. Instead of repeating the theme in its original key, I proceeded to introduce a new theme.

I played this composition in Milhaud's class, accompanied by Josepha Heifetz at the piano, who was a very gifted pianist and composer. When I came to the long-held note in my manuscript, Milhaud turned to the class, and without interrupting my playing, said 'the modulation is an indication of Murray Adaskin's wonderful musicianship.' I was so moved by his compliment that I almost burst into tears.

The *Canzona* was first performed by Murray in a faculty concert at the Music Academy of the West on 30 August 1949. It was the only student work on a program that included music by Bach, Mozart, Milhaud, Mendelssohn, and Hindemith.

Frances, who joined her husband in Santa Barbara during his second summer there, had a busy time practising new repertoire for her upcoming recitals and giving the occasional performance on campus and in the musicians' homes. It was as a result of one of these musicales that Roman Totenberg eventually introduced her to Peter Fritsch, which led to her recording of Hindemith's *Das Marienleben*. Milhaud felt a particular affection for the personality and artistry of Frances James. She was one of the few Canadian artists of the time to have in her repertoire the songs of Fauré, one of Milhaud's favourite composers. Murray remembers Milhaud's discourses on Fauré's music in class, illustrated by his singing of each song. That was the first time that Murray realized the extent of Fauré's artistry. It was in Santa Barbara that Frances learned Milhaud's song cycle *Rêves*, which she performed in concert both in the Music Academy of the West and later on the CBC, to the French composer's utter delight and satisfaction.

The Adaskins lived in the Gould Mansion, a large house they shared with Charles Jones and Soulima Stravinsky. Soulima, who was Igor Stravinsky's son, had a little boy nicknamed Zee-Zee, five years old at the time, who loved to stand outside Frances's door on the second floor of the mansion, listening to her practise. One day Zee-Zee decided to imitate the soprano's vocalizing of a chromatic scale, an act that greatly amused his grandfather, who was a frequent visitor to the mansion. On the occasion Igor Stravinsky turned to Frances and said, 'we have a twelve-toner in the family.' The Adaskins had frequent opportunities to meet with Stravinsky, but it was with Igor's son, Soulima, that Murray established a warm rapport that carried on through the Saskatoon days, when Soulima performed his father's piano sonata at the University of Saskatchewan.

The summers of 1949 and 1950 were spent thus, studying with Milhaud in Santa Barbara. Murray studied with him for one more summer session in Aspen, Colorado, in 1953. The Frenchman left an indelible mark on Murray's development as composer. By the time of his first exposure to Milhaud in 1949 Murray was already a recognized composer in Toronto, whose works had received public performances over the CBC. Upon his arrival in Santa Barbara, therefore, he was able to produce not only scores of music already written, but discs of full orchestral performances of these works, to the amazement of his fellow class-mates. After his visit to Toronto in 1951, when he was impressed by the CBC's encouragement of Canadian music, Milhaud was able to explain to his students the reason for Murray's recorded performances of his compositions: 'That is the way they do it in Canada,' he would say proudly.

In June 1951, Murray arranged for the CBC to do two broadcasts of Milhaud's music on the 'Wednesday Night' series, one an orchestral concert conducted by the composer, the other a chamber recital. The second concert featured the Dembeck String Quartet, with Madeleine Milhaud as narrator.[2] It was on this occasion that Frances James gave the Canadian *première* of the composer's *Rêves*.

Although Murray did not play in the CBC orchestra at that concert, he attended every rehearsal. He recalls one particular moment, which so vividly encapsulated the Frenchman's personality:

There was one passage in which he kept insisting that the orchestra was too loud. He never raised his voice, but simply said 'Gentlemen, it is too loud; make it pianissimo, please.' He managed to have the orchestra produce a sound that I had never heard from them before. There is a way of achieving a pianissimo that carries as if by magic. Suddenly, in the middle of the passage the drummer's metal folding chair collapsed on the cement floor. For the first time Milhaud shouted, 'Too loud!'

The orchestra went to pieces. He had a wit about him that was just really wonderful, and from then on the orchestra just fell in love with him. At another place in the same symphony, the concert-master had a two-bar solo, a very exposed part, which he performed with all the schmaltz he could muster; lots of vibrato that would melt the soul of a monster. Milhaud turned to the bassoon player, who was not playing and had a forty-bar rest, saying 'No schmaltz please!' The concert-master understood immediately and rectified his performance upon the return of the offending passage.

Milhaud had a wonderful way of talking to people, and of course he had such a strong personality that you listened to what he said.

One of Murray's longest works was composed during his period of study with Milhaud. The *Ballet Symphony*, scored for two flutes and piccolo, two oboes and English horn, two clarinets and bass clarinet, four horns, three trumpets, three trombones and tuba, percussion, piano, harp, and strings, was first conceived as a march – *March No 1 for Orchestra*, the first in a series of three – when commissioned in 1950 by the CBC for the 'Opportunity Knocks' program, produced by John Adaskin. It was at Milhaud's suggestion that Murray added other movements to it, converting it into a ballet. The work in final form has six movements: March, Allegro, Pas de Deux, Fugue, Adagio, and Finale (Rondo Allegro). Milhaud felt that ballet music would more readily find performance opportunities than a regular symphonic work. Ironically, Milhaud's suggestion, based on his own experiences and making considerable sense in Europe with its many ballet companies, was unsuited to the Canadian cultural climate. After the initial performance of the work in 1952 at a concert sponsored by the Canadian League of Composers, Murray approached the head of the Winnipeg Ballet for a possible choreography of the work, only to receive a non-committal response. The work was performed two more times within the next six years, never to be heard in a live performance again.

At the end of the third summer of studies with Milhaud, the French composer advised Murray that the time had come for him to stop taking lessons. Murray remembers Milhaud's words:

'You must stop studying. You must learn to create on your own.' Composing my next piece, after I had left Milhaud, was sheer torture. I almost cried in places, wishing I could get some advice, but I had to do it on my own. I had to solve these things on my own. And exactly what Milhaud predicted did happen. I acquired more confidence, became more mobile, and did not need to lean on teachers for advice. It gave me impetus and courage to do it my own way. It was one of the most cruel experiences I ever remember going through, but it served as an invaluable lesson to me.

Murray's friendship with Milhaud continued during his Saskatoon days, when he organized a concert at the University of Saskatchewan in commemoration of the composer's seventieth birthday.

THE CANADIAN COMPOSER SPEAKS OUT

The 1940s reverberated with rumblings of new sounds produced by the first generation of Toronto composers to have obtained most of their musical education in this country. This generation was to break with tradition and set new directions in Canadian music. A number of young composers, students and colleagues of John Weinzweig, were beginning to assert their individual style with Weinzweig in the lead, free of the fetters of nineteenth- and twentieth-century European post-Romanticism still propagated by prominent older musicians in Canada.

For most Toronto composers the 1940s constituted a decade of serious study of composition. Although in formative phases of their professional lives, they began to produce works of significance that were to set new standards for future generations of Canadian composers and were to shape the course of musical composition in this country. Murray Adaskin was one of the core group of energetic musicians surrounding John Weinzweig. In the late forties, this post-war student group was guided by their musical ideas and sense of nationalism. The more prominent of the group included Harry Freedman, Harry Somers, Barbara Pentland, and Godfrey Ridout. In Toronto, Weinzweig, who was only in his thirties at the time, assumed the role of mentor to many of this generation.

Harry Freedman, an English hornist, joined the TSO in 1946, concurrently with his initiation of composition studies with Weinzweig. A fellow composition student with Murray Adaskin, he produced between 1945 and 1950 a number of significant pieces for string and full orchestra. Barbara Pentland moved to Toronto in 1942 after studies at the Juilliard School of Music and in Tanglewood with Copland. Already in 1939 she had composed the *Five Preludes* and the *Rhapsody*, followed in 1941 by her *Piano Quartet* and *Studies in Line* for piano. Her work was chosen in 1942 for the first all-Canadian concert in New York, sponsored by the United States League of Composers.[3] The program of this important event also included compositions by Louis Applebaum, Hector Gratton, André Mathieu, Godfrey Ridout, and John Weinzweig. Pentland's biographers summarize her style of the 1940s: 'Her praise for the simple approach of Satie, the non-emotional music of Hindemith, and the rhythmic vitality of Stravinsky is in reality a description of her own objectives at that time.'[4] Later, in the mid-1950s, she adopted the serial technique.

Although only in his twenties during the epoch-making period, Harry Somers was involved in Canadian music making both as a pianist and as a composer. Two of his piano recitals at the Royal Conservatory of Music in Toronto hold considerable historical importance – one dedicated to the music of Barbara Pentland and the other of his own music. A Weinzweig student throughout the 1940s, Somers composed several significant works during this period, including two string quartets, a woodwind quartet, *Sketches for Orchestra*, *Scherzo for Strings*, and *North Country*.

Godfrey Ridout had composed and taught in Toronto since 1939. In addition to writing scores for radio dramas and for the National Film Board, and making symphonic arrangements of popular music for the CBC, he was involved in other cultural areas, contributing articles to publications and acting on the editorial board of the *Canadian Review of Music and Art*.

Other composers who lived outside of the Toronto area kept in contact with new developments in Toronto. These included such prominent figures as Louis Applebaum, music director of the National Film Board from 1942 to 1948 and later administrator of music at the Stratford Festival; Saskatchewan-born Robert Fleming, affiliated with the NFB first in Ottawa, then in Montreal; and Lorne Betts, who settled in Hamilton after his composition studies with John Weinzweig and became the city's most prominent musician. Another composer of film scores at this period was Eldon Rathburn. A native of New Brunswick, who studied composition, organ, and piano at the Toronto Conservatory of Music in the late 1930s, he spent three decades in Ottawa as staff composer for the National Film Board.

In Montreal a major musical force was Jean Papineau-Couture. Well established as a teacher of theory, *solfège*, harmony, and counterpoint, he was prolific throughout the 1940s in the writing of chamber, piano, vocal, and orchestral music. Other Montreal composers of the period include François Morel, Pierre Mercure, and Clermont Pépin. From 1946 to 1949 Pépin studied piano, composition, and conducting in Toronto; during this early period in his professional career he had already produced a number of significant works such as a piano concerto, a string quartet, and a symphony.

Montreal was also the home of conductor, composer, violinist, and teacher Alexander Brott, and of Violet Archer. Although she was later to settle in Edmonton, during the 1940s she was percussionist in the Montreal Women's Symphony Orchestra, and she commuted to New York and Yale in pursuit of her studies with Bartók and Hindemith respectively. Selected works of this period included her *Fanfare and Passacaglia, Sonata for Flute, Clarinet, and Piano, Fantasy for Violin and Piano,* and a string quartet.

The lot of the Canadian composer in the post-war era was not an easy one. Obtaining performances of their works was not a simple matter at a time when the conservative taste of audiences resisted being exposed to what was viewed as the avant-garde in music. The only way to have their works heard was for composers to organize and perform their own concerts, as happened with the Harbord Collegiate concert of 1947. The new generation was waiting to be heard, and the establishment of the Canadian League of Composers in 1951 was to provide a step toward satisfying this need.

In the 1940s and 1950s the Canadian Broadcasting Corporation provided a major and almost the sole source of support to young composers. As early as 1939 Samuel Hersenhoren conducted a series of fifty weekly concerts – 'Canadian Snapshots' – featuring new Canadian works. A year later CBC Montreal honoured J.J. Gagnier, Hector Gratton, and Claude Champagne with broadcasts of their music, while through the series 'Canadian Music in Wartime' the corporation commissioned local composers to provide music for radio drama.

Generally, during the war years Montreal-based Jean-Marie Beaudet and Toronto-based Samuel Hersenhoren were major proponents of new Canadian music on the radio. Throughout the 1943 and 1944 such programs as 'Music for Radio,' 'CBC Concert Hour,' 'Music of the New World,' 'Three Canadian Composers' Programmes,' and 'Canadian Music of the War Years' featured works of Pentland, Ridout, Cable, Weinzweig, Fleming, Champagne, Gagnier, Gratton, Coulthard, and Alexander Brott, among others.[5] Later, Neil Chotem, Morris Surdin, and Lucio Agostini were among the composers commissioned to write music for dramas presented on the 'CBC Wednesday Night' programs.

By 1952 the CBC Symphony Orchestra was formally established, even though throughout the previous decade a regular broadcasting orchestra had already been in existence. This was to be the body to play new Canadian compositions. Between 1952 and 1964 the orchestra consisted of approximately eighty players, about sixty per cent of whom were also members of the Toronto Symphony Orchestra.[6] Geoffrey Waddington, its founder and music director, intended the CBC to have a resident orchestra consisting of the best players in the country. Many Canadian works were commissioned during Waddington's tenure, creating a direct causal link between the number of symphonic works written by major composers during the 1950s and the existence of the CBC Symphony Orchestra.

Murray recounts his experiences with that orchestra:

In those days you were not only paid a commission fee to write the work, but you also knew that you were going to get a marvellous performance with many rehearsals. I can remember when one of the pieces that I wrote was my *Violin Concerto*, and I used a big orchestra for it. The last movement had complex, shifting metric beats: a bar in 2/4 alternated with 3/4 and 3/8. The players were able to read it at sight, almost as well as they did it at the performance. That was an indication of their high quality of playing. At Geoff's instigation they had performed so much contemporary music that a new breed of orchestral musician developed, to whom new music could present no difficulty.

Two other of Murray's works commissioned by the CBC preceded the composition of the *Violin Concerto*: the *Coronation Overture* and *Serenade Concertante*. The overture, written in 1953, was one of the Canadian works *premièred* on a special broadcast on 2 June in celebration of the coronation of the young Queen Elizabeth. A short time later it received another performance in Glasgow, under Waddington's baton. The *Serenade Concertante*, composed in Saskatoon in 1954, received its *première* with the CBC Vancouver Orchestra, conducted by John Avison.

The *Violin Concerto* was performed on the CBC in April 1956, with the composer conducting the orchestra. Dedicated to and *premièred* by Roman Totenberg, the first movement was written at Aspen during the summer of 1954, while the other two were completed at Canoe Lake the following summer. Totenberg, who loved the work, wanted to perform it for the BBC Sunday afternoon 'Home Service.' The piece, considered 'too advanced' by the BBC producer, never received an airing in Britain. The *Algonquin Symphony*, performed by Waddington in May 1958, was the last of the CBC-commissioned large orchestral works Murray composed in the 1950s.

The importance of the CBC Symphony Orchestra to Canadian music in the fifties is summarized succinctly in the following letter written by Murray to Terence Gibbs:

It [the schedule of programs by the CBC Symphony Orchestra during the 1958/9 season] is truly an impressive list and should be a matter of pride to all Canadian music lovers. The orchestra has grown to maturity in a miraculously short time, and this in itself is an indication of the artistic potential of this magic land of ours.

I also doubt whether the Canadian composer could have developed so quickly without the encouragement given him by the CBC Symphony Orchestra. Our composers have had the rare and valuable experience of hearing their music played superbly and intelligently. In fact, the Canadian composer may look upon the CBC Symphony Orchestra as a kind of symphonic patron.[7]

Within this context Frances James's performances in concert of songs written by Canadian composers assume an even greater historical significance. As noted earlier, throughout the 1940s she was the only Canadian singer to disseminate the music of her contemporaries. By incorporating them into her repertoire she performed them on her cross-country tours as well as on the radio. Her keen interest in the new compositional trends and her sincere belief in the contemporary Canadian composer made her a unique spokesperson for Canadian music.

The decade of the 1940s was a fertile period for the Canadian art song. Based on texts by Apollinaire, Walt Whitman, James Joyce, Anne Marriott, John Coulter, and Francis Jammes, among others, the form flourished. Composers produced individual songs as well as song cycles. Performances given by Frances James during this period include approximately sixty-five songs, most of them first performances, written by eighteen different Canadian composers, including Alexander Brott, Murray Adaskin, Lorne Betts, Neil Chotem, Jean Coulthard, Robert Fleming, Barbara Pentland, Harry Somers, and John Weinzweig.[8] Somers's *Three Songs* on a text by Walt Whitman – 'Look Down Fair Moon,' 'After the Dazzle of the Day,' and 'A Clear Midnight,' commissioned by Forest Hill Village – were *premièred* by Frances in 1946. Pentland's *Song Cycle*, five poems on a text by Anne Marriott – 'Wheat,' 'Forest,' 'Trains,' 'Mountains,' 'Cities' – was composed between 1942 and 1948. Frances *premièred* the first three of these songs in 1947. For a long time she was the only artist to sing Weinzweig's 'Of Time, Rain, and the World' (1947), three songs based on a text from Roget's *Thesaurus* and dedicated to her.

A landmark event in the history of contemporary music in this country occurred on 17 April 1947. The concert of contemporary music at Harbord Collegiate was the first such event to feature works by the young generation of Toronto composers. Sponsored by the Ontario Department of Education under the personal direction of Major Brian S. McCool, the concert was to benefit secondary school students. It had the strictly educational purpose of touring as many schools in the province as possible in order to introduce the students to contemporary music and to establish a closer rapport between high school students and Canadian composers and performers. This was projected as the first of a number of similar tours.[9] The program included Murray's *Sonata for Violin and Piano*, which he performed to the accompaniment of Louis Crerar; Somers's *Three Songs*, with Frances James accompanied by the composer;

Somers's piano sonata, *Testament of Youth*, performed by Reginald Godden; Pentland's *Studies in Line*, also performed by Godden; three songs from Pentland's *Song Cycle*, in which the composer accompanied Frances; and Weinzweig's *Sonata in One Movement for Violin and Piano*, featuring Hyman Goodman and Reginald Godden. All works were composed between 1941 and 1946.

The uniqueness of the concert was in the presentation of works by four contemporary composers, most of whom were also featured as performers, with Frances James providing the vocal solos. The event received widespread coverage in the local press, as the *Telegram*, the *Globe and Mail*, the *Toronto Star*, *Saturday Night*, and *Canadian High News* all reacted to it. The reception accorded these pieces in the press is representative of the public's and music critics' perception of Canadian music in the post-war reconstruction period. The *Telegram* saw the Adaskin sonata as a 'very charming work, indicating a certain sympathy for modern writing forms, but holding more closely to classical affiliation. Refinement and gentleness as well as clarity of expression are its principal characteristics.' It referred to Somers as a 'Canadian composer to be considered respectfully,' whose works showed a great deal of originality. Pentland's song cycle was seen as a very ambitious work, 'in a style peculiar to Miss Pentland and often remarkably effective, but surely very, very difficult to sing, with its phrases frequently left high in the air.'[10]

The *Toronto Star*'s Augustus Bridle seems to have been somewhat confused by the whole event. Usually elegantly articulate, the music critic was obviously groping for meaningful descriptive words: 'Adaskin's violin art was vibrantly facile ... the sonata was an interesting specimen of composer-art, rather more convincing in Crerar's pianism than in most of the picturesque violin fabrications ... Congratulations to the violinist who made so cleverly atmospheric a sonata, so interesting. The work was intellectual more than melodic, or violinic [sic] – or even rhythmically pianistic.'

To Bridle, Somers's songs would have been more effective as spoken verse, while Pentland's *Studies in Line* was 'graphically picturesque of four pianistic non-objectives.' He felt that where her songs were concerned, the composer 'has a very experimental talent for vocal forms compared to her obvious talent for pianologue art.' The Weinzweig sonata, although 'erratically written by a man conscious of latent dramatic power, as yet in impressive embryo,' was a 'brilliant example of how divergent violin and piano can be in this duo-graph form of composition.'[11]

John Jocom of *Saturday Night* saw in Adaskin's sonata features quite contrary to those described by Bridle. 'The violin part in the first movement had considerable lyricism despite unorthodox melodic patterns.' Harry Somers's

Three Songs 'matched lines of near-pantheistic meaning with completely impressionistic music.' Pentland's *Studies in Line* were 'unpretentious musical abstractions,' while Weinzweig's *Sonata* had a development 'containing some of the most provocative ideas and interesting expressions of them in the entire program.' However, Pentland's songs seemed to the critic to be the most offensive on the program, and he found some of the melodic phrases 'quite inappropriate.' He mused on the fact that 'even Frances James, with a notable ability to lyricize, must have found the going tough in those melodies.'[12]

Finally, Colin Sabiston of the *Globe and Mail* found Adaskin's *Sonata* with its 'fine, smooth tone' a pleasure to listen to. Pentland's piano pieces were 'pleasant but not particularly striking – in their appeal very suggestive of many of John Donne's short fragments of impressionistic verse, mildly sensory but not memorable.' However, he felt that she was a composer of great talent 'who is basically a romantic-impressionist, but determined, in her attachment to modernism, not to write a lyric phrase for the voice if she can help it.' Yet to Sabiston, Pentland's piano background to the songs, rich in colour and texture, glowed with an emotional warmth, 'not one shred of which is reflected in the melody assigned to the voice.' He expressed the wish that when she reached middle age, the composer might become more mellow in her currently rigid outlook toward lack of lyricism. Somers's piano sonata, in contrast, was seen as a deeply moving composition and an artistically sound work, imparting promises of even better works in the future.[13]

Viewed from today's vantage-point these divergent opinions in the press have to be taken not for their content, but for what they symbolize. The Canadian composer was indeed beginning to speak out, but the language and its message were not understood. Perhaps that is the nature of all art. The artist as a leader in the socio-cultural fabric of a country must create. The significance of those creations can be evaluated only after passage of time. Perhaps today, almost four decades later, we have attained the distance that will help us place the efforts of the first post-war generation of composers into some sort of perspective.

As a composer-performer, Murray played his *Violin Sonata* on a number of other occasions, especially during his 1949 tour with Frances James, when he incorporated it into his touring repertoire. Other performers of his sonata included Elie Spivak, Lorand Fenyves, and Albert Pratz. Murray also frequently played Weinzweig's *Sonata for Violin and Piano*, thus contributing to the dissemination of contemporary Canadian compositions.

A Toronto organization possessing a surprisingly broad vision of new music and Canadian culture in general – the Community Centre of the Village of Forest Hill – occupies an important position in the history of cultural developments in Toronto from 1946 to approximately the mid-1950s. This enlightened group of citizens, many of them professionals who volunteered their time for the cause of Canadian art, devised the daring (for the times) policy of commissioning Canadian compositions for their concert series.

As already mentioned, Harry Somers received the first commission to inaugurate the series. Murray Adaskin was asked to write a string piece for the 1951–2 season; he provided his *Sonatine Baroque* for unaccompanied violin. It received its first performance on 10 March 1952 by Eugene Kash, on a program that included baroque and eighteenth-century compositions played by Kash and harpsichordist Greta Kraus. The composer expressly devised the format of the work to make it suitable to the predominant musical style of the evening. Unfortunately, the performer did not seem to do the new piece justice, as seen from the following press review:

It sounded more like meditated destruction, with an accelerated breaking down of the original notes into shivering and violently agitated discords. This was repeated twice in the first section.

The second half of the sonatine was an unwinding of a rapidly played theme that ended slowly and comparatively serenely ... Much of the fault in last night's performance may lie with the violinist. Eugene Kash seemed so preoccupied with the notes that no thought went into the actual context ... he did manage to play exceedingly well some of the more difficult double-stopped passages.[14]

In actuality, this sonatine, published by Ricordi in 1961, is in the style of a baroque *sonata da chiesa*. In a predominantly tonal idiom, its dominant-tonic key areas are offset by layers of dissonances. The second movement is based on a long spun-out melody, while the last movement contains a fugal working out of the texture. The work was eventually dedicated to Murray's violin student, Andrew Dawes, who played it throughout the 1960s in Canada as well as in Geneva.

The importance of the Forest Hill concert series to the cultural fabric of Toronto at the time cannot be overstated. The series, which took place in the Forest Hill Collegiate auditorium, presented six annual events of an amazing variety. The programming was planned so that some musical numbers at each concert would be familiar to the audiences. The presence of younger listeners was encouraged, and a 'friendly coffee hour' following each program afforded an opportunity for the audience to meet the artists.

This highly enlightened concept, however, while supportive of the contemporary Canadian composer, fulfilled only a modest function within the void of opportunities for concert performances of new works facing composers in the late forties and early fifties. The time had come for the creation of a distinct organization for composers that would promote their music and further their professional interests. The idea for a Canadian League of Composers was thus formulated in 1951.

Murray remembers vividly those early days just before the formation of the League. It all started with a phone call he received from Reginald Godden, expressing concern that something had to be done to promote the music of John Weinzweig. Godden recommended that a group of young Toronto-based composers organize a recital consisting entirely of Weinzweig's music, and that this be presented as a surprise homage to the composer. Godden recommended a number of works suitable for such a recital, including the three songs *Of Time, Rain, and the World*, to be sung by Frances James; the violin sonata, to be performed by Murray; the *Israel Sonata* for cello and piano, to be played by Isaac Mamott and Leo Barkin; with Godden himself playing Weinzweig's piano sonata. The group asked George Brough to supply the piano accompaniment for the violin sonata. The flute and oboe divertimenti that Weinzweig had just completed were to be included on the program. Geoffrey Waddington was the general choice of the organizers for conductor, and the concert was to take place at the Toronto Conservatory of Music. Tickets were to be sent out by invitation. No fee was to be charged; the performers would donate their services for this concert in honour of Weinzweig. To keep the preparations from the composer, the group solicited the help of his wife, who would make sure that he attended the concert.

The idea generated much enthusiasm for the works of a composer who, according to Murray, was 'the bad boy of music in those days.' For the average and even the trained musician Weinzweig's music was difficult to understand. It was really the first serious writing in the twelve-tone idiom in Canada. Ettore Mazzoleni, the principal of the conservatory, lauded the idea with such verve that he offered his own services as conductor for the orchestral compositions. The orchestra assembled on that occasion consisted of players in the CBC symphony. As the group's regular conductor was Geoffrey Waddington, Mazzoleni's enthusiasm resulted in his substituting for Waddington for this concert. Waddington's contribution, however, was to ensure that the orchestra players received some remuneration, by persuading the CBC to broadcast the concert.

Murray recalls that the idea for a Canadian League of Composers was spurred on by the American League of Composers, whose president at that time was John Ward, composer of the opera *The Crucible*. As an organ of their league the Americans also published their own magazine, *Modern Music*, which was read avidly by the Canadian group. John Weinzweig and Louis Applebaum, who had been in contact with Aaron Copland (a prominent member of the American League of Composers), discussed the league concept as applicable in Canada, and the idea was then further developed by the young Canadians.

Murray recollects the formative days of the league:

We all got together and felt that since we had already made such an effort, it would be time to start thinking about a Canadian League of Composers. There were many meetings before the league got organized, and when we were faced with writing up the constitution, it was Philip Clark who wrote it for us. As controller of revenue for the province of Ontario, he was a very legal-minded person, and was able to help us tremendously with the actual legal wording. He was a great enthusiast for the whole idea of the league, and he did the same for other arts groups as well.

There was the question of what standards to set and how to define a contemporary composer. Do we include people like Leo Smith, for example? We invited Healey Willan to become our first honorary member. We were callow young people, and we felt that he was an old-fashioned English Wagnerian. As I think back on it now, I regret this attitude on our part. Were I to live through this again, I would certainly put up a fight against this. Then we had to decide whether Arnold Walter belonged in our group. There had to be a manifesto, and we were a group of strong-minded young people. We joined forces with the Montreal composers, and we said that Jean Papineau-Couture should be at the top of the list.

The constitution of the league, bearing the date of 7 December 1951, with its charter granted in 1952, carried the names of eight composers. The founding fathers were John Weinzweig, Louis Applebaum, Harry Freedman, Andrew Twa, Murray Adaskin, Harry Somers, Philip Nimmons, and Samuel Dolin. The three objectives set out in the constitution at that time included: to maintain the highest standards of musical composition; to foster the education of the general public in the field of contemporary music; and to encourage the establishment of scholarships in musical composition.

The league's primary aim was to present concerts of Canadian music both at home and abroad. To this purpose they organized concerts, such as the one in the Music Division of the New York Public Library in 1953, soliciting music from their members for these events. A letter to league members on 13 October 1953 called for scores for piano trio or solo piano, violin, or cello works for the New York performance. On a later occasion music for string quartet was requested from members for a performance in Los Angeles, organized by Albert Steinberg. The league functioned thus as a management organization for any national or international institution wishing to sponsor a concert of Canadian music.

Early in 1952 members of the league planned a concert involving a full orchestra. They had in mind the use of the Toronto Symphony Orchestra for an event to take place in Massey Hall. Murray Adaskin and John Weinzweig were delegated as the group's emissaries, to discuss the project with the orchestra's women's committee in an effort to persuade them to sponsor the concert:

We were assigned the job of trying to sell this idea to them of using the Toronto Symphony Orchestra for a program of Canadian music in Massey Hall. We were not particular as to who conducted it, although Geoff [Waddington] was our favourite because he was in the forefront of this movement at that time.

The meeting took place in one of the meeting rooms at the back of Massey Hall. John and I were invited into a large room where all the ladies were sitting around a big table. The president of the women's committee was a wealthy Torontonian. Two or three smiled encouragingly at us; the others looked either very stern or noncommittal. We presented our request. They asked such questions as what kind of audience we could expect to get, would they understand the music ...

We tried to explain that the time had come to start training an audience and that this was the best place to do it. Well, we were turned down flat. One of the ladies said that our time was up, and we were literally asked to leave. They had other things to do. John and I suddenly found ourselves on Victoria Street by the stage entrance to Massey Hall. We looked at each other and just burst out laughing at the complete defeat of our effort. However, we were young, enthusiastic, and did not easily take 'no' for an answer.

They resolved right then and there to find a means of raising the money themselves to buy the orchestra's services for one night. The concert of Canadian symphonic music was going to occur. From Jack Elton, the manager of the Toronto Symphony, they found out that five thousand would cover the expenses for such an event. Most of the money was raised singlehanded by Murray through his connections at the Royal York Hotel. Many of the local businessmen who frequented the dining-room admired the playing of the Toronto Trio, so that when Murray approached them with the request for funds it did not take him long to raise the money. Once the contributors were satisfied that this concert was for the good of Canada, they did not hold back in their contributions.

One man asked his secretary to write me a cheque for five hundred dollars. Suddenly I was bringing in these big cheques, and I think on one occasion John Beckwith said that almost anything could be done in Toronto as long as Murray Adaskin raised the funds. I said I was lucky, and I knew all these people who were glad to help me out in return for the pleasure they claimed to have received from my playing at the hotel.

Anyway, we hired the orchestra and asked Geoff Waddington to conduct it now that we called the shots. We had a marvellous women's committee of the League of Composers who sold tickets, and we had almost a full house.

That historic first orchestral concert of the league took place in Massey Hall on 26 March 1952. It was also broadcast on the Trans-Canada CBC network and beamed abroad through its International Service. The compositions presented on that occasion included Murray Adaskin's *Ballet Symphony*, Somers's *North Country*, Rathburn's *Images of Childhood*, Alexander Brott's *Violin Concerto* played by John Dembeck, Dolin's *Scherzo* (from his *Sinfonietta*), Freedman's *Nocturne* (from his *Symphonette*), and Walter Kaufmann's *Madras Express*. Murray remembers:

Whenever we went to Massey Hall we sat up in the gods. This time we bought the best seats in the house, and the MacMillans were sitting right beside us. Everybody felt that it was as if a breath of fresh air blew through the hall on that occasion. It was a very exciting evening and everyone generated so much enthusiasm. The next day Jack Elton phoned the League of Composers asking us to make this an annual event. Well, we could not do it because it was hard work to raise the money. We were a group of young artists, not businessmen, and to raise that kind of money on a regular basis required much effort. This was in the pre–Canada Council days. However, we agreed to make it an annual affair if the symphony's women's committee would raise the money. That went by the boards.

The *Ballet Symphony*, composed during 1950 and 1951 while Murray was studying with Milhaud in Santa Barbara and *premièred* at the league concert, is easily the longest of the composer's works. A suite that is neither a symphony nor a ballet, it combines in the finale themes and ideas from previous movements, which are then reviewed and more fully developed. It was one of the works chosen to represent Canada at the exhibition during the 1952 Olympics in Helsinki. Two years later Murray produced a second version of it suitable to a performance by the Edmonton Symphony under the baton of Geoffrey Waddington. In 1953 it received another performance by the CBC Concert Orchestra with George Crum conducting, while at the 1958 Stratford Festival it was included among the nineteen concerts of Canadian music recorded and presented by the International Service of the CBC.

Concerts of the Canadian League of Composers continued with great success, many of them in Eaton Auditorium. They took place not only in Toronto, but in several other cities including Vancouver, Stratford, and Montreal. In 1953 the group became affiliated with the International Society for Contemporary

Music. It also initiated the album *Fourteen Piano Pieces by Canadian Composers*, which was published in 1955 by the Frederick Harris company. The pieces, designed to be of practical use for teachers and pianists, were illustrative of the variety of styles in Canadian compositions.

John Weinzweig was the first president of the league. By 1953 its membership included – in addition to Louis Applebaum (vice-president), Harry Freedman (secretary), and Andrew Twa (treasurer) – Beckwith, Dolin, Morawetz, Nimmons, Ridout, and Somers in Toronto; A. Brott, Mercure, and Papineau-Couture in Montreal; Adaskin in Saskatoon; Pépin in Quebec; Blackburn, Fleming, Peacock, and Rathburn in Ottawa; Kaufmann in Winnipeg; Coulthard in Vancouver; and Betts and Kasemets in Hamilton.

In 1954 Murray, who had by then taken up residence in Saskatoon, was invited by the league to perform his *Violin Sonata* at their April recital in Eaton Auditorium. His accompanist on that occasion was Gordon Kushner. The same year two additional compositions by Murray were performed. On 4 December the Canadian Music Associates of Ontario presented at the Toronto Conservatory of Music a program of works by league members, including Murray's *Canzona and Rondo*, performed by violinist John Dembeck, with Mario Bernardi at the piano; and his *Sonata for Piano*, also performed by Bernardi. Composed four years earlier, and beamed to South America via short-wave on the International Service of the CBC, the sonata was dedicated to the pianist. A friend of the Adaskins, Bernardi accompanied Frances James on one of her 'Wednesday Night' concerts and provided the piano part for the recording in 1949 of Murray's *Canzona and Rondo* for the International Service of the CBC. In 1955 the Canadian Music Associates were once more the sponsors of a league concert that featured music by Murray Adaskin. On 8 February his *Serenade Concertante* was performed by Sir Ernest MacMillan and the Toronto Symphony Orchestra.

These early concerts of the Canadian League of Composers sparked much enthusiasm among the young performers who were its avid supporters. Pianist Arlene Nimmons and singers James Milligan, Trudy Carlyle, and Mary Morrison all participated individually or at times even combined forces with the Spivak and Dembeck quartets. The league received a major boost through the formation of the Canadian Music Associates (CMA), incorporated in 1954 to encourage the composition, performance, and publication of Canadian music. The CMA continued the work initiated by the Concert Committee of the league during the first three years of its existence. For the 1954–5 season the CMA numbered approximately fifty enthusiastic supporters of contemporary Canadian music. Their ambitious goals for the season included not only a series of two concerts and two Canadian film nights – one night with music scores by leading

Canadian composers – but also a plan to send a concert artist to Europe and the Latin American countries playing complete programs of Canadian works.

Murray Adaskin's apprenticeship and his maturing as a composer occurred amid some of the most exciting – and, in retrospect, important – developments in the history of Canadian music. Not only did he take part in determining the direction of these epoch-making events, but he played a major role in their evolution.

THE STRUGGLE FOR A CANADIAN CULTURAL IDENTITY

In the 1940s various arts groups in Canada became increasingly conscious of a common need: the development of a national cultural policy on the arts. The lack of government support through funding suggested an insensitivity on the part of the government toward the arts, and the Canadian populace manifested toward the arts what some artists termed 'a colossal indifference.' For example, Canadian composers had recognized that some form of organized support of their endeavours was essential to the propagation and preservation of Canadian music and that an organization was needed to promote Canadian contemporary music; accordingly, they formed the Canadian League of Composers. But each arts group, working in isolation from others, could only do so much.

Across the country artists began to organize in recognition that an outcry of unified voices is stronger than that of individuals. The early forties were a period of increasing communication among arts groups, leading to a unified expression of concern to the government in 1944. One of the earliest joint arts groups to be created was the Federation of Canadian Artists, founded as an outcome of a conference held at Queen's University in Kingston. The first conference of its type to be held in Canada (spearheaded by André Bieler, chairman of the Fine Arts Department at Queen's), it brought together representatives of several different art societies across the country. Its aim was to form a union of artists in order to strive toward an integration of the arts within the Canadian social fabric.[15]

One of the federation's plans was to be responsible for the creation of community art galleries across the country as an extension of the National Gallery in Ottawa. The creation of community art centres was also recommended as a means of providing creative stimulus and overcoming the sense of isolation experienced by artists removed from the large cities.

Throughout the 1940s artists were realizing the unifying potential of art within Canada's social and political scene. This potential had already been recognized two decades earlier by John Murray Gibbon, whose recognition that folk arts and traditions could serve as a means of unifying Canada resulted in the spectacular folk-music and folk-arts festivals. In contrast with Gibbon's endeavours, which enjoyed the financial backing of a large business corporation, the artists' manifesto of the forties was formulated at a time of minimal financial backing for the arts in most provinces.

A publisher's statement in the *Canadian Review of Music and Art* refers to the lack of support given the arts in Ontario, where in 1944, for example, the province was said to spend about $50,000 a year for art as compared to $620,000 a year spent by the province of Quebec. The publishers stressed the need for government support of arts and crafts in order to increase the earning power of a large segment of the population and to present Ontarians with an opportunity to enrich their lives through contact with art.[16]

The *Canadian Review of Music and Art* was a monthly publication, initiated in 1942 and published until 1948. The periodical was a major voice of artists in all fields, and published articles on Canadian cultural issues. Contributions came from musicians, architects, painters, poets, writers, and craftsmen. Today it stands as a document expressing the artists' emerging concern about the need for a national cultural policy. The founding editor was Christopher Wood, with L. de B. Coriveau, managing editor, and Godfrey Ridout, assistant editor. The editorial board included Marcus Adeney, Bettina Byers, John Coulter, Nicholas Hornyansky, Adolph Koldofsky, and Ettore Mazzoleni.

The *Canadian Review*'s first editorial expressed the need for post-war direction for the arts, such as the creation of a national library similar to the United States Library of Congress, a national orchestra like that of the BBC, a national opera, and a national theatre. It stated that while Canada had a wealth of talent, it lacked a single unifying force, a cultural national unity. In 1944 the periodical articulated its objectives:

1 To urge that arts and crafts be recognized in Canada as a vital part of the national economy, and that they be given centralized direction under a Ministry of Cultural Affairs.
2 To urge that opportunities be presented for proper instruction of arts and crafts to children.
3 To stress the importance of arts and crafts to Canadians on both cultural and economic grounds.
4 To interpret the work of the artist and craftsman to the public.

It went on: 'Hundreds of people are working today without encouragement and recognition. It is the intention of the *Canadian Review* to bring the work of these talented people in all parts of the country to the attention of the public. Thus, they may be encouraged to work with greater zeal and enthusiasm and thereby enrich our national life.'[17]

These objectives expressed what came to be the rallying cry of artists throughout the 1940s. The cry was to develop into a country-wide unifying cultural force, a broad sweep of growing momentum culminating, through a series of steps, in the creation of the Canada Council. This crown corporation was created in 1957 by an act of the federal government, to 'encourage and support the arts, humanities, and social sciences in Canada.'

That was in 1957. In the early 1940s, however, artists like John Coulter felt frustration at the situation in Canada, after reading reports in the Toronto *Globe and Mail* and elsewhere about the British Council for the Encouragement of Music and Arts. In his memoirs Coulter recounts his efforts to use the Arts and Letters Club, to which he belonged, as a lobbying group for the setting up of a similar council in Canada.[18] He thought the club was a logical organization to deal with the topic, which was in keeping with its charter. After considerable debate among members as to the extent of the club's involvement in community and cultural affairs, an advisory council of twelve professional artists and lay members, representative of each of the arts, was appointed.[19] Three recommendations were tabled by the council: the establishment of a nation-wide network of cultural centres; the making of strong representations to the federal government on behalf of the artist; and 'that the Club support in every possible way artistic activities of special merit both in and out of the Club.'

The agitation for recognition of the arts throughout 1943 and 1944 led to discussions in the press, in public lectures, in radio talks, and on panels. One radio panel discussion is excerpted in the December/January 1945 issue of the *Canadian Review of Music and Art*. CBC *Citizens Forum*, chaired by author Morley Callaghan, asked the question 'Can Canada Support the Arts?' of its panel members – sculptor Elizabeth Wyn Wood, writer John Coulter, and Toronto businessman W. Eason Humphreys.[20] Some of the more important points articulated during the debate pertained to the plight of the artist in Canadian society. Because of lack of audience support the artist was too often forced to seek more sympathetic audiences outside the country. Elizabeth Wyn Wood presented the problems in a most articulate and outspoken fashion:

It will cost us Canada if we don't support the arts ... We [are] asking for ... government assistance in the building of community cultural centers for the distribution of the arts – especially to remote districts; more adequate support of those institutions which serve both artist and public; better copyright laws for industrial design; the use of Canadian arts to make Canada better understood abroad ... Artists find it difficult to reach people. What we need is machinery by which we can get together ... [In this country] the fresh personality is dreaded ... the intellectual or the artist has neve been a Canadian hero.

Regarding the question of government subsidy of the arts, Wyn Wood felt that the services provided by five or six ministries should be centralized under a single ministry. In addition to simplifying the existing bureaucracy, she advocated moral support for the arts.

Once again, the CBC was in the forefront in responding to the need of the artists. In 1945 it created the Radio Canada International Service, with the intention of presenting Canadian culture abroad. Music and spoken-word transcriptions were distributed to radio stations across the world. One of the early musical events was the production in 1945 of a Canadian album of five 78-rpm discs including music of Healey Willan and Claude Champagne, under the baton of Jean-Marie Beaudet. A second album appeared the following year, including works by Coulthard, MacMillan, Weinzweig, and Tanguay.[21] Shortly thereafter, the Music Transcription Service was created. The policy was to distribute the recordings free of charge to overseas Canadian diplomatic missions, schools of music, and libraries.

Almost concurrently with the establishment of the Radio Canada International Service, the Canadian Foundation, an organization intended to stimulate interest in Canadian cultural activities at home and abroad, was incorporated by Dominion charter.[22] Its immediate purpose was to conduct a Canada-wide survey of all forms of assistance given to writers, musicians, composers, painters, sculptors, and other artists in order to devise a system of grants and awards to individuals and organizations. The intention was to build up a fund for the encouragement and support of the arts through contributions from private benefactors. Lawren Harris was one of the distinguished Canadians elected to membership in the foundation.

This was the organization approached by a group of people from the Arts and Letters Club for advice about practical ways of seeking government help.[23] George Pepall, Marcus Adeney, Herman Voaden, and John Coulter were advised by Walter Herbert, director of the foundation, to address themselves to the House of Commons Special Committee on Reconstruction and Re-establishment, presided over by J. Gray Turgeon, MP. Known as the Turgeon Committee, its purpose was to help members of the Canadian armed forces returning from the war to reinstate themselves into the social and economic fabric of their country. The result was that the group from the Arts and Letters Club joined fifteen arts organizations who prepared briefs to the Turgeon Committee.

This historic occasion is now frequently referred to as the 'March on Ottawa.' The arts groups involved in the March on Ottawa were the Royal Canadian Academy of Arts, the Royal Architectural Institute of Canada, the Sculptors' Society of Canada, the Canadian Society of Painter-Etchers and Engravers, the

Canadian Group of Painters, the Federation of Canadian Artists, the Canadian Artists' Association, La Société des Ecrivains Canadiens, the Music Committee, the Canadian Society of Landscape Architects and Town Planners, the Dominion Drama Festival, the Canadian Handicrafts Guild, the Canadian Guild of Potters, and the Arts and Letters Club. Sir Ernest MacMillan, a vocal spokesman for Canadian music and musicians, Elizabeth Wyn Wood, and John Coulter were among the leaders of the group. It was the first concerted effort in Canadian history by representatives from arts groups to articulate, through a united front, their collective requests to a parliamentary committee. The separate briefs were summarized in a composite brief read by John Coulter. It stressed the importance of the creative arts to the Canadian economy as a source of employment, and it deplored the lack of consideration given to art in this country, insisting that the best talents should be honoured at home and promoted abroad.

Three categories of recommendations were submitted to the committee: the first stressed the necessity for the creation of a governmental body to watch over all cultural activities; the second pertained to the need for establishment of community centres; and the third dealt with the relationship of the arts to national life.[24]

Coulter gives an eyewitness account of this momentous occasion:

I took a relatively small part in the ensuing discussion, being fascinated by the unfolding comedy; the incredulous surprise of the politicians at what they found themselves faced with. Presumably they had anticipated a tiresome forenoon of being amiably tactful to a clutch of fluttery featherbrains; artists, impractical footlers whose life was a fussy tangle of misunderstood reality and cloudy unattainable dreams. Instead they were confronted by a thoroughly informed team of citizens ... all of them with precisely calculated figures at their fingertips.[25]

The momentum built up on behalf of the arts among the arts organizations and in the public domain resulted in the creation of a Canadian Arts Council, an organization intended to continue the work of the sixteen groups. The body was formed on 5 December 1945 with Herman Voaden as chairman. A short time later, the Canadian Music Council was formed under the leadership of Sir Ernest MacMillan.[26]

As a result of the Turgeon Committee hearing and the general artistic ferment of the 1940s, the government launched an unprecedented, massive, and thorough investigation into Canada's cultural life. Realizing that the government of Great Britain had assumed partial responsibility for the support of its cultural institutions, and in response to the clamour for similar government support on home territory, the government of Canada appointed a royal commission to study the country's cultural resources. After almost a decade of polemics, organizing, and lobbying, the voice of the Canadian artist was finally heard by the government. On 7 April 1949 five distinguished Canadians were appointed as commissioners by Prime Minister Louis St Laurent with the approval of the privy council and the governor-general: the Right Honourable Vincent Massey, chancellor of the University of Toronto; Arthur Surveyor, civil engineer, Montreal; Norman A.M. MacKenzie, president, University of British Columbia; the Most Reverend Georges-Henri Lévesque, dean of the Faculty of Social Sciences, Laval University; and Hilda Neatby, professor of history and acting head of the history department, University of Saskatchewan.

The Royal Commission on National Development in the Arts, Letters and Sciences was also known as the Massey Commission, after its chairman, Vincent Massey. At the time of his appointment as chairman of the commission, Massey was recognized as a major patron of the arts in Canada, as a collector of Canadian art, and as a distinguished diplomat. Between 1935 and 1942 he was Canadian high commissioner in Great Britain and a delegate to the League of Nations. Regardless of where he was assigned as diplomat, he paid frequent visits to Canada, retaining an active part in Canadian cultural and political life. Upon the completion of his service on the royal commission, he accepted the post of the first Canadian-born governor-general (1952–9).

Father Lévesque, a Dominican, was a committed federalist and an important protagonist in Quebec's cultural revolution. According to Bernard Ostry, he was a man of tact and subtlety, and was a good political choice on the part of Louis St Laurent for such a cultural commission. Arthur Surveyor was chosen for his technical knowledge in the field of broadcasting, while both MacKenzie and Neatby were committed educators. Dr Hilda Neatby was an outstanding faculty member at the University of Saskatchewan, a Presbyterian, a Westerner, a Canadian nationalist, and a scholar of the highest ethical standards. Her colleagues regarded her as a formidable personality. A year after the Massey Commission report she published a highly controversial book, *So Little for the Mind*, an indictment of Canadian primary and secondary school education.

The broad scope of the commission's inquiry encompassed the needs of Canadian citizens with respect to science, literature, art, music, drama, film, and broadcasting. It thus penetrated all layers of the Canadian cultural fabric, and as such represented a significant move on the part of the Canadian government toward assessment of this country's cultural institutions and their potential.

The commission's method was to hold public hearings across Canada and to solicit briefs from individuals and organizations. Over the two years of work they held 224 meetings and read 462 briefs.[27] Their respondents included government institutions, universities, music and drama schools, provincial governments, national organizations, and local bodies such as arts groups, private radio stations, and individual artists. The commission also solicited critical reports from some eminent Canadians on the strengths and weaknesses in their disciplines as practised in Canada. These studies were found of such value that a selection was published in 1951 in a separate volume: *Royal Commission Studies: A Selection of Essays Prepared for the Royal Commission on National Development in the Arts, Letters and Sciences.*

The two volumes (the *Report* and the *Essays*) constitute the most comprehensive documentation of the state of culture in Canada up to the middle of the twentieth century. The first part of the bipartite *Report* was an assessment of the Canadian 'cultural landscape' – a stock-taking of the country's cultural and intellectual life. The second part contained recommendations to the federal government as to means by which the intellectual and cultural life of this country could be advanced. The need for government support of the arts and letters was obvious and long overdue, but the mode in which this support could be extended without government interference with freedom of artistic expression still needed to be worked out. Many of the weaknesses in Canada's cultural fabric uncovered by the Massey Commission reinforced the issues already raised by artists throughout the 1940s. The Commission's report with its subsequent recommendations merely formalized public recognition of these weaknesses. It constituted a vehicle for the transmission of arts groups' grievances to the government in the best democratic tradition, thus placing within the jurisdiction of the government the responsibility for improving the state of the arts and culture in Canada. A summary of some of the issues identified by the commission is relevant to the discussion of the general artistic climate of the 1940s, of which the Adaskins were a product.

Part 1 of the report was organized according to categories of agencies studied: mass media (broadcasting, films, press, and periodical literature); voluntary bodies and federal agencies (voluntary societies, galleries, museums, libraries, archives, historic sites, and monuments); scholarship, science, and the arts (universities, national scholarship, the scholar and the scientist, the artist and the writer); and cultural relations abroad (UNESCO and projection of Canada abroad).

In this part the influence of the United States on Canadian cultural life was acknowledged, particularly the grants from the Carnegie and Rockefeller foundations to help Canadian cultural endeavours. While Canadian indebtedness to the United States was considerable, its dependence on the southern neighbour was also seen as potentially harmful. Many Canadians had attended American universities for higher education, and the cultural importation in education, film, radio, educational philosophy, and periodicals was seen as potentially damaging to Canadian cultural independence.

The CBC was considered successful in the reinforcement of its three goals: an adequate coverage of an entire population; the creation of 'opportunities for Canadian talent and Canadian self-expression generally'; and 'successful resistance to the absorption of Canada into the general cultural pattern of the United States.'[28]

The National Film Board's post-war activities in educational documentaries were found praiseworthy, particularly because of its work in areas of little interest to the commercial producer. It was found inadequate, however, in servicing the needs of French-speaking Canada and in its lack of a centralized film library that would be composed of an archival and a reference section.

Voluntary societies such as the Canadian music festivals, Les Jeunesses Musicales, the Institute of International Affairs, the YMCA, and YMHA were seen to play a central role in the support and dissemination of culture. One of the functions of these societies was to teach Canadians how to cope with the problem of passive entertainment – leisure time – by requiring some degree of active participation from their members. The major criticism was that, of the $791,504 in federal aid given to the voluntary societies the year of the inquiry, only some $21,000 was allotted for cultural matters; despite the distribution of federal funds to these societies, the government was lacking in its support for arts and letters.

A similar lack of government support was found to hamper the operation of most of the other cultural institutions across Canada. The National Gallery, for example, founded in 1880, houses the most complete collection of Canadian art in the country. It disseminates knowledge about Canadian art through loans of its collections, and it arranges for exhibitions of art from abroad. One of the gallery's immediate needs was a new building with increased staff.

In addition to the National Gallery a network of local galleries was spread across Canada. Compared to their wealthy and established counterparts in the United States, Canada's resources in these galleries were slim. Travelling exhibitions were one of their chief functions. An interdependent relationship existed between the National and the local galleries on occasions when the National Gallery sent out travelling exhibitions for the benefit of the Canadian people as a whole.

The commission saw a need, too, for programs in art instruction for children and for publications in art. While generous grants made in the past by the Carnegie Corporation of New York for the development of educational programs in art museums were gratefully acknowledged, the continued educational function of art galleries was stressed. In addition, the interdependence of the creative artist and the art galleries was emphasized. Unlike the United States, where contemporary artworks were frequently purchased by private citizens, in Canada artists were more dependent on galleries for financial support.

Government financing of museums was also found scanty. Compared to the generous budget of American and British museums, the budget of the National Museum in Ottawa was minuscule, and the museum was inadequately housed and staffed. Yet it contained, among others, an important anthropological section rich in ethnology of the Iroquois, Eskimo, and West Coast Indian. It also housed an important collection of recordings of French-Canadian, Maritime, and Indian folklore.

Despite the fact that there were museums in some other Canadian cities and that some universities were acquiring museum collections, the number of museums relative to the Canadian population and resources was low. Little public money was granted for this purpose. The neglect of certain fields, such as the lack of a folk-museum in the Prairies to record Canadian history, threatened the destruction and loss of valuable materials that could only be preserved and cared for in such institutions.

The role of universities in Canadian society was also evaluated by the commission. By 1948 universities were reaching a crisis in funding partly because the federal grants to veteran students under the Veterans' Rehabilitations Act were about to expire, and partly because some provinces were ignoring the increasing demands of higher education.[29] The Massey commission pointed out that universities serve the national cause in many ways, one of them being acting as local patrons of arts, letters, and sciences. It recognized the national service rendered by universities, such as contribution to defence and scientific research, but warned that the humanities were in danger of being neglected. 'The purpose of a university is, through a liberalizing education, to enable persons to live more complete lives ... Academic courses stripped of the humanities lose enrichment as well as discipline. They provide for a living but not for the life which makes living worthwhile.[30] The commission noted a tendency toward a 'starvation' of the humanities at universities and stressed the importance of retaining the traditional character of the humanities. Higher salaries were paid to faculty in the sciences, engineering, and medicine than to those in the humanities.

The commission's assessment of the state of Canadian universities at the end of the 1940s creates a context for an understanding of Murray Adaskin's activities at the University of Saskatchewan starting in 1952, the year of the report's completion.

In their assessment of the creative arts in Canada, the commission quoted the following passage submitted in a brief by the Canadian Arts Council:

No novelist, poet, short story writer, historian, biographer, or other writer of non-technical books can make even a modestly comfortable living by selling his work in Canada.
No composer of music can live at all on what Canada pays him for his compositions.
Apart from radio drama, no playwright, and only a few actors and producers, can live by working in the theatre in Canada.
Few painters and sculptors, outside the field of commercial art and teaching, can live by sale of their work in Canada.[31]

This serious statement served as a guide for the commission's thorough examination of the creative arts: music, theatre, ballet, painting, sculpture, architecture and town planning, literature, publishing, folklore, handicrafts, and Indian arts.

The commission praised a number of achievements in the field of music, including the important role played by the CBC in Canadian music and in the employment of Candian musicians in particular. It noted, however, the hostility of audiences to new music. Despite the important Symposium on Canadian Music in Vancouver in 1950, which included four concerts of music by thirty-three Canadian composers, music by the contemporary Canadian composer was still too little known in Canada.

Only four orchestras – in Vancouver, Winnipeg, Toronto, and Montreal – were professional enough to be able to play the more difficult symphonic repertoire, and these were plagued by financial problems. There was as yet no published history of music in Canada, nor an adequate library of music. Few Canadian compositions were available in published form, and facilities for reproducing a composer's manuscript in order for it to be performed were inadequate.

The concerns of the composer were compounded by those of the performer. Frances James, as one of Canada's most eminent performing artists, was asked to make a submission to the royal commission. An abstract of her brief, quoted below, which was submitted on 1 March 1950, was incorporated into the commission's report:

SUBMISSION OF FRANCES JAMES TO
THE ROYAL COMMISSION ON NATIONAL DEVELOPMENT
IN THE ARTS, LETTERS AND SCIENCES

Mr Chairman and Commissioners:
  I have recently completed a coast-to-coast concert tour of Canada during which I gave sixteen song recitals. My income was $3200; my expenses (hotel and incidental, fees paid my manager and accompanist, and rail fares) were $2700. I therefore realized $500 from

my season's concerts. Supplementing this was my income from the Canadian Broadcasting Corporation. This was practically all absorbed by expenditures for clothes, accompanist's rehearsal fees, printing, photographs, and other expenses pertaining to my year's engagements. Since I could not live on this small profit, it is assumed that if I were not married and did not have a husband who supports me, I would either have to leave the country or give up singing.

I have quoted these figures from the financial statement of my year's concert activities to indicate the precarious situation in which a resident Canadian musician finds herself to-day. The implications of this situation are even more disturbing to the artist when she realizes that this is the reward of almost a life-time's preparation.

The American monopolies in the Canadian concert field, namely Community Concerts, Inc. in the eastern half of Canada, and the National Concert and Artists Corporation in the remaining portion, cover a minimum of 150 cities and towns in Canada. Each city has a series of concerts which the community organizes under the guidance of the American headquarters. No resident Canadian artist is included in any of these concerts. Those Canadians whose services are in demand in these communities have long ago chosen to leave Canada and acquire a reputation in the United States. Not only are resident Canadians prevented from concertizing before a wide Canadian audience, but millions of dollars are drained from the country.

As a remedy for this I would suggest that there be at least one resident Canadian artist on each series. Surely some form of national publicity could be used to create a demand for the musicians of a high artistic calibre who prefer to remain in Canada. In conversations I have had with leading citizens of these communities, I have learned that when this situation was brought to their attention, they were only too eager to co-operate by demanding a percentage of Canadian artists on their series.

This suggests the need for a central agency to represent all available resident artists, to effectively promote these artists, and supply any information required on lines similar to the function of the British Arts Council. I cannot recommend too strongly the need to publicize the Canadian artist to the Canadian people. If he were presented with as much promotion as the American agencies give their artists, I am sure he would be demanded and welcomed by organizations sponsoring concerts in Canada. It has been found many times that the wrapping on the package of the imported artist is more impressive than its contents. My hope is that Canadians, really capable ones, can be so wrapped and found to have every bit as exciting material inside as outside. No one is in favour of excluding fine artists from Canada, just as it would be foolish to encourage inferior artists because they are Canadians. Only the most capable, experienced, and seasoned Canadians who are able to stand in an international field, should be thus considered and encouraged to pursue their careers in the country of their birth.

As a resident Canadian musician, I should like to say that at present, the most important reason for an artist's remaining in Canada is the Canadian Broadcasting

Corporation. Through its policy of 'C.B.C. Wednesday Nights', and other programmes on the domestic network, as well as the policy of the International Service to have Canadians present Canadian music, the C.B.C. has an enviable record of accomplishment. Indeed, it is the most consistent source of encouragement to Canadian artists.

Because she was one of the few artists to have contact with Canadian music teachers and students in Canada's interior, contacts developed over her twenty-year period of touring the country, Frances was also asked to submit an additional brief to the commission. Its purpose was to point out the difficulties encountered by a Canadian artist in receiving adequate training in Canada and in retaining Canadian identity once this training has been completed whether in Canada or abroad.

Problems similar to those outlined in Frances James's brief were encountered by the theatre artist and the painter. Lack of encouragement of its native talent had driven many actors out of the country. The importance of a national theatre in Canada was stressed as an essential cultural resource. Canadian painters, for the most part, had felt isolated from the rest of the population, at a time when they made sincere efforts to reach out and communicate with the nation. A strong appeal from the Federation of Canadian Artists urged that the visual artist be provided with means of livelihood, stating that arts are not a luxury 'but an essential prerequisite to the development of a stable national culture.'

In addition to funding deficiencies on the part of the federal government toward many of the cultural organizations, the royal commission also reported a number of legislative restraints that imposed hardship on voluntary organizations, museums, and art galleries, as well as on scholars, scientists, artists, writers, and publishers. Writers, in particular, felt that they should be able to deduct from their income tax their expenditures for books, documents, and other tools used as part of their trade. They felt that expenses incurred in researching, writing, and preparing a book for publication should also be deductible for income tax purposes.

The *Report* of the Massey Commission is an extremely well-written document and a moving reinforcement of the commissioners' and the arts groups' convictions that culture represents the spiritual foundations of a country's national life. The sincerity of their concern for Canada's cultural welfare is perhaps best summarized in their own words: 'Canadian achievement in every field depends mainly on the quality of the Canadian mind and spirit. This quality is determined by what Canadians think, and think about; by the books they read, the pictures they see and the programmes they hear. These things, whether we call them arts and letters or use other words to describe them, we believe to lie at the roots of our life as a nation.'[32]

The conclusions of the report stated that Canada's cultural institutions were suffering from a 'lack of nourishment.' Canada was found to lag far behind other countries in the priorities given to cultural matters by the government. Varying reasons could have accounted for this attitude, including the relative youth of the nation, the geographical disposition of a scattered population, a dependence on the resources of the United States, and perhaps most serious of all, the tidal wave of technology that was seen as potentially damaging to a country with a young cultural tradition.

A number of separate recommendations were made regarding broadcasting, the National Film Board, and such federal institutions as the National Gallery, Museums, and Public Archives, the federal libraries, and historic sites and monuments. The most dramatic recommendation, however, one that has had far-reaching implications and that has very much affected the state of our culture at present, was the commission's recommendation that a body to be known as the Canada Council for the Encouragement of the Arts, Letters, Humanities, and Social Sciences be created 'to stimulate and to help voluntary organizations within these fields, to foster Canada's cultural relations abroad, to perform the functions of a national commission for UNESCO, and to devise and administer a system of scholarships.'[33]

The scholarships to which the above statement refers are discussed in a separate chapter of the *Report*, where the commission recommends that in addition to the already existent scholarships to students and researchers in the natural sciences, similar grants be given to post-graduate students and advanced researchers in the humanities, the social sciences and law, and in the creative arts. Finally, in the area of creative arts and related fields, the commission urged that a system of grants be made available for persons engaged in the arts and letters in Canada, as well as for those artists, musicians, and writers from abroad who wish to study in Canada.

The commission then proceeded with recommendations regarding the structure of the proposed Canada Council and some of its duties with respect to national and international activities.

Submitted in May 1951, the *Report* summed up a decade of artists' struggle to be heard, and represented a milestone in Canada's cultural development. The cultural community's demands for government assistance to the arts were about to be incorporated into a Canadian cultural policy.

The Canada Council was established on 8 January 1957 by an announcement in the Speech from the Throne and received royal assent on 28 March of that year. The final impetus for its creation was the receipt of about fifty million dollars in succession duties from the estates of two prominent Canadian citizens – Isaak Walton Killam and Sir James Hamet Dunn – who had recently died.[34] An account of the reaction of the press and of some members of Parliament, both for and against the creation of this crown corporation, would require another volume. For better or for worse, the relationship between government and culture in Canada had been initiated.

Thirteen years had elapsed from the meetings of the Turgeon Committee, through the exhaustive studies of the Massey Commission, to the establishment of the Canada Council. Most of the recommendations of the Massey Commission were eventually implemented by the Canada Council and other organizations. Some of the weaknesses in the cultural fabric identified by the commission were rectified over the years. In the three and a half decades succeeding the Massey Commission's work Canada has witnessed the establishment of some of its major cultural institutions. The Stratford Playhouse and its annual performing arts festival was inaugurated in 1953. The Canadian Music Centre was created in 1959, filling the need for a central repository for Canadian contemporary music to act both as a library and a centre for dissemination. John Adaskin was one of the centre's early presidents (1961–4). Ten years later a theatre and auditorium complex was built in Ottawa, to house an orchestra that was virtually state supported; the National Arts Centre was opened in 1969, with Mario Bernardi the resident conductor of the National Arts Centre Orchestra. For the inaugural concert Jean-Marie Beaudet, director of the centre, commissioned from Murray Adaskin his *Diversion for Orchestra*. The need for a central repository of musical Canadiana for the preservation of this country's musical documentation was answered through the establishment in 1970 of the Music Division of the National Library. Helmut Kallmann became its head.

Public consciousness in the cause of the arts and letters in this country was raised through the work of the Massey Commission. Today we are the beneficiaries of the momentum built up in the post-war years. However, the true heroes and heroines in the history of our culture in the twentieth century are the artists and musicians of the 1940s. Murray Adaskin, Frances James, and their cultural circle established highly successful careers at what was, perhaps, the most difficult time in Canadian cultural history. They were the ones to recognize the cultural deficiencies in this country. It is through their struggle for a recognition of the elemental dependence of a civilized nation on its cultural heritage that we today reap the benefits of their efforts. They are the true pioneers of Canadian culture in the twentieth century.

5

A Prairie renaissance of the arts: 1952–1973

THE UNIVERSITY OF SASKATCHEWAN

During the eventful years of the artists' struggle for recognition, the studies of the Royal Commission on National Development in the Arts, Letters and Sciences, and the formation of the Canadian League of Composers, Murray Adaskin continued in the employment of the Canadian Pacific Railway in Toronto. One fall day in 1951, Dr Francis Leddy from the University of Saskatchewan invited Murray to have lunch with him in a restaurant on Bloor Street near Avenue Road. The University of Saskatchewan at Saskatoon had advertised through the nationally known *Saturday Night* the position of a chair in music. The university was ready to initiate a music department and was searching for the right person to develop a music program. Dr Leddy, dean of arts and sciences at the University of Saskatchewan, was in Toronto to attend a scholarly conference. He used the opportunity to informally interview Murray, who, though he didn't know it, had been highly recommended to the university's search committee. Shortly after the lunch with Leddy, Murray was invited to Saskatoon for a formal interview.

After thirteen years of performing with the Toronto Trio at the Royal York Hotel, during which time his career had begun to move from full-time performance toward composition, Murray was intrigued with the possibility of a new orientation. An academic life, while demanding a concentrated period of time teaching during the winter and spring sessions, would nevertheless afford him an extended period during the summer when he could devote himself exclusively to composing. He travelled to Saskatoon with the intent of scrutinizing the faculty and the university as closely as the search committee intended to scrutinize him.

Murray recalls vividly the day in early January when he first visited the campus:

It was forty degrees below zero; a frightfully cold, clear, but beautiful sunny day. I met with the President, Dr W.P. Thompson, after which I was taken to dinner at the Bessborough Hotel, where the entire search committee was in attendance. Dining in this established and elegant hotel was an expensive undertaking. Filling the position of head of a newly established music department, however, was an important event, and the evening spent over dinner served more than a social function. It afforded the committee an opportunity to further study the candidate as a professional and as a human being. It was a rather hilarious evening, and they drew out of me all sorts of stories about my experiences as a performing musician. They wanted to see what I was all about, and I had them in fits of laughter.

Leddy had originally told me that the appointment was to be made sometime at the end of May or early June 1952, and that I should not expect immediate results after my interview. The next day, I was in Leddy's office at nine o'clock in the morning. He had just handed me some information about the university to look at when, suddenly, his phone rang. I was soon to find out that he had been summoned to the president's office where the entire search committee was assembled. Upon his return Leddy informed me that the president wished to see me. I had a curious sensation when I walked into Dr Thompson's office and saw all the people with whom I had had dinner the previous night. They all smiled at me with that cat-that-swallowed-the-canary look, and the president very solemnly said: 'Mr Adaskin, we have just decided to offer you the appointment of full professor with tenure at $5,600 annual salary. I wish the salary was higher, but that is all we can offer at the moment.'

It was only later that I found out that as a result of my having praised the beauty of the winter scenery in Saskatoon during the dinner on the previous night, one of the committee members told Dr Thompson: 'For God's sake let's offer him the job before the weather changes and shows him what Saskatoon can really be like.'

In the late summer of 1952, Murray and Frances Adaskin left Toronto to move into their new house in Saskatoon, which was to be their home for the ensuing twenty-one years. Murray's first glimpse of the University of Saskatchewan revealed a handsome set of greystone buildings in the collegiate Gothic style of architecture. The use of natural limestone as the predominant building material and the proliferation of imposing brick buildings lent the campus an intrinsic sense of unity. The university, prominently located on a 2,600-acre site on the north bank of the South Saskatchewan River, is a focal point for anyone looking from the old Bessborough Hotel across the wide, smoothly flowing river. A set of gracefully arching massive bridges provides a connecting link between the campus and the downtown area of the city. One part of the university land serves as campus, while the other is used for its experimental farm.

One of the first things Murray learned about the University of Saskatchewan was its long tradition of public service. As the major institution of higher learning within a fairly young, almost totally agricultural province, the university geared its direction and philosophy toward serving the needs of the province. Agriculture was one of its highest priorities, and it provided such services as soil and water analysis and horticultural and agricultural advice. Besides offering practical aid to the province's agricultural community, the university endeavoured to foster a spiritual and cultural atmosphere by providing leadership in its musical life. Music festivals had played an important role in Saskatchewan's cultural activities since the beginning of the century. In 1931, Arthur Collingwood, a Scot from Aberdeen who had previously been brought to Saskatoon as adjudicator for one of the festivals, was hired to initiate a music department at the university. His mandate was to create a link between the university and the community by working with the Saskatchewan Musical Association.

Collingwood brought to the Canadian Prairies his expertise as choirboy of Westminster Abbey and as student at Oxford, the Guildhall School of Music, and the Russian Conservatory of St Petersburg. Composer and conductor, he was responsible for the development of the local symphony orchestra, which was to assume new directions during the 1950s under the leadership of Murray Adaskin. Collingwood's tenure of the chair in music lasted until 1947, after which there was little in the way of formal musical activity at the university until Murray's arrival in 1952.

By the time of the Adaskins' arrival, the university was in the fourth decade of its existence. It was created in 1909, only four years after Saskatchewan was carved out of the Northwest Territories and established as an independent province. More than perhaps any other Canadian academic institution, the University of Saskatchewan was the product of one man's idealism and vision.[1]

Walter Murray, a Canadian from New Brunswick with a PH D in philosophy, came to Saskatchewan to found a university at a time when the population of the province was 325,000 and Saskatoon itself held only eight thousand people.[2] He was faced not only with establishing a philosophy and a purpose for the university, but even with such a basic decision as where it should be located. After settling upon Saskatoon, he proceeded to build up an institution whose basic philosophy was to serve the needs of the people of the province. His professional and personal life was entirely dedicated to his strong commitment to public service.

A focus on agriculture was to him a top priority in a province dependent on agriculture. The College of Agriculture was thus the first institution built, establishing the University of Saskatchewan as one of the earliest in Canada to have such a college on campus.

In assembling a faculty President Murray sought out scholars of stature in their fields – Canadian citizens with a PHD degree, who were imaginative, had strong personalities, and were capable of demonstrating leadership and of growing with the university. One of these appointments, as professor of biology in 1913, was that of W.P. Thompson, a PHD from Harvard. One of the oldest faculty members at the university, W.P. Thompson became its third president after Walter Murray's completion of his term in 1937. It was during Thompson's presidency that Murray Adaskin was hired as professor of music. Another academic appointed to the faculty by President Murray who was to prove influential in Murray Adaskin's life was the Rhodes scholar Francis Leddy. A former student at the university, Leddy, who had received a PHD in Classics at Oxford, was appointed to the Classics Department in the 1930s. Over a period of three decades Leddy became one of the university's most distinguished faculty members and held a number of administrative positions, from dean of arts and sciences to vice-president academic. He was one of the first members of the newly established Canada Council, and in 1964 took over the presidency of the University of Windsor.

Several other distinguished academics who had attained national and international prominence became Murray Adaskin's associates. Historian Hilda Neatby, whose service on the Massey Commission was mentioned in chapter 4, was one Rudolf Altschul, professor of anatomy, and Gerhard Herzberg, professor of chemistry, were others. Although he hired primarily Canadian faculty, Walter Murray's humanitarian impulses resulted in his appointment of two leading European researchers who were being persecuted by the Nazis: Altschul was offered a position in 1939, which he held until 1963, and Herzberg became affiliated with the institution during the war years and remained there until 1945. At a time when Canada's immigration laws would have made it impossible for people like Altschul and Herzberg to emigrate to this country, Walter Murray found the means to circumvent the rules. When Murray Adaskin made his acquaintance, Altschul, who was teaching in the College of Medicine, was conducting experiments on rabbits. Gerhard Herzberg, who later won a Nobel Prize, left Saskatoon for a position with Yerkes Observatory, University of Chicago, and then moved to the National Research Council in Ottawa.

To Walter Murray scientific research was a priority. Scientists were granted research money, equipment, and adequate space. By contrast, the arts faculty had to contend with large classes, cramped classrooms, inadequate library facilities, and crowded offices shared by several people. The seeming gulf between the arts and the sciences, however, was not an accurate reflection of the president's attitude toward the arts.

Recognizing the cultural value of the fine arts and believing that the arts and humanities should constitute a large portion of university life, Walter Murray encouraged art throughout the province by making the university a patron of the arts. He promoted painting by commissioning such local personalities as Gus Kenderdine and Ernest Lindner to create artworks for the university. Recognizing the talent of the young Saskatchewan painter Kenderdine, Walter Murray gave him a studio atop the newly built physics building. He also offered Lindner a job at the university, providing encouragement that affected positively the artist's professional life. In his search for fine paintings, some of which were donated by him to the university, Walter Murray started what is now its permanent art collection.[3] Through his efforts the university summer arts program at Emma Lake was established, an artists' summer workshop that trained many distinguished Saskatchewan painters. In 1925, as part of promoting the province's culture, President Murray arranged an exhibition of Saskatchewan artists at Hart House in Toronto. The catalogue for the exhibition was based on notes he provided.

The campaign to establish a chair in music also expressed the president's belief, which he had held since 1913–14 when he was president of the Saskatchewan Musical Association, that it was the university's role to further musical life in the province. This belief led him to request endowed funds from the Carnegie Foundation in New York for the purpose of establishing the chair. At the end of the 1920s there was no comparable Canadian foundation, and the province itself was not rich enough to provide funds for the university.[4] In recognition of Walter Murray's outstanding leadership, the Carnegie Foundation gave the University of Saskatchewan an endowed chair in music, which was subsequently filled by Arthur Collingwood. Additional funds requested by Collingwood for equipment, such as pianos, were used by Walter Murray toward a music reference library, and the re-establishment of a symphony orchestra, which was conducted by Collingwood.[5]

In 1949 W.P. Thompson became president of the University of Saskatchewan. A dedicated man of high principles, he continued the direction set for the university by Walter Murray. He believed that the development of pure and applied scientific research should be a priority and that, subsequently, the greatest need was to find accommodation on campus for scientists and engineers. Although he acknowledged the clamour of the arts and humanities faculty members about crowded working conditions, lack of facilities, the need for a central library and a new arts building, these needs could not be met readily. Throughout the 1940s the provincial government assumed a greater role in university affairs than previously, and while an engineering and medical building as well as the university hospital were in the plans, a fine arts building was not.[6] Even later, in a 1956 report from the university's forward planning committee presenting a list of building priorities on campus, the construction of an arts building was placed fourteenth in the list of fifteen projects.[7] The library, however, was completed in 1956 with the assistance of government funding, incorporating space to house the provincial archives.

The first wing of an arts building did materialize until 1959 on the occasion of the Golden Jubilee celebrating the university's first half-century. That year also marked the end of W.P. Thompson's tenure as president; the position was filled by a specialist in radiation chemistry, J.W.T. Spinks, from 1959 to 1974.

The period of Murray Adaskin's association with the University of Saskatchewan coincided with the presidency first of W.P. Thompson and then of J.W.T. Spinks. Although the composer arrived fifteen years after Walter Murray's retirement – and seven years after his death – the founder's legacy was still strongly felt. The University of Saskatchewan was Walter Murray's creation, and his philosophy was felt in every facet of its life. Over the twenty-one years of his association with the institution, Murray Adaskin carried on the tradition, creating a veritable cultural centre in the province. His contributions to the university were made possible through his tireless energy, his imagination, his professional expertise, and an idealism that met with a sympathetic response from an enlightened administration. The Adaskins' arrival in Saskatoon in 1952 marked the beginning of a cultural era for the university, the city, and the province unmatched in the history of their existence. Walter Murray's philosophy of the spiritual significance of the arts to the community found its exponent in Murray Adaskin, who became the driving force behind a Prairie renaissance of the arts.

A PERSONAL APPROACH TO ACADEMIC LIFE

The Adaskin house on University Drive, within walking distance of the university, was a tall, imposing building located in an old and established part of Saskatoon. Situated on a sprawling piece of property, the three-storey building faced a broad boulevard richly lined with trees. The back of the house was one street removed from an embankment, which sloped gracefully to the river some one hundred feet below. The third floor housed Murray's studio, a bathroom, and two guest rooms. Perhaps the most active part of the ten-room house, the third floor functioned as a veritable hotel when, over the two decades of Murray's association with the university, artists brought by him to perform in Saskatoon were offered accommodation in his home. For twenty-one years the house reverberated with laughter and good cheer, for it not only provided a setting for receptions after the innumerable concerts sponsored by Murray, but also served as a haven for visiting artists in need of the respite and warmth offered by the Adaskin hospitality. Benjamin Britten, Peter Pears, Soulima Stravinsky are but three names in an unending chain of distinguished visitors.

During Murray's first year at the University of Saskatchewan, the total student enrolment was 2,056.[8] He was chairman of a department of which he was the only faculty member, and enrolment in his two introductory music classes totalled thirty-four students. The music department, housed in the Soils and Dairy Building (later known as the John Mitchell Building), comprised a class-room and an office side-by-side. The somewhat austere conditions of a large empty class-room that could seat forty people were reflected in a first-year music department budget of seven thousand dollars. Murray had to start building a department literally from the ground up with a budget that seemed to defeat this mandate. Equipment was minimal. There was an upright piano in the composer's office where he taught his individual composition students, but there was no grand piano for the concerts the department was expected to give, the library was small, and the university lacked even such a basic teaching tool as a phonograph.

To Murray, these conditions presented a new type of challenge. His task was to build a music department, and this opportunity to create a program and communicate his love for his art to the younger generations held an excitement for him that was the focus of all his energy and enthusiasm. One of the first steps he took was to solicit the aid of the physics department in the building of a phonograph. A senior physics student was assigned the task of constructing a record-player with a good sound which was then placed in a plywood box. The quality of the unit was so exceptional that it served the music department for almost the entire period of Murray's tenure. The physics department also acoustically adjusted the sound in the large bare class-room by lining it with tiles.

Collaboration and dedication were the trademarks of the remarkable faculty assembled by W.P. Thompson during his ten-year presidency. The faculty got to know one another, and their dedication, their belief in working toward the good of their institution, benefited the university and the students. W.P. Thompson knew each member by name and took a personal interest in the professional endeavours of each. Murray remembers meeting Dr Thompson on winter mornings when the president would always stop to chat, despite the penetrating cold that transformed their words into mist:

I would come from my parking slot where they had plug-ins for cars, and the president would come from another direction. Our paths would converge, and after greeting me, he would say 'Murray, how are you getting along? I know that the main reason that you came here was to have time to compose. Are you finding that time?' Well, the truth of the matter was that of course I was not finding the time to write, but due to the nature of the academic year, I had long summers off from teaching. I knew that I would have five months each year available to me solely for the purpose of composing. Because Saskatchewan was an agricultural province where most students returned to their parents' farms as soon as weather permitted, classes ended earlier in the summer and started later in the fall. As a result, however, in the winter session classes were held straight through without a Christmas or Easter vacation. I did not mind the work in the winter as long as I had my summers off to compose. So all I said to Dr Thompson was that everything was going beautifully, and that I was just as happy as can be. He would then say to me, 'Now Murray, if there is any aspect of the work that turns out to be too much for you, do not hesitate to talk to me about it.'

I would walk away not touching the ground from that moment on. When a distinguished personality such as Dr Thompson makes this kind of comment to you, it obviously means that they are delighted to have you and that they like what you are doing. What more can one ask for? If I were dying, I would not have said a word of complaint to him. What a wonderfully smart man he was to deal with people in that manner.

W.P. Thompson was a scientist of international reputation, whose field was plant genetics, particularly in the development of rust-free wheat. He believed in hiring the best available scholars and researchers to head a faculty or a department. Many of the faculty attracted to the university during its period of post-war growth and development accepted, like Murray, the challenge of being involved in the growth and direction of a new program. The administration was looking for a faculty with a pioneering spirit, professionals willing to transplant their expertise to the university at Saskatoon. Many among the faculty and the administration were highly supportive of music, lending Murray the type of encouragement that was necessary for him to build the music program.

Francis Leddy, who was not an artist himself, was one of the moving spirits when it came to anything that dealt with the arts. Another prominent academic with a great understanding for music, and a close friend of the Adaskins, was Clarence Tracy. An internationally respected scholar, he was an authority on the works of Robert Browning and Richard Savage. Perhaps the closest of Murray's collaborators and friends at the University of Saskatchewan was the artist Eli Bornstein. Sensitive in spirit and gentle in demeanour, Bornstein came to the university in 1950 when the art department consisted of two people. His responsibilities at that time included all studio activity: drawing, painting, sculpture, and design. His professional activities in the early phase of his career – sculpture, painting, and print-making – reflected his interest in problems of realism. In the mid-1950s, Bornstein's interest in construction and abstraction led him increasingly toward the constructed relief medium. In the words and writings of Charles Biederman, he discovered a kindred perception of art and of new forms.[9] Bornstein's structurist work developed a uniqueness of style through the artist's deep commitment to colour and nature. While some works combined elements used in paintings and sculpture, others, particularly the larger artworks, attest to his interest in integrating art and architecture.[10]

Bornstein's love of music was the magnet that drew him to the creative efforts of Murray Adaskin. In Murray, the younger man found a father-figure and a kindred artistic spirit with whom he was able to share meaningful and stimulating conversations about music and art. Murray's open mind toward and interest in new directions in art was a great source of encouragement to Eli. Murray recognized in the artist's work 'a professional integrity that caused Eli to face a certain isolation from the artistic community as well as the public.' To Bornstein, the Adaskins' arrival in Saskatoon symbolized the start of a new era for a somewhat culturally conservative and traditional town. He remembers Murray's enthusiasm about contemporary music and his efforts to foster an understanding for contemporary music in the community. Murray was a factor in the artist's decision to remain in Saskatoon.

In February 1954, Murray and Eli staged a collaborative exhibition concert in Convocation Hall of the University of Saskatchewan. Accompanied at the piano by Mario Bernardi – a visitor to Saskatoon – Murray performed his own works: *Canzona and Rondo* and the *Sonata for Violin and Piano*. Bernardi then played the composer's piano sonata, and Murray performed his *Sonatine Baroque* for unaccompanied violin. While listening to the concert, the audience was surrounded by Eli Bornstein's sculptures, paintings, water-colours, drawings, and prints. The show was officially opened by W.P. Thompson, who, although not well versed in art or music, realized the importance of the event and wanted to show his support and appreciation for the concept developed by two of his senior professors.

The music and art departments continued their collaboration over the years by featuring annual joint recitals and exhibitions of the works of their students. The best compositions produced by Murray's class were performed by the music faculty as well as by professional musicians from the community, while artworks created by students in Eli's classes were displayed in the concert hall. The program covers were handsomely designed, at times in colour, by a leading art student. These collaborative recitals constituted a major university event.

The special rapport among faculty members was fostered and manifested in other areas of academic endeavour as well. One of these, the Joel Club, was a select group of twelve faculty members and downtown professionals, each representing a different academic discipline or area of interest. The purpose of the meetings held in the members' homes, twice a month, was to hear papers by its members, each of which was followed by a question-and-answer and discussion period. The group frequently discussed music and art, and read research papers prepared for presentation at scholarly conferences.

Another group within the University of Saskatchewan that became closely linked with Murray's sphere of activity was the medical faculty. At the time of Murray's arrival the College of Medicine had been in existence for six years. It offered a two-year program, after which the students transferred to another university to continue their medical studies. With Wendell McLeod as dean, the College of Medicine developed a high national and international profile. Dr McLeod was a gastroenterologist, originally from Winnipeg, with a degree from McGill. A friend of Norman Bethune, he was one of the first Canadians to visit China. His advanced ideas on preventive medicine led to his establishing a department of social and preventive medicine, a pioneering move for Canada. He had a strong interest in arts and music, and through those interests he became a good friend of the Adaskins.

McLeod spent the first year of his deanship travelling, with the purpose of recruiting an international faculty. The result was a clinical faculty that was a cosmopolitan group, as unusual situation for a small and relatively isolated city in the midst of the Canadian Prairies. The medical faculty, which had already acquired the anatomist Rudolf Altschul, included biochemist Charles MacArthur and pathologist Stewart Lindsay, who pushed for the development of a full medical school and who promoted a good medical-social system. Cardiologist Louis Horlick came from McGill University to join the faculty in 1954. A member of the university's board of governors, Dr Horlick still conducts research and has his own practice, serving as consultant for patients referred to him from all over the province. Other distinguished members of the medical faculty who belonged to the Adaskin circle were doctors William Feindel and Joseph Stratford, who established the Neurological Institute at the university. Feindel later became head of the Montreal Neurological Institute, taking over from Wilder Penfield at McGill; Stratford moved to the Montreal General Hospital. Later additions to the medical faculty included pediatrician and neurologist Hanna Sellers and pediatrician and cardiologist Frank Sellers. Husband and wife, in 1987 they had practices in Ottawa, and Dr Frank Sellers was also head of the College of Physicians and Surgeons in Toronto.

Apart from the pioneering spirit shared by this group of people and their dedicated efforts toward expanding the Faculty of Medicine, the question arises as to what sustained these highly qualified individuals' intellectual attention in a community the size of Saskatoon. The somewhat isolated location of the city made trips to a larger cultural centre for an infusion of concerts, art, or drama difficult. Yet many chose to stay in Saskatoon, although they could easily have found positions in places that were culturally more active. In fact, many declined such offers from other cities in favour of the University of Saskatchewan. An atmosphere of interaction and co-operation among faculty members, generated originally by the educational philosophies of two of the university's presidents – Walter Murray and W.P. Thompson – made working at the university a rewarding experience. As a result, a constructive force emerged that affected the university, the students, and the Saskatoon community.

For twenty-one years something unusual took place in the middle of the Canadian Prairies. Saskatoon assumed an active cultural life. Weekly concerts featured distinguished artists; large-scale musical events and festivals occurred, and a major art gallery was established. A broad circle of intellectuals was actively engaged in fostering the arts through their attendance at concerts, their support of community musical events and art exhibitions, and their interest in collecting Canadian art. While the university was responsible for drawing these exceptional scholars and doctors to the Prairies, selecting them carefully from a national and international panoply of specialists, two people in particular represented a focal point around which many of these intellectuals congregated: Frances James and Murray Adaskin. The timing of the Adaskins' arrival in Saskatoon was providential, for they supplied artistic perspective in this remarkable university community.

For two decades the thriving group of intellectuals constantly enriched one anothers' lives, as well as the university and the community. It was this 'enlightened circle' whose chemistry and personalities drew them into the spiritual sphere of the Adaskins, which in turn provided the stimulus for the Adaskins' work in the field of musical culture in the Canadian Prairies.

Murray approached his university commitments with a dedication that displayed a highly personal touch. He taught classes in composition and music appreciation within a program that was originally created exclusively as a service course within the university. Since a degree in music was not offered until 1967, over the first fifteen years of Murray's association with the University of Saskatchewan his students were non-music majors, who took the music appreciation course as part of their program of studies for an engineering or other university degree.

The music appreciation course, offered as a two-hour evening class, soon mushroomed to number more than four hundred students. Contemporary music assumed a central focus. The first term was usually devoted to the rudiments of music, while the second term focused on the study of works by one twentieth-century composer. The music of Charles Ives, Aaron Copland, Igor Stravinsky, Arnold Schoenberg, and Darius Milhaud was introduced. The presentation of live musical examples was an important ingredient in the course. Frances James was frequently enlisted to demonstrate selections from the art and contemporary song repertoire, and guest musicians, invited by Murray to perform Sunday evening concerts, were frequently recruited to play for the class. Since the department lacked a performance faculty, Murray's imaginative approach to the presentation of live music constituted for many of these young people a rare contact with the act of musical performance.

One of Murray's favourite composers, Stravinsky, and his music were frequent topics of study. On one occasion a concert of the Russian composer's music was planned to include the piano sonata that was also studied in detail by students in the music appreciation class. At the last minute the pianist originally scheduled to give the recital had to be replaced and the only person whom Murray considered capable of playing the Stravinsky sonata with only one week's advance notice was the composer's son, Soulima. Murray had made his acquaintance during his summer studies in Santa Barbara and felt free to call upon his friend for this occasion.

Shortly after Soulima's arrival in Saskatoon, Murray proudly informed him that his four hundred students listening to the performance knew the sonata inside out. He still vividly remembers that moment:

He looked at me with a very strange look, and on the night of the recital he said to me, 'Murray, would you mind if I put the music on the piano, and have you turn pages for me?' He had played this piece a million times; it was in his bloodstream, and he had in fact even recorded it. However, he had never expected more than a handful of people in the audience to be acquainted with the sonata. The fact that in this case the entire audience knew the work made him somewhat shaky.

So during the concert I stood beside him – he had put the music flat on the piano – and I kept turning the pages. But he never glanced at the music. He did not need to because he played it to perfection. His father had originally written it for himself, then taught it to Soulima, who had a crisp, marvellous rhythmic sense.

This was the kind of music he did so well. During his whole growing-up period as a pianist Soulima had not learned Chopin or Brahms because his father did not approve of their music. Only later in life did he discover Chopin, whose works he got to love. I remember hearing him play Chopin, an interpretation that was a bit on the dry side because he had never played this kind of romantic music where each note needed to be milked.

Soulima was a very interesting personality whose hands and face were the image of his father's.

In 1971 the music of Igor Stravinsky was once more the topic for the second term of the music appreciation class. The students became intimately acquainted with *L'Histoire du Soldat* and the *Octet for Wind Instruments*:

> They knew every note forwards and backwards, and could analyse the whole thing even though very few of them were musicians. What is even more interesting, they fell in love with the music because I played it, hammered it away at them for such a long time. They had also studied the music on records and heard live performances by musicians whom I brought to play for them.
>
> I remember the evening of the final examination on the fateful day of Stravinsky's death. The exam was to begin at 7 p.m., and the announcement of the composer's death was made on the six o'clock news. I stood at the door handing out the examination questions to each student who came through the door, and each of them had something to say to me about the event. Most said how deeply saddened they were to hear the news, which was of much more significance to them now that they had studied so much of Stravinsky's music. They thanked me at the end of the exam for bringing the world of Stravinsky to them in such a way that it would be with them forever. These were the deeply touching moments that made my teaching of this class so rewarding to me.

Right from the time he arrived in Saskatoon Murray's musical activities were multifaceted, penetrating various layers of the university and town community. In his second year of teaching, Murray organized and trained a small chamber music orchestra with players selected from among university students and Saskatoon musicians. In an effort to demonstrate to the group the importance of their endeavours and to encourage them in their work, he even engaged his friend Geoffrey Waddington that year to conduct one of their concerts. A letter sent to Murray from the conductor's wife after the concert captures the sincerity and symbolism in Murray's intentions. It mentions that while one day some of the members of his group would make even more important music and to greater audiences, it could never be offered with more humility, pride, and love than the music heard on this occasion. The program seemed to be the result of a different approach to music. The beauty of the sounds heard that night was the outcome of a desire to create something 'lovely to hear.'[11] That same year Murray gave twenty-eight half-hour Sunday afternoon broadcasts over a local radio station on topics related to music and musicians.

By 1955 Murray's department was granted a second full-time position, which was filled by Austin Clarkson. After three years, Clarkson left the University of Saskatchewan for New York, where he studied for a PH D in musicology at Columbia University before joining the music faculty at York University in Toronto.

With the addition of Clarkson, the music department was able to offer a greater variety of courses, including composition, theory, fundamentals of music, history of Western music, and music appreciation. Both musicians also lectured on aspects of their discipline to departments within the university when called upon to do so. Involving university students in the performance of music constituted an important part of Murray's and Austin's educational philosophy. This resulted in Austin's founding of the Engineers' Glee Club and the University Singers, and his conducting their annual concerts. Murray's University Chamber Orchestra tackled the score of Purcell's *Dido and Aeneas* in a concert performance that enlisted the services of Frances James. Annual staged performances of operettas were a highlight of the students' musical season. Although the preparation of a work such as *Brigadoon* was extremely time-consuming, the students' enthusiasm caused Murray to give unselfishly of his time. Frances Adaskin's letter to her friend Catharine Whyte, in Banff, presents an insider's account of one of these events:

Murray conducted the student operetta – *Blossomtime*– an enormous undertaking with dozens of rehearsals and many hours of work. Completely amateur cast – all students. Murray persevered and ended up by having the best show in history, with six performances at the Capitol Theatre, a large movie house which seats 1,200. The students made a profit for the first time in history. They are now prevailing on him to take it on again, and I am afraid that he is going to weaken ... As the students have been prone to regard the Music Department as something long-hair, he felt that by taking over this typical student effort he would get closer to them and gain their confidence ... The President and Murray's Dean are delighted, as this is the first time there has been any good influence [on the student body at large] by the faculty. Murray's years [with the Royal York Hotel] have been fruitful, for he is a born diplomat, and we find that is one of the prime requisites whether one is a university professor or a hotel musician.[12]

Murray's activities at the University of Saskatchewan were innovative and imaginative, all the more noteworthy considering his lack of prior university experience. Always ready to offer his assistance and encouragement to his students, Murray was quick to recognize exceptional talent and to mould a course of studies to suit the needs of that individual. One such student was Paul Pedersen, who later became dean of the School of Music at McGill University. Between 1954 and 1958 he studied at the University of Saskatchewan, first embarking upon a medical program while taking as many courses in the music department as it had to offer. His initial interest in composition received Murray's full support and encouragement, and it was at Murray's advice that Pedersen embarked upon a career in music.

The university could not at that time offer the talented young composition student a degree in music, and Murray knew that Paul's studies would have to be continued elsewhere. Murray was in a position, however, to offer him a course whose practical value would serve him in the future. He had advised his student to go to the faculty of music at the University of Toronto, and he knew that Paul's financial situation would make it necessary for him to earn money while pursuing his studies. Murray and Austin, therefore, designed a music calligraphy course for Paul, to teach him a revenue-making skill. Murray remember this episode:

In his course of studies with me Paul had shown ability by way of calligraphy. He was a very neat person. Austin and I decided to set up a calligraphy class for him so that by the time he arrived in Toronto we could write to the Canadian Music Centre and the CBC and recommend him as a copyist. Good copyists were hard to come by, and Paul was a good musician who would understand what was involved when dealing with orchestral parts.

While Paul did not receive official university credit for this course, we did manage eventually to have such a course approved for credit and to offer it on a regular basis.

Once in Toronto, Paul found himself working starting Friday nights almost through the night, all day Saturday, and at times even on Sundays to have orchestral parts ready for Lucio Agostini and all these composer-conductors who at that time had their own radio shows.

Pedersen obtained a PHD in musicology from the University of Toronto in 1970.

Another young person studying in Saskatoon during the early years of Murray's residence there who also benefited from the composer's belief in his talent and subsequent support was the pianist Boyd McDonald. At the time of the Adaskins' arrival the twenty-year-old McDonald was studying with the city's distinguished piano teacher Lyell Gustin. As performing musicians both Frances and Murray needed a good accompanist, and McDonald frequently filled this function. He accompanied Murray in a number of radio broadcasts and concerts in Regina and Winnipeg. He also helped out in performances of the university students' compositions at the Annual Exhibition of Music and Art concerts and appeared in a solo recital during the second year of the Sunday Evening Recital series. In 1961 he joined the piano faculty of the music department. The Adaskins had introduced Boyd to Darius Milhaud at Aspen the previous year, and Murray was even able to obtain a scholarship for him to study with the French composer. McDonald subsequently studied in Paris as a student of the famed Nadia Boulanger. Although he had saved up a considerable sum of money in preparation for this trip, he was about three hundred dollars short. It was with Murray's help that the missing sum was raised, making McDonald's sojourn in France possible. Murray recounts the event:

Three hundred dollars by today's standards is not much, but at that time it meant the difference between making it and not making it. I decided to speak to a wealthy neighbour of ours, Mr A.A. Murphy, owner of the radio station CFQC in Saskatoon. I went to see him and told him Boyd's story. Well, he did not know much about Boyd, but he said to me that if I thought that that was the right thing to do, he would help me get some money. He gave me $100. Then he picked up the phone right then and there and said to the person at the other end of the line, 'Bill, send me over a cheque for $100.' The other person must obviously have asked for a reason, for the gruff reply was, 'Mind your own god-damn business. Do I ask you for a reason when you ask me for money?' With that the receiver was slammed down. He turned to me and said, 'Okay, we have $200,' upon which he picked up the receiver again, dialed another number, and within two seconds I had the money for Boyd.

These businessmen may have had rough exteriors, but they all had hearts of gold.

In a letter to Catharine Whyte in 1958 Frances commented that 'Murray never stops working from the moment he gets up until the moment he goes to bed late at night.'[13] While this comment was made with respect to his summer composition activities at Canoe Lake, it reflected Murray's work ethic throughout the academic year as well. In addition to his administrative duties as head of an expanding department and as instructor of music appreciation and composition courses, his many activities included involvement with student performances such as operettas, lectures, and concerts for the university and town community; conducting the Saskatoon Symphony Orchestra; participation as board member in a number of national music organizations; and organizing three major concert series. Despite the amount of work during any single day, time was always found for encouragement and advice to individual music students.

Each of the three major concert series constituted an unusual undertaking not just for a university in the midst of the Canadian Prairies, but for Canada as a whole. Two of the three series took the form of festivals: the Golden Jubilee Music Festival, twenty-one concerts presented in the summer of 1959 in celebration of the university's fiftieth anniversary; and the Six Exhibition Concerts organized on the occasion of Canada's centennial. Concurrent with both events were the Sunday Evening Recitals, created, organized, and managed by Murray Adaskin for a period of almost twenty years, from 1954 to the end of his stay at the university.

At first featuring six concerts, the Sunday Evening Recitals expanded to eight and at one point even to ten concerts. The series, which took place in Convocation Hall, was usually sold out, because any concert staged by Murray was regarded by the community as an event of special significance. The hall itself, centrally located in a greystone building on campus, projected an intimate atmosphere. With a seating capacity of about 450, this little hall panelled in wood had a semicircular balcony reaching right to the stage.

For the Sunday Evening Recital series as well as the two festivals, Murray acted as manager, selecting the artists and writing to them to book them for the series. He viewed these university concerts as part of the educational process, and as such their organization and representation fell within his jurisdiction. He even engaged in fund-raising for the series, as well as organizing the social activities after each concert. Although some of these social events were delegated to other members of the university and town community, very frequently they took place in the Adaskin house at the hosts' own expense.

Most of the concert financing was done through ticket sales – usually ten dollars for adults and five dollars for students for the entire series. Any small deficit was then covered by the university. Murray found it feasible to operate on a minimal budget, because in most cases he was able to invite as guest artists his friends and professional connections who were willing to lower their fees. To compensate them for the effort of coming to Saskatoon, Murray would frequently organize for them a whole series of concerts in Canada's West. In other cases, he co-ordinated the timing of his friends' Saskatoon concerts with their previously scheduled concerts in nearby western cities. They would stop over in Saskatoon on their way to Eastern or Western Canada. In order to save the artists and the university the expense of a hotel bill, many musicians were guests at the Adaskin mansion. Murray functioned also as ticket vendor and carried the evenings' revenue to the cashier's office on Monday mornings. Many times he could be found sweeping the stage, or dusting and washing the piano keys with Frances just before a performance. Thus, Murray not only planned the Sunday evening concerts, but took care of every detail in this successful venture.

Over the two decades of recitals under Murray's management, the concerts featured artists of national and international reputation. The one stipulation upon which Murray insisted was that each program include some contemporary music.

With each passing year the concert grew in scope and perspective. Local and regional talent of the highest calibre was tapped in the presentation of the 1955–6 season: Boyd McDonald (piano), Peggie Sampson (cellist) from Winnipeg, Murray Adaskin (violin), Lauren Kolbinson (spinet), Frances James, Trudy Carlyle, and Howard Leyton-Brown (violin). Already in this early series contemporary music held priority on the programs. The audience was thus introduced to Samuel Barber's *Piano Sonata*, Bohuslav Martinu's *Seven Arabesques* for cello, John Weinzweig's and Aaron Copland's sonatas for violin and piano, Chester Duncan's *Six Songs*, Aaron Copland's *Emily Dickinson Songs*, and Schoenberg selections. Each concert also presented recognized masterpieces from the musical repertoire.

Murray appeared as soloist in two of these 1955–6 concerts, even experimenting with the sound of the spinet when he and his student Lauren Kolbinson played Niccolò Paganini's two sonatas originally written for violin and guitar in a violin-spinet combination. In an admirable example of collaborative effort, Murray also directed in that same year a concert performance of Purcell's opera *Dido and Aeneas*. All the participants were in some way connected to the university either as staff, faculty, or spouses. The conductor of the opera was Austin Clarkson, who enlisted the services of his University Singers and University Orchestra. Members of both groups were either students, graduates, or faculty. Boyd McDonald played the figured bass part for the occasion, using the spinet lent to the university by Lauren Kolbinson.

The success of the series, fed by Murray Adaskin's and the other participants' genuine enthusiam and love of music-making, led to its continued development in future years. In 1962 Murray organized a concert devoted entirely to the music of Darius Milhaud, as a commemoration of the French composer's seventieth birthday. Throughout the years following Murray's initial contact with Milhaud, their friendship had flourished. The Adaskins had been directly responsible for introducing Canadian radio audiences to his music when, in 1951, at Murray's instigation, the CBC broadcast two concerts dedicated to the French composer. Some years later Murray commissioned a work from Milhaud for the University of Saskatchewan's Golden Jubilee Festival, so that the summer of 1959 witnessed the world *première* in Saskatoon of his *Sonatine for Viola and Cello*, performed by Gerald Stanick and Peggie Sampson. When originally approached by Murray with the commission, Milhaud was quick to oblige his friend despite his numerous other concurrent commitments, particularly since the project allowed him to complete his self-imposed task of composing for all the major string chamber music combinations.

For his homage to Milhaud on his seventieth birthday, Murray infused the occasion with an informal atmosphere and a personal touch. His verbal comments to the audience during the evening communicated his understanding and love of this music to the assembled listeners. To Murray the audience was an extended family, with whom he wanted to share Milhaud's musical world. His success in the endeavour was mirrored in the closing remarks of the reviewer for the campus newspaper, *The Sheaf*: 'the program was, to use a colloquialism, a smashing success. Darius Milhaud has my respect, my appreciation, [and] my thanks.' As an additional personal touch, Murray collected the signatures of each member of the audience, appending them to a telegram that was sent to the French composer after the concert. The telegram read as follows:

Dec. 16, 1962, 11 p.m.

To Darius Milhaud
Music Dept.
Mills College
Oakland, California

Dear Milhaud, in order to honour you at the end of your 70th anniversary year, your Hymne de Glorification for solo piano, Dreams for voice and piano, Sonatine for flute and piano, Duo for two unaccompanied violins, and your Suite for violin, clarinet and piano were played tonight at the University of Saskatchewan by my friends Thomas Rolston, Edward Abramson, David Kaplan, Sylvia Stuart, Garth Beckett, Boyd McDonald and myself.

The undersigned enthusiastic audience join us in sending you good wishes and our admiration hoping that you will continue to write for many years to come and that you will enrich our lives with many more masterpieces.

Murray Adaskin
Frances Adaskin

The telegram contained close to one hundred signatures. Murray recounts Milhaud's reaction upon the presentation of this Saskatoon birthday bouquet:

You can imagine the fun when Milhaud answered the telephone to be told that there was a telegram from Saskatoon for him, and he of course said, 'Please read it to me.' [The operator] began with the message, and then started reading an endless list of names! Quite a few of them Ukrainian with difficult pronunciations! When Milhaud realized what it was all about he asked that the telegram be delivered to him, and the enclosed photograph shows him reading it with obvious relish. Though the wire cost me something like $50.00, his letter to me afterwards in which he said, 'You *would* think of such a thing,' made me very happy indeed.

Over the two decades of the Sunday Evening Recital series, Murray trained his audiences both to expect the unexpected and to hear and meet some of the more prominent internationally known artists. English oboe player Leon Goossens and guitarist and lutenist Julian Bream were favourites. Other artists were Peter Pears and Benjamin Britten. Britten's first visit to Saskatoon occurred at the invitation of the Kinsmen's Club, sponsors of the Celebrity Concerts. As friends of the Adaskins since their Toronto visit in the early 1950s, Britten and Pears stayed in the Adaskin home every time one or both passed through Saskatoon. Britten, who was a very private person, took no particular pleasure in the large receptions after the concerts and much preferred returning to his hosts' private quarters, where he, Pears, and the Adaskins would chat, sitting around a table over a cup of tea and some cheese until the early hours of the morning.

Murray recalls a particularly memorable day in 1961, when Benjamin Britten, who was in the last stages of work on his manuscript to the *War Requiem*, played the score at the piano:

It was the spring before the first performance of the *War Requiem*, which he wrote for the reconstructed Coventry Cathedral, which suffered damages during the war. He was planning to have as leading singers representatives of the three major nations involved in the war: German singer Dietrich Fischer-Dieskau, Russian Galina Vishnevskaya, and the British Peter Pears.

He had divided the orchestra into two separate groups and he questioned what their seating arrangements would be during the performance. One morning when Ben came down for breakfast he said to me, 'Murray, I brought the score of the *War Requiem*. Would you like to hear it?' I just about died. The two of us sat down on the piano bench, and he sang, shouted, played everything at once from the huge orchestral score.

It took a long time to play through the entire work. At the end he turned to me and asked for my advice as to how to place the orchestra. I said: 'Ben, you must feel strongly about how you are thinking about this work in the first place. Subconsciously you must know what you want. Why then don't you do it the way you want to do it and don't listen to anybody else!'

Britten's visits to Saskatoon occurred in the wintertime, and Murray recalls with affection how the British composer attempted to cope with the frigid Canadian Prairie winters:

Ben arrived in a coat given to him by friends that was originally worn by an officer in the Battle of Balaklava.[14] By this time it was a kind of a light green colour. I have no idea what its original colour was; you know how quickly cloth fades. It was a thick material, heavy as lead, that came right down to his heels. You could probably stand it up and it would have stood on its own. Now Ben was a thin man, a little taller than I, and he looked as if he was completely lost in this coat. Yet he just loved it and was very proud of it. Imagine carrying that thing! I would guess that it must have weighed forty or fifty pounds! Fran and I so enjoyed seeing his affection for it that we just roared with laughter. We always had to help him get it into the car.

The Sunday Evening Recital series was made possible primarily through Murray's extended network of contacts among well-known Canadian and international musicians. It was not a money-making enterprise and the artists were offered only a token sum. Money, therefore, was not the drawing card that attracted artists to Saskatoon. In many cases it was their friendship with the Adaskins that prompted them to brave the arctic chill of the Saskatoon winters in order to perform at the University's Convocation Hall.

Two other events organized by Murray, in the summer of 1959 and throughout 1967, presented concepts unique to the Canadian cultural scene. The year 1959 marked the fiftieth anniversary of the founding of the University of Saskatchewan. The institution itself organized a number of events to celebrate the occasion of its golden jubilee, and Murray, who felt that music was a fitting means to augment the celebrations, organized the Golden Jubilee Music Festival.

The six-week mammoth cycle extended from 1 July to 15 August 1959. It was so unusual in concept that it led Lauretta Thistle, music critic for the *Ottawa Citizen*, to exclaim, 'to quote a comic strip... what in the ever-lovin' blue-eyed world is going on in Saskatchewan? and how does Saskatoon persuade a world figure like Milhaud to write a work for it?'[15] What was 'going on' in Saskatoon was none other than Murray Adaskin's mind at work. In his gently persuasive and charmingly forthright manner Murray master-minded, organized, and directed the festival. Twenty-one concerts were given during the six-week period, the first three of which accompanied the meeting of the Learned Societies hosted by the University of Saskatchewan that year.

Twenty-one distinguished instrumentalists from the United States and Canada were invited to participate both as performers and as teachers. Murray's plan encompassed a six-week summer session for young instrumental students, to be invited from all parts of the province to study and participate in workshops and forum discussions with the distinguished visitors. The concentrated exposure to music during this period, both at the private tuition level and through the concerts, was to serve an educational purpose in the development of a new generation of Canadian orchestral players.

The summer faculty thus assembled by Murray Adaskin consisted of players of one each of the woodwind instruments, two horn players, one trumpeter, a trombonist, and a percussion player, a string quartet, and a bassist. The list included such luminaries as Rafael Druian, at that time concert-master of the Minneapolis Symphony; cellist Robert Jamieson, another principal from the same symphony; and Iowa pianist John Simms, who participated in almost every concert either as accompanist or as chamber music player. John Pepper, from the Los Angeles Philharmonic, acted as concert-master.[16]

The choice of the faculty who brought to Saskatoon the riches of their experiences with the Toronto, Montreal, Los Angeles, and Minneapolis symphonies was Murray's alone. He corresponded with them, extended the invitations, found housing for them – usually through the large network of the Adaskins' personal friends – organized their schedules, picked them up at the airport, and directed them through the six-week course of events.

The sixty young music students, whose attendance at the summer festival was made possible by scholarships raised by local service clubs at Murray;s instigation, were put up in private homes free of charge, where, for the duration of their stay, they were looked after by their hosts. Junior students were offered the opportunity to play in the Saskatoon Junior Symphony Orchestra. The more advanced students performed in some of the larger ensembles and with the Saskatoon Symphony Orchestra, each section of which was led by one of the visiting faculty. The total involvement with music at so many different levels offered the youth, most of whom had come from the province of Saskatchewan, an inestimable musical opportunity. Murray's real reward for all his hard work was the satisfaction of knowing what this opportunity afforded to the talented young musicians. Terence Helmer and Andrew Dawes were among the group of string players assembled in Saskatoon that year. Both distinguished themselves in the years to come as members of the Orford String Quartet.

The festival consisted of two to three concerts a week of mostly solo and chamber music. Several times the local symphony orchestra was incorporated into the events. The most striking aspect of this already unusual festival, however, was Murray's plan to commission twelve new works specifically for the occasion. Most of the new compositions were to be Canadian, but the plan was to include four works by composers representing different corners of the world: Benjamin Britten, England; Darius Milhaud, France; Charles Jones, the United States; and Luigi Nono, Italy. Because of the shortness of time, only one of the four planned new international works was conceived – the *Sonatine for Viola and Cello* by Milhaud. This fact did not decrease Murray's determination to infuse the program with contemporary international compositions: Elliott Carter's *Woodwind Quintet*, Luigi Dallapiccola's *Quaderno Musicale di Anna Libera*, Charles Jones's *Sonata for Violin and Piano*, Copland's *Four Dance Episodes* from *Rodeo*, and Barber's *Adagio for Strings* were some of the more recently composed works. In addition, Charles Ives's *Violin Sonata No 1* was performed by Druian and Simms, and one entire concert was devoted to the music of Igor Stravinsky.

Eight Canadian composers, including Murray Adaskin, provided compositions on commission for this historic event: Udo Kasemets (*Sinfonietta*, conducted on the occasion by the composer), Jean Papineau-Couture (*Pièce Concertante No 4* for solo oboe and strings, conducted by Roland Leduc), John Weinzweig (*Divertimento No 3* for solo bassoon and strings)[17], Sophie Eckhardt-Gramatté (*Duo Concertante for Cello and Piano*), and Robert Turner (*Variations and Toccata for Ten Instruments*); as well as Boyd McDonald and Paul Pedersen, both alumni of the University of Saskatchewan, whom Murray was especially pleased to offer their first professional commissions. A major Canadian group passing through Saskatoon was also incorporated into the program: the Montreal Bach Choir, conducted by George Little, made a brief appearance on its return from the Vancouver International Festival.

During the course of the festival both Murray and Frances participated as soloists. In addition to having several of his own compositions performed, Murray conducted on a number of occasions and played in a Haydn string quartet with Andrew Dawes, Gerald Stanick, and Peggie Sampson. Frances James made guest appearances in performances of Debussy and Milhaud songs. Surprisingly, audiences for these concerts seemed to be anything but conservative; their eclectic tastes resulted in sold-out houses.

The Saskatoon Golden Jubilee Music Festival, therefore, set a number of precedents. Very seldom had there been a concert series in Canada to present such a large number of contemporary compositions, and never had there been an occasion to commission such a substantial number of new Canadian works for performance during a six-week period. The programs were balanced with selections from the contemporary international, Canadian, and classical music repertoire. Two outdoor wind-ensemble concerts featured such little-known examples from the classical repertoire as compositions by, among others, J.C. Bach, Hassler, C.P.E. Bach, Paër, Zingarelli, and Poulenc.

With its goals to bring young Saskatchewan music students in contact with top instrumental teachers on this continent, to provide Saskatoon audiences with a first-class eclectic repertoire, and to foster Canadian music in particular, all as a means of celebrating the fiftieth anniversary of the university's existence, the festival was an unequivocal success. It provided Murray with an opportunity to put into practice a philosophy that constituted the very essence of his artistic being: to share his love of music with the world and particularly to encourage the talented younger generations to embark upon a musical career. Combined with these broad humanistic ideals was an elemental sense of nationalism and a belief in the quality of the creative impulses of Canadian composers.

It would not be an exaggeration to state that Murray Adaskin was, single-handed, the inspiration for, the motivating force behind, and the driving force during the University of Saskatchewan Golden Jubilee Music Festival. And he did it on a shoestring. The budget of thirty thousand dollars for the entire operation was raised in part through funds from the Canada Council and in part through approximately one hundred dinner and luncheon speeches given by Murray to the service clubs of the community. The national significance of his accomplishment cannot be overstated. The critic and composer Udo Kasemets sent the following evaluation to Murray in a private communication:

Looking back at the Festival and judging it from a distant perspective, I am even more convinced than before that it was a total success. All your aims were fulfilled in a magnificent way. When I sounded harsh on the 'Critically Speaking' (and also in my forthcoming articles for *The Star* and *The Journal*)[18] about the commissioned works, I think it marks also a success. If we have a great number of works performed we can start to look at them with critical eyes and we can set standards. With few odd performances here and there we can only be grateful that Canadian music is played at all and there is no chance for honest criticism. With a festival like yours the situation is completely different and we get a right to speak. Once more, my superlative congratulations to you, you great man![19]

The national response to such a milestone in Canadian culture was a mild interest at best. Norman Lucas, producer of CBC Winnipeg, taped the concerts, and some of the tapes were eventually aired on the Western network. Plans to produce a series of records of the performances did not materialize.

The summer of 1959 was rich in musical fare for Canadian audiences, for two other music festivals were unfolding concurrently with the one in Saskatoon: the Vancouver International Festival and the Stratford music season. The five-week Vancouver festival, in its second season, featured such internationally known artists as Bruno Walter and Herbert von Karajan, and commissioned works by Harry Somers, Pierre Mercure, and Robert Turner. Its ambitious scope resulted in its eventual financial downfall, but in 1959 it constituted a glamorous drawing card for tourists; the glitter of the occasion, occurring in the spectacular surroundings of mountain scenery and the Pacific Ocean, overshadowed the cultural events in a small town in the middle of the Canadian Prairies. As a festival held at a Canadian university, however, the Golden Jubilee Festival was of unique scope and proportions, and as a non-profit-making proposition the fact that the all-too-modest budget was not overspent is a credit to Murray Adaskin's organizational abilities. The festival will be remembered by the many people who experienced the personal touch of Murray's enthusiastic endeavours, just as the works commissioned for the occasion will remain as milestones for posterity.

Since its founding in 1909, the University of Saskatchewan had prided itself on its tradition of public service. Its mandate, to be close to the people of the province and to serve the whole province, was in the forefront of President Thompson's philosophy as he urged all faculty members to devote part of their time to community service. Murray Adaskin's philosophy of education was in total harmony with that of his university. His aim was to share his love for music with the lay men and women in the community. To him art was not an elitist discipline within the reach of only a select few; art and music existed for the betterment of life, and his strong community commitment was based on his wish to spread an appreciation of music to all people.

Murray's involvement with the Saskatoon Symphony Orchestra occurred over a period of five years. At the time of his arrival in Saskatoon this was a small community orchestra made up predominantly of enthusiastic amateurs who contributed their services free of charge. The symphony had no budget, and when its conductor, Victor Kviesis, left in pursuit of a paying job, Murray was asked to take over. By the end of his association with the symphony, Murray had built up its budget to the dizzying heights of four thousand dollars. One of his first contributions to his new activity was the idea, unusual in Canada at the time, of having the symphony commission one new Canadian work a season. At one of his luncheon addresses to the Saskatoon Cosmopolitan Club Murray described the struggle of Canadian composers for recognition. He pointed to the example of the Louisville (Kentucky) Symphony Orchestra, which had become known for its commissions of national and international compositions. After such a pep talk the club decided to sponsor a Canadian work. It presented the symphony with a cheque for two hundred dollars, the first in a number of annual commissions of Canadian compositions.

The president asked if he could present the cheque to the composer on stage. When he came backstage and saw all the music parts to the thick orchestral score, somewhat taken aback he asked whether that was the new piece. When I confirmed, he said, 'Gosh, I didn't know it was going to be anything like that! I thought that you would receive a sheet of paper with a melody on it!' Well now, that is how deliciously naive and sweet they were. He immediately said that the sum was not adequate, and right then and there he raised it to $250. Each year they kept raising it.

I always went to the Cosmopolitan Club's annual banquets in order to present a report on what happened to the commissioned piece and how it was received by the audience, musicians, and critics. One time someone sent us a program from a Philadelphia Symphony Orchestra concert with one of these pieces on it, and the program notes mentioned its Saskatoon *première* and that it was originally commissioned by the Cosmopolitan Club. When I read this acknowledgment to the Club members, their pride knew no bounds.

The first commission in 1958 was to Saskatoon-born Robert Fleming, who had already attained national recognition as a film composer. His parents were Saskatoon residents, and Fleming enjoyed a widespread reputation in his home town. The work produced for that occasion was his *Summer Suite*. Murray remembers this inaugural event: 'By this time we were holding the concerts in the big gymnasium. The place smelled a bit like running shoes and sweat, but it was a big hall and they put up a stage for us, one of those removable stages. Fleming conducted his own *première*, but I had to coach the orchestra beforehand so that by the time they faced the composer, the players knew what they were doing.'

For each commissioned work Murray invited the composer to conduct his own *première* performance and to meet the audience afterwards. In order to make the new composition more accessible to the audience, Murray would program it just before intermission, and repeat its performance after intermission: 'Each year after such a double performance people would come up to me to comment on how much better the orchestra played it the second time, while in fact they played it just as well at the rehearsal. It never occurred to the members of the audience that they could hear more things in the new composition the second time around.'

The commissioning of Canadian works continued for about ten years, to include Jean Papineau-Couture's *Trois Pièces* for orchestra and Harry Somers's *Picasso Suite*. In an acknowledgment of Murray's Saskatoon activities, Papineau-Couture wrote in a 1962 letter to the composer: 'I think it was very natural for me to dedicate the work to you. After all, you were at the very origin of it.' Violet Archer, Neil Chotem, Harry Freedman, Udo Kasemets, Eldon Rathburn, Talivaldis Kenins, and John Weinzweig were some of the composers who wrote commissioned works for the Saskatoon Symphony.

As part of his publicity campaign to raise financial support for the symphony, Murray arranged a number of events to promote greater understanding by the community of the musicians and their efforts. He arranged for the dean of medicine at the university, Dr T.H. McLeod, who was also chairman of the symphony board, to address a group of members of the community to explain the educational function and the financial needs of such an organization. Murray then proceeded to demonstrate to the group the capabilities of the different sections of the orchestra by having each play popular tunes. Educating the masses in an attempt to create an understanding of and empathy with music was never too far removed from Murray's consciousness.

Organizing the local junior symphony orchestra and arranging for the Saskatoon Kiwanis Club to purchase instruments for the young people and to donate scholarships for them was another of Murray's community activities. His fund-raising efforts on behalf of the junior symphony and the Saskatoon Symphony were embodiments of the philosophy that when there is a will to make something work there are no obstacles to it that can't be overcome.

Although other organizations, such as the Saskatoon Cosmopolitan Club and the Kinsmen's Club, sponsored concert series, Murray's managerial activities provided the major musical fare in the city for more than twenty years. Part of his audience consisted of members of the Adaskins' wide circle of friends, representative of a broad cross-section of disciplines. Doctors, lawyers, painters, businessmen, and academics congregated around the pair, and interacted to create a constructive force within the cultural life of the city. Among them were Murray's university friends, cardiologist Louis Horlick, nurse Ruth Horlick, artist Eli Bornstein, actress Chrisse Bornstein, dentist Sydney Gelmon, and social worker Miriam Gelmon. They combined forces with such leading citizens of Saskatoon as the president of radio and television station CFQC, G. Blair Nelson, painter Mary Nelson, lawyer Fred MacDermid, and painter Margaret MacDermid. A benefactor of many of the city's activities, Fred MacDermid had come to Saskatoon in 1907 as founder of the law firm MacDermid and Ferguson, which became the most reputable law firm in the city.[20]

With the Adaskins at the helm, this group of professionals and artists constituted some of the fund-raisers for what are now considered the city's main cultural institutions, the Art Gallery and the Arts Centre. They were among the group of people who devoted their free time to various boards and committees. Through their presence they supported Murray's concerts and all of the arts in the city. They were the pillars of culture in Saskatoon and constituted the enlightened circle around the Adaskins. In turn, the Adaskins enriched their lives. The Sunday Evening Recital series afforded them the opportunity of hearing good music as well as new music. They met the performers at the receptions that followed the concerts and were able to exchange stimulating ideas with interesting people in the musical world. The nature and the size of the town itself made possible this kind of communication, which in a larger city would have been considerably more difficult.

The post-concert Adaskin receptions became legendary. They often included as many as fifty people and were given in an elegant style with most of the expenses sustained by the hosts. Occasionally these events took place in the university president's home or in their friends' homes, making them a real community effort. The primary objectives shared by all these individuals were to support the arts and to improve the quality of life in the city.

The Adaskins' love for Canadian art and painting was infectious. They set a style and a tone among their friends that encouraged these men and women to purchase Canadian paintings. In addition to supporting such local artists as Ernest Lindner, Winona Mulcaster, Dorothy Knowles, and Bill Perehudoff, they invested in a number of paintings by the Group of Seven. One of the major figures on the Saskatoon art scene and a respected member of the Adaskin circle was Frederick S. Mendel. Born in Germany in 1888, he became the founder and chairman of the board of Intercontinental Packers, Ltd. In the 1920s he and his family had established meat-packing plants in Northern Germany, Poland, and Hungary. Their specialty was the production of bacon. Before the war Mendel lived in Berlin, surrounded by such leaders of contemporary culture as Kurt Weill and Bertolt Brecht. In 1934 he found it necessary to leave Germany because of the prevalent anti-intellectual and anti-Jewish atmosphere. He chose to settle in Saskatoon, where, in the 1940s, he purchased an empty plant and started a meat-packing business from the ground up. One of his daughters, Eva Mendel Miller, who had been an art student in Berlin, pursued her involvement with art on Canadian soil. It was under her influence that Mendel began his art collection, first of works by local Saskatchewan painters, then by such Canadians as Emily Carr and members of the Group of Seven. With his daughter acting as his consultant Mendel became a renowned collector of Canadian and European art.

Mendel was a philanthropist, always ready to help a worthy cause. To quote B.T. Richardson, from his introduction to Mendel's *Reminiscences*, 'business to him is an activity dealing in ideas, the paramount concern being not to accumulate money, but to use man's creative capacity to build and add to the livelihood of the people engaged in it.'[21] Mendel's recognition of Murray Adaskin's artistry and human worth was reflected in the incident with the Stradivarius, related in chapter 4, which cemented a close friendship between the two men.

The Mendels had converted a space on the floor above the offices in the meat-packing plant into a private art gallery, which frequently also served as the setting for a convention or reception. During the first decade of the Adaskins' residence in Saskatoon, the city had no official art gallery. Viewing of artwork was restricted to private collections, Mendel's own gallery, and the Arts Centre, which was run on a volunteer basis in rented stores and later in the basement of the King George Hotel. It was at Mendel's suggestion that a plan was devised for the construction of a permanent art gallery. He suggested a system of grants from various government organizations, which would be matched by a large donation from him. Women's organizations under the leadership of Margaret MacDermid, Mary Nelson, 'Bubs' Coleman, and others carried out rigorous fund-raising campaigns. The city, in turn, donated the choicest part of its land by the river bank to the art gallery. A conservatory of flowers was added to the gallery building by the city to provide colour and greenery during the winter. The cheerfulness of the conservatory vegetation brightened many a farmer's winter months and served as a point of attraction for families, who would come from within a radius of three hundred miles to see the flowers and the art exhibition.

Fred Mendel, after whom the art gallery was named, donated his Canadian collection to the institution. During the early years of its existence Murray Adaskin served on its board of directors, and Eli Bornstein was one of the artists whose works were exhibited there.

As part of its Canadian Centennial project Saskatoon received another major cultural institution. At the instigation of Mayor Sidney Buckwold, a multi-purpose auditorium was built in the centre of the city. During the time they lived in Saskatoon, therefore, the Adaskins witnessed an expansion of locales for the city's cultural activities from Convocation Hall, a small university auditorium with creaky parquet floors, to the most modern facilities. They and their friends were one of the primary motivating forces behind Saskatoon's cultural expansion.

Frances James became involved in a project of her own when, shortly after the opening of the Mendel Art Gallery, she embarked upon a campaign to raise money toward the purchase of a grand piano for the gallery's Art Centre. The small recital hall on the lower floor of the gallery, which because of its intimate atmosphere was an ideal location for chamber music concerts, lacked a piano. Through a number of musicales organized by Frances at which a silver collection was taken up, the Frances Adaskin Art Centre Piano Fund attained its goal to purchase a Bösendorfer.

Two activities in Saskatoon had fully absorbed Frances's time: teaching and acting as hostess for receptions held after the concerts organized by Murray. She became a member of the Music Teachers' Association, assuming its presidency for one year. Although the university music department did not have a voice teacher on the faculty, because of the stringent rules against nepotism she would not have been eligible to fill that position. Many of her private students, however, were either registered in various university programs or were relatives of faculty members. These were the singers recruited by Murray for his operatic presentations. Margaret Ready sang in Pergolesi's comic intermezzo *La Serva Padrona,* while Marnie Patrick and Bill Fleming starred in Hindemith's short comic opera *Hin und Zurück.* Frances's students also sang leading roles in the musical shows organized by the student association: *Brigadoon, Blossomtime,* and *West Side Story.* Sylvia Stuart and Greta Clark were among her other outstanding voice students, and the latter herself became a voice teacher in Saskatoon.

Throughout their careers the Adaskins have been sensitive in detecting talented young musicians and have helped and encouraged them in any way they could. The help Murray gave Boyd McDonald, a student, in his goal to study at Fontainebleau with Nadia Boulanger encapsulates the Adaskins' philosophy of life. This philosophy is aptly summarized in a letter from Frances to Catharine Whyte:

Murray and I have spent a good part of our lives trying to be good friends to our friends; to give to others the full measure of the many wonderful things that have come our way. We often wish we could do more [especially] now that we have so many young people, some of whom are so gifted yet have nothing to come and go on. We find that we have many avenues in Canada that we can open to give them help, though we ourselves are not able to materially help. In the eight years we have been in Saskatoon we have succeeded in placing many, many of them in wider horizons, and when they leave we always hope that they, in turn, will want to come back and use Saskatoon as a base from which they can give back to others the richness of their experiences, at the same time carrying on their own careers. This will be the only way we can develop a small but important cultural community. It is already paying off, for this summer Boyd and Sylvia McDonald have returned to Saskatoon after spending three years in Paris.[22]

The same letter also mentions as one of Murray's protégés Andrew Dawes, who was not only Murray's violin student, but a member of the Adaskin household for more than three years.

In the spring of 1960, preceding the Adaskins' sabbatical in Europe, Murray used the opportunity of Isaac Stern's concert engagement in Saskatoon to arrange an audition for the young violinist with him. At Stern's subsequent recommendation Dawes received names of three renowned European violinists to whom he could apply for lessons while in Europe with the Adaskins. One of these was Lorand Fenyves in Geneva, with whom Dawes studied for five years.[23]

Another teenager in the household was Susan Adaskin, daughter of Murray's brother John, who found the Adaskins' home a refuge in the year following her father's death. She displayed a talent for writing, particularly for poetry, which Murray encouraged.[24]

The Saskatoon period signified for both Adaskins a new stage in their professional activities. At the threshold of middle age, they entered a new life, turned over a new leaf. At an age when most people, happy to have found their goal, would have settled down to let life take its course, the Adaskins had the courage to leave behind highly successful careers and head toward the unknown.

While for Murray the Saskatoon years epitomized the most productive period of his professional career, for Frances they marked an abdication from the frenzied pace of her Toronto concert years. At age forty-nine, she was at the height of her vocal prowess and enjoyed a widespread national reputation. She was fully aware of the implications on her career that a removal from the centre of musical activities – the Toronto-Ottawa-Montreal triangle – might carry. At this stage in her and Murray's lives, however, she was prepared for the consequences.

During the first twenty years of their married lives Murray had held jobs as violinist. While performing gave him pleasure, his developing interest in composition made it increasingly difficult for him to combine his Royal York job with composing. For those twenty years the emphasis in their partnership had been on Frances's singing career while Murray's work as violinist earned a living for them both. When the opportunity presented itself for him to devote himself to composition, which, in effect, the university appointment made possible, Frances was prepared at this point to place primary emphasis on Murray's endeavours. His turn had come to embark upon the activity most musically fulfilling to him – to leave the sphere of the fiddler and the hotel performer and to acquire a greater freedom of professional opportunity. Frances decided to follow Murray on the path that was best for him.

Murray's salary at the university amounted to approximately one-third of the sum earned at the Royal York. The Adaskins accepted this steep cut in pay in the full realization that there would no longer be funds to cover the deficit incurred during any concert tours on which Frances might embark. Consequently, her concert activities became restricted to local appearances with the Saskatoon Symphony Orchestra, the university concert series, and occasional demonstrations of the vocal repertoire in Murray's music history classes. She continued her discussions of new repertoire through her correspondence with Emmy Heim until Heim's death in 1954. Although Frances's CBC commitments continued for a few years, travel between Saskatoon and Toronto proved too expensive. In 1953 she sang on the 'CBC Wednesday Night' series a program that included songs by Chester Duncan, and a year later she performed

Stravinsky's *The Rake's Progress*. Frances also made an attempt at establishing a local radio program of classical music, and in February-March 1953 she gave a series of broadcasts on radio station CBK entitled 'Songs with Frances James.'

The biggest musical problem Frances encountered in Saskatoon was the dearth of experienced pianists with whom she could work on a regular basis. In 1952 the local talents Boyd McDonald and Garth Beckett were still students. In later years McDonald and Mabel Sanda became Frances's regular accompanists. These first years in Saskatoon are best summarized in Frances's own words in a letter to Catharine Whyte of 16 April 1956:

My singing has been diminished and I am now a teacher of singing and a singer on the side. It has been a difficult re-adjustment but was inevitable, for when Murray was earning a good income at the Royal York I could indulge in what seemed to many a very busy and profitable career. The first year I came here I had a lot of radio work that took me back and forth to Toronto. With the coming of TV these programs have diminished or have been taken off entirely. Since radio was the bulk of my income it really paid most of my tours and Murray provided the rest. As my teaching interest increased I found it so absorbing and tiring that I had no time to practise or was too exhausted to try, so that last year I hardly sang at all … There has been such shameful teaching here that each pupil I have seems to be a problem. I feel at a complete loss sometimes … what to do, and would gladly have strangled the teacher who had so mangled a talented youngster. I am trying to keep my class down so I can teach longer lessons.

Throughout her two decades in Saskatoon Frances became involved with an ever-widening circle of voice students. Community service at all levels was thus an important aspect of both of the Adaskins' creative activities.

Murray took to heart President Thompson's belief that the greatness of a university depends upon the greatness of its faculty and upon the extent of the faculty's involvement with the community. Adjudicating at music festivals was one of the activities encouraged by W.P. Thompson, and in Murray's twenty-one years of service at the University of Saskatchewan he adjudicated at almost one hundred festivals in the provinces of Saskatchewan, Alberta, and Manitoba. Winnipeg, Calgary, and Edmonton, where the three largest festivals in Western Canada were held, called upon Murray to adjudicate musical events ranging from guitar and violin competitions to composition. It was through these festivals, in fact, that he discovered many gifted young violinists and composers who later studied with him, and whom he helped at a crucial stage in their development as musicians.

Murray's interest in the history and development of the violin as an instrument led to his writing an article in which he casually mentioned that an old violin brought from Europe by a grandfather or some other family member and stored in oblivion under the bed could well turn out to be a valuable rare instrument. The article was published in a farm paper called *The Western Producer*, which was read by every farmer in the three Prairie provinces. Before he realized what he had done, he was overwhelmed by hundreds of letters written by farmers, describing the violins they had unearthed in their households and asking his opinion of their worth. Eventually, Murray found it impossible to cope with the deluge of correspondence and printed a form letter explaining the difference between a modern and a rare violin, and pointing out the signs at the back of the instrument and at the scroll that could serve as identifying features.

The result of that particular educational attempt was an even more intensified period of activity as the farmers started bringing their instruments to his office for personal evaluation. Looking back at this episode in amusement, Murray now says: 'The amount of letters, correspondence, and appointments that I had from these people all over the place was just incredible; it never ended. I didn't know there were so many potential Strads and Amatis under people's beds!'

Giving talks on various aspects of music to local community groups, such as service clubs and women's organizations, was another of Murray's frequent activities. On one of these occasions, as a means of showing his audience the difference in sound between two rare and two home-made instruments, he conducted an experiment during which all four instruments were played. A successful Saskatchewan wheat farmer by the name of Steven Kolbinson was a collector of rare violins and had acquired a Del Jesu Guarneri. Kolbinson was also an amateur instrument maker, a hobby in which he enjoyed the support and partnership of Eddie Mather, a local gunsmith. During a public lecture on violins, Murray borrowed Kolbinson's newly acquired Guarneri and added his own Stradivarius and one violin constructed by each of Kolbinson and Mather. He reminisces:

In order to show off the violins I played the Adagio of Bach's first unaccompanied sonata on each of them and asked the audience to identify the two old instruments. Fran, who was in the audience, guessed my Strad as Eddie Mather's instrument, and it turned out that the two winners were Eddie and Steven. I will say this: I didn't cheat, but I tried to play my best on the new violins, because with the rare instruments you couldn't help but play well on them.

When I announced the results that most of the audience took their home-made violins to be the Strad and the Guarneri, tears of happiness started to roll down Eddie's and Steven's cheeks. This was the great moment of their lives. Everyone roared with laughter at the end when I announced what had happened. As a result of this episode, I became very close friends with these two men.

Kolbinson's ambition to acquire a quartet of instruments by the same maker was fulfilled when he managed to assemble four Amati instruments. One of these was acquired from Daisy Kennedy, one of the great English violinists of her time; the other had been in a private collection in France and had been smuggled into England during the Second World War. The viola, purchased by Kolbinson in France, had been constructed for a member of the Borghesi family and carried the family crest at the back. The cello, originally in the possession of the family of Clive, viscount of India, still carried the wax imprint of the Clive emblem. It was purchased in England after its discovery in the Earl of Plymouth's castle. Kolbinson's wish was for the university to use the Amatis and to form a quartet-in-residence in order to have these magnificent instruments played upon on a regular basis. His selling price was twenty thousand dollars for the group. In Murray's own words:

At that time $20,000 was a lot of money and our university could not easily dip into some reserve fund for that purpose. The negotiation took place over a period of almost a year. Final approval had to come from the university senate, whose members came from all over the province and included provincial government officials.

A tea-party was arranged in the vice-president's home. I remember sitting on the floor because there were so many people, and first I talked about violins, what was special about old violins, then about this Amati quartet. I must have been convincing enough because eventually the president phoned me and said that it was decided that they should buy them.

In my excitement it never occurred to me that we should have bows for each of the instruments. After the instruments were delivered I mentioned this to Kolbinson. He let me choose four from his fabulous collection of bows, offering them to me as a commission for selling the quartet. I proceeded to present them to the university. There were at least two Hill bows, and the four were probably worth around $700. Today each would be worth in the thousands.

After having procured four such precious instruments for the university Murray's next step was to find professional players to become the university's quartet-in-residence. Negotiations were initiated with the newly formed Orford String Quartet to become the regular players of the Amati instruments under the possible new title of 'Amati Quartet' of the University of Saskatchewan. The negotiations were cut short through an offer from the University of Toronto that the Orford Quartet could not refuse. For the ten years following their acquisition the instruments were only taken out of their vault for an occasional performance by a visiting musician. By 1969, however, the music department had acquired enough good string teachers to form a university Amati Quartet. With Murray Adaskin at the helm, the group included Norma Bisha, violin; Michael Bowie, viola; and Edward Bisha, cello. Several concerts were given locally and plans were laid for more extensive touring.

The episode of the Amati instruments once more highlighted Murray's capacity for pioneering efforts and his imaginative approach to music. After twenty-one years at the University of Saskatchewan, however, Murray's idealism found itself at odds with the cold realism of a new generation of academics. There was to be no permanent resident string quartet, and by 1973 its first violinist, Murray Adaskin, retired from his service at the university. With his retirement the only quartet of original Amati instruments in Canada was also retired, to gather dust and exist in obscurity at its university repository.

GROWTH OF THE MUSIC DEPARTMENT

Through his appointment as chairman of the music department Murray was faced with an awesome task – the creation, development, and direction of an academic unit within a major provincial institution of higher learning. His chairmanship was an appointment without term, implying the administration's full trust in his capabilities to develop and implement a philosophy of music education and to retain his administrative duties for the duration of his position at the university. Murray's administrative task was all the more difficult in light of the minimal budget received from the university for this purpose. During the first few years of the development of the music program Murray was able to hire only one faculty member – Austin Clarkson. Between them they offered courses in the fundamentals of music, history of Western music, composition, advanced composition, and music appreciation. By the time Clarkson left Saskatoon to work on a PHD in musicology at Columbia University, the music department had built up a student body averaging fifty students a year.[25]

In his administrative capacity Murray had set several goals for his department: he wanted it to develop into a centre for the teaching of composition, on the premise that of all the Prairie universities at the time Saskatoon was the only one offering serious work in the field of composition; he was pressing for the approval of a program for a bachelor's degree in music, preferably a degree in composition; he was stressing the need for more space and better facilities. Each year in his annual reports to the president Murray reiterated the need for a fine arts building to house the departments of art, drama, and music.

From an admistrative point of view, the years preceding his sabbatical in 1960–1 were the happiest for Murray. Throughout that period under his direction the department gradually evolved and expanded, while retaining an intimate character where each student could receive individual attention. After his sabbatical and throughout the remaining years of the sixties the department changed rapidly, resulting in an explosion in student enrolment.

The department's increased performance orientation was reflected in the hiring of performance faculty, which included among others a pianist, a cellist, a conductor, and a trumpet player. The number of courses expanded, and Murray's evening music appreciation classes became especially popular. A major event in the history of the music department occurred during 1964–5 with the amalgamation of the departments of music and music education. Murray anticipated that this event would not only expedite the university's decision to grant the music department a degree program but that plans for such a degree would evolve concurrently with those for a fine arts building.

During the first year of the amalgamation the student enrolment swelled to 914, with a total offering of ten courses in music and nine in music education. The faculty included Boyd McDonald, piano, and Michael Bowie, cello, with R.B. McFarland, David Kaplan, and R.J. Solem as additions from music education. An integration of courses took place, enabling the music department to offer in 1967 the B MUS, BA, and B ED degrees. An impressive array of performing groups sprang up under the guidance of faculty members, including the Greystone Singers, the Chamber Singers, the University Chorus, the Concert Band, the Varsity Band, the Recorder Ensemble, the Education Chorus, the Brass Ensemble, and the Summer School Chorus.[26]

Such an explosion in the structure of the music department understandably brought with it adminstrative problems and resultant tensions. The department had become too large and the individual teaching loads too heavy. More faculty members were needed to accommodate the growing number of students, and the existing facilities were becoming too cramped to be able to offer the students adequate service. Murray's level of frustation with the university was reaching critical proportions as his continued pleas for a fine arts building and for proper budget recognition went unanswered.

Finally, in 1966, pressures at the university as well as those imposed by his composition commitments forced Murray to withdraw from his administrative duties as head of the department. On 18 November he was appointed composer-in-residence, the first such appointment to be made by a Canadian university. His new position enabled him to continue his teaching while allowing him more time for consultation with his students and for his own creative work. He continued his managerial activities as organizer of the Sunday evening concert series and of a special festival of six Exhibition Concerts that was to occur as part of the university's Canadian centennial celebrations program.

The tempo and variety of Murray's activities during the twenty years at the University of Saskatchewan exhibited a relentless work ethic that could be matched by few. His efforts were fuelled by his enthusiasm and by an unshakeable belief in the necessity to contribute his share toward the improvement of the state of music in this country. Locally, he assisted in the formation of the Saskatoon Music Council, designed to establish closer contact among musical organizations in the city. Throughout the 1950s he belonged to several national organizations. In 1956 he was appointed to the membership selection committee of the Canadian League of Composers, which involved the study of scores submitted by prospective members. In 1959 he became a member of the national scholarship committee for the National Youth Orchestra in Stratford. In 1960 he became a member of the Composers, Authors, and Publishers Association of Canada. In the mid-1960s he became a Fellow of the Royal Society of Arts, London, member of the national advisory council of the National Youth Orchestra, and member of the board of honorary advisers for the Canadian Bureau for the Advancement of Music.

Murray's appointment to the board of the Canada Council in 1966 for a three-year term, however, was, he felt, the most challenging of all the national offices. The appointment itself came as a total surprise in the middle of the summer. Murray and Frances were at their Ontario summer cottage at Canoe Lake in Algonquin Park, their annual refuge from civilization, when one day the postmaster rushed over in her boat to announce an urgent telephone call from Ottawa for Murray. The Adaskins had purposely elected not to have a telephone in their cottage, and were therefore dependent on the little post office across the lake as their only contact with the outside world. Murray recalls this incident on a hot, drowsy July afternoon:

I hopped in my little boat and followed her across the lake wondering whom do I know in Ottawa who may be dying; the fact that it was urgent scared us. The postmistress sat in the office while I phoned. It was a funny old telephone which still operated by turning the handle and since it was a party line anyone could listen in. Finally I got through to Ottawa and said there was a message for me to call this specific number. Who was I calling? Well, it was the Parliament buildings, the office of Judy LaMarsh, the Minister of State. At my surprised exclamation 'Judy LaMarsh', the postmistress, who had been following every word I said, turned absolutely pink with excitement.

The conversation with Ottawa proceeded as follows: 'Mr. Adaskin,' she said, 'this is Judy LaMarsh speaking. I am terribly sorry, but I need your help.' I could not imagine what it could possibly be, so I told her to go on, that I would be honoured to do anything I can. 'An order-in-council has just come through appointing you to the Canada Council and I said to myself "My God, I haven't even asked the man yet!"

The meeting was to take place a week later, I think it was in Saint John, New Brunswick. Once a year they always had an out-of-town meeting in some different part of Canada to allow people in different cities to meet the members and unburden themselves to them.

And boy, did we have people unburden themselves! For three years I could not go to any social occasion anywhere that someone did not corner me to give me a piece of their mind because their niece or somebody else had applied for a scholarship and was turned down.

On 22 July 1966 Murray sent Judy LaMarsh his letter of acceptance, saying: 'Your telephone call reached me in the miniature post office of Canoe Lake and I can assure you that your call sparked the most delightful flurry ... as a result [of which] our local postmistress will never be the same again.'

Murray considers his term of the council as an extremely interesting and rewarding learning experience. He looks back on those days with a sense of accomplishment, for he was directly responsible for recommending a higher Canadian music content for orchestras funded with council money:

One year I produced statistics on the number of orchestras that we were helping, the total amount of money granted to them, the number of concerts they gave per year, and the number of Canadian works included in their programs. I came up with some startling figures. The bulk of the money went to the six top orchestras – Toronto, Montreal, Quebec, Winnipeg, Edmonton, Vancouver – and it was a lot of money. I discovered that a total of approximately two hundred concerts a season presented about twelve hundred works, three of which were Canadian.

At my mention of these statistics everyone on the Council was horrified, as if I had dropped a bomb on the table. For a couple of stunned moments there was dead silence among the twenty-one members. Afterwards one man put his arm around me as we walked out and said, 'Thank God for people like you sitting on the council!'

As a result of Murray's investigation into Canadian content, the council also discovered that a similarly disproportionate number of artists employed by this country's orchestras was also non-Canadian. This resulted in a policy recommending the percentage of Canadian personnel of each orchestra funded by the council. At first this created a ripple of discontent among conductors, who viewed the new policy as an attempt by the council to dictate the contents of their concert seasons to them. Eventually the policy was implemented; it is still in operation today.

Two other events during the 1960s exerted considerable influence on Murray: his sabbatical from university teaching in 1960–1 and a visit to Rankin

Inlet with Eli Bornstein in 1965. After his first seven years of work for the music department, as well as festival organization, concert planning and implementation, assistance to students, and community activities, Murray welcomed his right as an academic to take a one-year leave from the university in order to be able to concentrate for an uninterrupted period of time on his creative endeavours. He and Frances decided to spend the year in Europe, where they visited England, Switzerland, and northern Italy. The bulk of their time was spent in Morges, a little town twenty-five miles from Geneva that was of particular significance to Murray because of its association with Igor Stravinsky. The Russian composer, who had resided in this small, peaceful Swiss community during the war, had written a number of his works there, including Murray's favourite, *L'Histoire du Soldat*.

The Adaskins' decision to spend their sabbatical in Morges was facilitated through the offer of her home made by a Polish noblewoman, introduced to them by their friend Boris Roubakine in Lausanne. Madame Turczynska, widow of the scholar who collaborated with Paderewski on the new Polish edition of works by Frederick Chopin, was the owner of a modern villa with all such conveniences as oil heating, a dishwasher, and clothes washer. Paderewski had also at one time owned a large estate in Morges at which he entertained most of the crowned heads of Europe. In this charming villa in a town filled with musical history, Murray was able to settle down happily at his composition projects. It was there that he completed his *Concerto for Bassoon and Orchestra* and the *Capriccio for Piano and Orchestra*.

During this period in Europe the Adaskins met several musician friends and made the acquaintance of Luigi Dallapiccola and Roger Sessions. One evening, while dining in a Florentine pensione, Murray and Frances overheard a young boy, sitting with his parents at the next table, ask his father what he was writing at the time. At the father's response that he was working on his fifth symphony, Murray almost dropped his fork. One man's introduction stating, 'I am Roger Sessions from Princeton,' was countered by 'I am Murray Adaskin from Saskatoon.' Moments like that made the sabbatical the kind of rejuvenating experience needed by both Adaskins at that particular stage in their careers.

Five years later the opportunity presented itself for Murray to visit the Canadian Arctic. Affiliated with the University of Saskatchewan was the Institute for Northern Studies, which operated an Arctic Training Centre at Rankin Inlet on the west coast of Hudson Bay. The university's newly formed anthropology department had appointed to its faculty Dr Robert Williamson, who brought with him extensive Arctic experience and a knowledge of Inuit languages. Williamson, who was also in charge of the Arctic Training Centre, urged Murray to visit Rankin Inlet in order to tape the traditional Inuit songs, because he saw the rapid disappearance of old customs under the influence of southern life-styles.

Realizing that Rankin Inlet held interest for Eli Bornstein, Murray invited his friend to accompany him on a trip to the north that lasted ten days.

It was terribly cold and we shivered the whole time while we were there, mainly because we did not bring the right clothing. We did not realize what type of clothing has to be worn in that fascinating wind-swept part of the world. Nevertheless, this was a wonderful trip for us, and I reprimanded myself for waiting this long, until I was in my fifties to see our stunningly, strikingly beautiful Arctic. I came back with lots of tapes of songs sung by an old couple; the woman's name was Qalala and the man's Nilaula. The first piece that I wrote upon my return was an orchestral composition called *Qalala and Nilaula of the North*.

Our object was to write an opera on an Eskimo theme and incorporate the folk-music collected during the trip. Eli wanted to do the designs, sets, and costumes.

While the opera did not materialize, Murray's northern experiences, such as having a real Inuit parka hand-made for him by an Inuit woman, watching a seal hunt, lunching in an igloo on sardines and hardtack – special hard biscuits dipped in tea in order to soften them and make them edible – and riding in a dogsled across the white vastness of the land, became an indelible part of his Canadian consciousness. To him it was a deeply moving experience.

The beginning of Murray's term as newly appointed composer-in-residence in 1966 was devoted to the organizing at the president's request of another major music festival, this time as part of the university's celebration of Canada's centennial. The six Exhibition Concerts, as they were called, took place between May and December 1967, each devoted to the music of a leading Canadian composer. Concurrently with the performances of the composers' works were exhibitions of their manuscripts, publications, photographs, and other memorabilia pertinent to their professional work. Once more, in keeping with his personal style, Murray devised a unique idea: a thoroughly Canadian music festival in honour of Canada's centennial, on a model that had never before been presented in Canada. His intention was to highlight six distinguished Canadians and present them to the audience in a human as well as a professional perspective in order to create as complete a picture of each composer as possible.

In a letter outlining this project to the university's Centennial Planning Committee, Murray offered the following rationale:

The main object of such a series of concerts is to enable our audience to get a complete look at the composer from every point of view and therefore reach a better and deeper understanding of his work.

A general complaint in the world of music today is that there seems to be such a wide gap between the living composer and his audience. The sincere music lover rarely meets a live composer nor is he often given the opportunity of hearing the composer discuss or 'explain' his music. Surely this is the kind of cultural project our university should be proud to present as part of its centennial celebrations.

The choice of the six composers could be easily and quickly made, but an important point is that we make the splendid gesture of inviting at least two and perhaps three composers from French Canada.

The musical programmes would consist of solo and chamber-music works. For obvious reasons large-scale pieces would not be practical nor financially feasible ...

Saskatoon will be acclaimed in Canada for being the first to make the opportunity available of taking a close and intimate look at their composers while at the same time honouring them.[27]

The composers were to be guests of the university and were expected to be involved in the interpretation of their works as performers, conductors, or commentators. They were invited to remain on campus for several days following the event in order to meet students and faculty. The exhibition of memorabilia was to include items pertaining to professional friends, teachers, and students – anything that would contribute to the delineation of the composer's inner profile. The six composers whose participation Murray solicitated for this occasion accepted with enthusiasm. They included Jean Papineau-Couture from the University of Montreal, John Weinzweig from the University of Toronto, Barbara Pentland from the University of British Columbia, Bernard Naylor from Winnipeg, Clermont Pépin from the Conservatoire de Musique et d'Art Dramatique, Montreal, and Eldon Rathburn from the National Film Board in Ottawa. The choice of compositions and of performers was left up to each composer.

The programs for each event were also conceived imaginatively. Murray had asked the composers for a line from one of their manuscripts in their own handwriting, with their signature appended to it. These were then printed as designs for the cover pages of each of the six programs. The fund-raising for this event was also carried out single-handed by Murray, who obtained money from the Centennial Fund in Ottawa, from the Canada Council, and from the university. Combining these funds with proceeds from the ticket sales, he was able to cover all the expenses and emerge with a balanced budget.

The concerts featured a wide array of Canadian performers, where local artists combined with such guests as the UBC Faculty Quartet from Vancouver, the Toronto Woodwind Quintet, and the Gabora String Quartet from Montreal. Sopranos Rose-Marie Barbeau and Louise Lebrun, cellist James Hunter, and violinist Liliane Garnier were among the soloists, along with Frances James, who sang Weinzweig's *Of Time, Rain, and the World*, as the person to whom the work was originally dedicated and who gave it its *première* performance twenty years earlier.

In order to familiarize the audience with this repertoire, Murray made it a point, whenever possible, to repeat after intermission one of the pieces performed in the first half of the evening. The fifteen-minute intermission gave the audience an opportunity to view the exhibition of the composer's memorabilia, creating a context for the replaying of some of the music previously heard on the program. In the concert of music by Jean Papineau-Couture, for example, all three of his pieces – *Aria pour Violon Seul, Quatrains, Suite pour Violon Seul* – were repeated. During the Weinzweig evening, at which his Divertimentos nos 1 and 3, his three songs, and the *Woodwind Quintet* were played, it was the quintet that received the repeat performance. Pépin's concert included his *Variations for String Quartet, Cycle-Eluard* (for soprano and piano), *Suite for Violin, Cello, and Piano*, and *String Quartet No 2*. The question-and-answer period after intermission, led by the composer, was followed by a repeat of his *Cycle-Eluard*. Similarly, in the Barbara Pentland concert, the audience had a chance to communicate with her during her introductory remarks to her *Trio Con Alea*, a work commissioned for *première* performance during Canada's centennial year. Her other works included *String Quartet No 1, Shadows, Caprice*, and *Fantasy*. The concert of music by Bernard Naylor included, in addition to his *String Trio* and *'Emily' Variations and Fughetta for Violin and Piano*, song cycles for soprano and piano (*Presences* and *Suite for High Voice and Piano* on poems by C. Day Lewis), and a newly composed work *Not so Far as the Forest* for soprano and string quartet *premièred* in England just three months earlier.

Perhaps the most original of the six concerts was the last, featuring the music of Eldon Rathburn, staff composer for the National Film Board of Canada. Since by then he had written more than one hundred film scripts, it was logical to present him to the audience within the context of his music for film. Four films were shown – *Canon*, produced by Norman MacLaren; *Sky* by John Seeney; *City of Gold* by Tom Daly; and *Labyrinth* (Chamber 3) by Roman Kroiter, which was used at Expo in Montreal. Rathburn was on stage, in front of the large screen, explaining every detail of his film-composing techniques. The National Film Board made available for the occasion a number of exhibits and film-strips, including some footage from silent films. It also provided the services of two technicians, who brought much of the needed equipment with them.

The Exhibition Concerts series was a monumental success and is today of considerable historical value. It was acclaimed by the participating composers as one of the most interesting projects ever offered to them, and the series constituted the first showcase of its type for a Canadian composer. Judging by its enthusiastic reception by the audience, Murray envisioned that this type of showcase-festival could become a regular feature at universities across Canada. To him, universities would have been obvious locales for similar celebrations of Canada's distinguished composers.

Murray had planned to have each of the six programs filmed for television for presentation later as half-hour television shows. Unfortunately, the media did not seem to share his enthusiasm. Geoffrey Waddington, who was one of the few media people to recognize the importance of Murray's endeavours, was unequivocally rejected by those in CBC management whom he tried to interest in taping the concerts for national radio broadcasts. To Murray he quoted one of his superiors as saying: 'Did you say Saskatoon, Geoff? What the hell are you talking about?' Nevertheless, Waddington did somehow manage to get the Winnipeg branch of the CBC to send an engineer and a producer to tape some of the concerts and give a few broadcasts for the Prairie region of the CBC. Except for local newspaper reviews, there was no national coverage of the concerts. Despite the fact that through his unique showcase of Canadian composers Murray had placed Saskatoon in a prominent position in the Canadian musical world, to the rest of the country, ironically, Saskatoon was still an island whose location isolated it from the hubbub of centennial celebrations in Toronto and Montreal, somehow diminishing the importance of its musical contributions. This major historical event remained unnoticed by the rest of Canada, a curious reflection of the mode in which Canadians viewed themselves and their culture.

The year of the Exhibition Concerts marked the beginning of the end of Murray's happy association with the University of Saskatchewan. The changing educational direction of the music department and the realities of an academic atmosphere shaped by a younger generation of faculty, whose sphere of endeavour progressively distanced them from the philosophic orientation of the early university presidents, Walter Murray and W.P. Thompson, contributed to Murray Adaskin's frustation and disillusionment. One wish began to dominate his life, and that was the yearning to retire from the university environment, which he no longer found congenial, in order to be able to devote all his energies to composing. By 1969 he decided that early retirement was the only solution to his dilemma. He was discouraged from this course of action by the university's controller of revenue and the president, both of whom advised

Murray to stay until his next sabbatical. Early retirement would have adversely affected his pension calculations. In January 1973 Murray received his sabbatical from the University of Saskatchewan at full pay for the spring term. His association with the university had ended to his satisfaction and benefit, and on 15 January he and Frances were free to move into their new home in Victoria, British Columbia. Throughout their careers they had gravitated geographically in a westward direction. For Frances it had been a steady progression from the Maritimes, through Quebec and Ontario to Saskatchewan. For Murray the westward shift began in Toronto. It is small wonder, therefore, that Victoria, the beautiful garden city on Canada's west coast, would complete the Adaskins' migratory cycle.

6

The compositions of the Saskatoon period

Murray Adaskin's Saskatoon years were a fertile period in his development as composer. Approximately sixty-five per cent of his total output – about forty compositions – was written during this period. Many of his works were either created or completed at Canoe Lake, the Adaskins' summer refuge from the hectic pace of the academic year, where Murray found the necessary peace of mind to devote himself full-time to composition. At the height of his creative powers, Murray reached his full potential, developing in the process an identity as a uniquely Canadian composer. Many of what he considers his strongest works were written in this period, particularly the *Algonquin Symphony*, *Divertimento No 3*, the bassoon and violin concertos, and – what is perhaps his most popular work to date – the *Serenade Concertante*.

Through its large number of commissions of Murray's compositions, the CBC proved very supportive of and encouraging to his endeavours. Throughout the 1950s and 1960s three individuals in particular were responsible for the propagation of Canadian compositions by commissioning them, procuring first performances, and ensuring subsequent live performances of these works on the radio network: Geoffrey Waddington, John Peter Lee Roberts, and – particularly in the case of Murray's music – Tom Taylor. In 1947, Waddington had been appointed music adviser and consultant to the CBC English network. With his appointment as music director of the CBC in 1952 he assumed a powerful role in Canadian musical life, holding the responsibility for radio music programming and for hiring performers for these programs. The additional responsibility of directing and conducting the CBC Symphony Orchestra from 1952 to 1964 resulted in his exerting considerable control over music broadcasting in Canada. John Roberts, who had been music producer at CBC Winnipeg, assumed in 1957 the position of program organizer with the CBC in Toronto. In 1965 he took over Waddington's position as radio network supervisor, Serious Music Department. Tom Taylor started his broadcasting career in Winnipeg shortly after the war, and in the late fifties held the position of executive music producer, Serious Music Department, for the Prairie region.

Each of these men was an enthusiast for and a staunch believer in Canadian music and in the necessity to support Canadian composers by commissioning works and by introducing them to the public. The following letter from Geoffrey Waddington to Murray Adaskin characterizes this attitude:

As part of its plans to mark the Coronation of Her Majesty the Queen, the CBC is commissioning from a number of Canadian composers works to mark the occasion. These are to be given their première performance as part of our special broadcasting around coronation week.

We would like to invite you to write an overture for full symphony orchestra of approximately six to eight minutes in duration ...

We feel this provides the Corporation with an especially fitting way to mark an historic occurrence and that it offers a particularly interesting opportunity for Canadian music ... We hope that whenever possible and feasible inspiration should be from our Canadian life and background.[1]

This enlightened CBC policy toward Canadian composers, while still in evidence during the early 1970s, was particularly strong during Murray's years in Saskatoon. A large percentage of Murray's works were commissioned by the CBC, received *première* performances in either its Toronto, Winnipeg, or Vancouver studios, and were heard in subsequent live performances on the radio. Waddington conducted first performances with the Toronto CBC Symphony Orchestra of at least four of Murray's compositions: *Suite for Orchestra, Ballet Symphony, Coronation Overture,* and *Algonquin Symphony.* John Avison, conductor of the CBC Vancouver orchestra, *premièred Serenade Concertante.* On a later occasion he played the piano to Murray's violin part in *Canzona and Rondo,* performed in a six-week series of chamber music programs by members of the Canadian League of Composers, produced for the CBC by Robert Turner.

Eric Wild, as conductor of the CBC Winnipeg Symphony Orchestra, figured prominently in the Adaskin compositions performed on the Prairie network and produced by Tom Taylor. As an admirer of Murray's compositions, Taylor had set himself the task of airing as many of the works on the Prairie network as possible. Since the regional network included Alberta, Saskatchewan, and Manitoba, Murray was seen as the Canadian composer most representative of that region. In fact, by the time he retired in 1979, Taylor had almost succeeded in broadcasting Murray's entire *oeuvre.* Some shows were produced during the summer festival he started in conjunction with summer school at the University of Manitoba, which included a series of six or seven chamber music and choir concerts per season. While the festivals were significant public events eliciting wide audience support, many of Murray's works were also performed in the studio with the CBC Winnipeg orchestra. Taylor was instrumental in commissioning, through John Roberts, and producing the *première* performances of Murray's opera, *Grant, Warden of the Plains,* and his orchestral work, *Qalala and Nilaula of the North.*

During the fifties and sixties, therefore, the CBC emphasized live broadcasting of works by domestic composers. Because of such people of vision as Waddington, Roberts, and Taylor, who had the courage to support programming of Canadian music, these were fruitful years in the history of twentieth-century Canadian composition.

Another project of the CBC, initiated in 1945, was the recording on discs of Canadian works and performances by domestic artists. Later known as Radio Canada International, the function of the project was to distribute these discs to radio stations, organizations, and libraries abroad, thus disseminating national culture outside of Canada. At the Stratford Festival in 1958, nineteen concerts were recorded for the International Service of the CBC, including Murray's *Serenade Concertante,* conducted by Sir Ernest MacMillan, and his *Suite for Orchestra* and *Ballet Symphony,* under the baton of Geoffrey Waddington.

In addition to being prolific during his Saskatoon period, Murray diversified, writing with equal care and intensity for small and large orchestra, soloist and orchestra, chamber groups, instrumental solos and duos, voice, and compositions for young musicians. An overview of the works in each category is presented below. Detailed information on each work may be found in appendix B.

WORKS FOR ORCHESTRA

The three earliest orchestral works – *Suite for Orchestra, Suite for Strings,* and *Ballet Symphony* – were written during the period of Murray's composition studies with Weinzweig and Milhaud. The *Suite for Orchestra* acquired considerable popularity through its numerous performances. At its *première* in 1949 it elicited an angry response from one listener, who went to the trouble of sending the following telegram: 'First performance of your work received with revulsion. Have you seen a psychiatrist.' Inexperienced in coping with such vehement reactions at that early stage in his creative career, Murray discussed the incident with Milhaud. The next day, in a gesture that required few words, but whose meaning firmly implanted itself in Murray's memory, his mentor pulled out a small clipping from Nicholas Slonimsky's *Dictionary of Musical Invective*, in which a composer was lambasted in even stronger terms than Murray was in the telegram. The composer was Beethoven, and the work his *Ninth Symphony*.

The three-movement *Suite for Strings*, with its Fugue, Ostinato, and Finale, was Murray's only conscious attempt at the twelve-tone idiom. While popular with contemporary European composers, the idiom did not feel natural to him and was not used as a compositional process again. The *Ballet Symphony*, also conceived as a multi-movement suite, exhibits in the finale a technique that became a feature of the mature Adaskin compositional style: themes and ideas from the previous five movements are recalled and motivically developed.

Two of the earliest orchestral works written during Murray's Saskatoon period are the *Coronation Overture* and the *Serenade Concertante*. Each is less than ten minutes long, devised to suit the requirements of the occasion for which it was written. The *Coronation Overture*, composed in honour of the coronation of Queen Elizabeth II, was first performed in 1953. Murray could not know at that time that thirty years later this work would be performed in the presence of the queen, with the composer in the audience, on the occasion of the royal couple's visit to Victoria. George Corwin conducted the University of Victoria Orchestra in University Centre on campus, in what was for Murray a profoundly moving experience. According to the composer, one of the highlights of his life occurred when he and Frances were presented to the queen after the concert.

The completion of the *Serenade Concertante* followed the *Coronation Overture* by one year. One of Murray's compositions to attain the broadest national and international hearing, this work was performed all across Canada as well as in such disparate locations as Detroit, Jerusalem, Hartford (Conn), Munich, and Mexico City. Some of its conductors were John Avison, Sir Ernest MacMillan, Victor Feldbrill, Lee Hepner, Alexander Brott, Walter Susskind, and the composer himself. It was also recorded, along with two other Canadian works, on the Columbia label with the CBC Symphony Orchestra, conducted by Walter Susskind. The subsequent review in *The American Record Guide* is one of the few intelligent statements in the media pertaining to Murray's compositions, indicative of the reviewer's understanding of contemporary music: 'Adaskin's contribution is a charmer, superbly fashioned and superbly finished. Its bitter-sweetmeat of thirds and sixths is a neat delight ... The Serenade is properly disciplined, its charm not corrupted by any attempt to cut capers. In its sculptured chasteness Adaskin's piece is probably the best on the recording.'[2]

This work was also the subject of one of the more positive statements about

Murray Adaskin's music by a leading Toronto critic. After hearing *Serenade Concertante* performed by the Toronto Symphony Orchestra in 1955, John Kraglund said: 'The work was modern, but rather as Stravinsky's *Petrushka* is modern. Of the pieces by Adaskin we have had an opportunity to hear, this seemed to us one of the most pleasant in its erratically rhythmic humour, which alternated with tenderly plaintive passages that were neither cold nor bleak.'[3]

This favourable opinion was retained and with the passing of time even intensified, when almost thirty years later the same reviewer encountered the work once more: 'Most sections of the TS [Toronto Symphony] had a chance to feature their soloists in the charming, lightweight *Serenade Concertante* by Canadian composer Murray Adaskin. In style, the Serenade showed influences of the Classical period (by way of Ibert), with tuneful motifs projected most vividly by the winds. To retain these tuneful fragments, for whistling on my way to the office I found it expedient to forgo yet another hearing of Tchaikovsky's *Romeo and Juliet*, which completed the programme.'[4]

Perhaps the most enlightening review was offered by J. Dorsey Callaghan in the *Detroit Free Press*:

The *Serenade Concertante* by Murray Adaskin was a refreshing addition to the contemporary literature ... The idiom is that by which coming generations will probably recognize the creative genius of the mid-twentieth century.

In this case there is no striving after effect for its own sake. The melodic contours are definitely of our time, but the composer is not loath to employ conventional means such as ending the entire work with a text-book resolution.

It came as a surprise, and a pleasant one at that. One gets a bit weary of the obvious avoidance of the older forms ... It may be that Adaskin's composition is a sign that so-called modern music is maturing.[5]

Two orchestral works of major proportions were completed in the two years preceding Murray's sabbatical from his university duties: the twenty-three-minute *Algonquin Symphony* and the somewhat shorter *Saskatchewan Legend*. The *Algonquin Symphony* stands today as a major Canadian work of the twentieth century. With its superbly colourful orchestration, its allusions to Canadian context and bird-calls, it is a master work at par with some of the paintings of the Canadian Group of Seven. It was conceived at Canoe Lake in Ontario's Algonquin Park and written in evocation of the area.

The cottage at Canoe Lake, originally constructed to the Adaskins' specifications in 1945, was a rustic, wooden structure with walls and floors of solid cedar. The high, beamed ceilings, the hand-carved wooden furniture, and the pot-bellied stove in the main sitting-room exuded an atmosphere well suited to the serenity of the surrounding trees and lake. In the absence of electricity, the lamps, refrigerator, and stove were operated by gas. To accentuate the sought-after isolation from civilization, there were no roads leading to the cottage. The only way for the city visitor to reach it was by boat from the Portage Store past the village of Dwight.

Nestled at the bottom of a slight incline by the water's edge was a small, one-room log cabin, which contained a piano, a stove, a desk, and a single bed. The austere premises served as Murray's studio, in which he worked on most of his compositions. The piano was a Heintzman upright, originally a player piano, bought by the Adaskins for one hundred dollars and converted into a regular piano.

This particular area of Algonquin Park holds considerable historical significance, as it once provided a favourite locale for such members of the Group of Seven as A.J. Casson, J.E.H. MacDonald, Lawren Harris, who had built a cabin near the present Portage Store, and Tom Thomson, whose drowned body found in Canoe Lake generated many a local legend. The Adaskins' closest neighbours were the Charles Matthewses, staunch supporters of the Group of Seven in the early part of this century, whose frequent visitor over the years of the Adaskins' annual Canoe Lake pilgrimages was A.J. Casson.

At the time of this book's writing A.J. Casson is in his late eighties, Matthews is nearing his hundredth birthday, and the Adaskins are no longer able to cope with the rigours of the rustic life at Canoe Lake. The cottage, built on leased park property, is slated for destruction within the next twenty-five years in a relentless effort by the park's officials to restore the park to its natural state, destroying in the process a great deal of Canada's cultural history. During the 1950s, 1960s, and 1970s, however, the area resounded with Murray's music as he tested his compositions at the piano. The many happy years spent at Canoe Lake and the many happy memories of the call of the loons, the song of the white-throated sparrow, and the rapping of the woodpecker, of watching the sunrise and sunset on the lake, and of living in the vastness of Ontario's spectacular back country are embedded in his compositions. The *Algonquin Symphony* serves perhaps as the best example of these phenomena and bears a direct connection to Canoe Lake and the Taylor Statten summer camps for children located at the opposite end of the lake.

Taylor Statten was a Wesleyan Methodist whose love for outdoor activities led him to the establishment on Canoe Lake in 1921 of Camp Ahmek, a woodcraft camp for boys intended as a training centre for future Canadian leaders. Statten's special emphasis there was on Indian lore. Three years later, Ethel Statten, his wife, founded Camp Wapomeo, a training camp for girls on Little Wapomeo Island. The Stattens assumed the Ojibway names of Gitchiahmek (Great Beaver) and Tonakila ('you first') respectively. To all of his friends, however, Taylor Statten was known as 'The Chief.' He was a remarkable educator, a man of high moral standards, with an intense love for the outdoors. He made every effort to promote music, theatre, and art at the camps and even employed Lawren Harris as camp artist at one time. The annual pageants created by Statten served as means to teach the children about Canadian history, and many a young aspiring Canadian musician spent several seasons as camp counsellor, responsible for performing solo or in chamber ensembles for camp musicales.

The Adaskins were always welcome guests, frequently contributing to Camp Ahmek's musical life. In 1953 Murray composed an evening song, the 'Hymn of Thanks,' to words by A. Eustace Haydon, which was adopted as the camp's standard evening hymn. Murray recounts an experience in 1982, long after the Chief had died. Standing on his dock, he saw a group of young campers paddling by in their canoe. He engaged them in a conversation, during which he asked them if they still sang the 'Hymn of Thanks' in the evening. When they confirmed this, he told them that he composed it. Their eyes lit up as they started to sing it for him from their canoe. In the calm of the evening twilight a wonderfully touching bond was created between the younger and the older generation, bridging the gap between the past and the present.

The warm bonds of friendship constituted for the Adaskins part of the magic of Canoe Lake. Murray nurtured a particular respect for the Chief, and both Adaskins were frequent observers of his Indian ceremony around the council ring, where he sang two distinctive Indian tunes: 'Hiawatha's Farewell' and the 'Omaha Tribal Prayer.' When the *Algonquin Symphony* was commissioned by the CBC in 1956, Murray's first thought was to create a work suggestive of the atmosphere and spiritual climate of Algonquin Park and Canoe Lake, with special allusions to Tom Thomson. The Chief proved very supportive of Murray in this endeavour and procured through friends manuscript copies of the two Indian tunes to enable him to incorporate them into the symphony.

Shortly after Murray received the material he also received news of Taylor Statten's death. Murray decided then that his new work would be a tribute to the Chief's memory. In time, the *Algonquin Symphony* became one of the most successful Canadian tone-poems, an abstraction of the essence of Canadian history in the area.

The first of the symphony's three movements was used as a canvas on which the composer etched his impressions of the Chief's spiritual characteristics. The second movement, based on the tune 'Hiawatha's Farewell,' is conceived in the manner of a requiem, with the eerie cry of the loon and passing references to the 'Hymn of Thanks' interspersed. The first occurrence of Hiawatha's tune includes the beginning portion of the text, 'Mourn Ye Not for My Departure, Mourn Ye Not, I Go upon a Journey Forever.' The third movement, based on the 'Omaha Tribal Prayer,' contains passing references to common sounds by the lake: an orchestra of frogs, the knocking of the woodpecker, the high-pitched song of the white-throated sparrow, and the distinctive call of the loon.

One year after the completion of this monumental work, Murray finished at Canoe Lake the *Saskatchewan Legend*, commissioned by the Golden Jubilee Committee of the University of Saskatchewan for the celebration of the institution's fiftieth anniversary. The first performance took place in September 1959 with the Saskatoon Symphony Orchestra, conducted by the composer. Murray recalls an interesting episode connected with this *première*: 'The first performance was greatly helped by extra players from Winnipeg, Regina, Edmonton, and Vancouver. The Vancouver player – George Zukerman, bassoon – just happened to pass through Saskatoon from Prince Albert, and we procured a bassoon for him after 6:00 p.m. ! ... We played the work twice and received a fine reception from the audience.'

Like the *Algonquin Symphony*, this work, entirely based on two Saskatchewan folk-songs, has a typically Canadian flavour. Recommended to Murray by Dr Richard Johnston, the two songs, 'Desjarlais' Reel' and 'Riel Song,' were in the collection of Saskatchewan folk-songs in the National Museum of Canada. The composition attained considerable popularity throughout the sixties at its performances by such groups as the Detroit Symphony Orchestra under Paul Paray, the Winnipeg Symphony under Victor Feldbrill, and the Toronto Symphony Orchestra, conducted by the Israeli Gary Bertini. At one of its Regina performances the music was choreographed as a ballet danced by four members of Laura Davis's dance group. The four soloists represented the 'Spirit of Dedication,' 'Spirits of Rebellion,' and 'Spirit of Simplicity.'

In a letter to Murray, critic and composer Udo Kasemets reported on a 1962 Stratford performance of the work by the National Youth Orchestra and on the enthusiasm with which the youngsters played it: 'Hearing them play the alert rhythms of your work and spin the lines of the long soli, I came to the conclusion that young people should play mainly contemporary music, not spend their time on Rossini and Tchaikovsky.'[6]

Ten years elapsed before Murray wrote his next major orchestral work, *Qalala and Nilaula of the North*. Commissioned by the CBC, it was intended for broadcast on the network's 'Tuesday Night' program in commemoration of Canada's national day, 1 July in 1969. It was written for a small orchestra of twenty-one players: a woodwind quintet, fourteen strings, and two percussion players. Murray's trip to Rankin Inlet three years earlier served as its inspirational source, with the work based on musical material from the tapes on which he recorded the songs of two Inuit elders named Qalala and Nilaula. Murray recalls Qalala as an eighty-five-year-old woman, and Nilaula as a man with a smiling and kindly face, looking much older than his years. 'He sang of how his relatives urged him to leave his home at Repulse Bay and move with them to Rankin Inlet, and how as a result, it changed his life.' His song ended with 'the truth of the past is not the truth of the present.'

The composition is based on three main melodic ideas. Nilaula's tune is heard at the opening of the piece, while Qalala's contrasting material is incorporated later; the third element derives from an ancient game of throat rhythms played by Eskimo women, with nonsense words accompanying guttural sounds constantly repeated in ostinato patterns. The *première* performance of this work was conducted by the composer. In the same year Murray completed the *Diversion for Orchestra (An Entertainment)*, an eight-minute work commissioned by Jean-Marie Beaudet, director of the National Arts Centre, for its new resident orchestra on the occasion of its inaugural concert. At the time of the commission the orchestra had just been formed, the only orchestra in North America to be almost entirely supported by the state. Consisting of only forty-four players, the goal of Canada's national orchestra was to perform works from the baroque, classical, and contemporary repertoire, and its mandate was to engage in frequent cross-country tours. Mario Bernardi, its first resident conductor, *premièred* the *Diversion for Orchestra* and performed it on several subsequent tours.

The players in this new orchestra were carefully selected from among the best applicants, many of whom were called back from studies or engagements abroad. Murray moulded his composition to suit the special nature of the group. In order to feature the various instruments in their solo capacity and give them a chance to display their individual abilities, he cast the work into a rondo form: A-B-A-C-A. The sectional outline allowed for the newly appointed first-desk players to be introduced to the audience through brief solo passages written for them. The B section (Lentamente) begins with a flute solo, followed by a duet between the oboe and bassoon, and ending with two oboes and two bassoons. A brief clarinet cadenza brings the section to a close. In the C section (Vivace) various families of instruments are juxtaposed, ending with the timpani, which creates a bridge to the return of the full orchestra. As the title implies, the work was intended as nothing more pretentious than an entertainment for a chamber ensemble. It was Murray Adaskin's special way of paying homage to Canada's young national orchestra.

Two other symphonic works were created in close succession: the four-and-a-half-minute *Fanfare for Orchestra* was commissioned for the opening of the auditorium of the Saskatchewan Centre of the Arts at Regina; the longer work, *There Is My People Sleeping,* was a CBC commission for performance on the two-hour documentary program intended by the CBC as a homage to the composer on his retirement. The somewhat unusual title derived from the book of ethnic poems and drawings by Sarain Stump, a full-blooded Indian artist living in Alberta. The idea was recommended to Murray by Catharine Whyte, who was very fond of this poetry.

Despite their shortness three other pieces must be mentioned in this category of symphonic music: marches number one, two, and three for orchestra. The first two were commissioned by John Adaskin for his radio program, 'Opportunity Knocks.' Exuding a Chaplinesque spirit they were not intended as stylized march music but rather as humorous openings to radio programs. The third one, composed in Victoria almost thirty years later, was written at the suggestion of Paul Freeman, conductor of the Victoria Symphony Orchestra, for a dual celebration of the composer's seventy-fifth birthday and the Duncan Musical Society's twenty-fifth anniversary. The festivity of the occasion was magnified by the birth of a first child to Catherine Lewis, a voice student of Frances James. The triple celebration was captured in a joyous quotation of the 'Happy Birthday' tune, played in the coda by the tuba. A review in Victoria's *Monday Magazine* encapsulates the spirit of the piece: 'Irreverent, witty, and at the same time eminently humane, it seemed to give as much pleasure to the members of the orchestra as to the audience. We don't have space to mention all the elegant bits of fun crammed into the brief march, but an ocarina solo ... and a few phrases from 'Happy Birthday' bravely sounded by the tuba were especially memorable.'[7]

WORKS FOR SOLOIST AND ORCHESTRA

Four significant compositions fall into this category: *Concerto for Violin and Orchestra, Concerto for Bassoon and Orchestra, Capriccio for Piano and Orchestra,* and *Divertimento No 4 for Trumpet and Orchestra.*

Started at Aspen in 1954 and completed the next year at Canoe Lake, the violin concerto was written for Murray's friend Roman Totenberg, who also *premièred* it with the CBC Symphony under the composer's baton. Totenberg was very fond of the work, and of the second movement in particular, with its great warmth and use of instrumental colour through sensitive scoring. The expressive solo violin line that spins its way through the movement culminates in a lengthy cadenza. At Totenberg's request this movement was rescored for a smaller ensemble of solo violin, flute, clarinet in B-flat, bass clarinet, string quartet, and bass to enable him to perform it more frequently.

The bassoon concerto and the *Capriccio for Piano and Orchestra* were composed by Murray during his sabbatical leave in Morges, Switzerland in 1960. The piano work was written for the famous British pedagogue, pianist, and adjudicator Kendall Taylor; the bassoon concerto was commissioned by George Zukerman, who *premièred* it in 1961 with the Vancouver Symphony Orchestra, conducted by Irwin Hoffman. The internationally known Canadian virtuoso adopted the work into his repertoire and performed it frequently on his world tour to Australia, Israel, Europe, and across Canada. In a recent letter to the Adaskins, Zukerman wrote: 'It's still the major 20th-century work for the instrument as far as I'm concerned. The proof is not only in my opinion, but in the fact that here is a 1960 composition which didn't have its first and final performance in the year of its premiere.'[8]

The *Divertimento No 4 for Trumpet and Orchestra* is the fourth of a series featuring various combinations of solo instruments. The first *Divertimento* was written for two violins and piano; the second for violin and harp; the third for violin, horn in F, and bassoon. Murray composed two more in Victoria, one for two guitars and chamber orchestra and one for percussion and orchestra. The trumpet work was written for Murray's colleague at the University of Saskatchewan, Dr Lawrence House. In the composer's own words: 'The solo part makes use of the rather rarely heard piccolo trumpet as well as the B-flat (or C) trumpet. Written in one movement of contrasting sections the Divertimento begins and ends with a motif reminiscent of the white-throat, that spunky little sparrow whose song is interpreted by New Englanders as "Old Sam Peabody, Peabody, Peabody," but in Algonquin Park, Ontario, where this work was composed, the song is interpreted as "I love Canada, Canada, Canada." No doubt the true sentiment of any decently brought up white-throated sparrow!'

CHAMBER MUSIC

Murray was also prolific in the category of chamber music, composing works for three to nine instruments. His *Divertimento No 1* was commissioned by his brother Harry and first performed by the two brothers and Frances Marr Adaskin, piano, at the Vancouver Art Gallery in 1956. A one-movement work with a cadenza for piano and one for the two violins, its opening material exudes a youthful exuberance, in keeping with the memory of childhood, when Murray and his brother performed the Pleyel violin duet Opus 48. The whole work is based on a cadential motive from the duet (appendix A, ex 1), which lends the piece an uplifting opening.

Two other trios were composed during the Saskatoon period: *Divertimento No 3* for violin, French horn in F, and bassoon, and *Trio for Flute, Cello, and*

Piano. Commissioned for a commemorative concert marking the first convocation to take place at the University of Regina, *Divertimento No 3* was recorded some time after the event for Radio Canada International by Taras Gabora, violin; George Zukerman, bassoon; and Barry Tuckwell, French horn. The three-movement composition is still one of the more popular works in the contemporary trio repertoire. The second work was composed for the Alberta Chamber Trio, in such a manner as to display each instrument's characteristics in solo passages and in combination with its partners.

Of the two quartets, one is the *Introduction and Rondo* for piano, violin, viola, and cello, while the other is a three-movement string quartet. The former was composed for a competition sponsored by the Vancouver Festival for that combination of instruments, held in the summer of 1958. Murray was later to find out that his piece was considered to be the best but could not be awarded first prize because it was too short. The string quartet, commissioned by the CBC for the Canadian String Quartet and completed in 1963, is a three-movement composition in which the third movement displays considerable rhythmic and motivic similarity to the rondo movement of the piano quartet. One of the many comments this work elicited after its first performance alluded to its sense of freshness and joy: 'It should be called Spring quartet (Primavera). It sounds so full of burgeoning life and joy and yet so elegant. Lyrically eloquent, the music has a distinctive personalized quality ... so refreshing to hear after all the contemporary works we've heard this year, many of them coarse in sound, grossly exaggerated in style, with their pathetic tone rows stretched out of all proportion in attempts at tension.'[9]

Another chamber work was completed in the same year as the string quartet. The *Cassenti Concertante*, a quintet for oboe, clarinet, bassoon, violin, and piano, was commissioned by the Canada Council for the Cassenti Players, a group directed by George Zukerman. This was one of three compositions written by Murray that feature the bassoon in either solo or chamber music context. Two of the three were composed with Zukerman in mind, and all three were subsequently adopted by him as part of his repertoire. The *Cassenti Concertante* was taken on tour throughout California, to Winnipeg, and to Montreal where it was performed at Expo 67. A reviewer in the *Winnipeg Free Press* made the following observation: 'I enjoyed the Adaskin piece with its strong dissonant ... chords from the piano, its dry Stravinskyan textures and tight control of his misplaced accents. The more Adaskin one hears the more it is apparent that here at least is a voice with a recognizable stylistic consistency. That in itself is no mean achievement.'[10]

Rondino for Nine Instruments, originally composed as part of a CBC-TV program conducted by Mario Bernardi, is a delightful, dance-like five-minute work intended to hold the interest of the broader, television-viewing audience. It features a woodwind quintet and a string quartet, which appear together at the beginning and end of the composition, while throughout the rest of the piece the two families of instruments are contrasted with each other, emphasizing colour and individual solo appearances. The composer states that this is a rondo 'without any developmental complications.'

WORKS FOR ONE AND TWO INSTRUMENTS

Three compositions fall within the category of instrumental solo: *Sonata for Piano*, *Sonatine Baroque* for unaccompanied violin, and *Two Pieces for Viola da Gamba*. Both *Sonata for Piano* and *Sonatine Baroque* are early works predating the Saskatoon period. The pieces for viola da gamba were composed at the end of Murray's stay in Saskatoon for a friend and respected artist, Peggie Sampson. After a recent hearing of the pieces, Lauretta Thistle, the long-time reviewer for the *Ottawa Citizen*, who has sustained throughout the years her interest in the Adaskins' professional activities, expressed her impressions of these compositions as performed by Peggie Sampson:

He has written with great facility for her instrument and produces two vastly different pieces. The first is a sort of chaconne, or perhaps lament, contrasting double-stopped passages with single-note phrases and using strumming on open strings.
    The second consists of free-flowing long-lined melodies with ... a pleasant geniality.[11]

All four of the compositions for two instruments involve the violin: *Sonata for Violin and Piano*, *Canzona and Rondo*, *Divertimento No 2*, and *Two Portraits for Violin and Piano*, the latter two dating from the Saskatoon period. In a rather unusual combination for violin and harp, *Divertimento No 2* has a structure of A-B-A and coda with an expressive harp solo in the B section and a violin figuration in the A sections reminiscent of Fritz Kreisler's coquettish manner. Also delightful are the *Two Portraits*, in which the bold gesture in the melodic line of the first *Portrait* (ex 2) is counterbalanced by a tender gesture in the second. Humorous, naive, suggestive of the carefree, floating gestures of a skater, the second *Portrait* is cast in rondo format.

WORKS FOR VOICE

Despite the fact that his wife is a singer, Murray wrote little for voice. Apart from a song dating from the Banff days, and *Epitaph* (1948), both of which were dedicated to Frances James, one other vocal work exists; *Of Man and the*

Universe is, in effect, a trio for mezzo-soprano, violin, and piano. Composed as a commissioned piece for Canada's centennial celebrations at Expo 67, the text is based on quatrains IX and X from 'Of the Nature and State of Man with Respect to the Universe,' by the early eighteenth-century English poet Alexander Pope.

The composition denotes a strong sense of structural unity. Each of the three instruments (voice included) is treated as an equal partner with an equal involvement in the generic development and transformation of the germinal material. The broad gestures of the opening statement in the piano outline the intervals of the fourth, seventh and ninth, which are of primary importance to the piece. The contrasting ideas expressed in the poem are highlighted through the structural divisions in the composition. For example, the majesty inherent in the opening statement, 'The great directing mind of all ordains,' is reflected in a vocal line of ascending leaps of an eleventh and a ninth that command attention (ex 3). For emphasis this opening vocal statement is set apart from the rest of the text by instrumental passages that precede and follow it. The text continues: 'All are but parts of one stupendous whole / Whose body nature is and God the soul. / That changed thro' all, and yet in all the same / Great in the earth as in the ethereal frame.' A piano cadenza separates this from the next statement just as, in an attempt at structural parallelism, a violin cadenza assumes a similar function with a later statement of the text.

The whole piece is more tonally oriented and is one of the few manifestations of vertical harmony rather than of purely evolving horizontal lines. The interval of a fourth outlined horizontally in the opening piano figures (ex 4) assumes a harmonic function within a progression of chords based on the descending fourth (ex 5). The pitches B-flat, E-flat, and A–D outlining the first two fourths in example 4 are transformed into the descending harmonic pattern in example 5 based on descending fourths D–A, and C–G. The composition exudes a sense of drama in its successful representation of the contrasting meanings of the text among the three soloists.

A second centennial project commissioned by the CBC was Murray's opera, *Grant, Warden of the Plains*, a major undertaking and his longest composition. The CBC was planning to produce a short opera from each of its regional networks during Canada's centennial year, and Murray's was to be presented at the CBC Winnipeg studios with Tom Taylor as producer. The commission stipulated that the work, on a topic of regional history, be confined to one hour's duration, employing forces of chamber music proportions. A Winnipeg poet was recommended to provide the libretto for the opera; although she had no previous experience at writing for opera, Mary-Elizabeth Bayer had developed a reputation as a warm-hearted and appealing poet, who was at that time also director of the Manitoba Centennial Commission. As a descendant of one of the

Selkirk settlers, she had become an authority on the history of the Red River area.

The story chosen for the opera was that of the Métis leader Cuthbert Grant, son of a Scottish trader employed by the North West Company, and a Cree mother. Born in 1793 at Aspen Creek on the Upper Assiniboine, Grant was sent to Scotland to obtain his education. He returned to the West at age nineteen as a dashing young rake and a *bon vivant*, quickly acquiring a reputation as a daring trader with the North West Company, a good rider, and a skilled hunter. Grant's character seemed full of contradictions: reared a Presbyterian, he eventually assumed the Catholic religion; at first a loyal member of the North West Company, upon its assimilation into the Hudson's Bay Company, he assumed a major role with the rival organization. Accused of murder and treason as a young rebel who led the native people against Governor Robert Semple and shot him at Seven Oaks, Grant became a respected guardian of the peace as warden of the Plains in the Assiniboia district.[12] In a similar contradictory light Grant, who had engaged in relationships with at least two native women, each of whom bore him a child, settled down in a permanent and respectable church marriage with a devoutly Catholic woman.

As a Métis leader, Grant was considered by his people to be a hero, whose fame preceded that of Louis Riel. One of the early heroes of Canada's West, he witnessed the transition of the West from a fur trade frontier to part of a developing nation.[13]

The opera takes up Grant's story several years after the massacre at Seven Oaks. He has attained a good position with the Hudson's Bay Company, whose governor is George Simpson, and is surrounded by friends who are traders and adventurers. Two thoughts are torturing him: the memory of the massacre and his role in the event (as expressed in his song 'That Day of Dark Remembering'), and his indecision as to whether to go West as a free spirit and trader, or settle at his present location and ask Maria to marry him ('Soon, Soon I Must Decide'). His rival in love is Alexander Macdonnell, a man full of hate and jealousy, who never misses a chance to belittle or slander Grant. Maria, however, loves Grant and is willing to forgive him his past if he will convert to her religion. The love triangle is highlighted against a backdrop of settlers at the fort, fur traders with the company, and Governor Simpson, who extends to Grant the offer to become warden of the Assiniboine region. The dilemma is resolved with Maria's willingness to marry Grant (in their duet 'This Is the Time of Forgiveness'), his duel with Macdonnell who has incited the confrontation, and his ultimate decision to settle down as warden and keeper of peace. Grant's magnanimity is evidenced through his sparing of Macdonnell's life, proof that he is worthy of Maria's affection and of his new position.

Although Murray Adaskin received the commission for the opera three years before the projected performance date, it was not finished until September 1966, because of some difficulties with the libretto. At first the libretto was too broad in scope, presenting too large a canvas, with a number of side-issues that added unnecessary complications to the plot and would have extended its scope beyond the prescribed one-hour limit. Several drafts had to be submitted, and Murray had to seek advice about the dramatic structure of the libretto from Herman Geiger-Torel, stage director for the opera school at the Toronto Conservatory of Music. Maria's 'Autumn Song' was one of the earliest text excerpts that Murray received from the author, prompting him to set it as a separate unit before the rest of the opera. This soprano aria, a lyrical duet for bassoon and voice, was first performed at the Winnipeg Art Gallery before the opera's *première*. It has received several performances over the years, and is a favourite piece with bassoonists.

Finally, in the summer of 1966, with the pressure of deadlines weighing heavily upon him, Murray was able to set the entire script to music. That summer the Adaskins extended their stay at the Canoe Lake cottage until the end of September to enable Murray to finish the work. To accelerate the copying procedures, the parts had to be distributed among copyists across Canada because of the urgency for the performers to start rehearsals. The opera received its *première* broadcast on the CBC National Radio Network on the 'Tuesday Night' program, 18 July 1967, under the baton of Victor Feldbrill. Bass-baritone Peter van Ginkle sang the role of Cuthbert Grant, soprano Nona Mari that of Maria McGillis, and bass Paul Fredette that of Alexander Macdonnell. The opera was dedicated to the memory of Murray's Banff friend, painter Peter Whyte, who had died in the year of its completion.

The *première* was received with considerable enthusiasm all across Canada. Comments ranged from 'one of the most outstanding music programs to have ever come from the West'[14] to '... a successful and gripping theatre work. The singing ... [and] appealing use of chorus seemed to be perfectly balanced and beautifully paced. Even without the advantage of a stage production I found the dramatic intensity of the last half quite overwhelming.'[15] Herman Geiger-Torel also responded: 'It is a wonderful score, full of warmth, poetry and drama. I was immensely impressed.'[16]

The opera employs a chorus of twelve to sixteen singers and a small orchestra consisting of string quartet with double bass, piccolo, flute, oboe, clarinet, bassoon, horn, two trumpets, trombone, percussion, and piano. The soloists include, in addition to the three principal singers, the old lady (narrator) who speaks Bungay, a hybrid of English mixed with Cree inflections; John, John Also and Robert – three traders and friends of Grant – two tenors and a bass;

Governor Simpson, a bass; and Pierre Falcon, a lyric tenor with a French-Canadian accent.

This one-act opera represents a highly unified musical unit, which interweaves songs by each of the soloists with spoken dialogue and measured voice patterns spoken to orchestral accompaniment. The chorus has a dual role: like that in a Greek play it comments on various parts of the action, and as participant in the action, it represents the settlers. A particularly striking section is the men's chorus, 'A Song for the Settlers,' accompanied only by timpani and percussion. In a continually fluctuating metre the first part, 'My Love Is the Land I Defend, Land of My Birth,' serves as a majestic introduction to the robust and catchy alliteration of 'Dig Deep Dig Down' (ex 6). Its function as commentator is particularly prevalent in the opening scene, where it sings to an orchestral background alternately in unison and in parts. For dramatic emphasis the chorus reverts to spoken text with orchestral accompaniment at 'and vengeance for old crime and greed for gold.'

A successful dramatic device in this opera is the use of a narrator, the old lady who speaks Bungay. She characterizes a ghost, a voice that seems to emerge from the old graveyard. Hers is not a singing role, but she articulates in metric speech patterns dictated by the accents and inflections of the underlying text. The vocal speech rhythms are notated and the voice speaks to the accompaniment of the orchestra. Her part is to be performed by a professional actress who has been taught the correct Bungay accent.

Chorus and narrator are combined very effectively at the opening of the opera. The scene, set in a graveyard, projects an other-worldly atmosphere through the opening choral statement, 'Gather the magic of the moon ... Still in the awe-filled night. Respect the echo of the dead whose signs are in modest graves beside the weathered county church ...' While the melodic material continually unfolds in the orchestra, stage directions call for 'moonlight that filters through the night, resting on a weather-beaten gravestone from which emerges the voice of an old lady of the past [the narrator] who now unfolds the story.'

Through the introduction of the ghostly voices at the cemetery, the opening scene creates a sense of timelessness, which is contrasted to the active portions of the story that develop in a series of flashbacks. The function of the narrator is to set a context for the introduction of each of the characters or situations. The drama thus falls into four major sections, each preceded by the narrator's explanations: from the opening graveyard scene to the end of Grant's first presentation of 'Soon, Soon I Must Decide,' from Maria's 'Autumn Song' to the beginning of the ball, the entire ball scene, and the duel scene between Macdonnell and Grant. Each of these units resembles a tableau ready to come to life after the introduction of the characters by the narrator. Each tableau depicts the personalities of the protagonists and projects local colour – particularly evident in the scene at the ball. This dramatic device, with the narrator providing the link between two different time periods through the use of flashbacks, the chorus as commentator, and the creation of the tableaux, suggests an affinity between this opera and such hybrid genres as Berlioz's *Damnation of Faust*.

One of the highlights of the opera is the scene of Governor Simpson's ball at Fort Garry. Long and colourful, it takes place alternately within and outside the ballroom. The tune of an Irish reel pervades the texture, which juxtaposes different metres, creating a lively and gay atmosphere. Sounds of violins tuning are heard from the orchestra before the music for the reel bursts forth. The governor's guests are entertained by 'A Song for the Settlers' and by Pierre Falcon's 'The Legend of White Horse Plain.' Contrasted with the joyful atmosphere is Grant's inner turmoil and indecision. His 'Soon, Soon I Must Decide' recurs twice during the ball scene, culminating in his duet with Maria, which presents the resolution to his agony. The announcement of Grant's acceptance of Governor Simpson's offer to be warden of the plains is made at the ball simultaneously with the announcement of his engagement to Maria. The ball scene ends with the chorus pronouncement 'Make Them a World.'

The shortest of the four scenes, the description of the concluding duel, is confined entirely to the narrator and a chorus of men's voices. Neither Maria nor Grant makes a solo appearance after their duet.

The composer's innate sense of musical unity manifests itself on a number of different levels: repetitions of musical phrases within a choral unit; quotations of parts of the opening chorus at the end of the opera, which create a sense of balance between the beginning and the end of the work; and the triple appearance of Grant's pivotal statement, 'Soon, Soon I Must Decide.' The germinal idea in his song – the melodic outline of a seventh – is used as a unifying device in the duet as well as in the chorus. 'Make Them a World,' and the transformation of this idea, symbolize the various stages of Grant's inner turmoil (ex 7).

The melodic contour in the first two statements in example 7 is delineated by a descending seventh while the next three statements outline an ascending seventh reached through three superimposed thirds. The same germinal idea appears transformed in the duet, where it signifies a resolution to his anguish. By forgiving him, Maria provides the answer he was seeking (ex 8). A further rhythmic transformation of the motive creates a sense of peace and a spiritual union between the two protagonists at the end of the duet (ex 9). A final transformation of the same motive occurs in the choral 'Make Them a World' (ex 10). The process of motivic transformation, therefore, serves as a further unifying device in this work.

Folk elements pervade both the text and the music of this truly Canadian opera. In addition to dealing with figures from Canadian history, recounting the story of an Indian legend, and placing the action within Fort Garry, the sense of colour is heightened through allusions to such pioneer foods as pemmican and bannock. The use of Bungay, French, and French-Canadian accents contributes to the national flavour of this opera, as do the two musical numbers based on folk-like material: 'Come Let Us Sing of the Service,' performed by the quartet of fur traders, and the reel in the ball scene.

One of the arias from this opera, Macdonnell's 'Night is No Longer Summer Soft,' was re-scored in 1970 for band, on the occasion of a band clinic held in Saskatoon. The opera itself received no performances after its initial radio broadcast, despite the fact that Geiger-Torel saw its potential as a televised production.

WORKS FOR YOUNG MUSICIANS

In keeping with his lifelong interest in introducing young people to music and in encouraging young musicians in their endeavours, Murray Adaskin has composed a number of works specifically aimed at performance by violin students and high school bands and orchestras. His *Three Pieces for Violin and Piano* ('Quiet Song,' 'Dedication,' 'Dance') and the *Daydreams for Violin and Piano* were intended as a projected series of works for young violinists, each of which was to be a study of a different type of technical problem couched in such musical terms as to make it palatable to the performer. *Daydreams* has also been transcribed for alto saxophone and piano. Two further works belong to this group of educational pieces: *Calisthenics for Violin and Piano* and *Legato and Ricochet for Violin and Piano*. A *Toccatina for Piano* was published by the Waterloo Music Company as number 9 in *Horizons – Music by Canadian Composers*, Book 1, intended for grades three to five. Each of the nine pieces in this collection was written on a different scale pattern by a different Canadian composer; the composers are George Fiala, Louis Applebaum, Violet Archer, Robert Fleming, Carleton Elliott, Brian Cherney, Richard Johnston, Robert Turner, and Murray Adaskin. The pieces are aimed at acquainting the beginning piano student with the sound of music not based upon traditional scales. Murray's study is a short, humorous one-page work based on polyrhythms and emphasizing the 'Oriental' scale of augmented seconds.

A work with a similar purpose is *The Prairie Lily* for voice and piano, intended for use by schoolchildren in Saskatchewan and included in Book 6 of

Basic Goals in Music (McGraw-Hill). *Essay for Strings,* written for a high school string orchestra, and the band transcription of the aria 'Night Is No Longer Summer Soft' from Murray's opera, *Grant, Warden of the Plains,* were performed at various band clinics and music educators' conferences. Perhaps the most popular of his educational pieces, the *Rondino for Orchestra,* was commissioned by the Canadian Music Centre as suitable for a junior orchestra. After a recent performance of it by the Vancouver Youth Orchestra, Murray received a letter from the president of the Junior Symphony Orchestra in Vancouver, which read, in part: 'It is the time given and interest demonstrated by persons such as yourself which makes the youth orchestra movement in Canada the most vital and dynamic of all such movements in the Western world.'[17]

GENERAL STYLISTIC FEATURES

The characteristic most common to all Murray Adaskin compositions, whether they stem from the pre-Saskatoon, the Saskatoon, or the Victoria period – that typically Adaskin stamp – is a sense of joy and fun. Unassuming and unaffected, each work is based on a natural progression of ideas, in an embodiment of the composer's principle to follow the ideas wherever they may lead him just as one follows a rolling ball. A Chaplinesque sense of humour and wit lend most of his works an expression of youthful optimism that transcends limitations of age. Coupled with the wit is an amiable warmth, captured in his sense for linear continuity and the long line. The composer is a melodist at heart, a tendency equally prominent in his writing for solo instruments and in instrumental combinations. Expressiveness is at the forefront of each composition, and is attained through his immense knowledge of the capabilities of each instrument to which he assigns a wide range of expression, a feature revealed particularly in an orchestral context. Murray Adaskin is a master of orchestration, a skill acquired in the three decades as orchestral musician that preceded his composition studies. Coupled with an innate talent for instrumental colour, his orchestration skills place him among the best instrumental composers on today's Canadian music scene. He is not an experimental composer; his instruments are treated within the confines of their idiomatic capacities, pointing to the fact that much can still be said musically by using conventional – that is, non-electronic, non-aleatoric, non-computer – means.

What sets Murray Adaskin apart from many contemporary composers is that his works are written with affection and sincerity, and that each is an embodiment of a personal expression toward the individual or group for which it is created. The *Coronation Overture,* for example, with its middle section an exuberant reel in square-dance tempo, was inspired by his memories of an evening in Rideau Hall where the then Princess Elizabeth, a happy young woman, was seen on television square-dancing with Prince Philip. Throughout the overture, which is based on the two-measure quotation of 'Long to Reign over Us,' Murray's homage to the human being is coupled with his homage to the symbol represented by the queen. Through its motivic and rhythmic transformations the identity of the familiar melodic excerpt is never completely obvious. The full orchestral texture of the opening section is warmed through a series of superimposed thirds and – by inversion – sixths, extracted from the familiar tune. The slowly evolving material that also horizontally delineates the interval of the third (exs 11a and 11b) is immediately transformed into 6/8 metre at the beginning of the square-dance section (ex 12). Two further transformations follow in the oboes and in the violins, backed by most of the brass instruments (exs 13 and 14).

Other works similarly exhibit an individual atmosphere or distinctive musical climate: the *Algonquin Symphony*, as a tribute to Taylor Statten, embodies the composer's special feelings of affection toward the man and the geographic region of Ontario associated with him; the *Diversion for Orchestra*, with its homage to the young members of the new national orchestra, displays his sense of national pride. The *Serenade Concertante* was purposely created as a simple and forthright work, suitable to the small chamber orchestra available to John Avison at the time. As the broadcast for which the piece was commissioned was to consist entirely of Canadian works – still a relatively novel idea in 1954 – Murray planned to communicate a mood of careless amiability to the radio audiences. On other occasions meaningful memories are embedded in his compositions, such as the profound effect of his trip to the Canadian Arctic (*Qalala and Nilaula*), glimpses into childhood performances of violin duets with his brother (*Divertimento No 1*), and memories of his cantor grandfather, one of whose prayers was fondly remembered in the *Fanfare for Orchestra*.

Despite the allusions to extra-musical ideas that, on occasion, even include sounds from nature, Murray Adaskin's music is at no time intended as program music. It would, in effect, constitute a total misrepresentation of his compositional idiom to describe it as such. The personalized impulses become abstracted in a manner similar to that of Robert Schumann in his *Abegg Variations*, where references to his personal world are abstractly embedded in his musical textures.

Instruments are always treated with great care, particularly when they appear within an ensemble context. They are often featured in a soloistic fashion, and only occasionally are all instruments in a symphonic work used simultaneously. In such instances the purpose is to punctuate a texture for rhythmic or dramatic reasons. In the middle section of the *Saskatchewan Legend* (mm 62–82) passages in oboe solo alternate with similar solos in the horns, violins, and violas. The linear direction of the interweaving melodic material lends this section a spatial effect through its transparent textures. A similar type of soloistic instrumental treatment is evidenced throughout the violin concerto. As an example, the first-movement orchestral introduction, which precedes the entry of the solo violin, opens with an imitative dialogue between the bassoons and flutes, which is then taken up by the violins and cellos in the same imitative fashion. The orchestration of the slow movement sets a warm tone, which is intensified through the expressiveness of the solo violin line. The colour in the orchestral introduction to this movement is generated through the superimposition of the B-flat trumpet playing in thirds over the viola and cello lines. The melodic continuum is then transferred to oboes playing in thirds followed by the flutes, and the introduction is concluded by lower woodwind passages. Examples of similar techniques abound throughout the third movement.

Perhaps the best instance of soloistic treatment of instruments may be found in the *Serenade Concertante*, where the frequently juxtaposed wind and string families also feature individual instruments in a concertante fashion. This is clearly exemplified in the first eight measures, which generate the basic motivic and rhythmic materials for the entire piece. The opening eight-measure statement weaves out one long melody, which is shared by the solo clarinets and oboes in alternation. A counter-melody, evolving in the solo bassoon simultaneously with the melody, delineates a clearly contrapuntal texture. The opening statement sets up a dualism between the melodic line and the constituent germinal ideas that generate its continuum (ex 15). Three basic elements are introduced within the first two measures: the simple triad D, F, A in the clarinet (see a in ex 15), the A, B-flat, A motive in the bassoon delineating the interval of a second (see b in ex 15), and its altered inversion, the interval of the seventh (see c in ex 15). Each of these germinal ideas undergoes immediate transformation after its initial statement as shown in a^1 and a^2 of ex 15, which are derivatives of the opening triad, and b^1, derivative of b. According to the composer, the curve and rhythm of the first two measures determine the characteristic flow of the rest of the piece.

After the initial statement of the melodic material in the solo clarinet, oboe, and bassoon, the melody is spun out lyrically in the first and second violins. Throughout the piece there is a continual thinning out and thickening of the texture as individual instruments or groups interject and interweave motivic material.

In addition to exemplifying Murray Adaskin's unique approach to his treatment of instruments within an orchestral context, the *Serenade Concertante* serves as an excellent example of the composer's developmental techniques. A stamp of his compositional style is a natural sense of inner unity whereby an entire movement or – as occurs frequently in a multi-movement work – the entire composition is based on a germinal idea stated initially in the first few measures of the work. Rhythmic and melodic transformations of this idea serve as a unifying and a structural device throughout the work. The three elements identified as a, b, and c in the *Serenade Concertante* (ex 15) are further transformed in mm 11 and 12 in the material performed by the bassoons in contrast to the singing line of the violins (ex 16). The opening figure of the trumpet solo a few measures later is a combination of motives a and b (ex 17). The compositional craft is evidenced in the skilled manipulations of these germinal ideas, lending the composition an air of a natural evolutionary process. Despite the tight weave of his musical textures, Murray's compositions never sound contrived.

The introductory melodic idea of the Andante Sostenuto of the piano quartet serves as an example of a melodic line of great warmth. In beautiful counterpoint, the violin and viola engage in an amiable dialogue, joined by the cello. Embedded in this line is the motive that serves as the basic germinal unit of the entire composition (ex 18a). Its identifying characteristics, the two rising fourths followed by a falling second or, alternately, a falling third, are recognizable in examples 18b and 18c, which are transformations of 18a. In a further transformation it becomes the basic material of the Rondo movement (ex 18d), where, because of its new context and spiccato articulation, it assumes a new identity.

The *Divertimento No 3* has perhaps the most remarkable display of inner unity within a work, based on a motive that is transformed in such a way that each of the three movements assumes its own distinctive character. The germinal idea for the entire work, stated in the violin in mm 1–3 (ex 19), is, in effect, a descending four-note unit consisting of three whole steps and a half-step: A-G-F-E. It is then transformed throughout the work rhythmically and intervallically in a number of ways. In the second movement the four notes appear out of order so as to emphasize the semitone relationship of the pattern, which is now transposed to the pitches E-D-C-B (ex 20). The interval of the second becomes the basis of the B section of this movement, which is cast in the form of A-A-B-A and coda. In the third movement the descending unit is embedded within the opening figures played pizzicatto and staccatissimo. This movement also serves as a summation of the germinal idea through its full statement in long note values of the first-movement opening theme, which is repeated three times in the French horn to a jazzy, ostinato pattern set up in the bassoon (ex 21). The A sections of both previous movements are then restated in reverse order in the third movement. The Divertimento ends with the A section of the first movement, lending the work a unifying arch. The inherent sense of symmetry is created through a process whereby a melodic continuum is created out of a juxtaposition of smaller germinal units, which are further atomized and transformed throughout the work only to be assembled again at the end of the whole and presented in the original context. Each movement ends with a triad, in which the interval of a fifth constitutes the basic sound, filled in with a superimposed third or sixth in the following manner: Movement 1 = B, F-sharp, A; Movement 2 = E-flat, B-flat, G; Movement 3 = B, F-sharp, D. This work has a depth of perspective that transcends the light-hearted element suggested in its title, *Divertimento*.

The work of Murray Adaskin displays a classical sense of structure. His compositions are cast in one, two, or three movements, and are conceived as a sonata, concerto, overture, capriccio, divertimento, rondo, trio, quartet, and the like. Such titles as *Sonatine Baroque, Canzona and Rondo,* and *Serenade Concertante* are indicative of his classical orientation. His sense of structural balance and symmetry within each movement is demonstrated in his predilection for A-B-A and rondo forms. The violin concerto, for example, is cast in A-B-A form. The eight-and-a-half measure orchestral introduction contains a short passage in canonic imitation between the flutes and bassoons, which is subsequently transferred to the strings and completed by the woodwinds. The first solo violin statement overlaps with the end of the orchestral introduction. It is a continuous, uninterrupted melodic line that unfolds over twenty-two measures. The second violin statement begins to unfold after an orchestral interlude, working out over thirty-three continuous measures a melodic line that features harmonics and double stops. The third statement, cadenza-like and quasi-improvisatory, unfolds over sustained notes in the orchestra. The first movement concludes with a repetition of the initial eight-measure orchestral introduction followed by parts of the first violin statement. The violin material is treated in a unique way. The emphasis is on the lyrical capabilities of the solo instrument, and the entire movement is structured in such a way as to allow the violin to soar and dance above the orchestral texture. The surprise element in the repeat of previously stated material is manifested in a rhythmic twist, where a shift in the metric accent gives rise to a new inflection within a motivic restatement, as illustrated in the two passages from the violin concerto cited in examples 22a and 22b.

A similar sense of symmetry is shown in the bassoon concerto. The first movement espouses an A-B-C-A-B structure, in which the A could be considered an exposition introducing the two basic themes of the movement: theme 1 is stated in contrapuntal imitation between the solo bassoon and the muted trumpets; theme 2 is introduced in the oboe (mm 10–15). The B section could be considered as developmental since its various rhythmic transformations of theme 2, such as syncopation and offbeat accents, lend it a more active function. It is interlaced with bravura passages for the bassoon. A lengthy cadenza for the solo instrument may be considered as the c section, which is followed by a repeat of theme 1 in A, this time re-orchestrated for the piccolo and bassoon, ending the entire movement with its most active portion, B.

Sonata form is seldom encountered in an Adaskin composition, and on occassions where it seems to occur, as in the first movement of the *Algonquin Symphony*, it is a manifestation of a very individual approach. The opening idea, shared among the instruments in the woodwind section where each portion of the melody is continued by a different instrument, takes eleven measures to unfold (ex 23). This may be considered the first subject material. With its transparent contrapuntal texture in which instrumental colour is emphasized, this section exudes a sense of peace, serenity, and spaciousness. The second subject material consists of two themes derived from the opening material, as shown in examples 24a and 24b. The development section, which also contains a fleeting fugato passage, is based on transformations of motives from subject 1. Instrumental colour is the predominant element here, and occasional derivative themes are performed soloistically in order to feature the timbres at opposite ends of the sound spectrum of such instruments as the piccolo and bass clarinet.

The recapitulation sees the return of the two major themes in reverse order, with theme 1 in a totally new context, most of it shared by solo and tutti violins. Because of the continuous developmental process of the opening material, the overall sonata form framework seems to be of secondary importance. The emphasis is on orchestral colour, texture, and thematic treatment, which lends the movement a feeling of organic growth. A coda ends the movement.

The Adaskin harmonic vocabulary displays a fondness for dissonant counterpoint. Seldom is there a sense of vertical harmonic progression within a broader tonal context. A tonal orientation is not one of the composer's operative criteria. A chord, a triad with added notes, or a tone cluster is treated as an independent entity. The specific flavour of his textures results from the continuously unfolding, horizontally conceived superimposed lines. Linear counterpoint is the primary mode of expression, and where chordal texture occurs, the resultant sound is a vertical crossroads of horizontal dynamics rather than a premeditated structural event.

The Adaskin melodic line projects some very distinctive features. It is frequently disjunct, consisting of large intervals that, when combined with the specific rhythmic outline, give rise to a broadly sweeping melodic curve of great energy. One such example may be found in the first violin line of the third movement of the string quartet at measures 15–21 (ex 25), or in the broad gestures of the opening violin statement in the first *Portrait* of *Two Portraits* (ex 2). The rhythmic motion and intervallic configuration in the dialogue between the bassoon solo and the trumpet at the opening of the bassoon concerto create two intertwining lines of great flexibility and amiability (ex 26). The broad sweep in the melodic curve is also attained through a combination of disjunct and conjunct motion to create a melody of tenderly lyrical character, as in the opening measures of the violin solo of the first movement of the violin concerto (ex 27).

Rhythmic vitality is another stamp of the Adaskin style. Cross-rhythms, offbeat accents, and syncopations make his compositions at times difficult to perform, particularly by a larger group. The third movement of the violin concerto, with its continuous metric fluctuations of 2/4, 3/8, 5/8, presents the conductor and the orchestra with a challenge. Ostinato patterns are a frequent occurrence both as repetitions of five or six-note cells (ex 28) or as one- or two-note pitches (as in the opening measures of the *Diversion for Orchestra*). The dance-like character and the rhythmic verve of an Adaskin musical motive are best evidenced in the *Serenade Concertante*. The melodic ostinato pattern seldom recurs in the same rhythmic configuration. The pattern, which begins on the downbeat in example 29, shifts to the offbeat in example 30, where newly introduced rhythmic accents lend it a new character. The same pattern undergoes further rhythmic transformations, as seen in examples 31 and 32. Such rhythmic treatment lends a passage a light-hearted, dance-like, humorous, and at times jazzy effect.

The manifestation of these techniques in the *Diversion for Orchestra* lends the work an air of good-natured bounciness. The basic compositional principle is the germinal unit, consisting of either a rhythmic ostinato or a short motivic idea. Both are clearly defined through their juxtaposition in the individual instrumental groups. The jubilant tone set at the opening of this composition matches the festive occasion for which it was composed. The leap of a fifth in the timpani, followed by a dramatic roll, introduces a three-measure ostinato pattern based on the interval of a second, which is treated in a rhythmically syncopated fashion by the full orchestra. Alternating 2/4 and 3/4 metres lends the A section a sense of rhythmic fluctuation and flexibility. The melodic snippets heard throughout the A section are either an outgrowth of the horizontal play of seconds or transformations of one another. Example 33 juxtaposes two such ideas, the first of which, a, is encountered in two transformed versions in close succession in example 34. The interval of the seventh delineated in mm 47–8 in the oboes and strings is merely an altered inversion of the interval of the second, which serves as basis of the A section of the composition.

Such rhythmic treatment is often the result of an impish sense of humour, which is at times witty, whimsical, or Chaplinesque. The sense of fun is also evident in such works as the *Rondino for Nine Instruments* or the second of the *Two Portraits* for violin and piano. Murray Adaskin has an inborn sense for the timing of humorous moments: a joke is never carried beyond its effective limits. The many Charlie Chaplin movies watched as a boy left a profound impression on the mature man, and the Chaplinesque features embedded themselves into the composer's subconscious creative process.

When one considers the scope and intensity of Murray's university commitments during the academic year, the volume and variety of works composed during his Saskatoon period are indeed prolific. They denote a life totally dedicated to work within a situation where work, seen as a labour of love, signified pleasure. The process was to continue after his retirement from the University of Saskatchewan with the Adaskins' move to Victoria, when the city accepted into its folds two lives in busy retirement.

7

Two lives in busy retirement:
Victoria, BC

On 15 January 1973 the Adaskins moved into their new residence in Victoria, Canada's westernmost city. They were no strangers to this part of the world. Throughout their careers as performing artists they had made annual pilgrimages to the city to give recitals and visit friends. Their decision, therefore, to retire in Victoria, away from the bitter cold of the harsh Prairie winters, did not come as a surprise. Their love of nature, greenery, serenity, and an aesthetic atmosphere resulted in their acquiring a corner plot of land and an imposing house on Devon Road in the Uplands, an established, fashionable part of the city.

Rejoicing that at last he would be able to devote himself entirely to composition, Murray set up a studio with a small upright piano, in the basement of the house. Frances, who was intending to continue her voice coaching, albeit on a reduced scale, set up a basement studio at the other end of the house where the sounds of the grand piano would not disturb the composer's creative processes. The stage was set for a quiet, comfortable life of moderate musical activities.

It did not take long, however, for Victoria's musical community to realize the significance of harbouring in its midst two Canadian musical figures of such stature. Combined with their natural tendency toward involvement in the cultural aspects of their community, the Adaskins began to notice increasing demands on their time, which they met with willingness and co-operation. Their move to Victoria, therefore, signified the beginning of a third major phase in their artistic careers: a retirement that was – and still is – musically so active that it could easily compete with a full-time career of persons thirty years their junior.

A city of almost a quarter of a million people, whose history goes back little more than 130 years, Victoria in 1973 enjoyed a well-developed musical life fed by several diverse cultural institutions. The Conservatory of Music and the music department at the University of Victoria were the major educational institutions for musicians. The conservatory, the older of the two, had developed under the directorship of its principal and vice-principal, Robin and Winifred Wood, into a major training school for young performers in the West. Both Woods were renowned pedagogues, performing artists, and widely respected adjudicators at music festivals. Winifred Wood also functioned as head of the piano section at the conservatory. In 1973 the University of Victoria was only in its tenth year as an autonomous institution, and the fledgling music department was being developed under the skilled directorship of Phillip T. Young, brought in from Yale to build up a strong music unit within the university, offering graduate and undergraduate programs in performance, composition, and music history/musicology.[1]

The Victoria Symphony Orchestra had just changed its status from the largest community orchestra in British Columbia to a semi-professional organization with a small nucleus of full-time professional players. Some of these musicians were also employed by the conservatory and the university. The conductor under whom this change occurred and the orchestra season expanded was Laszlo Gati, who was followed in 1979 by Paul Freeman, formerly of the Detroit Symphony Orchestra. Other organizations contributed to the city's active concert life: the Victoria Musical Arts Society continued the tradition set in the 1930s by the Victoria Ladies' Musical Club, which had sponsored a number of concerts by Frances James; and concerts by the Victoria Choral Society and the annual music festival had begun to gather momentum.[2]

Murray Adaskin had not been in Victoria long before he received a phone call from Robin Wood. Two of the three members of the conservatory violin faculty had departed rather abruptly, leaving behind many violin students who needed instruction and guidance in order to complete the year. Murray, who could not refuse such a request to help out, found himself teaching a full load of students for the remainder of the school year. In the following years, it was the university that needed the services of both Adaskins. Murray was asked to teach an orchestration class as a replacement for faculty members on sabbatical leave, and Frances, in addition to teaching voice through the conservatory, was asked to take a number of voice students from the university.

Although Murray did not continue the pace of full-time violin teaching set during his first year in Victoria, he was in demand by parents of highly gifted children to coach their youngsters. He, therefore, continued to teach on a small scale, often cultivating a talented violin student for admission into the string class at the University of Victoria. The same pioneering spirit that led him to the University of Saskatchewan compelled him to continue his activities as violin pedagogue in Victoria. His concern with the function of music students as valuable future consumers of music and educated listeners was transferred to the Victoria scene.

Cultivating the idea of beauty in the young generations was an essential part of Murray's educational philosophy. This was not only manifested in his approach to teaching but also in the works he composed for young musicians. The *Adagio for Cello and Piano* was commissioned by Robin Wood as a test-piece suitable for students at the grade viii to x level to be used in the Victoria Music Festival. The *Three Tunes for Strings* was commissioned by the Oak Bay Strings, thirty-six young people between the ages of thirteen and nineteen. In each case, Murray's goal was through these works to foster in young students the love and enjoyment of music-making and to develop good string playing.

His activities as adjudicator at music festivals did not cease with his move westward, and his services were much in demand during the Victoria Festival. For Murray, adjudicating opened another channel through which to reach the young generation. It was through such festivals that three composition students came from the Prairies to study with him in Victoria. All three eventually studied with Rudolf Komorous at the university and became successful musicians: by 1987 David MacIntyre had become an established faculty member at Simon Fraser University, Mark Ellestad completed his master's degree in composition at the University of Victoria, and Rod Sharman received his *Reifendiplom* – the equivalent of a doctorate – from the Institut für Neue Musik in Freiburg, Germany.

To the young musicians Murray extended unshakeable moral support and encouragement in their musical endeavours, which were frequently of great significance to their development as musicians. One of his teaching methods was to talk about music with such affection that his words stirred and inspired his students, who would leave the studio with a sense of awe. In retrospect, Mark Ellestad compares those student days with Murray Adaskin to opening a door only to find himself in an enchanted garden.

Frances had a similar charismatic effect on her students. Through her association with both the university and the conservatory – contrary to her original intentions – she had assembled a considerable voice class and was invited on a number of occasions to give master classes at the conservatory. Stepping into the Adaskin house, a veritable art gallery of Canadian works, was to her students an enriching experience in the exposure it offered them to art and culture. The quiet home with its profusion of cut flowers provided beautiful surroundings, and the artist's extensive concert experience served the voice students as an inspiration in their own endeavours. In her enthusiasm toward teaching, Frances would frequently call upon Murray to join her and the student in the studio to share in the joy of a convincing interpretation of a musical work. Within such an atmosphere time stood still, and the students shared with the Adaskins the magic of the creative act in music.

Frances always felt that it was her responsibility as a Canadian performer to pass on to her students the advantages she had gained through her studies with Hayes, Kurenko, and Heim. She wanted to share the benefits acquired from her radio and concert experiences, and, above all, she wanted to introduce her students to the world of contemporary Canadian as well as non-Canadian music. Two students in particular benefited from this atmosphere – Jane MacKenzie and Catherine Lewis. Both became busy performers developing national and international reputations. In 1987 Lewis is specializing in contemporary music, while MacKenzie is much in demand in Europe as an opera and oratorio singer.

As part of their support for their students the Adaskins often helped them attain the next phase of their musical studies by writing letters of recommendation, by enlisting the help of their personal friends, or simply by advising the students about their careers when such advice was needed. Close to one thousand letters of recommendation were written in the Adaskins' house in Victoria on behalf of their students as well as of musicians from all across the country.

The Adaskins' students were not the sole recipients of the couple's support and encouragement. Their commitment and total dedication to music and to those whose lives are touched by music are still today evidenced through their attendance at practically all musical events in the city. Murray's concern for the welfare of the Victoria Symphony Orchestra led to his serving on the symphony society's board of directors and to his frequent involvement with fund-raising activities on behalf of the orchestra.

Despite his many activities in Victoria, Murray Adaskin has continued his prolific composition, and at the time of the writing of this biography, at age eighty-one he is still working on new compositions. Up to the present, twenty-five works, or almost a third of his total output as composer, have been written during his years of 'retirement' in Victoria. The Victoria works, many of which were commissioned by local groups, fall into five categories: instrumental, orchestral, chamber, solo with orchestra, and voice with orchestra. In the 'instrumental' category, violin, piano, clarinet, and cello are featured as solo instruments. Of the two pieces for violin and piano the single-movement *Israeli Violin Piece T'Filat Shalom (A Prayer for Peace)* stems from 1974. It was originally composed for Jeff Krolik, an Adaskin violin student who followed his teacher from Saskatoon to Victoria in order to continue his studies with the master. Krolik's father, vice-president of the Canadian branch of the Canadian Jewish Council at the time, commissioned the composition through the council for Jeff, who played it in Jerusalem. The *Impromptu for Violin and Piano* was composed for Mark Neumann, another former violin student, who performed it at his graduating recital at the University of Victoria's School of Music. Another composition written for students during Murray's Victoria period was the four-hand work, *Rankin Inlet – Eskimo Song*.

One of Murray's outstanding works is the *Sonata for Cello and Piano*, composed for Windsor cellist Dr T.C. Akeley. It incorporates as its slow movement the *Adagio for Cello and Piano*, written shortly after Murray's arrival in Victoria. *Premièred* at the University of Windsor School of Music in 1981, it met with instant acclaim: 'The core of Adaskin's work, the adagio in the second movement is a remarkably lyrical piece of spellbinding beauty ... Adaskin wrote a jewel for the piano-cello repertory and the duo of Akeley and Butler polished it to extraordinary brilliance.'³ Among the international artists to have adopted this work into their repertoire is Tsuyoshi Tsutsumi, who, with Ronald Turini at the piano, gave it a superb rendition during the 1985 Victoria International Festival.

The *Nocturne for Clarinet and Piano* was commissioned in 1975 by the International Clarinet Congress through a grant by the Ontario Arts Council, and was *premièred* at the congress by Stanley McCartney, clarinet, and Mark Widner, pianist. The *Ontario Variation for Solo Piano*, while conceived as part of a fascinating project, suffered an obscure fate. It was to have constituted one of a set of variations for piano written by a number of composers born in Ontario throughout a forty-year period. The originator of the idea, a member of the theory and composition department at the University of Western Ontario, had planned to have the variations published along with analytical comments by the representative composers. Although Murray's contribution to the volume was sent to the editor, the entire project seems to have died.

The orchestral works category varies in size of ensemble from strings only (*Three Tunes for Strings*), and strings and harpsichord (*In Praise of 'Canadian Painting in the Thirties'*) to larger ensembles (*Nootka Ritual for Orchestra, Dance Concertante*, and the short *March No 3 for Orchestra*). While *In Praise of 'Canadian Painting in the Thirties,'* commissioned by the Chamber Players of Toronto through a Canada Council grant, met with a number of subsequent performances including the National Arts Centre Orchestra, conducted by Lukas Foss, and several performances in Victoria, the *Dance Concertante for Orchestra* did not bring the composer much joy. It was originally envisioned as a concerto for orchestra for the Windsor, Ontario, symphony. Subsequently, the conductor requested that it be changed into a concertante for woodwind quintet and orchestra. After a number of requests for further alterations such as a cadenza for bassoon and one for the clarinet in the third movement, the conductor suggested that because of the length of the piece a cut should be made in it. The composer, unhappy about the cuts and alterations to which his composition was submitted, did not attend the *première*.

The chamber music written in Victoria can be classified as three wind quintets, two brass fanfares, and two more works in the divertimento series. Commissioned by the University of Victoria's Pacific Wind Quintet, the three-movement *Quintet for Woodwinds* was performed by them on a number of occasions in Vancouver and Seattle.[4] The three-movement *Bassoon Quintet*, commissioned by the CBC for George Zukerman and the Purcell String Quartet, fared even better than the previous quintet.[5] In the composer's words: 'There is no intended relationship between this work and the *Concerto for Bassoon and Orchestra* of 1960 (also written for George Zukerman) except for an intense affection for the instrument. I merely wished to produce a work of inner intensity and warmth, yet employing a minimum of means and consciously culling out redundant and virtuosic passages.' It was *premièred* on a broadcast of 'Arts National' recorded in the CBC Vancouver studios with producer George Laverock, and has since received several major performances including one at the Victoria International Festival with Zukerman and members of the Quartet Canada.

The third of the quintets, *Music for Brass Quintet*, was commissioned by Lawrence House for a performance at the 1977 Summer Festival in Guelph, Ontario. Because of its affiliation with Guelph, the birthplace of the great Canadian tenor Edward Johnson, Murray dedicated the composition to the singer's memory and based it on a one-and-a-half measure quotation from *Pelléas et Mélisande*, an opera often sung by the tenor.

Of the two shorter brass works, the *Fanfare for Brass Quintet* was commissioned by Tom Taylor as a one-minute theme for 'Festival Celebrations,' a series of weekly broadcasts on the CBC-AM network, September through November 1977. The *Brass Fanfare for a Wedding* was written as a wedding gift to Victoria Nelson, daughter of the Adaskins' Saskatoon friends Blair and Mary Nelson, in fulfilment of a promise made to the bride as a child. The work was performed by Larry House and a group of players from the University of Saskatchewan, on the patio of the Nelsons' house overlooking the South Saskatchewan River with a magnificent view of the broad Prairies beyond, a majestic setting for the music and for the occasion.

Of the two divertimenti for solo instruments and orchestra, *Divertimento No 5* for two guitars and chamber orchestra was commissioned by one of Murray's former Saskatoon composition students. In a letter to Murray, Peter Mc-

Allister, one of the two guitarists states: 'Your work for two guitars and chamber orchestra is incredible, not only because you write for the nature of the guitar so remarkably well, but because the whole piece flows from beginning to end beautifully ... This *Divertimento No 5* will be played many, many times. I am sure that a lot of conductors will jump at the chance to play such a great piece by you. I can assure you that this work will remain in our repertoire for the rest of our lives, and it, as the first work ever by a Canadian composer for 2 guitars and orchestra will hold a very special place in our hearts forever.'[6]

The *Divertimento No 6 for Percussion and Orchestra* was *premièred* at the University Centre Auditorium of the University of Victoria in February 1985. As part of the Victoria Symphony Orchestra's 'Discovery Series' featuring contemporary compositions, the work was written for percussionist Salvador Ferreras and conducted by George Corwin of the university's School of Music.

The most important of the Victoria compositions, and a significant contribution to the international repertoire of works for narrator and orchestra, is *The Travelling Musicians*. Based on the Brothers Grimm fable *The Musicians of Bremen*, the story deals with the lot of a donkey, dog, cat, and rooster, who have been discarded by their masters because, given their advanced age, they can no longer provide the services expected of them. Each decides to create a new living through his/her musical activities. The donkey can play the flute, the dog can play the timpani and bark, the cat has a fondness for the glockenspiel, and the rooster can sing. Dejected, they eventually meet on the road, comfort each other, decide to provide mutual company, and form a quartet.

Their path leads the hungry foursome into the woods, to a house with a table bedecked with the most magnificent food. Their glance through a window reveals a band of robbers feasting around the table and counting their stolen money. The quartet's first attempt to scare the robbers out of the house proves successful. They enter the house and continue feasting where the robbers left off. No sooner have they eaten and dropped off to sleep than the robbers return. Through their concerted efforts the four partners succeed once more in scaring the robbers away, this time by having them believe that the house has been taken over by a terrible witch. From that moment onward the robbers never return and the musicians rediscover happiness in their new premises through their music-making activities. The text ends with these touching lines: 'And any day, if you happen to pass that house, / whether it be morning, noon or night, / you will hear the musicians making their music for all who care to listen / or for no other reason than the sheer joy of it. / For no other reason than the sheer joy.'

The fable has been adapted to a poetic text by the renowned Victoria poet P. K. Page. Considered today as one of Canada's foremost poets, her reputation dates back to the forties when she was still a member of the Montreal 'Preview Group.' She has since earned many prizes for her poetry, including an Order of Canada in recognition of her achievements. Some of her collections include *Poems Selected and New* (Anansi, 1974) and *Evening Dance of the Grey Flies* (Oxford, 1981).

The text to *The Travelling Musicians* is no ordinary libretto; as a literary work it could well stand on its own. It combines with the music, which is moulded to the sounds and meaning of each word, to provide a rare coherence and unity of the arts of music and words. The text has a musical quality created through the careful choice of words, each with its specific rhythm and sounds contributing to the musical flow and imagery of the whole. Witness the following excerpt:

> This time they were in such high spirits that they danced as they went
> although Donkey was lame
> and Dog had an ache
> and Cat had a pain
> in the tip of her tail
> and Rooster, alack,
> had a crick in his neck
> and his joints were as stiff
> as an iron weather-vane.
> Yet they danced till all four
> could not dance one step more!

On one level this is a simple fable for children, while on another it is a moving and compassionate parable of the human condition told with a delightful touch of humour. The composition attests to the fact that some of the more complex thoughts on life can be expressed with great dignity using eminently simple means. The composition employs a full orchestra with a pronounced percussion section and requires a narrator who also sings. The orchestral introduction sets a warm tone through its emphasis on thirds, creating a static, suspended motion. Out of this initial statement evolves a melody that is developed by different groups of instruments over the next twenty-five measures. The vocal line consists of a rhythmic speech part, which occasionally breaks into song. At times the orchestra plays a passive role, providing only sustained chords as a background to the narrator's line. For the most part, however, the orchestra assumes an active role in the story by either engaging in Chaplinesque effects that punctuate and enhance certain words, or by imbuing the story with a sense of motion. Some of the humorous effects include melodic units representative of each animal – such as the purring of the cat or the crowing of the rooster – or an instrumental figure representative of a knock on the head or the twitter of birds.

The timing, or the pacing, of the episodes in the story provides the work with its unity. Three moments in particular highlight the composition: the section conveying the chaos and noise as the four animals crash through the glass, scaring the robbers out of the house (mm 380–6); the dancelike statement by the orchestra illustrating the animals' delight as they feast on the 'mouthwatering bites' spread out on the table (ex 35); and the sleep scene (mm 425–32). The last is particularly effective in its expression of the sounds of the travelling companions. The dramatic flow of events is suspended when, after their feast, each of the companions finds an appropriate spot for the night. The text indicates that not a sound was to be heard. Musically, however, the silence is conveyed through sporadic snippets of melodic and rhythmic figures played in triple piano by individual instruments, representing the sound of snoring and other noises in the dead of night. Unity is further projected in the composition by the introduction at its conclusion of some of the purely orchestral material that was heard at its opening.

The work has an immediate appeal to the general audience. The composer becomes a magician who, through an innate sense for the pacing of the humorous events, embellishes and projects the images in the text, manipulating the listener's involvement with the story, from a fast-paced chaotic set of events, through a suspension of motion in the sleep scene, to an increase in tension as robber John returns, to the serenity of the ending with its call of the loon. *The Travelling Musicians* is one of the best compositions of its genre in the twentieth century. *Premièred* on 22 January 1984 in Victoria, it was narrated by the soprano Catherine Lewis, for whom the vocal part was written. Paul Freeman conducted the Victoria Symphony Orchestra.

While the *première* of the work was taped by the CBC for a later performance on 'Mostly Music,' this broadcast differed considerably from the type of reception a new Adaskin work would have been given two decades earlier. By the 1970s CBC policy toward the commissioning and performing of contemporary Canadian music had changed. The period of the fifties and sixties, when Canadian works were solicited to celebrate a variety of national occasions, had come to an end. By the early eighties it became obvious that, plagued by financial difficulties, the CBC could no longer perform the function of patron of the arts or pursue its policy toward Canadian music with fervour equal to that of its early days. Changing times and improved technology do not necessarily lead to an improved artistic climate. Murray, whose career as a performer at first paralleled the evolution of early broadcasting in Canada, and whose career as a composer was to a great extent moulded by the CBC, lived through the whole gamut of the history of broadcasting and of the CBC itself. He experienced the evolution of its various policies toward the arts and Canadian content, and he was a beneficiary of the heyday of the CBC's encouragement and support of live broadcasts of Canadian music. He was, therefore, well aware of the potentially adverse effect of the gradual change through the 1970s in the CBC attitude toward the Canadian composer. The nature of the works Murray composed for Victoria and the fewer performances these new works received in comparison with those of previous years attested to this fact. He continued to compose, but in the absence of what used to be his major support, his works, for the most part written for local individuals and groups, received less national exposure than those from the Saskatoon period.

The Canada Council is one of the few remaining federal institutions in this country to offer cultural support to its artists, and many of Murray's Victoria compositions were indeed commissioned by the council. There exists in Canada today, however, a phlegmatic attitude toward its artists. Murray and the generation of composers dating from the forties have established a tradition of Canadian music. Weinzweig, Papineau-Couture, Pépin, Pentland, Morawetz, Coulthard, Beckwith, and Somers have created a body of compositions that can be viewed as the classical repertoire of Canadian works. These are the works that should be accepted by today's audiences and by the younger composers as recognized products of the post-war generation of Canadian composers. As such they should be performed and recorded on a regular basis, and the recordings should be made available commercially. The *Anthology of Canadian Music*, compiled by Radio Canada International, serves such a purpose, but because of its re-issuing of discs recorded during the CBC's earlier years, the technical production and level of performance are not always consistently high. In 1985 a collection of Murray Adaskin's recorded works was issued in the *Anthology* series.

On the more positive side of the cultural scene, the CBC SM-5000 series is a commendable project of the highest quality, featuring Canadian performers and, occasionally, composers. Despite this series, however, the post-war generation of Canadian composers has not yet received the recognition due to them from today's society. Although Murray Adaskin's works are frequently performed in Victoria and occasionally in other parts of Canada, they should in effect constitute a standard part of today's concert repertoire. Compositions such as the *Algonquin Symphony* or the more recent *Travelling Musicians* are still for the most part unknown to Canadian audiences and musicians. Since conductors do not perform them with their symphony orchestras, and no recording exists of either of them (except for one movement from the

Algonquin Symphony), these two important works, which easily rank with compositions by international composers, could be doomed to obscurity. Canada has yet to recognize its traditions, and it has yet to discover a sense of their importance and value. The artists' struggle for recognition in the 1940s seems to have come full circle. In the post-war period they fought for government support of the arts, for improved conditions for the creation and display of their art, and for public recognition of the arts. Over the next three decades they began to reap the benefits of their labours, as the arts in Canada began to flourish within a social climate more sympathetic to them. In the mid-1980s, however, the clock seems to have been turned back several decades as the economic cutbacks to our cultural institutions leave the arts in a precarious position once again. Moreover, the cutbacks appear to reflect a more utilitarian mood in society.

A composer's legacy is the sum total of the impact he or she has exerted on contemporary society as well as the impression the works leave on future generations. Evaluations of a composer's *oeuvre* in posterity are made possible on the basis of availability of published editions of the music, frequent live performances, and the existence of recorded performances that disseminate the music to a broad audience. While the magnitude of Murray Adaskin's impact on his contemporaries as educator, performer, and composer is visible today, one wonders how his legacy is to be transmitted to future generations. A very small proportion of his works exists in published editions. These include *Serenade Concertante, Algonquin Symphony, Saskatchewan Legend, Sonatine Baroque,* and three of the pieces for young students.[7] The others are in manuscript form only in their Canadian Music Centre repository.

Murray has never found the business aspect of his profession to be very palatable. In today's society composers need to be business-oriented or to have an agent to contact publishers, to ensure that catalogues listing the compositions are up-to-date, to communicate on an ongoing basis with national and international artists to interest them in performing the composers' works, and to promote their compositions to recording companies. Murray has found time for many things throughout his busy career, but the pursuit of publicity for his works has not been one of them. In a 1971 letter, Keith MacMillan of the Canadian Music Centre notified Murray of his intention to include his *Daydreams* (for alto saxophone and piano) in the new syllabus of the Royal Conservatory of Music of Toronto, which was in the process of being drafted. The inclusion, however, was conditional on the work's being available in published form by the time of the publication of the syllabus. The letter, dated 30 September, stressed that since the syllabus committee's choice could not be delayed beyond 15 October, the decision regarding a publisher had to be confirmed within two weeks of the writing of the letter. Murray's response, which exemplifies the general predicament of the contemporary Canadian composer, is quoted below:

Dear Keith:

Your letter concerning my *Daydreams* for Saxophone and Piano reached me this morning. While I should be more than pleased to have it listed by the Conservatory, you must realize that I have hoped for a publisher interested in my music for the past 10 years, yet found none. So your suggestion that I find one to publish the above piece within the next ten days is positively humorous. This is partly my reason for favouring the plan put forward recently that the Canadian Music Centre publish works such as these. Having said this, I'm afraid therefore that you'll have to count me out – a decision I make with real regret.

Other problems primarily related to the reception of his compositions plagued the composer. The impression left on the audience by the first performance of a work is of considerable importance to its life span. A bad performance can destroy the chance for the piece to receive a good press review or to be evaluated on its own terms. It also can contribute to a communication gap between the composer and his audience, by making it more difficult for the audience to understand the composer's ideas at first hearing. Too often Murray experienced orchestral performances of his works where, two weeks before the *première*, the conductor had not even glanced at the new composition. One of Murray's long-standing irritants is the fact that too little rehearsal time is devoted to a contemporary piece when, precisely because of its newness, it requires more rehearsals than a work from the standard repertoire with which the players are familiar.

In Murray's experience, today's composer is continually faced with rejections. Conductors often reject the composers' appeal for performances of their works; critics often view new works with suspicion, displaying through their at times overly harsh reviews a surprising lack of support for Canadian works; performers may give the work no more than one airing. Occasionally, when a touring artist incorporates a work into his repertoire, a composition does stand a chance of repeated performances. Murray Adaskin has been fortunate throughout his career to have had such performers as Roman Totenberg, Lorand Fenyves, George Zukerman, Geoffrey Waddington, and a producer like Tom Taylor to propagate and disseminate his compositions.

Murray's experiences as a composer in Canada have run the whole gamut from rejection of his works to enthusiastic response from audiences and individuals; from dismal press reviews to acclamations; from being hurt to being elated. He has grappled successfully with all situations and has emerged a stronger individual, whose unshakeable belief in this country's artistic and social institutions should serve as an example to many. The country, in turn, has recognized his achievements and his contributions to his society through the many honours awarded to him throughout his career.

How does Murray evaluate his position as a composer in twentieth-century Canada? In keeping with the sense of modesty by which he has been guided all his life, he has no strong feelings about his importance. He does not view himself as an innovator, but rather compares himself to the pool of composers of any given period who create good music by taking advantage of existing idioms. His philosophy is that many seeds need to be planted to make it possible for one composer of major stature to emerge. Hundreds of composers in the eighteenth century paved the way for one genius like Mozart. The number of Murray's compositions that may survive for posterity will be dependent largely on circumstances. In his opinion, Stravinsky's early compositions would not have survived because of public apathy, had he created them in Toronto. In Paris in the early decades of this century, however, the public participated in musical events. The resultant polemics were an indication of a lively involvement on the part of the public with the creative arts.

Murray abides by the principle that his music is directed to the listener. A good composition must sound uncontrived, as if it was created that way. It must have a natural flow from the beginning to the end, and the listener must not be aware of the craftsmanship of the work. Music must have a magic that will mesmerize people, for musical expression encompasses all thoughts that cannot be put into words.

Murray does not believe in approaching the writing of a new composition with a preconceived notion of its structure. He does not believe that it is possible for any composer to mentally conceive the composition in its entirety before it is transferred onto paper. One must have flexibility to change direction in the middle of the creative process, to 'learn to kick the ball from where it lies.' To Murray, starting a new composition and staring at the blank page can be a nightmare, just as knowing how to end it can be. 'I always suffer over a title because I don't want it to mean something the music does not convey. I suffer over that and can go for weeks before I can finally decide on an acceptable title.'

Another of Murray's important principles is that he must be true to himself. One of his greatest desires in writing music has always been to discover his own way of doing it, without imitating a style or following a trend introduced by a respected colleague. While realizing that one must be aware of prevalent compositional trends, Murray feels that it is important when composing to aim to please only oneself and not to try to impress others.

256 Frances James and Murray Adaskin

A number of composers have influenced Murray's approach to the creative process, among whom Igor Stravinsky and Darius Milhaud rank very high. Murray was first exposed to Stravinsky's *L'Histoire du Soldat* in the mid-1930s, when he heard a record of it through a friend who brought it from Paris.

By this time I had read about the *L'Histoire* but had no idea of what it sounded like. If I ever was hit by a bolt of lightning and if ever one's life could be changed in a flash, that's what it did to me. I simply could not believe the sheer beauty of it, and I can remember thinking how was it possible that I had to wait so long before being exposed to this piece. In Toronto this type of new music was not as yet being performed.

I can also remember hearing for the first time Milhaud's *La Création du Monde*. It is a wonderful piece, which uses the saxophone in the most enchanting way. It conjured up an entirely new feeling about the instrument than we had in North America at the time. In France they looked upon it as an orchestral instrument with its own distinctive colour, while with us, the saxophone was still associated with the dance band and the foxtrot.

Pieces like *La Création du Monde* and *L'Histoire du Soldat* were milestones in the history of music, which changed the course of music.

George Gershwin, Kurt Weill, and Charles Ives are three more composers whose music is dear to Murray's heart. And he can still be moved to tears by a superb performance of such a song as 'Johnny', from Benjamin Britten's *Cabaret Songs*. Of his own generation of composers, Charles Jones and John Weinzweig are of particular significance to him. Of the younger generation, Bruce Mather has earned Murray's admiration. 'Everything I have ever heard by Bruce has that quality of uniqueness and genuineness about it. It is avant garde, but it is real.'

As for his own music, Murray offers some very specific opinions: 'While it may not have great depth, it does have a kind of human element and always at some point a Chaplinesque quality emerges. I love that kind of humour; I love that unexpected twist of events. When it wants to come out in the music, I let it, and the older I get the less I suppress it. I just go ahead and do it my own way.'

This belief in writing music in his own way is the quality that gives the compositions of Murray Adaskin their special stamp. By remaining true to himself, by adhering to the compositional principles developed over the years, and by refusing to follow fads, Murray has always stood alone amid the compositional trends in Canada. If his compositions have not received the acclaim and recognition they deserve from younger contemporary composers, it is because they were, and still are, considered 'out of fashion,' that is, different from the music defined as the avant-garde of the times. One of Murray's colleagues goes so far as to evaluate him as the true avant-garde because he has had the courage to stand alone, while those considered as today's avant-garde are the real conservatives in their beliefs and their tendency to imitate fashionable trends.[8]

Many features of Murray Adaskin's style denote a neoclassic orientation. And yet, while he does not avoid the use of such older forms as rondo, sonata, suite, overture, and the like, his music cannot be labelled traditional. Established concepts and precepts are moulded by him into a contemporary idiom, creating in the process a distinctive twentieth-century language, a Canadian orientation with a specific Adaskin style. While his compositions are frequently structured in ABA form, which lends them a recognizable repetition of material, this seeming simplicity of structure on one level is balanced on the other by extreme skilfulness in the manipulation of motives. Short germinal ideas presented at the outset of a composition are subjected to a continuous process of rhythmic and intervallic transformation, which is the essence of the Adaskin developmental technique within a composition.

A skilful orchestrator, Murray employs the instruments of an orchestral work sparingly, with the priority always uppermost in his mind of bringing out the specific colour or feature of a particular instrument or group of instruments. Very seldom do all of the instruments in an orchestral work play together. His textures are, therefore, very clear because of his treatment of orchestral instruments in a quasi-soloistic fashion. His inimitable sense of humour is a feature seldom encountered in contemporary music, which at times seems to take itself too seriously.

Murray's music is infused with freshness, joy, imagination, and sincerity. An incident connected with his *Suite for Strings* typifies his sincerity and musical integrity. His only attempt at composing in the twelve-tone idiom, this suite never felt to him like part of a natural process. As a result, when the opportunity presented itself to have the piece performed, he turned it down. The specific nature of the ensemble for which the work was written solicited considerable interest from conductors of string groups, including Boyd Neel and later Benjamin Britten, who wanted to perform the piece at the Aldeburgh Festival. As late as 1973 Murray stated in a letter to the supervisor of music and record libraries of the CBC: 'I have never been really pleased enough with this work to want to have it publicly performed, and so it's with genuine regret that I must tell you that while I do have the parts and the score, I would prefer not having it performed at this time. I do so hope that whoever wants to see it will choose something else of mine.'

Above all, Murray Adaskin is a truly Canadian composer whose position in the development of music in his country may be equated with that of Aaron

Copland in the United States. Early in his career as composer, Murray asked Darius Milhaud how one writes music representative of one's country. In other words, how could he write truly Canadian music? His French mentor asked him whether he loved Canada, whether he had travelled throughout the country, and whether he had developed a feel for the land and its people. Upon receiving a positive response from Murray, Milhaud assured him that he did not need to make conscious attempts at writing music that was Canadian, because his love for the country would manifest itself subconsciously. Darius Milhaud was right in his prediction, for there is probably no other Canadian composer who has so successfully and so frequently incorporated into his music allusions to the Canadian landscape and ethos. The Canadian evocations translated into abstract terms – as in the opening and closing orchestral passages from *The Travelling Musicians* – combine with transliterations into musical terms of the call of the loon and other birds typical of the Canadian landscape. The majestic yet lonely cry of the loon permeates so many of the Adaskin compositions that it may be interpreted as symbolic of his feelings toward the austere and magnetic beauty of his country's natural resources.

The sense of tranquillity and space mirroring Canada's geographic vastness is reflected in such works as *Algonquin Symphony, Saskatchewan Legend, Qalala and Nilaula of the North,* and *The Travelling Musicians.* Ontario, the Prairies, the Inuit of the North, and French Canada – as embodied in the quotation from the French-Canadian folk-song 'Le Petit Rocher' in his *Capriccio for Piano and Orchestra* – are interwoven into his works like individual patches in a huge pan-Canadian quilt. One of his few compositions on a non-Canadian topic, *The Travelling Musicians* assumes a Canadian identity in its purely orchestral passages. More than that, however, despite the German origin of the tale, the plot, in reality, deals with the human condition, with those features of the fable that transcend national boundaries to encompass all of humanity. The poem and the music present a unified appeal for a universal community of human beings, a spiritual kinship of humankind that places Murray Adaskin in the same spiritual sphere as Mozart and Beethoven.

Apart from the sentiments toward his country exhibited in his compositions, Murray's unshakeable belief in the quality of Canadian music and its function as a building-block of this country's musical culture has motivated his indefatigable lifelong work on behalf of the Canadian composer and of contemporary music in general. In violin performances of works by his colleagues, his involvement in creating the Canadian League of Composers, his mammoth efforts in organizing two festivals in Saskatoon, his pronouncements on behalf of Canadian music while functioning as a member of the Canada Council, the emphasis on Canadian and other contemporary music in his music classes at Saskatoon – in all these endeavours Murray Adaskin can be singled out as the quiet rebel within Canada's cultural scene. His national activities were part of a natural impetus. He had no political motives, for Murray Adaskin is not politically minded. His motives were idealistic, guided by his love for and belief in everything that Canada represents.

Coupled with this attitude was his belief in sharing his love of music, both with audiences and with the students whose music-making he encouraged. This philosophy is as evident today as it was thirty years ago. Both Murray and Frances still unselfishly share their vast experiences with students at the university or conservatory in Victoria when they are invited to address classes there. Both have dedicated their lives to Canada. Their patriotism and nationalism extend support to all individuals who work toward the promotion of culture in this country. The Adaskins never hesitate to reach out to people whom they may not have met but whose contribution to this country has in some way moved them. They are prompt in communicating their feelings in letters motivated by a sense of artistic kinship and patriotic gratitude. The warmth expressed in their letters, the tone of encouragement and sincere interest in individuals whose achievements they praise, display their pride in being Canadian.

Nor have the passing years diminished Murray and Frances's interest and involvement in every aspect of life around them. Athirst for knowledge, they readily accept new ideas and are open to understanding the quickly changing world around them. No generation gap exists between them and their younger friends, and they are blessed with the capacity to make new and retain old friends that transcends the boundaries of age and time.

Frances James's and Murray Adaskin's youth coincided with the Depression and the war years. Though they were deprived of the opportunity to pursue formal education in music, their careers served as their artistic apprenticeship. They were self-educated and from their experience they each learned more than they could ever have learned through any formal studies. Their careers were totally chiselled from Canadian soil. Each is a pioneer who paved the way for future generations of musicians. Throughout their careers the motivating force was their belief in this country's cultural potential and their concern for its cultural institutions. Relentless workers, they contributed their enormous energy and dedication to the betterment of their community and its institutions, and to their students. These outstanding musical personalities gave of themselves with selflessness, humility, and modesty. Their innovative, creative ideas shaped society around them, as they still do today.

In June 1984 Frances James received recognition for her lifelong contribution to and impact on Canada's musical life in the form of an honorary doctorate from the University of Victoria. Her husband, also a recipient of an honorary doctorate on that occasion – his fourth such degree – stood proudly beside her. A month later she was honoured by the Canadian Musical Council for her distinguished career.

Gradually Canada is recognizing the remarkable contribution made by these two artists to its culture. In Victoria a television documentary and a CBC short-wave radio interview with Frances James have been prepared. On 22 September 1984, eleven years after his retirement from the campus, Murray returned to Saskatoon to receive his fifth honorary doctorate from the University of Saskatchewan. As he walked down the aisle in Convocation Hall, the walls reverberated with memories, silent echoes of twenty-one years of music-making.

While the present is a time for reflection, there is no room for nostalgia in Murray's life. To him the past is merely a building-block to the future, which he approaches with irrepressible optimism. As Murray and Frances celebrate their fifty-sixth wedding anniversary in 1987, the future merely represents a continuation of the remarkable process of growth that has symbolized the course of their lives. Many pages in their book of life have yet to be filled. The Adaskins' attitude toward life is aptly echoed in the concluding lines of *The Travelling Musicians*:

> And any day, if you happen to pass that house,
> whether it be morning, noon or night,
> you will hear the musicians making their music for all who care to listen
> or for no other reason than the sheer joy of it.
> For no other reason than the sheer joy.

APPENDIX A

Musical examples

This appendix contains the musical examples referred to by number in chapter 6. The examples from *Serenade Concertante* and *Algonquin Symphony* are reproduced by permission of G. Ricordi & Co.

Example 1

Example 2

The great di-rec-ting mind, the great directing mind, of
all   or -   dains.

Example 3

cantabile e legato

Example 4

Example 5

Example 6

Example 7

Example 8

Example 9

Example 10

Example 11a

Example 11b

Example 12

Example 13

Example 14

Example 15

Example 16

Example 17

Example 18

Example 19

Example 20

Example 21

Example 22a

Example 22b

Example 23

Example 23 (continued)

Example 24a

Example 24b

Example 25

Example 26

Example 26 (continued)

Example 27

Example 28

Example 29

Example 30

Example 31

Example 32

Example 33

Example 34

Example 35

Example 35 (continued)

Catalogue of compositions by Murray Adaskin

The number in parentheses following each title gives the approximate duration of the work in minutes and seconds. The first date and location indicate when and where the work was composed. Where no publisher is given, the composition exists only in manuscript form in the Canadian Music Centre. Orchestral instruments are listed in the following order: soloist – flute, oboe, clarinet, bassoon – horn, trumpet, trombone, tuba – timpani, percussion, harp, harpsichord, piano – strings. Movements are separated by commas; tempo changes and sections within one movement are separated by dashes. The catalogue lists, where relevant, recordings of individual works. 'Anthology' indicates the work is included in the album of Murray Adaskin's compositions in *Anthology of Canadian Music* (ACM 23), Monique Grenier executive producer, Montreal, Radio Canada International.

ABBREVIATIONS

b. – bass	timp. – timpani
c. – cello	va. – viola
perc. – percussion	vl. – violin

ORCHESTRAL

Suite for Orchestra (12'05")
1948, Toronto. First performance: 22 June 1949 in Toronto on the CBC national network, radio orchestra, conducted by Geoffrey Waddington. One movement: Fast – Slowly – Scherzo (Fast). Instruments: 3.2.2.2 – 4.2.2.0 – timp., perc., harp – strings. Recorded: RCI-17 CBC Orchestra, conducted by Roland Leduc (1958). Anthology. Dedicted to Geoffrey Waddington.

Suite for Strings (15')
1949, Toronto. First performance: 10 July 1950 in Vancouver, CBC Vancouver, radio

orchestra, conducted by Albert Steinberg. Three movements: Fugue, Ostinato, Finale. Instruments: 12 vl. 4 va. 4c. 3b.

March No 1 for Orchestra (3')
1950, Toronto. Commissioned by the CBC for the 'Opportunity Knocks' program. First performance: 19 June 1950, radio orchestra, conducted by John Adaskin. One movement. Instruments: 3.3.3.3 – 4.3.3.1 – timp., perc., harp, piano – strings. Dedicted to 'My brother John.'

Ballet Symphony (24'50")
1951, Toronto. First performance: 26 March 1952 in Massey Hall by the Toronto Symphony Orchestra, conducted by Geoffrey Waddington. Six movements: March, Allegro, Pas de Deux, Fugue, Adagio, Finale (Rondo Allegro). Instruments: 3.3.3.3 – 4.3.3.1 – timp., perc., harp, piano – strings. Recorded: RCI-71 Toronto Symphony Orchestra, conducted by Geoffrey Waddington (1958). Anthology.

March No 2 for Orchestra (3')
1953, Saskatoon. Commissioned by the CBC for the 'Opportunity Knocks' program. First performance: 2 March 1953, radio orchestra, conducted by John Adaskin. One movement. Instruments: 3.2.2.2 – 2.3.2.1 – timp., perc. – strings. Dedicated to Tamar and Susan.

Coronation Overture (9')
1953, Saskatoon. Commissioned by the CBC for Coronation Day broadcast. First performance: 2 June 1953 in Toronto on the CBC national network by the CBC Symphony Orchestra, conducted by Geoffrey Waddington. One movement: Maestoso – Square Dance Tempo – Maestoso. Instruments: 3.3.3.2 – 4.3.3.1 – timp., perc., harp – strings.

Serenade Concertante (7'25")
1954, Saskatoon. Commissioned by the CBC Vancouver Orchestra. First performance: 16 April 1954 by the CBC Vancouver Orchestra, conducted by John Avison. One movement: Moderato. Instruments: 2.2.2.2 – 2.1.0.0 – strings. Published: Ricordi, Toronto 1956. Recorded: Columbia ML5685 and ML5921, CBC Symphony Orchestra, conducted by Walter Susskind (1961); also RM222, Toronto Symphony Orchestra, conducted by Sir Ernest MacMillan. Anthology. Dedicted to Catharine and Peter Whyte.

Algonquin Symphony (23')
1958, Canoe Lake, Algonquin Park. Commissioned by the CBC. First performance: 3 May 1959 in Toronto, by the CBC Symphony Orchestra, conducted by Geoffrey Waddington. Three movements: Allegretto, Lento Sostenuto, Largo – Allegro – Largo –

Allegro. Instruments: 3.3.3.2 – 4.3.3.1 – timp., perc., harp – strings. Published: Ricordi, Toronto 1962. Recorded: Dominion 1372, and Citadel CT-6011, Toronto Philharmonia, conducted by Victor Feldbrill, third movement only (1962). Written in memory of Taylor Statten (1882–1956).

Saskatchewan Legend (12'50")
1959, Canoe Lake, Algonquin Park. Commissioned by the Golden Jubilee Committee, University of Saskatchewan. First performance: 27 September 1959 by the Saskatoon Symphony Orchestra, conducted by the composer. One movement: Allegro moderato – Poco meno mosso – Tranquillo – Tempo I. Instruments: 3.2.2.1 – 2.3.3.1 – timp., perc. – strings. Published: Ricordi, Toronto 1961. Dedicated to Dr and Mrs W.P. Thompson.

Qalala and Nilaula of the North (25')
1969, Saskatoon. Commissioned by John Roberts for the CBC, for the commemoration of Canada Day, 1 July. First performance: 1 July 1969 in Winnipeg on the CBC 'Tuesday Night' series, by the CBC Winnipeg Orchestra, conducted by the composer, produced by Tom Taylor. One movement: Adagio – Allegretto – Tempo I – Adagio. Instruments: 1.1.1.1 – 1.0.0.0 – 2 perc. – 14 strings (21 players). Dedicated to John, Christina, and Noel Roberts.

Diversion for Orchestra (An Entertainment) (8'30")
1969, Canoe Lake, Algonquin Park. Commissioned by Jean-Marie Beaudet, director of the National Arts Centre. First performance: 7 October 1969 in Ottawa at the inaugural concert of the National Arts Centre Orchestra, conducted by Mario Bernardi. One movement: Allegro con spirito – Lentamente – Tempo primo. Instruments: 2.2.2.2 – 2.2.0.0 – timp., perc. – strings. Recorded: SM-294, Edmonton Symphony Orchestra, conducted by Pierre Hétu (1975); also SM-333, National Arts Centre Orchestra, conducted by Mario Bernardi (1977). Anthology.

Fanfare for Orchestra (4')
1970, Saskatoon. Commissioned by the Saskatchewan Centre of the Arts, Regina. First performance: 20 August 1970 in Regina at the official opening of the Centre's auditorium, by the Regina Symphony Orchestra, conducted by Howard Leyton-Brown. One movement. Instruments: 2.2.2B-flat.2 – 4F.3.3.1 – timp., perc. – strings. Recorded: SM-163, conducted by Eric Wild, CBC Symphony Orchestra. Anthology. Dedicated to Victor Feldbrill.

There Is My People Sleeping (12')
1971, Saskatoon. Commissioned by Carl Little for the CBC. First performance: March 1971 in Toronto on the CBC 'Tuesday Night' series as part of a two-hour documentary

program on the composer, by the CBC Symphony Orchestra, conducted by the composer. One movement: Adagio. Instruments: 2.2.2.2 – 2.2.0.0 – perc. – strings. Dedicated to the memory of Edward A. McCourt (1907–72).

Nootka Ritual for Orchestra (8')
1974, Victoria. Commissioned by the Nanaimo Symphony Orchestra through a Canada Council grant. First performance: 17 April 1974 in Nanaimo by the Nanaimo Symphony Orchestra, conducted by Tom Petrowitz. One movement: Maestoso. Instruments: 2.2.2.2 – 2.2.2.0 – timp., perc. – strings. Dedicated to Tom Petrowitz.

In Praise of 'Canadian Painting in the Thirties' (21')
1975, Victoria. Commissioned by the Chamber Players of Toronto through a Canada Council grant. First performance: 24 January 1976 in Toronto by the Chamber Players. Three movements: Paraskeva Clark (Lento e cantabile), Louis Muhlstock (Adagio), Charles Comfort (Allegretto – Tempo giusto). Instruments: strings, harpsichord.

March No 3 for Orchestra (5')
1981, Victoria. Commissioned by Dr Paul Freeman. First performance: 29 March 1981 by the Victoria Symphony Orchestra, conducted by Paul Freeman. One movement. Instruments: 3.2.2.2 – 4.3.3.1 – timp., perc. – strings (piccolo replaces ocarina in B if unavailable). Dedicated to Paul Freeman.

Dance Concertante for Orchestra (12'30")
1983, Victoria. Commissioned by the Windsor Symphony Society through a Canada Council grant. First performance: April 1983 by the Windsor Symphony Orchestra, conducted by Laszlo Gati. One movement: Andantino – Allegro moderato – Andantino. Instruments: 3.2.2.2 – 4.3.3.0 – timp., perc. – strings.

Divertimento No 8 for Concert Band (11')
1986, Victoria. Commissioned by the Saskatchewan Music Educators Association. First performance: 18 October 1986 in Regina, by the Honours Band of the Province of Saskatchewan, conducted by Howard Cable. Dedicated to Dr J. Francis Leddy.

SOLO AND ORCHESTRA

Concerto for Violin and Orchestra (17'35")
1955, Aspen, Colorado, and Canoe Lake, Algonquin Park. First performance: 30 April 1956 in Toronto by the CBC Symphony Orchestra, conducted by the composer, Roman Totenberg, violin. Three movements: Allegro moderato, Andante, Allegro. Instruments: solo violin – 2.2.3.2 – 2.2.1.0 – perc. – strings. Dedicated to Roman Totenberg.

Concerto for Bassoon and Orchestra (14'55")
1960, Morges, Switzerland. Commissioned by George Zukerman. First performance: 5 February 1961 by the Vancouver Symphony Orchestra, conducted by Irwin Hoffman, George Zukerman, bassoon. Three movements: Allegro moderato, Andante semplice, Allegro giusto. Instruments: solo bassoon – 3.2.2.0 – 2.2.2.0 – timp. – strings. Recorded: SM-143, CBC Vancouver Chamber Orchestra, conducted by John Avison, George Zukerman, bassoon. Anthology. Dedicated to George Zukerman.

Capriccio for Piano and Orchestra (19')
1961, Morges, Switzerland. First performance: 20 January 1963 on the CBC national network, by the CBC Symphony Orchestra, conducted by John Avison, Kendall Taylor, piano. One movement: Lento – Allegro – Meno mosso – Allegro – Andante semplice – Tempo primo – Allegro. Instruments: solo piano – 3.2.2.2 – 4.3.3.1 – timp., perc. – strings. Dedicated to Kendall Taylor.

Divertimento No 4 for Trumpet and Orchestra (11'37")
1970, Canoe Lake, Algonquin Park. Commissioned by the Saskatoon Symphony Orchestra through a grant from the Cosmopolitan Club. First performance: 24 August 1970 by the Saskatoon Symphony Orchestra, conducted by the composer, Dr Lawrence House, trumpet. One movement: Adagio – Adagietto – Adagio – Allegro – Scherzando – Adagietto – Adagio. Instruments: solo trumpet – 2.2.2.2 – 2.2.0.0 – timp., perc. – strings. Dedicated to Dr Lawrence House.

Divertimento No 5 for Two Guitars and Chamber Orchestra (16')
1980, Victoria. Commissioned by Don Wilson and Peter McAllister through a Canada Council grant. First performance: 12 December 1981 by the Saskatoon Symphony Orchestra, conducted by Glen Fast, Don Wilson and Peter McAllister, guitars. One movement: Allegretto – Allegro – Allegretto. Instruments: 2 guitars – 1.1.1.1 – 1.1.1.0 – perc. – strings.

Divertimento No 6 for Solo Percussion and Orchestra (16'20")
1984, Victoria. First performance: 28 February 1985 at the University Centre of the University of Victoria by the Victoria Symphony Orchestra, conducted by Dr George Corwin, Salvador Ferreras, percussion. One movement: Allegro con brio – Andante – Allegro con brio – Cadenza – Allegro con brio. Instruments: percussion – 2.2.2.2 – 2.2.1.1 – strings. Dedicated to Dr George Corwin.

T'Filat Shalom – A Prayer for Peace (6'45") (Transcribed for solo violin and orchestra)
1986, Victoria. Transcription commissioned by George Laverock. First performance: 23 April 1986 at the Orpheum Theatre in Vancouver, for a CBC broadcast on the theme of

world peace, by the CBC Vancouver Symphony, conducted by James Frankhauser, Campbell Trowsade, violin. Instruments: solo violin, 0.2.0.0 – 0.2B-flat.0.0 – strings.

CHAMBER MUSIC

Divertimento No 1 for Two Violins and Piano (11')
1956, Canoe Lake, Algonquin Park. Commissioned by Harry Adaskin. First performance: 20 November 1956 at the Vancouver Art Gallery, Harry and Murray Adaskin, violins; Frances Marr, piano. One movement: Allegro moderato. Dedicated to Harry and Frances Adaskin.

Introduction and Rondo, Quartet for Piano and Strings (9')
1957, Saskatoon. First performance: 21 July 1959 as part of the Saskatoon Golden Jubilee Concerts, Rafael Druian, violin; Albert Falkove, viola; Robert Jamieson, cello; John Simms, piano. Two movements: Andante sostenuto, Allegro.

Rondino for Nine Instruments (4'20")
1961, Saskatoon. Commissioned by CBC-TV. First performance: 25 March 1962, CBC-TV, by players from the CBC Symphony Orchestra, conducted by Mario Bernardi. One movement: Allegro con spirito. Instruments: flute, oboe, clarinet in B-flat, bassoon, horn in F, 2 violins, viola, cello. Recorded: RCI-215, Chamber Ensemble of the Winnipeg Symphony Orchestra, conducted by Victor Feldbrill; also RCA Victor, CC1009. Anthology. Dedicated to Charles Jones.

String Quartet No 1 (19'50")
1961, Saskatoon. Commissioned by the CBC. First performance: 25 March 1963 on the CBC 'Distinguished Artists Series,' by the Canadian String Quartet (Albert Pratz and Bernard Robbins, violins; David Mankovitz, viola; Laszlo Varga, cello). Three movements: Allegro, Adagio, Allegro. Dedicated to the memory of Emil Mendel (1891–1963).

Cassenti Concertante (9'15")
1963, Saskatoon. Commissioned by the Cassenti Players through a Canada Council grant. First performance: 19 January 1964 in Convocation Hall, University of Saskatchewan, by the Cassenti Players (George Zukerman, director and bassoon; Warren Stannard, oboe; Kenneth Lee, clarinet; Arthur Polson, violin; Harold Brown, piano). One movement: Adagio maestoso – Allegro ma non troppo – Meno mosso e tranquillo – Tempo II – Adagio. Dedicated to Eli Bornstein.

Divertimento No 3 for Violin, Horn in F, and Bassoon (11'50")
1965, Saskatoon. Commissioned by the Regina Campus of the University of Saskatchewan through a Canada Council grant. First performance: 20 May 1965 in Regina, Howard Leyton-Brown, violin; Mel Carey, horn; Thomas Schudel, bassoon. Three movements: Adagio maestoso, Un Poco Allegretto e Grazioso, Moderato. Instruments: violin, French horn in F, bassoon. Recorded: RCI-405 with Taras Gabora, violin; Barry Tuckwell, French horn; George Zukerman, bassoon (1975). Anthology.

Trio (1970) for Flute, Cello, and Piano (17'30")
1970, Canoe Lake, Algonquin Park. Commissioned by the Alberta Chamber Trio through a Canada Council grant. First performance: 21 April 1971 at the University of Western Ontario, by the Alberta Chamber Trio. (Gloria Saarinen, piano; Werner van Zweeden, flute; Talmon Herz, cello). Three movements: Allegro moderato, Lento, Allegro giusto.

Quintet for Woodwinds (13'30")
1974, Victoria. Commissioned by the Pacific Wind Quintet through a Canada Council grant. First performance: 19 January 1975 at the School of Music of the University of Victoria, by the Pacific Wind Quintet (Eileen Gibson, oboe; Jesse Read, bassoon; Tim Paradise, clarinet; Richard Ely, French horn; Lanny Pollet, flute). Three movements: Allegretto – Andantino – Allegretto, Andante – Andantino – Andante, Allegro ma non troppo.

Fanfare for Brass Quintet (7')
1977, Victoria. Commissioned by producer Tom Taylor for CBC Winnipeg as a theme for a series of CBC broadcasts in 1977.

Music for Brass Quintet (8')
1977, Victoria. Commissioned by Dr Lawrence House through an Ontario Arts Council grant. First performance: April 1977 at the Guelph Summer Festival, by the Toronto Brass Quintet (Lawrence House and Stephen Chenette, trumpets; George Stimpson, bassoon; Kenneth Knowles, trombone; J. Kent Mason, tuba). One movement.

Bassoon Quintet for String Quartet and Bassoon (21'25")
1977, Canoe Lake, Algonquin Park. Commissioned by the CBC for George Zukerman, bassoon, and the Purcell String Quartet. First performance: 19 April 1978 at the CBC Vancouver studios, by the Purcell String Quarter (Norman Nelson, Joseph Peleg, violins; Phillippe Etter, viola; Ian Hampton, cello) and George Zukerman, bassoon, produced by George Laverock. Three movements: Andante amabile e molto moderato,

Adagio, Allegro giocoso. Dedicated to 'My wife Frances James, celebrating our 47th anniversary.'

Brass Fanfare for a Wedding (1'45")
1981, Victoria. First performance: 24 July 1981 at the home of Blair and Mary Nelson, of Saskatoon, on the occasion of the wedding of their daughter, Victoria; Lawrence House and Miles Newman, trumpets; Mel Carey, French horn; Mike McCawley, tuba; Stewart Smith, trombone; Darrell Bueckert, percussion.

Divertimento No 7 for Two Celli and Piano (7')
1985, Victoria. First performance: 8 November 1985 at Langley Community Music School, Langley, BC, by Ian Hampton, cello; Susan Round, cello; Arlie Thompson, piano.

INSTRUMENTAL: SOLO

Sonata for Piano (9'10")
1950, Toronto. First performance: 21 February 1950 for the International Service of the CBC, Louis Crerar, piano. Four movements: 'With Free and Gentle Motion,' Moderato, Lento, Finale. Dedicated to Mario Bernardi.

Sonatine Baroque for Solo Violin (8'55")
1952, Toronto. Commissioned by the Forest Hill Community Centre Concert Series. First performance: 10 March 1952 in Toronto, by Eugene Kash, unaccompanied violin. Three movements: Adagio, Andante, Presto. Published: Ricordi, Toronto 1961. Tape: Andrew Dawes. Anthology. Dedicated to Andrew Dawes.

Two Pieces for Viola da Gamba (9')
1972, Canoe Lake, Algonquin Park. Commissioned by Peggie Sampson through a Canada Council grant. First performance: 1972 at Canoe Lake by Peggie Sampson. Two movements: Adagio, Allegretto. Recorded: Music Gallery Editions, Toronto (1974). Dedicated to Peggie Sampson.

Rankin Inlet – Eskimo Song (5'10")
1978, Victoria. A wedding gift for Geraldine and Claude McLain, B MUS graduates from the School of Music, University of Victoria. One piano, four hands.

Eskimo Melodies (5'10")
1980, Victoria. Rewritten from the four-hand version of *Rankin Inlet* for Walter Prossnitz, who performed it during his first China tour.

Ontario Variation for Solo Piano (3')
1980, Victoria. Commissioned by Jack Behrens, University of Western Ontario, through an Ontario Arts Council grant. Intended as one of six variations by six different composers, on a theme by Jack Behrens. Never performed.

INSTRUMENTAL: TWO INSTRUMENTS

Sonata for Violin and Piano (15'15")
1946, Toronto. First performance: 17 April 1947 at Harbord Collegiate, Toronto, Murray Adaskin, violin; Louis Crerar, piano. Three movements: Moderato, Andante, Rondo Allegro. Recorded: SM-211, with Lorand Fenyves, violin; Pierre Souverain, piano (1975). Anthology. Dedicated to Louis Crerar.

Canzona and Rondo (7')
1949, Santa Barbara. First performance: 18 October 1949 in Toronto, on the International Service of the CBC, Murray Adaskin, violin; Mario Bernardi, piano. Two movements. Recorded: RCA Victor 221, with Marta Hidy, violin, and Chester Duncan, piano (1965). Anthology. Dedicated to Roman Totenberg.

Divertimento No 2 for Violin and Harp (4'45")
1964, Canoe Lake, Algonquin Park. First performance: 17 January 1965 in Toronto, Hyman Goodman, violin; Erica Goodman, harp. One movement: Allegretto – Andante – Tempo giusto. Dedicated to the performers.

Two Portraits for Violin and Piano (13')
1973, Victoria. Commissioned by the CBC for Lorand Fenyves. First performance: 19 November 1975 in Toronto on the CBC, by Lorand Fenyves, violin; Patricia Parr, piano. Two movements: Allegro moderato ma con brio, Allegretto. Tape: CBC performance by Lorand Fenyves, violin; Patricia Parr, piano. Anthology. Dedicated to Lorand Fenyves.

Adagio for Cello and Piano (8')
1973, Victoria. Commissioned by the Victoria Conservatory of Music through a Canada Council grant. First performance: February 1973 in Victoria, by James Hunter, cello; Robin Wood, piano. Transcribed for cello and orchestra in 1975.

Israeli Violin Piece T'Filat Shalom (A Prayer for Peace) (6'45")
1974, Victoria. Commissioned through the Canadian Jewish Council for violin and piano. First performance: 15 April 1974 in Jerusalem by Jeff Krolick, violin. One movement: Adagio.

Nocturne for Clarinet and Piano (7')
1978, Victoria. Commissioned by the International Clarinet Congress through an
Ontario Arts Council grant. First performance: 10 August 1978 in Toronto, by Stanley
McCartney, clarinet; Mark Widner, piano. One movement. Dedicated to Avrahm
Galper, former first clarinet of the Toronto Symphony Orchestra.

Sonata for Cello and Piano (16'15")
1981, Victoria. Commissioned by Dr Tom Akeley, University of Windsor, through a
Canada Council grant. First performance: 3 October 1981 at the School of Music,
University of Windsor, by Dr Tom Akeley, cello; Gregory Butler, piano. Three
movements: Allegro, Adagio, Scherzando. Anthology: Tsuyoshi Tsutsumi, cello;
Ronald Turini, piano. Dedicated 'In memory of my Brother John,' 1908–1964.

Impromptu for Violin and Piano (10')
1982, Victoria. Commissioned by Mark Neumann. First performance: 3 March 1983 at
the School of Music, University of Victoria, by Mark Neumann at his B MUS graduating
recital, with Jonas Kvarnström, piano. One movement: Andante.

FOR YOUNG MUSICIANS

Three Simple Pieces for Violin and Piano
1963, Canoe Lake, Algonquin Park. No 1: *Quiet Song* (2'40") published: Leeds Music
(Canada) Ltd; No 2: *Dedication* (3'10") dedicated to Karen Gelmon; No 3: *Dance*
(2'10"). First performance of all three: March 1963 at Convocation Hall, University of
Saskatchewan, by Roman Totenberg, violin; Boyd McDonald, piano.

Rondino for Orchestra (6'30")
1964, Saskatoon. Commissioned by the Canadian Music Centre. First performance: 9
March 1965 in Toronto by the North Toronto Collegiate Orchestra, conducted by
Douglas Couke. One movement: Stately and Rhythmic. Instruments; 3.2.3.1 – 4.4.1.0
– piano – strings. Dedicated to 'My brother John.'

The Prairie Lily (2'15")
1967, Saskatoon. Based on a poem by Hugh Blakeney. Commissioned by the Zonta
International Centennial Project Committee, Regina. First performance: 30 October
1971 in Toronto in Christ the Saviour Cathedral Hall. Instruments: voice, piano.
Published: McGraw-Hill 1968.

Daydreams for Violin and Piano (3')
1968, Canoe Lake, Algonquin Park. Fourth in a projected series for young musicians.

Published: Sonante Publications, Toronto 1979. Transcribed in 1972 for saxophone and piano, and clarinet and piano.

Calisthenics for Violin and Piano (3')
1968, Canoe Lake, Algonquin Park. Fifth in a projected series for young musicians. Dedicated to Jeff Krolik.

Legato and Ricochet for Violin and Piano (3')
1968, Canoe Lake, Algonquin Park. Sixth in a projected series for young musicians.

Night Is No Longer Summer Soft (2'30")
1970, Canoe Lake, Algonquin Park. Commissioned by Robert Hordern for a band clinic in Saskatoon. First performance: February 1970 by the 'A' Band of the Saskatoon School Music Teachers' Association, conducted by Herb Jeffrey. Instruments: 7.2.13.2 – 4.9.9.3 euphoniums – 4E-flat alto sax, 2B-flat tenor sax, 1E-flat baritone sax – perc. Transcription of the bass aria by the same title from *Grant, Warden of the Plains*.

Toccatina for Piano (25")
1971, Saskatoon. Incorporated as No 9 in *Horizons – Music by Canadian Composers*, published by the Waterloo Music Co 1973.

Essay for Strings (5'30")
1972, Victoria. Commissioned by the Oak Bay Junior–Senior High School Orchestra of Victoria. First performance: September 1972 at the British Columbia Music Educators' Association Conference. One movement: Allegro (Tempo di marcia).

Three Tunes for Strings (8')
1976, Victoria. Commissioned by the Oak Bay Strings of Victoria through a Canada Council grant. Three movements: Rankin Inlet (Eskimo Song), Meyerke, My Son (Jewish song), When the Ice Worms Nest Again (thought to have been written by Robert Service, c 1911 in the Yukon).

VOCAL, CHORAL, OPERA

Epitaph (2')
1948, Toronto. Text by Guillaume Apollinaire, translated by Bertha Ten Eyck James. First performance: 13 June 1952 in Toronto, Frances James, soprano, and Louis Crerar, piano. Recorded: on that occasion, RCI–74. Anthology. Dedicated to Frances James.

Hymn of Thanks (1'30")
1953, Canoe Lake, Algonquin Park. Text by Professor A. Eustace Haydon. Written for

Camps Ahmek and Wapomeo for unison voices and piano. Published: Boosey and Hawkes, 1955. Dedicated to Taylor and Ethel Statten (Chief and Tonakela).

Autumn Song (Aria from *Grant, Warden of the Plains*) (5')
1965, Saskatoon. First performance: 1965 at the Winnipeg Art Gallery, Tom Elliott, bassoon; Phyllis Thompson, soprano.

Of Man and the Universe (9'33")
1967, Canoe Lake, Algonquin Park. Based on a poem by Alexander Pope. Commissioned by the CBC for Expo 67 in Montreal. First performance: May 1967 during 'CBC Week,' at the Place des Arts, Montreal, Joan Maxwell, mezzo-soprano; Arthur Polson, violin; Ross Pratt, piano.

Grant, Warden of the Plains (58')
1966, Canoe Lake, Algonquin Park. Libretto by Mary-Elizabeth Bayer. Commissioned by the CBC for the 1967 Centennial celebrations. First performance: 18 July 1967 in Winnipeg with the CBC Winnipeg Orchestra, conducted by Victor Feldbrill, produced by Tom Taylor. Cast: Cuthbert Grant – Peter van Ginkle (bass-baritone), Maria McGillis – Nona Mari (soprano), Narrator – Evelyn Anderson, Alexander MacDonnell – Paul Fredette (bass), John – Ed Evanko (tenor), John Also – Peter Koslowsky (tenor), Robert – Robert Pubblo (baritone), Pierre Falcon – Wilmer Neufeld (baritone), Governor Simpson – George Waite (baritone). One act. Instruments: 2.1.1.1 – 1.1.1.0 – timp., perc., piano – strings. Dedicated to the memory of Peter Whyte (1905–1966).

The Travelling Musicians (20')
1982, Victoria, and Canoe Lake, Algonquin Park. Narrative by P.K. Page, based on *The Musicians of Bremen* by the Brothers Grimm. First performance: 22 January 1984 in Victoria by the Victoria Symphony Orchestra, conducted by Paul Freeman. Narrator – Catherine Lewis, soprano. One movement. Instruments: narrator – 2.2.2.2 – 2.2.1.1 – timp., perc. – strings.

First or early performances given by Frances James of works by Canadian composers

		Date of earliest performance
Adaskin, Murray	*The Shepherd* (Blake)	1934
	Epitaph (Apollinaire)	1948
Brott, Alexander	*Songs of Contemplation* (R.M. Milnes)	1946
Betts, Lorne	*Three Songs* (James Joyce)	1949
	Five Songs (James Joyce)	1950
	Six Songs (James Joyce)	1951
Chotem, Neil	*Three Songs for Voice and Instrumental Ensemble* (Michel Conte); *The Song of Solomon*	1951
Coulthard, Jean	*Rain Has Fallen All the Day* (James Joyce)	1947
	Two Songs of the Haida Indians (Constance Skinner)	1944
	Two Sonnets for Violin, Voice, and Piano (Shakespeare)	1940s
Crerar, Louis	*Blow, Blow Thou Winter Wind* (Shakespeare)	1952
	Four Shakespeare Songs	1952
Dainty, Ernest	*The Brook* (Tennyson)	1935
	My Ladye's Glove (John Hale)	1934
	A number of other songs	
Duncan, Chester	*Six Songs* (various authors, including A.J.M. Smith and W.H. Auden)	1953
Fleming, Robert	Many of his songs, including *Three Songs Dedicated to Alexandra Belugin: Immortal Sails* (A. Noyes); *The Trusting Heart* (D. Parker); *Courage* (W. De La Mare)	1943

Jones, Charles	*Fragment* (Shelley); *Rain over Rahoon*	
	(Joyce); *The Lent Lily* (A.E. Housman)	1945
Jones, Kelsey	Song Cycle *Euridice* (George Johnson)	1951
Key, Harold Eustace	*A Garden Is a Lovesome Thing*	1941
	In Flanders Fields (John McCrae)	1941
	Also, arranged by Key, the ballad opera	
	Christmas with Herrick	1929
MacMillan, Sir Ernest	*Two Christmas Carols*	1946
	Ode to England (Charles Swinburne)	1941
	Also, arranged by MacMillan, the ballad opera	
	Prince Charming	1931
	A number of other songs	
McNutt, Walter	*Two Songs* (H.E. Foster)	1936
McIntyre, Paul	*Four Poems of Walter De La Mare*	1950
Morawetz, Oscar	*I Love the Jocund Dance* (W. Blake)	1949
	Piping down the Valley Wild (W. Blake)	1947
Naylor, Bernard	*Suite for High Voice and Piano* (C. Day Lewis)	1947
	King Solomon's Prayer for voice and orchestra	1953
Ouchterlony, David	*She Walks in Beauty*	1941
Pentland, Barbara	Song Cycle (Anne Marriott)	1947
Somers, Harry	*Three Songs* (Walt Whitman)	1947
Weinzweig, John	*Of Time, Rain, and the World* (words taken	
	from Roget's *Thesaurus*)	1947
Willan, Healey	A number of songs	
	Premières of *Transit through Fire*	1942
	and *Deirdre of the Sorrows*	1945
	Ballad operas arranged by Willan:	
	Prince Charlie and Flora	1929
	The Order of Good Cheer (Victoria version)	1930
	The Ayrshire Ploughman	1930

Content of air-check discs
recorded by Frances James for the CBC

These recordings were made between 1945 and 1954 and represent a variety of CBC broadcasts. They are now transcribed onto tapes for the sake of preservation and are located in the Music Division of the National Archives in Ottawa. Of the fifty-nine tapes in the collection, forty contain concerts by Frances James Adaskin. The others are recordings of the Adaskin Trio, Murray Adaskin as conductor and performer, and teachers and students.

TAPE 1   with John Newmark, piano

John Weinzweig	*Time; Rain; The World*
Barbara Pentland	From *Song Cycle: Wheat; Mountains*
Jean Coulthard	From *Three Songs for Medium Voice: Rain Has Fallen All the Day*
Charles Jones	*Rain over Rahoon; The Lent Lily*
Lorne Betts	*Three Songs: Lean out of the Windows; Rain Has Fallen All the Day; I Heard an Army Charging upon the Land*
Harry Somers	From *Three Songs: Look down Fair Moon; After the Dazzle of Day*

TAPE 2   with Earle Moss, piano

John Weinzweig	*Time; Rain; The World*
Charles Jones	*Chant; Rain over Rahoon*
Bernard Naylor	*A Child's Carol; Roseberries; Twenty Years Near Past*

TAPE 3   with Mario Bernardi, piano

Lorne Betts	*Five Songs: My Love Is in a Light Attire; O, Cool Is the Valley Now; In the Dark Pine Wood; Winds of May; O, It Was out by Dooney-Carney*

Murray Adaskin   *Epitaph*
Jean Coulthard   *Two Songs of the Haida Indians: Song for Fine Weather;*
                        Love Song
Paul McIntyre   *Four Poems of Walter De La Mare: Alone; The Moth;*
                        Rachel; The Song of Soldiers
          with Sir Ernest MacMillan, piano
Ernest MacMillan   *I Sing of a Maiden That Is Matchless; Sonnet* (Elizabeth
                        Barrett Browning)

TAPE 4   with CBC Winnipeg Orchestra, conducted by Eric Wild
Bernard Naylor   *King Solomon's Prayer* (first performance)
          with Boyd McDonald, piano
Chester Duncan   *Six Songs: Beside One Dead; From the Hazelbow; A Simple*
                        Love Lyric; Saturday and Sunday; The One; A Riddle

TAPES 5–7   with CBC Opera Company, conducted by Geoffrey Waddington
Igor Stravinsky   *The Rake's Progress* (first performance in Canada)
                        Frances James: 'Anne'

TAPE 8   with Earle Moss, piano
John Weinzweig   *Time; Rain; The World*
Charles Jones   *The Ploughman; Rain over Rahoon; The Lent Lily*
Bernard Naylor   *A Child's Carol; Roseberries; Twenty Years Near Past*

TAPE 9   with Boyd McDonald, piano
Robert Schumann   *Schöne Wiege Meiner Leiden,* op 24, no 5; *Er ist's,* op 79, no
                        23; *O, ihr Herren,* op 37, no 3
Barbara Pentland   From *Song Cycle: Wheat; Mountains*
Jean Coulthard   *Rain Has Fallen All the Day*
Darius Milhaud   *Rêves: Marronniers; Toi; Confidence; Mistral; Longue*
                        Distance; Jeunesse
Harry Somers   From *Three Songs: Look down Fair Moon*

TAPE 10   with Leo Barkin, piano
W.A. Mozart   *Alleluja*
Robert Schumann   *Abends am Strand,* op 45 no. 3; *Aus den Östlichen Rosen,* op
                        25 no 25; *O, ihr Herren,* op 37 no 3; *Mondnacht,* op 39 no
                        5; *Schöne Wiege Meiner Leiden,* op 24 no 5
Claude Debussy   *Fêtes Galantes: En Sourdine; Fantoches; Clair de Lune*
Claude Debussy   From *Chansons de Bilitis: La Chevelure*

TAPE 11   with Dr Arnold Walter, piano
Claude Debussy   *Ariettes Oubliées: C'est l'Extase; Il Pleure dans Mon Coeur; Chevaux de Bois; Green; Spleen*
Claude Debussy   *Chansons de Bilitis: La Flûte de Pan; La Chevelure; Le Tombeau des Naïades*

TAPE 12   with the Mendelssohn Choir, conducted by Sir Ernest MacMillan
G.F. Handel   *Messiah* (incomplete)

TAPE 13   with Earle Moss, piano
John Weinzweig   *Time; Rain; The World*
Claude Debussy   *Baudelaire Poems: Le Balcon; Harmonie du Soir; Recueillement; La Mort des Amants*

TAPE 14   with Earle Moss, piano
Claude Debussy   *Chansons de Bilitis: La Flûte de Pan; La Chevelure; Le Tombeau des Naïades*
          with Murray Adaskin, violin
Jean Coulthard   Sonnet 18 of Shakespeare, dedicated to Frances and Murray Adaskin: *Shall I Compare Thee to a Summer's Day; When My Love Swears That Is Made of Truth*

TAPE 15   with Earle Moss, piano
Healey Willan   Excerpts from *Deirdre of the Sorrows*
Benjamin Britten   Arias from *Peter Grimes*
          with Dr Arnold Walter, piano
Henry Purcell   *Blessed Virgin's Expostulation*

TAPES 16–21   with CBC Opera Company, conducted by Geoffrey Waddington
Benjamin Britten   *Peter Grimes*

TAPE 22   with Earle Moss, piano
Darius Milhaud   *Rêves* (first Canadian performance, recorded 1950): *Marronniers; Toi; Confidence; Mistral; Longue Distance; Jeunesse*
          with Leo Barkin, piano
Darius Milhaud   *Rêves* (recorded 1951)

TAPE 23 with CBC Symphony Orchestra, conducted by Geoffrey Waddington
Benjamin Britten *Les Illuminations: Fanfare; Villes; Phrase; Antique; Royauté; Marine; Interlude; Being Beauteous*

TAPE 24 Songs arranged by Bernard Naylor
Black Eyed Susan
John Goss Collection *Love Will Find a Way*
Lady John Scott *Think on Me*

TAPE 25 with Murray Adaskin, violin; Louis Crerar, piano
Murray Adaskin *Canzona for Violin and Piano*

TAPE 26 Adaskin Trio with Frances James
Franz Schubert *The Trout*, D.550; *Ave Maria*, D.839
Cyril Scott; Arr.
Arnold Bax *Lullaby; O Dear, What Can the Matter Be?*

TAPE 27 Adaskin Trio with Frances James
Franz Schubert *Gretchen am Spinnrade*, D.118
Harold Eustace Key *A Garden Is a Lovesome Thing*
Roger Quilter *Love's Philosophy*

TAPE 28 with Montreal Little Symphony, conducted by Bernard Naylor
Gerald Finzi *Dies Natalis* (first Canadian performance 1948)

TAPES 29–33 with Radio Opera conducted by Ettore Mazzoleni
Healey Willan *Deirdre of the Sorrows*

TAPE 34 with Earle Moss, piano
Hugo Wolf *Auf einer Wanderung*
J. Brahms *Wir Wandelten*, op 96, no 2
Hugo Wolf *Verschwiegene Liebe; Gesegnet Sei*
J. Brahms *Minnelied*, op 71, no 5; *Nachtigal*, op 97, no 1
Bernard Naylor *C. Day Lewis Suite: Missing; Now She Is like the White Tree-Rose; Rest from Loving and Be Living; Twenty Years Near Past*
Arnold Schoenberg *Three Songs: Erhebung*, op 2, no 3; *Aufgeregten*, op 3, no 2; *Traumleben*, op 6, no 1

TAPE 35   with Gordon Kushner, piano
Robert Schumann   *Abends am Strand,* op 45, no 3; *Aus den Östlichen Rosen,* op
                               25, no 25; *Frühlingsnacht,* op 39, no. 13; *Mondnacht,* op
                               39, no 5; *Sehnsucht,* op 51, no 1

TAPE 36   with Boyd McDonald, piano
Chester Duncan   *Six Songs: Beside One Dead; From the Hazelbow; A Simple
                               Love Lyric; Saturday and Sunday; The One; A Riddle*
Claude Debussy   From *Fêtes Galantes: En Sourdine; Fantoches; Clair de
                               Lune*
Claude Debussy   From *Chansons de Bilitis: La Chevelure*

TAPES 37 and 38   with George Brough, piano
Paul Hindemith   *Das Marienleben*

TAPE 39   with Louis Crerar, piano
Paul Hindemith   *Nine English Songs* (first performance in Canada, 1946)
Elinor Remick Warren   *Sweet Grass Range* (July 1938)
                               (Frances James singing and whistling with accordion
                               accompaniment on the Banff Springs Hotel golf course.
                               Two takes)

TAPE 45   The Adaskin Trio, which consisted of Louis Crerar, piano; Philip Spivak,
           cello; and Murray Adaskin, violin; with guest artists
           Catherine Wright, contralto, and Frances James, soprano
           An evening at the Banff Springs Hotel (early 1930s)

Notes

1 *Encyclopedia of Music in Canada* 550
2 Letter from Alfred Whitehead to Frances James, 17 October 1970
3 Whitehead was forced to leave Montreal for reasons of health in the early 1940s. Between 1947 and 1953 he was head of music at Mount Allison University.
4 2 June 1926
5 25 April 1926
6 For a fascinating account of the railways and the life-style offered to their passengers see Hart *The Selling of Canada* 87.
7 J.M. Gibbon 'Scot to Canadian.' A copy of this autobiography is located in the Archives of the Canadian Rockies.
8 Hart *Diamond Hitch* 145
9 'Riders to Blaze New Rockies Trail' *Montreal Gazette* 28 July 1925
10 Gibbon 132–3
11 A summary of Gibbon's own experiences is in the booklet *Tribute to a Nation Builder* (Composers, Authors and Publishers Association, Toronto 1946).
12 The quartet included Marchand and Emile Boucher (tenors) and Miville Belleau and Fortunat Champagne (basses).
13 For list of dates of these festivals, see *Encyclopedia of Music in Canada*.
14 This long, woven sash, or the *ceinture fléchée*, was worn around the waist by the coureurs de bois, lumbermen, and habitants. It was very strong in order to support loaded canoes during portages. Because of the use of wax during the weaving process, the ends could be moulded into dishes and used as food containers.
15 The winners were listed in the program of the 1928 Quebec Festival. Document c 71593 in the Public Archives, Ottawa.

16 Program brochure of the Old English Yuletide Festival and Sea Music Festivals, Victoria 1929, 7, located in the CPR Corporate Archives, Montreal

17 See Giles Bryant *Healey Willan Catalogue* no 3.

18 Bryant no 21

19 Peter F. Bishop 'Canadian Music Criticism from 1918 to 1939 as shown in *The Toronto Star* and *Saturday Night*.' Unpublished MA thesis, University of Victoria 1979, 52

20 For more information on J. Campbell McInnes, see Ian Montagnes *An Uncommon Fellowship*.

21 *Encyclopedia of Music in Canada* 576

22 CBC *Program Schedule* 16 July 1944

23 CBC *Program Schedule* 28 June 1944

24 Quebec *Canadian Folk Song and Handicraft Festival* brochure, 1928. Ottawa, Public Archives, C 71593

25 *Encyclopedia of Music in Canada* 290

26 For personal reminiscences, see Harry Adaskin *A Fiddler's World* 119

27 *Encyclopedia of Music in Canada* 924

28 *Encyclopedia of Music in Canada* 983

29 Ibid 408

CHAPTER 2

1 Bart Robinson *Banff Springs: The Story of a Hotel* 63

2 Robinson 18

3 *Canadian Review of Music and Art* 1: 6 (October 1942) 19

4 Ibid

5 *Calgary Daily Herald* 13 August 1934

6 *Calgary Daily Herald* 27 August 1934. The authorship of this work has since been attributed to Leopold Mozart.

7 *Calgary Daily Herald* 7 August 1941

8 Such a concert was presented at the Art Gallery on 21 January 1938.

9 *Toronto Star* 10 January 1937

10 *Saturday Night* 3 February 1938

11 *Montreal Gazette* 17 January 1936

12 Stated by Mrs Gwendolyn Koldofsky in an interview with the author on 25 August 1983

13 She participated on at least three occasions: 1934, 1935, and 1937.

14 'Musical Events' *Saturday Night* 25 March 1937

15 *Toronto Star* 4 March 1936

16 *A Brief History of the* CBC 1

17 A.J. Black *Chronology of Network Broadcasting in Canada 1901–1961* 2
18 Black 4
19 Black 9
20 Black 14
21 Gibbon 'Scot to Canadian' 182
22 *Canadian G.E. Monogram* 2: 5 (September – October 1931) 6
23 *A Brief History of the* CBC 5
24 Reports of the CBC for 1936
25 Reports of the CBC for 1936, and CBC program schedules
26 This anecdote was related to the author by Murray Adaskin, who recalls it as a story circulated among Toronto musicians at the time.
27 Charles C. Hill *Canadian Painting in the Thirties* 11
28 Hill 14
29 Vincent Massey *What's Past Is Prologue* 87
30 Hill 51
31 Letter from Paraskeva Clark to Frances James Adaskin, 17 April 1975

CHAPTER 3

1 *Montreal Gazette* 19 April 1943
2 The date of the concert was 9 January 1944.
3 *Canadian Review of Music and Art* 2: 9–10 (October–November 1943)
4 Canadian Broadcasting Corporation *Annual Report, 1939–1940*
5 John Weinzweig generously imparted much of this information about wartime radio dramas to the author.
6 The author heard a recording of some of the broadcasts at the home of John Weinzweig; they are rare documents of how these radio dramas sounded at the time.
7 CBC *Program Schedule* 28 December 1941
8 Barbara Pentland's music was broadcast on 1 March 1943, and that of Arnold Walter, Robert Fleming, Frank Harris, and Graham George throughout January 1944.
9 Tom Archer 'The Listening Room' *Canadian Review of Music and Art* 3: 5 and 6 (June–July 1944) 32
10 'British Opera on the Radio' *Saturday Night* 12 January 1942
11 John Coulter *In My Day: Memoirs* 171
12 Coulter 177
13 *Toronto Star* 14 April 1942
14 Coulter 178
15 Gibbon 'Scot to Canadian' 192
16 Letter from John Murray Gibbon to Frances James, 15 December 1944
17 *Port Arthur News-Chronicle* 16 February 1938

18 'Over the Teacups' *Toronto Star* 15 April 1946
19 24 January 1948 16
20 *Windsor Daily Star* 23 October 1944
21 Isabel C. Armstrong *Ottawa Citizen* March 1938
22 *Saturday Night* 27 September 1949
23 See Ronald Hambleton 'Cancer Kills Voice Teacher after Year' *Globe and Mail* 12 October 1954. In this obituary Hambleton presents a moving eulogy to Madame Heim.
24 Some of this repertoire may be heard on the two-disc Vanguard recording, *The Art of Roland Hayes*, with Reginald Boardman at the piano.
25 Boston: Little, Brown 1943
26 Letter from Roland Hayes to Frances James, 4 August 1944
27 Letter from Roland Hayes to Frances James, 31 December 1947
28 Letter from Roland Hayes to Frances James, 4 January 1945
29 'World of Music' *Winnipeg Free Press* 24 December 1948
30 The Montreal performances took place on 19 February 1946 and 26 April 1947, the Ottawa performance on 29 April 1947.
31 Letter from Sir Ernest MacMillan to Frances James, 6 May 1970
32 *St Matthew Passion* was performed in Convocation Hall.
33 These performances occurred in 1942, 1943, 1944, 1946, and 1949.
34 *Toronto Star*, 30 December 1942
35 Charlesworth's appraisals appeared in the *Globe and Mail*, 29 December 1943, and *Saturday Night*, 30 December 1943, respectively.
36 Pentland, who had left Winnipeg two years earlier, had by 1944 become an active contributor to the Toronto musical scene.
37 Toronto *Telegram* 12 November 1946
38 Rose MacDonald *Telegram*, 12 June 1943
39 The date of the reviews in the *Toronto Star* and *Saturday Night* was 12 June 1943.
40 *Herald Tribune*, 21 January 1951
41 *Canadian Forum*, February 1951
42 Ten years later Fritsch reissued Frances James's original recording as a single disc, under the number LL97.
43 The series lasted until 23 October 1963 as 'CBC Wednesday Night.' On 27 October 1963 its title was changed to 'CBC Sunday Night,' and two years later it was renamed 'CBC Tuesday Night.'
44 CBC *Program Schedule*, 'Music 1949–50'
45 William A. Taylor 'Radio, Television: News and Reviews' *Musical Courier* 1 March 1948

46 The author had the privilege of winning in the piano category of the first Trans-Canada Talent Festival in 1959. The winner in the voice category was Cornelius Opthof. The producer was John Adaskin.
47 Thomas Archer 'Deirdre of the Sorrows' *Radio World* 11 May 1946
48 Archer
49 The *première* of *Les Illuminations* took place on 14 July 1948, and that of *Rêves* on 22 March 1950.
50 This performance took place on 13 June 1951.
51 Bernardi accompanied her in a 1950 broadcast of music by Canadian composers.
52 The orchestral part, demanding many rehearsals, was bravely tackled by Geoffrey Waddington. The chorus was led by Richard Johnston, then a professor of music at the University of Toronto, while Herman Geiger-Torel coached the singers. The all-Canadian cast was headed by Frances James as Ellen Orford and William Morton as Peter Grimes. Edmund Hockridge, Eric Tredwell, Gordon Wry, and Nellie Smith were some of the other principals.
53 'Canadians Do Well by Peter Grimes' *Toronto Star* 13 October 1949
54 'Response: Peter Grimes' *CBC Times*, week of 30 October 1949
55 *Saturday Night* 1 November 1949
56 Alan Blyth *Remembering Britten* 13–15
57 Terence Gibbs 'The New CBC Opera Season' *CBC Times*, week of 11 September 1949
58 Letter from Terence Gibbs to Murray and Frances Adaskin, 28 January 1971
59 S.R.M., *Winnipeg Tribune* 10 January 1950
60 'Music or No Music' *Vancouver Province* 3 February 1947
61 *Encyclopedia of Music in Canada* 370
62 The letter to which Frances James is referring is printed below:

November 18, 1948

Dear Mrs. Adaskin:

Mr. Jarrett has given me your letter enquiring about bookings at the Copper Cliff Club.

We have not had artists from outside the district perform at the Club for several years as larger organizations such as the Community Concert Association in Sudbury arrange this type of program.

Should there be any change in our policy we will be glad to get in touch with you.

Yours truly,

Chairman,
Entertainment Committee.

63 J.V. McAree 'Obstacles Confront Canadian Musicians' *Globe and Mail* 5 July 1949; Anne M. McDonagh, 'Sidelights on the Community Concerts Controversy' *Monthly Bulletin of the Royal Conservatory of Music of Toronto* October 1949

CHAPTER 4

1 The expression was coined in later years by Murray's friend Eli Bornstein, when he saw Marcel Ray's photographic portrait of Milhaud.
2 Members of the Dembeck String Quartet were John Dembeck and Stanley Kolt, violins; Robert Warburton, viola; and Cornelius Ysselstyn, cello.
3 Sheila Eastman and Timothy J. McGee *Barbara Pentland* 39
4 Eastman and McGee 42
5 The programs are listed in CBC *Times* 1943 and 1944.
6 *Encyclopedia of Music in Canada* 168
7 Letter from Murray Adaskin to Terence Gibbs, 4 May 1959
8 For a detailed list of songs *premièred* by Frances James see appendix C.
9 Colin Sabiston 'Warm Reception Given Canadian Music Series' *Globe and Mail* 18 April 1947
10 'Five Canadians' Compositions on Program' *Telegram* 19 April 1947
11 'Canadian Composers Featured at Harbord' *Toronto Star* 18 April 1947
12 'Program Plan Introduces Canadian Compositions to Keen Audiences' *Saturday Night* 10 May 1947
13 Sabiston
14 *Globe and Mail* 11 March 1952
15 'The Federation of Canadian Artists' *Canadian Review of Music and Art* 3; 5–6 (June–July 1944) 16
16 'Ontario Does Not Sponsor the Arts' *Canadian Review of Music and Art* 3: 7–8 (August–September 1944)
17 *Canadian Review of Music and Art* 3: 3–4 (April–May 1944)
18 Coulter *In My Day* ch 13
19 The members of the advisory council were Sir Ernest MacMillan, Marcus Adeney, W.J. Raymond Card, B.R. Coon, Nicholas Hornyansky, F.S. Haines, G.E. Jackson, Bertram Brooker, Earle Grey, Edmund Watson, I.D. Carson, and Eason Humphreys.
20 Some of this discussion is recorded in *Canadian Review of Music and Art* 3: 11–12 (December–January 1945) 15–20.
21 *Encyclopedia of Music in Canada* 167
22 The foundation's officers included Justice Joseph T. Thorson, president; George Glazebrook, vice-president; A. Davidson Dunton, treasurer; Margaret J. Cameron, secretary; and Walter B. Herbert, director.
23 Coulter 203

24 'Art Organizations Petition Parliament' *Canadian Review of Music and Art* 3: 3–4 (April–May 1944) 10
25 Coulter 207
26 Bernard Ostry *The Cultural Connection* 56
27 Royal Commission on National Development in the Arts, Letters and Sciences *Report* 8
28 Royal Commission *Report* 40
29 Ostry 59
30 Royal Commission *Report* 138
31 *Report* 182
32 *Report* 271
33 *Report* 377. For the political events that occurred from the submission of the royal commission report until the actual establishment of the Canada Council see Ostry *The Cultural Connection*.
34 Ostry 67

CHAPTER 5

1 For more details about the history of the university, see David R. Murray and Robert A. Murray, *The Prairie Builder: Walter Murray of Saskatchewan*.
2 Michael Hayden *Seeking a Balance, University of Saskatchewan, 1907–1982* 19
3 Murray and Murray 168–9
4 Murray and Murray 184
5 Murray and Murray 188
6 Hayden 211
7 Hayden 227
8 Hayden 214
9 Kazimir Karpusko *Eli Bornstein: Selected Words* (Saskatoon: Mendel Art Gallery 1982) 6
10 This is particularly evident in *Structurist Relief in Fifteen Parts* (1962), commissioned for the Winnipeg International Air Terminal and displayed on its south wall, and in the *Four Part Vertical Double Plane Structurist Relief* (1979–82), commissioned for the administration building of the Wascana Centre Authority in Regina.
    Bornstein's many national and international exhibitions include those at the Montreal Museum of Fine Arts, the Museum of Contemporary Art in Chicago, the National Gallery in Ottawa, and the Centre Culturel Canadien in Paris.
11 The letter is located in the archives of the Music Department, Walter Murray Library, University of Saskatchewan.
12 Letter from Frances James to Catharine Whyte, 16 April 1956
13 Letter from Frances James to Catharine Whyte, 5 August 1958

14 Balaklava is a Crimean village near Sevastopol in the Soviet Union. From 1854 to 1855 during the Crimean war it housed the British headquarters.

15 *Ottawa Citizen* 28 February 1959

16 Other participating artists included Lois Carkeek and Howard Leyton-Brown, violins; Robert Falcove, viola; Peggie Sampson and Barbara Draper, cellos; Robert Charbonneau, bass; Jacqueline Marçault, piano; Bethany Beardsley and Frances James, sopranos; Harry Dahlem, baritone; Helmut Seemann, flute; Franz Zeidler, clarinet; Phil West, oboe; Jane Taylor, bassoon; James Schmitt and John Scecina, French horns; Gerald Conrath, trumpet; Billy Walls, trombone; Thomas Gauger, percussion. Conductors included Murray Adaskin, James Bolle, and Geoffrey Waddington.

17 Only one movement of Weinzweig's *Divertimento* was completed on time.

18 See Kasemets's review, 'The Saskatchewan Summer Festival of Music, 1959' *Canadian Music Journal* 4: 1 (Autumn 1959) 14–23.

19 Letter from Udo Kasemets to Murray Adaskin, 12 August 1959

20 Fred MacDermid died in April 1986, at the age of 101.

21 *The Book and Life of a Little Man: Reminiscences of Frederick S. Mendel*

22 The letter is in the Catharine Whyte collection, Archives of the Canadian Rockies, Banff.

23 Dawes is one of the original members of the Orford String Quartet, formed in 1965.

24 Susan became a successful broadcaster with the CBC in Winnipeg, and is currently with the CBC in Vancouver.

25 Music Dept *Annual Reports* 1953–8. University of Saskatchewan Archives

26 Music Dept *Annual Reports* 1967–8. University of Saskatchewan Archives

27 Letter from Murray Adaskin to Professor O.L. Symes, 6 April 1966

CHAPTER 6

1 Letter from Geoffrey Waddington to Murray Adaskin 20 January 1953

2 The reviewer was Arthur Cohn, in the February 1965 issue of *American Record Guide* (Salem Research, Rd 2, Box 59A, South Road, Millbrook, NY 12545).

3 *Globe and Mail* 5 January 1955

4 *Globe and Mail* 9 January 1984

5 *Detroit Free Press* 29 January 1955

6 Letter from Udo Kasemets to Murray Adaskin, 21 September 1962

7 Review by Richard Todd, 3 April 1981

8 Letter from George Zukerman to Murray and Frances Adaskin, 2 January 1982

9 Letter from Naomi Adaskin to Murray Adaskin, 26 March 1963

10 Review by Jeffrey Anderson, 5 October 1967

11 *Ottawa Citizen* 1 April 1983

12 The massacre at Seven Oaks occurred in 1816, on the outskirts of today's Winnipeg. Twenty-one colonists were killed along with Governor Semple in the attack on the Selkirk settlers by the Métis and the Nor'Westers. The settlers were seen as representing interests of the rival Hudson's Bay Company.

13 This information appeared in the CBC *Times* 15–21 July 1967.

14 Telegram from John Roberts to Tom Taylor

15 Letter from Bruce Mather to Murray Adaskin, 19 July 1967

16 Letter from Herman Geiger-Torel to Murray Adaskin, 19 July 1967

17 Letter from Mrs P. Chamber to Murray Adaskin, 1 May 1981

CHAPTER 7

1 By 1980, the university was still only one of seven in Canada to offer through its music department a doctoral degree in musicology.

2 Since 1982 the Victoria Choral Society has been directed by Dr Bruce More from the School of Music, University of Victoria.

3 Harry Van Vugt *Windsor Star* 10 October 1981

4 Members of the Pacific Wind Quintet in 1974 were Tim Paradise, clarinet; Eileen Gibson, oboe; Jesse Read, bassoon; Richard Ely, French horn; and Lanny Pollet, flute.

5 Members of the Purcell String Quartet in 1977 were Norman Nelson, first violin; Joseph Peleg, second violin; Phillippe Etter, viola; and Ian Hampton, cello.

6 Letter to Murray Adaskin, 14 November 1980

7 For more information on publishers of these compositions see appendix B.

8 The evaluation is that of Bruce Mather, in a discussion with the author.

Bibliography

Adaskin, Harry *A Fiddler's World: Memoirs to 1938.* Vancouver: November House 1977
– *A Fiddler's Choice: Memoirs 1938 to 1980.* Vancouver: November House 1982
Adaskin, John 'Radio Production in Relation to Symphony Broadcasting' *Canadian Review of Music and Art* 1 (April 1942)
Adaskin, Murray 'The Fiddle and the Player' *Saturday Night* 21 April 1945
– 'Can Hockey Tactics Be Applied to Symphony Orchestras?' *Saturday Night* 28 April 1945
– 'Analysis of *Serenade Concertante*' Toronto: Canadian Music Centre 1961
– 'The University in Audience Training' *Music across Canada* 1:5 (June 1963)
– 'Victoria: More Beauty than Meets the Eye' *Musicanada* 35 (April 1978)
Adeney, Marcus 'Music in Post-War Canada' *Canadian Forum* June 1945
Aide, William 'Murray Adaskin' in Keith MacMillan and John Beckwith (eds) *Contemporary Canadian Composers.* Toronto: Oxford University Press 1975
Bishop, Peter Frederick 'Canadian Music Criticism from 1918 to 1939 as shown in the *Toronto Star* and *Saturday Night*' unpublished MA thesis, University of Victoria 1979
Black, A. *Chronology of Network Broadcasting in Canada 1901–1961.* Ottawa: CBC Information Services 1961
Blyth, Alan *Remembering Britten.* London: Hutchinson 1981
Bornstein, Eli *The Structurist.* University of Saskatchewan 1961–
Bradley, Ian L. *Twentieth-Century Canadian Composer.* Agincourt, Ont: GLC 1977
Brewster, F.O. 'Pat' *They Came West.* Banff: Altitude Publishing 1979
– *Weathered Wood.* Banff: Altitude Publishing 1977
– *Wild Cards.* Banff: Altitude Publishing 1982
Bridle, Augustus *A Story of the Club.* Toronto: Arts and Letters Club 1945
Bryant, Giles *Healey Willan Catalogue.* Ottawa: National Library 1972
Canadian Pacific Corporate Archives, Montreal. Festival Programs

Canadian Radio Broadcasting Commission. *Annual Reports.* 1933–6

CAPAC *Tribute to a Nation-Builder: An Appreciation of Dr J.M. Gibbon.* Toronto 1946

CBC *Annual Reports of the Canadian Broadcasting Corporation* 1936–44

– *A Brief History of the Canadian Broadcasting Corporation.* Ottawa: Public Relations Office, July 1976

– *Broadcasting in Canada: History and Development of the National System.* Ottawa: CBC Information Services 1961

CBC Times Eastern Region Programme Schedules, 1948–1960

– Prairie Region Programme Schedules, 1948–1960

– Western Region Programme Schedules, 1950–1970

Chalmers, Floyd S. *Both Sides of the Street: One Man's Life In Business and the Arts in Canada.* Toronto: Macmillan 1983

Charlesworth, Hector 'Order of Good Cheer Revived' *Saturday Night* 9 June 1928

Clarke, F.R.C. *The Life and Music of Healey Willan.* Toronto: University of Toronto Press 1983

Coulter, John 'Words for Music' *Opera Canada* September 1965

– *In My Day: Memoirs.* Toronto: Hounslow Press 1980

CRTC 'Bibliography' *Some Canadian Writings on the Mass Media.* Ottawa 1974

Duval, Paul *A.J. Casson: His Life and Works, a Tribute.* Toronto: Cerebrus/Prentice-Hall 1980

Eastman, Sheila, and Timothy J. McGee *Barbara Pentland.* Toronto: University of Toronto Press 1983

Edinborough, Arnold *A Personal History of the Toronto Symphony* [Toronto, 1971]

Edwards, C.A.M. *Taylor Statten: A Biography.* Toronto: Ryerson Press 1960

Egantoff, Bill 'Our Composer-in-Residence, Murray Adaskin' *The Sheaf* (University of Saskatchewan) 16 December 1966

Fraser, Esther *Wheeler.* Banff: Summerthought 1978

French, Maida Parlow *Kathleen Parlow: A Potrait.* Toronto: Ryerson Press 1967

Gibbon, John Murray 'Scot to Canadian: One of More than a Million.' Unpublished autobiography, 1951

– *Canadian Mosaic: The Making of a Northern Nation.* Toronto: McClelland and Stewart 1938

– *Canadian Folk Songs Old and New.* London: J.M. Dent and Sons 1927

Gooch, Bryan N.S. Interview with Murray Adaskin, in *Anthology of Canadian Music,* Radio Canada International, Monique Grenier, executive producer

Goudge, Helen *Look Back in Pride: A History of the Women's Musical Club in Toronto.* Toronto 1972

Hart, E.J. *Diamond Hitch: The Early Outfitters and Guides of Banff and Jasper.* Banff: Summerthought 1979

– *The Selling of Canada: The CPR and the Beginnings of Canadian Tourism.* Banff: Altitude Publishing 1983

– *The Brewster Story: From Pack Train to Tour Bus.* Banff: Brewster Transport Company Ltd 1981

Hayden, Michael (ed and annot) *So Much to Do, So Little Time: The Writings of Hilda Neatby.* Vancouver: University of British Columbia Press 1983

– *Seeking a Balance: The University of Saskatchewan 1907–1982.* Vancouver: University of British Columbia Press 1983

Helm, MacKinley *Angel Mo' and Her Son Roland Hayes.* Boston: Little, Brown 1943

Hill, Charles C. *Canadian Painting in the Thirties.* Ottawa: National Gallery 1975

John Adaskin Project: Towards New Music in Education. Toronto: Canadian Music Centre 1968

Kallmann, Helmut 'First Fifteen Years of Canadian League of Composers' *Canadian Composer* 7 (March 1966)

Kallmann, Helmut, Gilles Potvin, and Kenneth Winters (ed) *Encyclopedia of Music in Canada.* Toronto: University of Toronto Press 1981

Kalman, Harold *The Railway Hotels and the Development of the Chateau Style in Canada.* Victoria: Maltwood Museum 1968

Kasemets, Udo 'The Saskatchewan Summer Festival of Music, 1959' *Canadian Music Journal* 6:1 (Autumn 1959)

King, Carlyle *The First Fifty: Teaching, Research, and Public Service at the University of Saskatchewan 1909–1959.* Toronto: McClelland and Stewart 1959

MacMillan, Sir Ernest C. (ed) *Music in Canada.* Toronto: University of Toronto Press 1955

– 'Music in Canada,' Royal Commission on National Development in the Arts, Letters and Sciences, 1949–1951, *Royal Commission Studies* Ottawa: 1951

MacMillan, Keith 'Music on the CBC: The English Service Division of CBC Radio' *Musicanada* 31 (February 1977)

Mason, Lawrence 'Festival Proves Revelation of Riches of Canadian Music' *Toronto Globe* 23 May 1927

Massey, Vincent *What's Past Is Prologue: The Memoirs of the Right Honourable Vincent Massey.* Toronto: Macmillan 1963

Mellen, Peter *The Group of Seven.* Toronto: McClelland and Stewart 1970

Mendel, Frederick S. *The Book and Life of a Little Man: Reminiscences of Frederick S. Mendel.* Toronto: Macmillan 1972

Montagnes, Ian *An Uncommon Fellowship: The Story of Hart House.* Toronto: University of Toronto Press 1969

'Murray Adaskin – A Portrait' *Musicanada* 1:1 (May 1967)

Murray, David R., and Robert A. Murray *The Prairie Builder: Walter Murray of Saskatchewan.* Edmonton: NeWest 1984

Ostry, Bernard *The Cultural Connection.* Toronto: McClelland and Stewart 1978

Pentland, Barbara 'On Experiment in Music' *Canadian Review of Music and Art* 12 (August–September 1943)

Robinson, Bart *Banff Springs: The Story of a Hotel*. Banff: Summerthought 1973

Royal Commission on National Development in the Arts, Letters and Sciences 1949–1951 *Report*. Ottawa: Edmond Clouthier 1951

– *Royal Commission Studies: A Selection of Essays Prepared for the Royal Commission* ... Ottawa: Edmond Clouthier 1951

Royal Conservatory of Music *Conservatory Quarterly Review* 1918–35

– *Toronto Conservatory of Music Bulletin* 1935–47

– *Royal Conservatory of Music of Toronto Monthly Bulletin* 1948–64

Savage, Richard 'Murray Adaskin' *Canadian Composer* 10 (September 1960)

Schulman, Michael 'Murray Adaskin' *Musical Portrait, Murray Adaskin*. CAPAC, a Fiftieth Anniversary Project

– 'A Birthday for Adaskin' *Canadian Composer* 164 (October 1981)

Skelton, Geoffrey *Paul Hindemith: The Man behind the Music, a Biography*. London: Gollancz 1977

Solway, Maurice *Recollections of a Violinist*. Oakville, Ont: Mosaic Press 1984

Spinks, J.W.T. *A Decade of Change: The University of Saskatchewan 1959–1970*. Saskatoon: University of Saskatchewan 1972

Walter, Arnold (ed) *Aspects of Music in Canada*. Toronto: University of Toronto Press 1969

Whyte, Jon (ed) *Catharine Robb Whyte, Peter Whyte Commemorative Portfolio*. Banff: Peter and Catharine Whyte Foundation 1980

Index

Abramson, Edward, 190
Academy String Quartet, 25, 29; *see also*
   Canadian Academy of Music
Adamson, Bertha, 25, 29
Adaskin, Frances Marr, 43, 226
Adaskin, Gordon, 23, 24
Adaskin, Harry, 23, 24, 25, 26, 29, 30,
   62, 97, 100, 226
Adaskin, John, 19, 23, 24–5, 28, 30, 36,
   59, 60, 74, 79, 81, 82, 105, 144, 171, 225
Adaskin, Leslie, 23
Adaskin, Murray, viii
– acquires Stradivarius violin, 135–6
– and Saskatoon community, 187, 196–8,
   200, 204
– and Saskatoon Symphony Orchestra,
   187, 196–8
– and Canadian visual artists, 64, 65–7,
   69–71, 180, 199
– appointed to Canada Council, 208–9
– as conductor, 18; of Saskatoon
   Symphony Orchestra, 187, 196
– as member of Canadian League of
   Composers, 153, 154–5, 157, 158
– as member of Trail Riders, 10
– as teacher in Victoria, 243, 244
– as violinist: at Banff, 19, 29, 33, 34,
   35, 36–7, 39–40, 41, 42; for radio
   broadcasts, 51, 77; in theatres, 26–8;

in Toronto, 43, 45, 56–7, with Toronto
   Symphony Orchestra, 30, 49–50,
   59–60, 60–1, with Toronto Trio, 62–4,
   136
– at Institute of Northern Studies,
   210–11
– childhood and education of, 23–4,
   26–7; education in Europe, 32
– composition studies, 134; with Charles
   Jones, 44; with Sir Ernest MacMillan,
   137–8; with Darius Milhaud, 101,
   141–5; with John Weinzweig, 138–9
– his philosophy of composition and
   education, 196, 255, 259–60
– musical influences on, 256
– on faculty of University of
   Saskatchewan, 166, 173–4, 175, 178,
   179, 202–3, 215; assists students,
   185–7; forms Amati Quartet, 205–6;
   heads music department, 177, 182–3,
   184–5, 200, 206–7; organizes
   Centennial Exhibition Concerts,
   211–14; organizes Sunday Evening
   Recital series, 187–92; organizes
   Golden Jubilee Music Festival, 192–3,
   194–5; holds receptions for concert
   artists, 188, 198–9
– on performers and conductors, 49,
   54–5, 75

– style of, 235; developmental techniques, 238; melody, 241; orchestration, 236–7, 257; rhythm, 241; structure, 239; tonal language, 240
– works: *Adagio for Cello and Piano*, 245, 247; *Algonquin Symphony*, 148, 216, 217, 220, 221, 222–3, 236, 240, 252, 253, 258, 270–2 (Ex 23, 24); 'Back the Attack,' 74; *Ballet Symphony*, 144, 156, 217, 218; *Bassoon Quintet*, 248; *Brass Fanfare for a Wedding*, 248; *Calisthenics for Violin and Piano*, 234; *Canzona and Rondo*, 142, 180, 217, 228, 239; *Capriccio for Piano and Orchestra*, 210, 225, 226, 258; *Cassenti Concertante*, 227; *Concerto for Bassoon and Orchestra*, 210, 216, 225, 226, 239–40, 241, 248, 273–4 (Ex 26); *Concerto for Violin and Orchestra*, 148, 216, 225, 239, 241, 269–70 (Ex 22), 274–5 (Ex 27, 28); *Coronation Overture*, 148, 217, 219, 235–6, 266–7 (Ex 11, 12, 13, 14); *Dance Concertante for Orchestra*, 247–8; *Daydreams for Violin and Piano*, 234, 253–4; *Diversion for Orchestra (An Entertainment)*, 171, 224, 236, 241–2, 279–80 (Ex 33, 34); *Divertimento No 1 for Two Violins and Piano*, 216, 226, 236; *Divertimento No 2 for Violin and Harp*, 226, 228; *Divertimento No 3 for Violin, Horn in F, and Bassoon*, 226–7, 238–9, 268–9 (Ex 19, 20, 21); *Divertimento No 4 for Trumpet and Orchestra*, 225, 226; *Divertimento No 5 for Two Guitars and Chamber Orchestra*, 226, 248–9; *Divertimento No 6 for Solo Percussion and Orchestra*, 226, 249; *Epitaph*, 98, 139, 228; *Essay for Strings*, 235; *Fanfare for Brass Quintet*, 248; *Fanfare for Orchestra*, 24, 224–5, 236; *Grant, Warden of the Plains*, 218, 229–34, 235, 264–6 (Ex 6, 7, 8, 9, 10); 'Hymn of Thanks,' 222; *Impromptu for Violin and Piano*, 247; *In Praise of 'Canadian Painting in the Thirties,'* 71–2, 247; *Introduction and Rondo, Quartet for Piano and Strings*, 227, 238, 268 (Ex 18); *Israeli Violin Piece T'Filat Shalom*, 246–7; *Legato and Ricochet for Violin and Piano*, 234; *March No 1 for Orchestra*, 144, 225; *March No 2 for Orchestra*, 225; *March No 3 for Orchestra*, 225, 247; *Music for Brass Quintet*, 248; *Nocturne for Clarinet and Piano*, 247; *Nootka Ritual for Orchestra*, 247; *Of Man and the Universe*, 228–9, 262–3 (Ex 3, 4, 5); *Ontario Variation for Solo Piano*, 247; *The Prairie Lily*, 234; *Qalala and Nilaula of the North*, 211, 218, 223–4, 236, 258; *Quintet for Woodwinds*, 248; *Rankin Inlet – Eskimo Song*, 247; *Rondino for Nine Instruments*, 226–7, 242; *Rondino for Orchestra*, 235; *Saskatchewan Legend*, 220, 223, 237, 253, 258; *Serenade Concertante*, 38, 148, 157, 216, 217, 218, 219–20, 236, 237–8, 239, 241, 253, 267–8 (Ex 15, 16, 17), 276–8 (Ex 29, 30, 31, 32); *The Shepherd*, 47, 98, 137; *Sonata for Cello and Piano*, 247; *Sonata for Piano*, 157, 228; *Sonata for Violin and Piano*, 135, 139, 149, 150, 151, 157, 180, 228; *Sonatine Baroque for Solo Violin*, 152, 180, 228, 239, 253; *String Quartet No 1*, 227, 241, 272 (Ex 25); *Suite for Orchestra*, 141, 217, 218; *Suite for Strings*, 137, 139, 140, 219, 257; *Three Pieces for Violin and Piano*, 234; *Three Tunes for Strings*, 245, 247; *Toccatina for Piano*, 234; *The Travelling Musicians*, 249–51, 252, 258, 260, 281–2 (Ex 35); *Trio for Flute, Cello, and Piano*, 226–7; *Two Pieces for Viola da Gamba*, 228; *Two Portraits for Violin and Piano*, 228, 241, 242, 261 (Ex 2)

Adaskin, Samuel, 23, 24, 26

Adaskin, Susan, 201–2, 310
Adeney, Marcus, 43, 59, 159, 161
Agostini, Lucio, 147, 186
Aird Commission, 52
Akeley, T.C., 247
Alarie, Pierrette, 122, 124
Alberta Chamber Trio, 227
Aldrick, H.A., 93
Allan, Andrew, 104
Allen, Sir Hugh, 14
Altschul, Rudolf, 175, 181
American League of Composers, 153, 154
American Opera Company, 20
Anderson, Marian, 89
Apollinaire, Guillaume, 139, 149
Applebaum, Louis, 78, 110, 146, 153–4, 157, 234
Archer, Thomas, 106
Archer, Violet, 197, 234; *Fanfare and Passacaglia*, 147; *Fantasy for Violin and Piano*, 147; *Sonata for Flute, Clarinet, and Piano*, 147
Arthur, Jack, 36
Arts and Letters Club, 67, 106, 162
Aspen Summer School, 140, 148, 186
Association of Canadian Clubs, 22
Auer, Leopold, 62
Auric, Georges, 140
Avison, John, 120, 219, 236

Bach, C.P.E., 194
Bach, J.C., 194
Bach, J.S., 45, 142, 204; *Air on the G String*, 138; *Ave Maria* (Bach-Gounod), 18, 40; *B Minor Mass*, 48, 50; *St John Passion*, 48, 49; *St Matthew Passion*, 19, 20, 48, 49–50, 94, 134
Bacharach, Burt, 141
Balfe, Michael: *The Bohemian Girl*, 79
Ballad operas, 15–17; *At the Court of James v*, 16; *The Ayreshire Plough-man*, 16–17, 19, 20; *Bound for the Rio Grande*, 16; *The Chester Mysteries*, 16; *Christmas with Herrick*, 16; *Hugh the

Drover*, 17, 19, 78; *Indian Nativity Play*, 16; *The Jolly Beggars*, 13, 16, 18, 20, 21; *Mary Queen of Scots*, 16; *Order of Good Cheer*, 16; *Prince Charlie and Flora*, 16, 17, 21; *Prince Charming*, 16, 19
Bampton, Rose, 79, 126
Banff School of Fine Arts, 24
Banff Springs Hotel, 5, 6, 7, 12, 14–15, 17, 31, 33, 34–5, 36–7, 135; artists at, 37–8; music festivals at, 20, 21, 35; royal visit to, 41–2; *see also* Canadian Pacific Railway, hotels
Banff Springs Hotel Quintet(te), 19, 33
Banff Springs Trio, 36, 40, 41, 134; *see also* Toronto Trio
Barbeau, Marius, 11, 14, 19
Barbeau, Rose-Marie, 213
Barber, Samuel: *Adagio for Strings*, 193; *Piano Sonata*, 189
Barkin, Leo, 28, 120, 153
Barry, Ernest, 106
Bartók, Béla, 43, 147; *Contrasts for Violin, Piano, and Clarinet*, 35
Battle, Rex, 53
Bauman, Norbert, 105
Bax, Sir Arnold, 17, 43, 47
Bayer, Mary-Elizabeth, 229–30
Beatty, Sir Edward W., 11, 14
Beaudet, Jean-Marie, 57–8, 79, 81, 82, 105, 147, 161, 171, 224
Beck, Jean, 13
Beckett, Garth, 190, 203
Beckwith, John, 155, 157, 252
Beecham, Sir Thomas, 63, 80
Beethoven, Ludwig van, 258; *Archduke Trio*, 35; *Fidelio*, 5; *Missa Solemnis*, 48, 50, 51; *Ninth Symphony*, 219; string quartets, 26, 52
Bell, Billie, 22, 53
Benjamin, Arthur: *The Devil Take Her*, 78–9; *A Tale of Two Cities*, 105, 112
Benny, Jack, 35, 58
Berg, Alban, 88, 113

Bernardi Mario, 109, 113, 120, 157, 171, 180, 224, 227
Bertini, Gary, 223
Bethune, Norman, 65, 181
Betts, Lorne, 149, 157
Biederman, Charles, 180
Bieler, André, 158
Bisha, Edward, 206
Bisha, Norma, 206
Blackburn, Maurice, 157; *Canadian First*, 78
Blackstone, Milton, 14, 25, 31
Bohm, Jerome, 101
Bornstein, Eli, 179–80, 198, 200, 210, 211, 309
Boughton, Rutland: *The Immortal Hours*, 79
Boulanger, Nadia, 186, 201
Bowie, Michael, 206, 207
Boyle, Harry J., 105, 112
Brahms, Johannes, 44, 45, 82, 83; *Botschaft*, 47; *Hungarian Dances*, 40; *Das Mädchen Spricht*, 47; *Requiem*, 5, 50
Brault, Cédia, 18, 20
Brault, Victor, 11
Bream, Julian, 191
Brecht, Bertolt, 199
Brennand, Tom, 43
Brewster, Jim, 37, 42
Bridle, Augustus, 43, 50, 54, 95, 99, 150
British Broadcasting Corporation (BBC), 21
Britten, Benjamin, 85, 94, 102, 110, 113, 178, 191–2, 193, 257; *Albert Herring*, 84, 92, 105; *Cabaret Songs*, 256; *Les Illuminations*, 108, 109; *Let's Make an Opera*, 105; *Peter Grimes*, 84, 85, 92, 105, 110, 112, 114, 116; *Saint Nicolas Cantata*, 111; *War Requiem*, 191; *Young Apollo*, 57
Brockington, Leonard, 57
Brooker, Bertram, 64
Brott, Alexander, 74, 147, 149, 157, 219; *Violin Concerto*, 156; *War and Peace*, 78

Brough, George, 102, 120, 153
Brown, Donald, 112
Brownlee, John, 79
Brymner, William, 46
Buckwold, Sidney, 200
Burnett, Robert, 15
Burns, Robert, 13, 15, 20
Burt, Allan, 16–17
Bushnell, Ernest, 105
Button, Henry, 17
Byers, Bettina, 159

Cable, Howard, 77, 147
Calgary String Ensemble, 58
Callaghan, Morley, 160
Cameron, Dan A., 18
Campbell, Finley, 17
Campbell, Francean, 78
Campbell, Wishart, 22
Canada Council, vii, viii, 108, 156, 160, 170–1, 175, 195, 208–9, 212, 227, 247, 252, 258
Canadian Academy of Music, 25, 29, 31–2
Canadian Artists' Association, 162
Canadian Arts Council, 162, 167
Canadian Broadcasting Corporation (CBC), vii, 31, 53, 111, 113, 114, 115, 137, 140, 143, 146, 160, 165, 167, 168–9, 186, 214, 248, 257; CBC Concert Orchestra, 156; CBC Opera Company, 105, 111–12, 113; CBC Radio Canada International, 98, 157, 161, 218, 227; CBC Symphony Orchestra, 30, 55, 139, 144, 147–9, 153, 216, 218, 219, 225; 'CBC Tuesday Night,' 223, 231; 'CBC Wednesday Night,' 103–4, 108, 109, 111, 113, 143, 202; establishment of, 57–9, 'Festival Celebrations,' 248; and Frances James, 42, 91, 99, 105, 106, 143; and Murray Adaskin, 216, 217, 222, 227; music broadcasts 1940s-50s, 105–6, 110–11, 147; music broadcasts 1970s-80s, 251–2; wartime programs, 74–84

Canadian Concert Association, 45, 126
Canadian League of Composers, 113, 144, 147, 153–8, 172, 208, 258
Canadian Music Associates (CMA), 157–8
Canadian Music Centre, 171, 186, 235, 253, 254
Canadian Music Council, 162, 260
Canadian National Railway (CNR), 51, 52
Canadian Pacific Railway (CPR), 3, 6–7, 12–14, 15–17, 18, 19, 34, 38, 41, 46, 47, 84, 115, 172; hotels, 5, 6, 7, 8, 42, 62; sponsored broadcasts, 21, 51, 52–3; sponsored concert series, 17–18, 19; sponsored music festivals, 10–14, 22
Canadian Radio Broadcasting Commission (CRBC), 21, 22, 52, 57
Canadian Review of Music and Art, 36, 74, 146, 159
Canadian String Quartet, 227
Canoe Lake (Algonquin Park), 61, 65, 66, 148, 187, 208–9, 216, 220–1, 223, 231
Carlyle, Trudy, 112–13, 157, 188
Carr, Emily, 69–70, 199; Klee Wyck, 70
Carter, Elliott: Woodwind Quintet, 193
Cassenti Players, 227
Casson, Alfred, J., 65, 68, 221
Celebrity Concert Series, 121, 191
Chailley, Marcel, 32
Chamber Players of Toronto, 247
Champagne, Claude, 147, 161; Suite Canadienne, 14
Charlesworth, Hector, 17, 21, 22, 44, 49, 57, 95, 99
Château Frontenac, 5, 6, 10–11, 12; see also Canadian Pacific Railway, hotels
Château Lake Louise, 14–15, 35; see also Canadian Pacific Railway, hotels
Cherney, Brian, 234
Chopin, Frederick, 40, 183, 210; Etude in A-Flat, 83
Chotem, Neil, 147, 149, 197
Chuhaldin, Alexander, 56–7, 58, 137
Churchill, Winston, 73
Clapperton, Walter, 4, 5, 52, 86

Clark, Greta, 201
Clark, Paraskeva, 32, 65–6, 71, 72
Clark, Philip, 32, 66, 154
Clarkson, Austin, 184–5, 186, 189, 206
Clough, H.B., 9
Cocteau, Jean, 140
Collingwood, Arthur, 174, 176
Collins, Buddy, 27
Columbia Concerts Incorporated, 121
Comfort, Charles, 64, 65, 68, 71
Community Concert Series, 121, 122, 123–33, 168
Composers, Authors, and Publishers Association of Canada (CAPAC), 84, 104, 208
Les Concerts Symphoniques de Montréal, 81
Connor, Ralph. See Gordon, Rev Charles W.
Conservatoire de Musique et d'Art Dramatique, 212
Copland, Aaron, 85, 105, 113, 141, 145, 154, 182, 258; Emily Dickinson Songs, 189; Rodeo, 193
Cordon, Norman, 50
Coriveau, L. de B., 159
Corwin, George, 219, 249
Coulter, John, 79, 106, 107, 108, 149, 159, 160, 161, 162
Coulthard, Jean, 85, 147, 149, 157, 161, 252; Two Shakespeare Sonnets, 135; Two Songs of the Haida Indians, 97, 98
Crerar, Louis, 19, 36, 39, 63, 81, 105, 120, 139, 149, 150
Crum, George, 156
Czaplinski, Henri, 31–2

Dainty, Ernest, 54, 78
Dalhousie University, 117
Dallapiccola, Luigi, 210; The Prisoner, 105, 112; Quaderno Musicale di Anna Libera, 193
Daly, Tom, 213
Daunais, Lionel, 81, 106

Davies, Gordon, 66
Davies, Robertson, 79
Davis, Gordon, 107
Davis, Laura, 223
Dawes, Andrew, 152, 193, 194, 201
Deacon, John, 20, 21–2, 39
Debussy, Claude, 33, 43, 47, 86, 90, 93, 116, 137, 140, 194; *Ariettes Oubliées*, 96; *Chansons de Bilitis*, 94, 95, 109; *La Demoiselle Elue*, 109; *L'Enfant Prodigue*, 91; *Pelléas et Mélisande*, 248
Delius, Frederick, 47, 48, 109
Dembeck, John, 156, 157
Dembeck String Quartet, 143, 308
Dempsey, Jack, 92
Desjardins, Jeanne, 81
Detroit Symphony Orchestra, 48, 223, 244
Dolin, Samuel, 154, 157; *Sinfonietta*, 156
Donay, Harvey, 53
Dowland, John, 81
Doyle, Deirdre, 28
Druian, Rafael, 193, 194
Dubinsky, Isadore, 31, 59
Duncan, Chester, 202; *Six Songs*, 108, 189
Duncan, Douglas, 68–9
Dunn, Sir James Hamet, 170
Dunton, Davidson, 104
Duparc, Henri, 43, 47
Durey, Louis, 140
Dusseau, Jeanne, 14, 18, 19, 20, 22, 47, 87

Eaton Auditorium, 43, 44, 48
Eckhardt-Gramatté, Sophie-Carmen: *Duo Concertante for Cello and Piano*, 194
Eddy, Nelson, 58
Edmonton Symphony Orchestra, 156
Edmonton Varsity Musical Club, 117
Edward, prince of Wales, 35
Eisdell, Hubert, 48, 49
Elgar, Sir Edward, 48; *La Capricieuse*, 30–1

Elizabeth II, 148, 216, 219, 236
Ellestad, Mark, 245
Elliott, Carleton, 234
Elman, Mischa, 63
Elton, Jack, 155, 156
Empire Theatre (Toronto), 28, 33
L'Ensemble Instrumental de Montréal, 58

Faith, Percy, 22, 28, 56, 138
Faucght, Anne, 3
Fauré, Gabriel, 43, 90, 143
Federation of Canadian Artists, 158–9, 162, 169
Feldbrill, Victor, 219, 223, 231
Fenyves, Lorand, 151, 201, 254
Ferreras, Salvador, 249
Fiala, George, 234
Finzi, Gerald, 94; *Dies Natalis*, 93, 109
Fischer-Dieskau, Dietrich, 191
FitzGerald, Lemoine, 66–7
Fleming, Amy, 17, 20, 22, 79
Fleming, Bill, 201
Fleming, Robert, 78, 97, 146, 147, 149, 157, 234; *Summer Suite*, 197
Forest Hill Community Centre, 97, 151–2
Fortier, Achille, 11, 14
Fort William Music and Arts Club, 117
Foss, Lukas, 247
Fredette, Paul, 231
Freedman, Harry, 141, 145, 154, 157, 197; *Symphonette*, 156
Freeman, Paul, 225, 244, 251
French, Ward, 122; correspondence with Frances James, 123–33
Fricker, Herbert A., 48, 50, 51, 59, 95
Fritsch, Peter H., 101, 102, 143

Gabora, Taras, 227
Gabora String Quartet, 231
Gagen, R.F., 46
Gagnier, J.J., 147
Gagnon, Clarence A., 12
Garcia, Albert, 75
Gardiner, Glenn, 112

Garnier, Liliane, 213
Gati, Laszlo, 244
Gay, John: *The Beggar's Opera*, 78
Gee, A.K., 121
Gee, Fred M., 121
Geiger-Torel, Herman, 112, 231, 234
Gelmon, Sydney and Miriam, 198
General Electric (GE), 21, 54
George VI, 41–2
George, Graham, 78
Gershwin, George, 256; *Rhapsody in Blue*, 27
Gibbon, John Murray, 5, 6, 8–9, 13–14, 15, 17–18, 19, 38, 39, 41, 42, 46, 47, 53, 74, 78, 81, 82–4, 115, 158–9; *Brahms and Schubert Songs Transplanted*, 83; *Canadian Folk Songs Old and New*, 11; *Love Song from the Caravan*, 18; *Magic of Melody*, 83; *Northland Songs*, 19, 47; *Prince Charlie and Flora*, 16; *Songbook of the Trail Riders of the Canadian Rockies*, 10; *see also* Canadian Pacific Railway
Gibbs, Terence, 105, 109, 110, 111, 113, 114, 148
Gilbert and Sullivan, 80; *The Gondoliers*, 52; *The Mikado*, 52
Ginkle, Peter van, 231
Gluck, Christoph Willibald von: *Orfeo ed Euridice*, 83, 111, 112
Godden, Reginald, 45, 54, 81, 124, 138, 150, 153
Goldschmidt, Nicholas, 112
Goodman, Benny, 35
Goodman, Hyman, 43, 59, 62, 150
Goossens, Eugene, 79
Goossens, Leon, 191
Gordon, Rev Charles W., 15, 37
Goss, John, 17, 20
Gounod, Charles: *Ave Maria*, 18, 40; *Faust*, 5
Graham, George, 78
Grant, Cuthbert, 230
Gratton, Hector, 78, 146, 147

Gray, Enid, 20, 22
Greene, Lorne, 77
Grosart, Alistair, 76
Group of Seven, 16, 30, 44, 65, 67, 96, 199, 220, 221
Gustin, Lyell, 186

Hahn, Emmanuel, 65, 66
Haig, Jean, 16, 20, 22, 79
Halle, Adam de la: *Le Jeu de Robin et Marion*, 13
Ham, Albert, 32
Ham, George, 7
Hambourg, Boris, 25, 31, 43, 54
Hambourg Conservatory, 31–2
Hambourg Trio, 58
Handel, George Frederick, 40, 45, 75; *Acis and Galatea*, 78, 79, 82; *Joshua*, 82; *Judas Maccabaeus*, 82; *Messiah*, 4, 5, 50, 59, 84, 87, 92, 94, 95, 96, 134; *Rodelinda*, 47; *Samson*, 82; *Semele*, 82; *Solomon*, 82
Harris, Frank D., 78
Harris, Lawren, 44, 64, 65, 70, 161, 221, 222
Hart, E.J., 7
Hart House, 43, 44, 45, 135, 176
Hart House String Quartet, 11, 14, 17, 18, 19, 20, 25–6, 45, 48, 52, 58
Hassler, Hans, 194
Haydn, Franz Joseph: *Toy Symphony*. *See* Mozart, Leopold
Haydon, A. Eustace, 222
Hayes, Roland, 87, 89–90, 91, 99, 121, 246
Head, Michael, 18
Heather, Alfred, 16, 17, 18, 53; Light Opera Company, 19, 21, 22, 39
Heifetz, Jascha, 96
Heifetz, Josepha, 141, 142
Heim, Emmy, 48, 50, 87, 88–9, 91, 99, 101, 109, 112, 202
Heins, Donald, 59
Helmer, Terence, 193
Hepner, Lee, 219

Hersenhoren, Samuel, 28, 30, 59, 62, 76,
  77, 78, 81, 82, 147
Herzberg, Gerhard, 175
Hess, Myra, 48, 95
Hess, Willy, 30
Hesson, Jeanne, 50
Hewetson, Herbert, 17, 18, 20, 21
Hill, Charles, 65, 71
Hindemith, Paul, 85, 93, 94, 100, 102,
  105, 146, 147; *Hin und Zurück*, 201;
  Das Marienleben, 44, 91, 99–100, 101,
  102, 120, 143; *Nine English Songs*, 106,
  116
Hockridge, Edmund, 111
Hoffman, Irwin, 226
Hoffmannsthal, Hugo von, 88
Hofmann, Josef, 29–30
Holst, Gustav, 48
Honegger, Arthur, 140
Hood, Florence, 17
Horlick, Louis and Ruth, 198
Hornyansky, Nicholas, 159
Horowitz, Vladimir, 29
House, Lawrence, 226, 248
Hughes, Rosemary, 47–8
Humphreys, W. Eason, 160
Hunter, James, 213

Ibert, Jacques, 220
Imperial Order of the Daughters of the
  Empire, 117
Institute of International Affairs, 165
International Society for Contemporary
  Music, 156
Ives, Charles, 141, 182, 256; *Violin
  Sonata No 1*, 193–4

Jackson, A.Y., 12, 44, 64, 65, 68, 74
James, Bess Louise, 3, 8
James, Frances, vii
– and women's musical clubs, 45–6,
  116–17
– association with Canadian visual artists,
  64, 65–7, 69–71, 199–200

– as teacher, 112–13; in Saskatchewan,
  200–1; in Victoria, 243–6, 259–60
– as touring concert artist, 117–21
– childhood and education of, 3–5;
  musical education, 4–5, 86–7, 89, 90–2
– correspondence with Ward French of
  Community Concert Series, 121,
  123–33
– dress of, 85–6
– her submission to the Massey
  Commission, 167–9, 171
– performances of: in Banff, 5, 6, 8, 9–10,
  14–15, 19–20, 34, 36, 37, 39, 40, 41,
  42; on CBC radio, 58, 79, 82, 84, 103,
  105, 106, 108, 112, 115; in CPR ballad
  operas, 16–17; in CPR concert series, 18,
  38; in CPR music festivals, 22; on radio,
  21, 22, 51, 53, 54; in Santa Barbara,
  142–3; in Saskatchewan, 183, 185, 188,
  194, 202–3; in Toronto, 43, 44, 45,
  47–51, 59; on tour, 117–21
– *premières* in Canada: of Canadian
  works, 78, 79–80, 85, 93, 98, 106–8,
  139, 149, 153, 213; of non-Canadian
  works, 85, 93–4, 96–100, 101–2, 111,
  113
James, Frederick W., 3
James, Robert, 3
James, Ruth, 3
Jamieson, Robert, 193
Jammes, Francis, 149
Jefferys, C.W., 71
Jennings, Charles, 53, 54, 83, 97, 105, 112
Les Jeunesses Musicales, 165
Jobin, Raoul, 79, 124
Jocom, John, 150
Johnson, Bernard, 112
Johnson, Edward, 22, 248
Johnston, Richard, 223, 234
Jones, Charles, 43–4, 47, 140, 143, 193,
  256; *Sonata for Violin and Piano*,
  193
Jones, Kelsey, 85
Joyce, James, 149

Kallmann, Helmut, 171
Kaplan, David, 190, 207
Karsh, Yousuf, 95
Kasemets, Udo, 157, 195, 197, 223; *Sinfonietta*, 194
Kash, Eugene, 59, 62, 152
Kaufmann, Walter, 157; *Madras Express*, 156
Kenderdine, Gus, 176
Kenins, Talivaldis, 197
Kennedy, Daisy, 205
Kennedy, Margaret, 15, 17
Kennedy-Fraser, Marjory, 15, 17
Ketèlbey, Albert: *In a Persian Market*, 28
Key, Harold Eustace, 9, 18–19, 33, 39; *Christmas with Herrick*, 16, 18; *In Flanders Fields*, 18
Killam, Isaak Walton, 170
King, William Lyon Mackenzie, 41
Kinsmen's Club, 117, 191
Knowles, Dorothy, 199
Kolbinson, Lauren, 188, 189
Kolbinson, Steven, 204–5
Koldofsky, Aldolph, 19, 30, 33, 44, 48, 49, 159
Koldofsky, Gwendolyn Williams, 17, 19, 44, 47, 120
Komorous, Rudolf, 245
Kraglund, John, 220
Kraus, Greta, 152
Kreisler, Fritz, 40, 228
Kresz, Geza de, 25, 48
Kresz, Norah de, 48
Krieghoff, Cornelius, 12
Kroiter, Roman, 213
Krolik, Jeff, 246–7
Kunits, Luigi von, 25, 29, 31–2, 43, 45, 52, 59
Kurenko, Maria, 91–2, 113, 121, 246
Kushner, Gordon, 157
Kviesis, Victor, 196

Laderoute, Joseph Victor, 41
Laliberté, Alfred, 11

LaMarsh, Judy, 208–9
Lambert, George, 20, 21, 106
Landowska, Wanda, 80
Lapp, Horace, 36, 39, 42, 58
Laval University, 163
Laverock, George, 248
Law, Eileen, 95
Lawes, Henry, 81
Lay, Nelson, 75
Lebrun, Louise, 213
Leddy, Francis, 172, 173, 175, 179
Leduc, Roland, 194
Lehmann, Lotte, 48, 131
Lévesque, Georges-Henri, 163
Lewis, Catherine, 225, 246, 251
Leyton-Brown, Howard, 188
Lichtenstein, Clara, 4–5
Lindner, Ernest, 176, 199
Lismer, Arthur, 12, 16, 17, 31, 44, 64, 65, 68
Liszt, Franz, 4; *Die Lorelei*, 109
Little, George, 194
Little Symphony of Montreal, 81, 93
Loring, Frances, 65
Lucas, Norman, 195
Lunenburg Ladies' Trio, 58

McAllister, Peter, 248–9
McCartney, Stanley, 247
McCool, Major Brian S., 149
McCowan, Dan, 36
McCrae, John, 18
MacDermid, Fred, 198
MacDermid, Margaret, 198, 200
McDonald, Boyd, 109, 186–7, 188, 189, 190, 194, 201, 203, 207
MacDonald, J.E.H., 38, 221
MacDonald, Rose, 97
McFarland, R.B., 207
McFee, Allan, 75
McGill Conservatorium, 4, 5
McGill Operatic and Choral Society, 52
McGill Quartet, 58
McGill University, 4, 5, 185

Machaut, Guillaume de, 89
McInnes, J. Campbell, 11, 14, 16, 19, 20, 44, 48, 49, 79
MacIntyre, David, 245
MacKenzie, Duncan, 4
MacKenzie, Jane, 246
MacKenzie, Norman A.M., 163
MacLaren, Norman, 213
McLean, J.S., 67
McLeod, T.H., 197–8
McLeod, Wendell, 181
MacMillan, Andrew, 112
MacMillan, Sir Ernest, 11, 17, 18, 19, 20, 29, 45, 48, 49–50, 51, 57, 59, 60, 61, 62, 75, 79, 82, 88, 92, 95, 96, 134, 157, 161, 162, 218, 219; as arranger, 16, 19, 43, 47, 53; as composition teacher, 137–8; Ode to England, 94–5, 97; Six Bergerettes du Bas Canada, 14
MacMillan, Keith, 253–4
MacMillan, Winnifred, 17
McNutt, Walter, 78
Mahler, Gustav, 113; Symphony No 4 in G Major, 95
Malcolm, Scott, 45, 54, 124
Malcuzinski, Victor, 95
Malenfant, Cosima, 81
Mamott, Isaac, 153
Marchand, Charles, 11, 13
Mari, Nona, 231
Marr, Frances, 43, 226
Marriott, Anne, 149
Marshall, Lois, 94, 96
Marter, Eric de la, 14
Marinu, Bohuslav: Seven Arabesques, 189
Massey, Vincent, 25, 67, 68, 87, 163
Massey Commission, 123, 163–71, 172, 175
Massey Hall, 48, 59, 94, 155, 156
Mather, Bruce, 109, 256
Mather, Eddie, 204
Matheson, Ruth, 20, 22
Mathieu, André, 146

Matthews, Charles, 62, 68
Maxted, Stanley, 18, 20, 21, 22, 53, 54
Maynard, Dorothy, 89
Mazzoleni, Ettore, 80, 106, 107, 108, 112, 153, 159
Mendel, Fred, 136, 199–200
Mendelssohn-Bartholdy, Felix, 142; Andante Espressivo in C Minor, 40
Mendelssohn Choir (Toronto), 48, 59, 79, 95
Mercure, Pierre, 146, 157, 195
Metropolitan Opera, 57, 75, 80, 111
Milhaud, Darius, 44, 85, 101, 102, 105, 109, 140–5, 156, 182, 186, 189–90, 193, 194, 218–19, 258; La Création du Monde, 256; Duo for Two Unaccompanied Violins, 190; Fête de Montmartre, 47; Fumée, 47; Hymne de Glorification, 190; Rêves, 108–9, 143, 190; Sonatine for Flute and Piano, 190; Sonatine for Viola and Cello, 189, 192, 193; Suite for Violin, Clarinet, and Piano, 190
Miller, Eva Mendel, 199
Milligan, James, 157
Milne, A.A.: When We Were Very Young, 18
Milne, David, 67–8, 69, 136
Montreal Arts Association, 74
Montreal Bach Choir, 194
Montreal Symphony Orchestra, 57, 81
Montreal Women's Symphony Orchestra, 147
Moore, Mavor, 77
Morant, Nick, 35–6, 37, 38
Morawetz, Oscar, 157, 252
Morel, François, 146
Morgan, Ernest, 20–1, 106
Morrison, Mary, 157
Morson, Beatrice, 16, 53
Morton, William, 79, 81, 82, 95, 106, 107, 111, 112
Moss, Earle, 97, 109, 120
Mozart, Leopold: Toy Symphony

(formerly attributed to Franz Joseph Haydn), 41
Mozart, Wolfgang Amadeus, 131, 142, 255, 258; *Don Giovanni*, 112; *Exsultate, Jubilate*, 18; *The Magic Flute*, 83
Muhlstock, Louis, 65–6, 71
Mulcaster, Winona, 199
Murray, W.E. Gladstone, 57
Murray, Walter, 174–5, 177, 182, 214
Music Academy of the West (Santa Barbara), 44, 101, 109, 140, 142
Music Committee, 162
Mussorgsky, Modest, 89, 140

National Arts Centre, 171, 224; National Arts Centre Orchestra, 171, 247
National Carbon Company Studios, 25
National Concert and Artists Corporation, 168
National Film Board (NFB), 165, 170, 212, 213
National Gallery, 46, 66, 71, 158, 165, 170
National Library, 171
National Museum, 166, 223
National Research Council, 175
National Youth Orchestra, 208, 223
Natzke, Oscar, 75, 79, 87, 95
Naylor, Bernard, 81, 93–4, 120, 212; *C. Day Lewis Suite*, 98; *'Emily' Variations and Fughetta for Violin and Piano*, 213; *From Feathers to Iron*, 108; *King Solomon's Prayer*, 116, 117; *Not so Far as the Forest*, 213; *Presences*, 213; *String Trio*, 213; *Suite for High Voice and Piano*, 108, 213
Neatby, Hilda, 163, 175
Neel, Boyd, 140, 257
Nelson, G. Blair, 198
Nelson, Mary, 198, 200
Nelsova, Zara, 95
Neumann, Mark, 247
Newmark, John, 120

New Symphony Orchestra (1923–7). *See* Toronto Symphony Orchestra
New World Chamber Orchestra, 81
Nimmons, Arlene, 157
Nimmons, Philip, 154, 157
Nono, Luigi, 193
Noxon, Gerald, 77

O'Brien, Oscar, 14, 18; *Canadian Folk Songs Old and New*, 11; *Love Song from the Caravan*, 18
Ogilvie, Will, 64
O'Hara, Geoffrey, 11
Oldfield, Frank, 54
Onovski, Joyce, 36
Ontario Arts Council, 247
Ontario College of Art, 37
Order of Trail Riders of the Canadian Rockies, 8–10; *see also* Gibbon, John Murray
Orford String Quartet, 193, 205, 310
Orloff, Captain Boris, 76–7
Ostry, Bernard, 163
Ottawa Choral Society, 87, 95

Paderewski, Ignacy Jan, 210
Paër, Ferdinando, 194
Paganini, Niccolò, 189; *Caprices*, 61
Page, P.K., 249–50
Papineau-Couture, Jean, 146, 154, 157, 212, 252; *Aria pour Violon Seul*, 213; *Pièce Concertante No 4*, 194; *Quatrains*, 213; *Suite pour Violon Seul*, 213; *Trois Pièces*, 197
Paquin, Marie-Thérèse, 74, 120
Paquin, Ulysse, 20
Paray, Paul, 223
Parlow, Kathleen, 61–2, 135
Patrick, Marnie, 201
Patterson, Lisette, 87
Paulee, Mona, 124
Payne, Marjory, 58
Pears, Peter, 111, 178, 191
Pedersen, Paul, 185–6, 194

Peerce, Jan, 95
Pelletier, Wilfrid, 13–14, 57
Pentland, Barbara, 77, 78, 85, 97, 98, 147, 212, 252; *Caprice*, 213; *Fantasy*, 213; *Five Preludes*, 145–6; *Piano Quartet*, 145–6; *Rhapsody*, 145–6; *Shadows*, 213; *Song Cycle*, 116, 149, 150, 151; *String Quartet No 1*, 213; *Studies in Line*, 145–6, 150, 151; *Trio Con Alea*, 213
Pepall, George, 161
Pépin, Clermont, 78, 146, 157, 212, 252; *Cycle-Eluard*, 213; *String Quartet No 2*, 213; *Suite for Violin, Cello, and Piano*, 213; *Variations for String Quartet*, 213
Pepper, John, 193
Perehudoff, Bill, 199
Pergolesi, Giovanni Battista: *La Serva Padrona*, 201
Perrins, D.H.C.: *Scena for Soprano, Baritone, and Orchestra*, 5
Phillips, Walter, 38
Piastro, Michel, 80, 96
Pierné, Gabriel: *Children's Crusade*, 94
Plamondon, Lucien, 17
Plamondon, Rodolphe, 17, 20
Pleyel, Ignaz: violin duet Opus 48, 226, 261 (Ex 1)
Pope, Alexander, 229
Poulenc, Francis, 140, 194
Pratt, E.J., 31
Pratz, Albert, 59, 61, 151
Price, Bruce, 7
Primrose, William, 61
Prokofiev, Sergey: *Love for Three Oranges*, 22
Puccini, Giacomo: *La Bohème*, 112
Purcell, Henry, 81; *Dido and Aeneas*, 78, 185, 189
Purcell String Quartet, 248, 310

Quartet Canada, 248
Le Quatuor de Montréal, 58

Queen's University, 96, 117
Quilter, Roger, 5, 18, 47, 81

Rachmaninoff, Sergey, 18, 63
Ramsay, Captain Alexander, 16
Rathburn, Eldon, 78, 146, 157, 197, 212, 213; *Images of Childhood*, 156
Ravel, Maurice, 43, 109
Ray, Marcel, 36
Ready, Margaret, 201
Richardson, B.T., 199
Ridout, Godfrey, 77, 78, 145, 146, 147, 157, 159
Riel, Louis, 230
Rilke, Rainer Maria, 88, 91, 99
Roberts, John Peter Lee, 105, 216, 218
Rolston, Thomas, 190
Romanelli, Luigi, 58
Roubakine, Boris, 210
Rousseau, Henri, 139–40
Rowe, Jean, 17
Royal Canadian Academy of Arts, 161
Royal Commission on National Development in the Arts, Letters and Sciences. *See* Massey Commission
Royal Conservatory of Music of Toronto, 17, 19, 25, 29, 30, 31–2, 56, 61, 80, 100, 111–12, 153, 157, 253; opera school, 106, 108, 112; string quartet, 53, 58
Royal Society of Arts (London), 208
Royal Victoria College (Montreal), 4; *see also* McGill Conservatorium
Royal York Hotel (Toronto), 12, 16, 17, 31, 36, 53, 73, 134, 139, 155, 172; *see also* Canadian Pacific Railway, hotels
Rungius, Carl, 38
Russell, G. Horne, 46

Sabiston, Colin, 151
St Laurent, Louis, 163
Sampson, Peggie, 188, 189, 194
Sanda, Mabel, 203
Saskatchewan Centre of the Arts, 24, 225

Saskatchewan Cosmopolitan Club, 196–7, 198
Saskatchewan Musical Association, 174, 176
Saskatoon Kiwanis Club, 198
Saskatoon Music Council, 208
Saskatoon Symphony Orchestra, 187, 193, 196, 197, 202,̓ 223
Satie, Erik, 140, 146
Scherman, Paul, 77, 81
Schoenberg, Arnold, 88, 105, 182, 189; *Aufgeregten*, 108; *Erhebung*, 108; *Gurrelieder*, 113; string quartet, 29; *Traumleben*, 108
Schubert, Franz, 40, 44, 82, 83, 89, 93, 131; *An die Musik*, 47; *Die Forelle*, 47; *Gretchen am Spinnrade*, 47
Schumann, Robert, 113; *Abegg Variations*, 236; *Träumerei*, 83
Schumann-Heink, Madame, 29
Schuster, Frank, 75
Scott, Cyril, 5, 18
Scott, Howard, 79, 80
Seeney, John, 213
Seitz, Ernst, 54, 78
Serkin, Rudolf, 95
Sessions, Roger, 210
Shandor, Arpad, 96, 123, 131
Sharman, Rod, 245
Shaughnessy, Sir Thomas J., 7, 8
Sherman, Louis, 28
Sibelius, Jean, 30, 48, 94
Simms, John, 193, 194
Simoneau, Leopold, 122, 124
Simon Fraser University, 245
Simpson, Charles W., 13, 16
Simson, Fraser, 18
Slater, Montague, 110
Smith, Leo, 14, 43, 45, 59, 60, 137, 138, 154
Smith, Nellie, 106
Smyth, Dame Ethel, 17
Solem, R.J., 207
Solway, Maurice, 30, 59

Somers, Harry, 76, 85, 98, 109, 138, 145, 152, 154, 157, 195, 252; *North Country*, 146, 156; *Picasso Suite*, 197; *Scherzo for Strings*, 146; *Sketches for Orchestra*, 146; *Testament of Youth*, 150, 151; *Three Songs*, 97, 149, 150–1
Spinks, J.W.T., 177
Spivak, Elie, 59, 128, 151, 157
Spivak, Philip, 36, 59–60
Standard, Paul, 38, 41
Stanick, Gerald, 194
Statten, Ethel, 221–2
Statten, Taylor, 221–2, 236
Steinberg, Albert, 140
Stern, Isaac, 95, 201
Stewart, George, 80
Stewart, Reginald, 47–8, 54
Stratford Festival, 146, 195, 218
Strauss, Richard, 31, 40, 93
Stravinsky, Igor, 85, 143, 146, 182, 183–4, 255; *Firebird*, 43; *L'Histoire du Soldat*, 184, 210, 256; *Octet for Wind Instruments*, 184; *Petrushka*, 43, 220; *Piano Sonata*, 183; *The Rake's Progress*, 84, 92, 105, 112, 113, 203
Stravinsky, Soulima, 178, 183
Stuart, Sylvia, 190, 201
Stump, Sarain, 225
Sumberg, Harold, 30, 43, 59, 81
Surdin, Morris, 147
Surveyor, Arthur, 163
Susskind, Walter, 219
Swetnam, Dorothy, 120

Tagliaferro, Edith, 28
Tailleferre, Germaine, 140
Tait, R.S., 16
Taylor, Kendall, 226
Taylor, Tom, 105, 216–17, 218, 229, 248, 254
Tchaikovsky, Pyotr Ilyich, 223; *Capriccio Italien*, 40; *Romeo and Juliet*, 220
Thistle, Lauretta, 192, 228
Thom, Ruth. *See* Dusseau, Jeanne

Thomas, Lowell, 73
Thompson, W.P., 173, 175, 176, 177, 178–9, 182, 196, 203, 214
Thomson, Hugh, 110
Thomson, Tom, 67, 221, 222
Toronto Conservatory of Music. *See* Royal Conservatory of Music of Toronto
Toronto Society for Contemporary Music, 99
Toronto Symphony Orchestra (TSO), 29–30, 51, 52, 57, 59–60, 62, 79, 81, 92, 94, 95, 109, 134, 147, 155, 157, 220, 223
Toronto Trio, 19, 31, 45, 46, 51, 58, 62, 64, 73, 134–5, 155, 172
Toronto Woodwind Quintet, 213
Toscanini, Arturo, 61
Totenberg, Roman, 101, 143, 148, 225, 254
Tourel, Jennie, 100
Tracy, Clarence, 179
Tsutsumi, Tsuyoshi, 247
Tuckwell, Barry, 227
Tudor Singers (Montreal), 45, 48
Tudor String Quartet (Winnipeg), 58
Turczynska, Madame, 210
Turgeon, J. Gray, 161; Turgeon Committee, 161–2, 163, 171
Turini, Ronald, 247
Turner, Robert, 195, 217, 234; *Variations and Toccata for Ten Instruments*, 194
Twa, Andrew, 154, 157

United Nations Educational, Scientific, and Cultural Organization (UNESCO), 164, 170
United States League of Composers, 146
University of British Columbia (UBC), 117, 118, 163, 212, 213
University of Manitoba, 108, 218
University of Montreal, 213
University of Regina, 227
University of Saskatchewan, 113, 143, 145, 163, 166, 172, 173, 174, 180–1,
196, 203, 205, 208, 210, 214, 215, 226, 242, 248, 260; Golden Jubilee Music Festival, 188, 189, 194–5, 223; music department, 176, 184–5, 189, 205–7
University of Toronto, 44, 68, 80, 98, 163, 186, 205, 212
University of Victoria, 219, 244, 245, 247, 248, 249, 259, 320
University of Western Ontario, 96, 117, 247
University of Windsor, 175, 247
Upper Canada College, 87, 98

Vancouver International Festival, 195, 227
Vancouver Symphony Orchestra, 81, 226
Vancouver Youth Orchestra, 235
Vaughan Williams, Ralph: *Benedicite*, 94; *Five Mystical Songs*, 20; *Hugh the Drover*, 17, 19, 78; *Sea Symphony*, 20
Victoria Choral Society, 244, 320
Victoria Conservatory of Music, 244, 259
Victoria Festival Quartette, 18
Victoria International Festival, 248
Victoria Musical Arts Society, 117, 244
Victoria Music Festival, 244, 245
Victoria Symphony Orchestra, 225, 244, 246, 249, 251
Vidal, Pierre, 14
Vishnevskaya, Galina, 191
Voaden, Herman, 97, 161, 162
Vogt, A.S., 19
Vogt, Augustus, 95

Waddington, Geoffrey, 25, 30–1, 54–6, 58, 75, 80, 102, 105, 109, 110, 112, 114, 139, 147, 148, 153, 155, 156, 184, 214, 216, 217, 218, 254
Wagner, Richard, 48, 140; *Die Meistersinger*, 75; *Die Walküre*, 50
Waizman, Louis, 31, 138
Walcott, Charles D., 9
Walter, Arnold, 44, 78, 97, 98–9, 100, 112
Walter, Bruno, 195
Walton, Sir William, 43, 48

Ward, John: *The Crucible*, 153
Warlock, Peter, 5, 43
Watson, Jean, 124, 126
Wayne, Johnny, 75
Weill, Kurt, 199, 256
Weinzweig, John, 63, 76, 77, 78, 82, 85, 98, 134, 138–9, 141, 145, 146, 147, 153–4, 155, 157, 161, 197, 218, 252, 256; *Divertimento No 1*, 139, 213; *Divertimento No 3*, 194, 213; *Israel Sonata*, 153; *Of Time, Rain, and the World*, 97, 108, 149, 153, 213; *Sonata in One Movement for Violin and Piano*, 150, 151; *Three Songs*, 213; *Violin Sonata*, 135; *Woodwind Quintet*, 213
Welsman, Frank, 29, 32
Whitehead, Alfred E., 4, 5, 50, 58, 79, 81, 95, 106, 303
Whitman, Walt, 97, 149
Whyte, Catharine, 37–8, 185, 187, 201, 203, 225
Whyte, Peter, 37–8, 231
Widner, Mark, 247
Wild, Eric, 217
Willan, Healey, 5, 11, 47, 81, 97, 108, 138, 154, 161; *The Ayreshire Ploughman*, 16–17, 19, 20; *The Chester Mysteries*, 16; *Deirdre of the Sorrows*, 85, 105, 106–8, 110, 112; *Indian Nativity Play*, 16; *Order of Good Cheer*, 16; *Prince Charlie and Flora*, 16, 21; string quartet, 43; *Symphony No 1*, 43; *Transit through Fire*, 78, 79–80, 82, 106, 107; directs Tudor Singers, 45, 48
Williams, Gwendolyn. *See* Koldolfsky, Gwendolyn Williams

Williamson, Robert, 210–11
Wilson, Allan, 16
Wilson, Milton, 101
Wilson, Tom, 8, 37
Winnipeg Ballet, 144
Winnipeg Symphony Orchestra, 223
Wolf, Hugo, 93, 101, 116, 117
Women's musical clubs, 42–3, 45–6, 116–17; Ladies' Musical Club, Halifax, 98; Montreal Ladies Morning Musical Club, 46, 117; Women's Musical Club of Toronto, 44; Vancouver Women's Musical Club, 46; Victoria Ladies' Musical Club, 117, 244; Women's Musical Club of Winnipeg, 116
Wood, Christopher, 159
Wood, Josephine, 18, 20, 22
Wood, Robin, 244, 245
Wood, Winifred, 244
Wright, Catherine, 17, 20, 22
Wyle, Florence, 65
Wyn Wood, Elizabeth, 65, 66, 160–1, 162

Young, Phillip T., 244
Young Men's Christian Association (YMCA), 9, 165
Young Men's Hebrew Association (YMHA), 165
Ysaÿe, Eugène, 30, 32
Ysaÿe, Gabriel, 32
Ysselstyn, Cornelius, 31, 36, 97

Zingarelli, Niccolò, 194
Zuckerkandl, Victor, 100–1, 103, 120
Zukerman, George, 223, 226, 227, 248, 254